Mastering Aesop

Mastering Aesop

Medieval Education, Chaucer, and His Followers

❦

Edward Wheatley

University Press of Florida

Gainesville · Tallahassee · Tampa · Boca Raton
Pensacola · Orlando · Miami · Jacksonville

Copyright 2000 by the Board of Regents of the State of Florida
Printed in the United States of America on acid-free paper
All rights reserved

05 04 03 02 01 00 6 5 4 3 2 1

Library of Congress Cataloging-in-Publication Data

Wheatley, Edward.
Mastering Aesop: Medieval education, Chaucer, and his followers /
Edward Wheatley.
p. cm.
Includes bibliographical references and index.
ISBN 0-8130-1745-9 (alk. paper)
1. English literature—Middle English, 1100-1500—History and
criticism. 2. Fables, Greek—Adaptations—History and criticism.
3. English literature—Middle English, 1100-1500—Greek influences.
4. Chaucer, Geoffrey, d. 1400. Nun's priest's tale. 5. Lydgate, John,
1370?-1451?—Knowledge—Literature. 6. Henryson, Robert,
1430?-1506? Morall fabillis of Esope the Phrygian. 7. Fables, English—
History and criticism. 8. Education, Medieval—Great Britain.
9. Animals in literature. 10. Aesop's fables. I. Title.
PR347 .W48 2000
820.9'001—dc21   99-056399

The University Press of Florida is the scholarly publishing agency for the
State University System of Florida, comprising Florida A&M University,
Florida Atlantic University, Florida International University, Florida
State University, University of Central Florida, University of Florida,
University of North Florida, University of South Florida, and University
of West Florida.

University Press of Florida
15 Northwest 15th Street
Gainesville, FL 32611–2079
http://www.upf.com

Contents

Preface

This work contributes to the ongoing examination of several closely related topics that have emerged in medieval studies during the last twenty years: the influence of Latin texts and commentaries on vernacular authors, theories of translation, the nature of medieval pedagogical practice, and the study of manuscripts as exemplars of unique, individual readings. To twenty-first-century readers, a detailed examination of these topics in relation to the humble Aesopic fable must necessarily appear to lower the tone of such elevated areas of inquiry, but I hope to show that it provides a rich area of exploration: although some manuscript evidence relating to curricular fable betrays juvenile readers acquiring basic Latin language skills, more mature readings of Aesopic fable draw upon the same types of scholastic discourse and hermeneutic activity as the reading of Virgil's *Aeneid* or Ovid's *Metamorphoses*.

While these highly respected classical Latin texts and others have been studied in light of their medieval scholastic commentaries and subsequent vernacular "translations," the primary-school canon has not received so much attention, in spite of the survival of a remarkable number of exemplars of the canonical texts studied in late medieval grammar schools. One of those texts was a collection of Latin fables in elegiac verse generally introduced by a dedicatory epistle from the legendary Roman emperor Romulus. He claims to translate the work of Aesop, whose legendary biography as a slave who wins his freedom survived through the Middle Ages. This biography, along with theories about fable from classical and medieval authorities, helped to determine the reception and use of the elegiac Romulus in the grammar-school canon; I examine these texts in the opening chapters here.

The heart of my study of the elegiac Romulus is in commentaries from one hundred manuscripts of this fable collection (some clearly the work of grammar-school pupils) and several incunables of the fables that were intended for a school audience; appendices reproduce some of these texts. These documents suggest a surprisingly sophisticated range of pedagogical practices. I trace fable commentary and classroom conventions into the field of discourse inhabited by some of their closest descendants, the vernacular fables of medieval Britain. The Middle English fables of Geoffrey Chaucer and John Lydgate—*The Nun's Priest's Tale* and *Isopes Fabules*— and Robert Henryson's Middle Scots collection, *Morall Fabillis*, are clearly indebted to the scholastic fable tradition in a variety of ways. All of Lydgate's fables and most of Henryson's are translations of apologues from the elegiac Romulus. More importantly, as former students of Latin fable, Chaucer, Lydgate, and Henryson brought to their mature writing an understanding of the conventionally defined discursive field that this mode of discourse could inhabit. Chaucer and Henryson acknowledged their understanding of the boundaries of that field while working to broaden them; Lydgate seemed unable to move beyond the discursive limits that he inherited from school texts. The last three chapters of this work position these three poets within what proves to be a much more expansive discursive space than modern readers might otherwise assume.

An earlier version of Chapter 4 appeared under the title "Commentary Displacing Text: *The Nun's Priest's Tale* and the Scholastic Fable Tradition" in volume 18 (1996) of *Studies in the Age of Chaucer*. It is reprinted by permission of the New Chaucer Society. The first half of Chapter 6 originally was published as "Scholastic Commentary and Robert Henryson's *Morall Fabillis*: The Aesopic Fables" in *Studies in Philology*, volume XCI, number 1, Winter 1994; Copyright 1994 by the University of North Carolina Press. It is used by permission of the publisher.

Aaron E. Wright's *The Fables of Walter of England, Edited from Wolfenbüttel, Herzog August Bibliothek, Codex Guelferbytanus 185 Helmstadiensis* (Toronto: Pontifical Institute of Medieval Studies, 1977) came to my attention too late in the process of writing this book to be taken into account here. Readers seeking a transcription of a glossed and commented manuscript of all sixty of the elegiac Romulus fables will find this excellent edition invaluable.

This work has been underwritten by the Andrew W. Mellon Foundation Faculty Fellowship in the Humanities at Harvard University, the National Endowment for the Humanities, the American Philosophical Society, and the Dean of the Faculty and the Trustees of Hamilton College.

I owe thanks for support of this project to numerous mentors, colleagues, and friends. At the University of Virginia, Hoyt N. Duggan, A. C. Spearing, and Barbara Nolan helped with the initial stages of the project;

Derek Pearsall made useful suggestions as the work progressed. Alastair J. Minnis's comments on an earlier version of this work resulted in a substantially stronger book. Colleagues at Hamilton College, especially Bonnie Krueger, Maureen Miller, Carl Rubino, Bonnie Urciuoli, and Thomas A. Wilson, offered advice and inspiration. Professor Emeritus Jean D'Costa commented extensively and perceptively on the manuscript. Harvard Mellon Faculty Fellows Christopher Bongie, Dagmar Herzog, Mary Jaeger, and Jennifer Fleischner, under the generous-spirited leadership of Professor Richard Hunt, read and commented on a draft of Chapter 1 during a memorable year of scholarly exchange; I owe special thanks to Jennifer for suggesting the witty title of the book. During wide-ranging peregrinations among European manuscript libraries, the weary pilgrim found hospitality and companionship with many kind friends: Felicity Lawrence, Matthew Bullard, Kate Parkin, Bill Hamilton, Elisabeth Delavaud, Friedhelm and Steffi Marx, Patrizio Tua, Makiko Tsukada, Cathy Lencioni, Gianni Peirano, and Somchart Chungsiriarak. Research assistants Nick Mastrocinque, Matthew D. Williamson, and Lew Gleich helped immeasurably at Hamilton; Luke Roman did the same at Harvard.

My parents, Bill and Mary Wheatley, have kept the faith as I undertook graduate study and this project; my thanks seem a paltry return. My greatest gratitude and devotion belong to Mary Mackay, who, during years of work on this project, always managed to transform my beastliness into something resembling proper human behavior. This book is for her.

Introduction

Between late 1260 and early 1262, a teacher of grammar and rhetoric in Padua, Rolandino Patavino, wrote *The Chronicles of the Trevisan March*, in which he traced the tyranny of the recently deceased Ezelino da Romano, a supporter of Emperor Frederic II.[1] In Book VI, the chronicler describes the events in Padua during 1249, the year before Frederic's death, when the office of *podesta* had been filled by Ansedesio dei Guidotti, Ezelino's nephew ("... the essence of evil ... the root of wrongs, [and] the deadly poison that is close to the serpent's tail," according to the not impartial chronicler).[2] Part IV of Book VI, bluntly entitled "Of some men arrested for verses," includes the following episode:

> Every day many knights and burghers gathered in the hall of the podesta's palace and conversed. There was a sparrowhawk on a perch in the hall, which a man of education saw and was reminded of some verses in a book called Aesop, which he recited. Someone who liked the verses wanted to have them in writing. Without guile he showed them to someone else and the judge of the podesta, Bonaventura dei Carrazoni, a citizen of Bergamo, cordially listened to the verses and read them and had no suspicion of them; in fact, he listened to them with a good bit of pleasure. But someone innocently mentioned these verses to the podesta, and so finally the content of these verses was given a bad interpretation. Since Ansedesio had been spending his nights and days diligently looking for an excuse to scatter the people of Padua, a task that had been committed to him, as his actions showed, on the basis of these verses he had his own judge Bonaventura arrested and imprisoned, along with many notaries and other persons who had listened to the verses, and some judges, too. .... This was the character of those verses:

Verses of Aesop
The doves accept as king a hawk to fight against the kite; the king
hurts worse than the foe. They soon begin to complain about the
king, because it would have been much better to suffer the wars
of the kite than die without a single blow.[3]

When the tyrant Ezelino later visits Padua, the relatives of those imprisoned
for fable telling attempt to ransom the prisoners, but Ezelino, furious at
their presumption, greets them with a small army. Nearly all of the petition-
ers flee in fear, and the two who remain are jailed. Ezelino then calls his
knights and infantry together and delivers a speech defending himself
against the accusation inherent in the fable: "He said that he was not a
hawk that wanted to devour doves, but a father who intended to cleanse his
house; he knew how to expel scorpions, to sweep out tadpoles, to crush and
batter the heads of serpents."[4] The populace remains unconvinced by his
"soft words," skepticism that proves well-founded. Later in the year,
Ezelino orders the judge Bonaventura decapitated, and then he demands the
execution of at least nine more men held in prison "because of those verses."
The imprisoned survivors of the fable-telling incident "were transferred to
worse dungeons and chained with harsher fetters."[5]

This episode is significant not merely because it is one of the cruelest
incidents associated with fable in the Middle Ages. It also shows that fable
provided a site for hermeneutic free-play in both the historical contextualization of a narrative and the interpretations given to it: the "educated
man" clearly targets Ezelino with the story but assumes that it will be taken
only as sly irony, a literary entertainment to console suffering citizens of
Padua; this attitude leads to a series of retellings that ends with the fable
"innocently mentioned" to Ansedesio. Only then, according to Patavino,
was "the content of [the] verses . . . given a bad interpretation." But if both
the "educated man" and Ansedesio understand the fable to refer to the
tyrant, why is one interpretation acceptable and the other "bad"? Aside
from the chronicler's foreshadowing of the "bad" events which the fable
sets in motion, the interpretation is "bad" because it began with a fable, an
example of moral literature, and ended with the immoral action of Ansedesio throwing its hearers into prison. Thus the reading is "bad" because
it contravenes not only the chronicler's political agenda but also the most
fundamental medieval understanding of literature, that it should lead to
moral action.

Ezelino's guilt is strongly implicated by this chronicler because the tyrant
reacts to the educated fable teller's verbatim reproduction of the fable, not

a specially tailored paraphrase that might have pointed to the ruler more clearly. Since the teller refrained from adding any particularized clues about whom the hawk represents, Ansedesio's response betrays the fact that he, too, sees his uncle as tyrannical. But even though Patavino aims to paint Ezelino as a tyrant, the chronicler betrays the fact that the ruler, like the fable teller, is educated: the tyrant's response is conventionally rhetorical, akin to medieval forms of scholastic interpretation. He counterargues by citing other texts that relate to the fable, and in their use of animal metaphors, these texts, both proverbial and biblical, meet the fable on its own territory.

This deadly instance of fable telling serves to remind modern readers that in spite of its current status, fable has been considered important at other times in Western history. In the Middle Ages, fables were taught in schools, quoted in sermons, depicted in manuscript margins, painted onto walls,[6] and told and retold by the literate and illiterate alike. Such historical information signals the first intellectual leap that we as modern readers must make in confronting this subject: we must be able to imagine an era during which fable was taken seriously as a vehicle for social, political, and religious communication.

The fable quoted by the educated man in Patavino's chronicle came from a collection which was taken very seriously indeed: the curricular text on which this book focuses was the most popular Latin fable collection in Europe from the thirteenth through the fifteenth centuries. This collection, based upon an earlier prose Romulus recension, was probably written in the late twelfth century; it exists in more than 170 manuscripts, mostly from the fourteenth and fifteenth centuries.[7] The popularity of the collection, the contents of which remained remarkably stable over these centuries,[8] was so firmly established before the advent of printing that it appeared in at least fifty editions and printings from five countries before 1500, and several more in the early sixteenth century.[9] Published in Léopold Hervieux's monumental five-volume compilation expansively entitled *Les Fabulistes Latins depuis le siècle d'Auguste jusqu'à la fin du moyen âge* and in editions by Bastin and Warnke,[10] the sixty elegiac verse fables have been printed and discussed under several titles: the "elegiac Romulus" (the title which I prefer to use, as it highlights the verse form and authorial pedigree which one branch of introductory material creates for it); the *Anonymus Neveleti,* for the sixteenth-century editor Isaac Nevelet, whose 1610 edition of the fables provided the basis for La Fontaine's renowned translations; or the fables of Gualterus Anglicus (Walter the Englishman), whose authorship is suggested in some manuscripts to which Hervieux gave special credence;[11] and the

Aesopus moralizatus, though in the later Middle Ages that name was applied to the collection only when it was accompanied by a commentary.[12]

As shown by the fables reproduced and translated in Appendix 1, this collection generally does not diverge from modern conceptions of fable, and, in fact, some of the fables from Book 1 of the elegiac Romulus (the first twenty tales in the collection) are still among the best-known representatives of fable generally. The widespread popularity of these fables during this period must be attributed to their presence in the grammar-school classroom, where the "educated man" in the chronicle by Patavino (himself a teacher of grammar and rhetoric) probably first learned the text he recited. Hitherto the collection has been superficially studied in its curricular context by historians of education within particular countries or regions.[13] The first three chapters of this book, however, will give a broader overview of the attitudes and practices surrounding the reception and appropriation of the verse Romulus collection as a Latin curricular text; I will draw upon evidence from across Europe, since the consistency of the fables' inclusion in the European grammar-school curriculum implies a certain consistency of pedagogical approach.

I undertake this literary-historical study with several assumptions. The first is that in the Middle Ages as now, fable was viewed as universal intellectual property, usable by anyone confident enough to appropriate it and put her personal stamp on it. Even so, as Annabel Patterson has argued in *Fables of Power: Aesopian Writing and Political History,* appropriation of fable does not take place in a literary-historical vacuum, and the literary history that a fabulist privileges when approaching fable largely determines the nature and function of his literary product. In the Middle Ages, appropriation of fable highlighted a tension not only between fable's pagan past and its medieval Christian present, but also between divergent views about the nature of fable's founding father Aesop and the roles which his literary offspring could legitimately play in a Christian community. Within the smaller world of medieval grammar schools, both of these tensions were exacerbated by the canonical place of fable early in a child's education: no other "classical" narratives were given to such inexperienced Latinists to memorize, paraphrase, and interpret. However, transmission and interpretation of fable took place under the control of schoolteachers. To these teachers fell the responsibility of reinforcing the classical fable canon, helping students distinguish between less authoritative folktale and fully authoritative Aesopic fable; furthermore, these pedagogues bore the duty of teaching acceptable methodologies for diminishing (but never, of course, effacing) the tensions between paganism and Christianity, authority and appropriation. The texts which helped to define the reception and function of the fable in the later Middle Ages are the subjects of the first three chapters of this book, and these texts determined many of the techniques of translation and appropriation used by medieval vernacular fabulists, including Geoffrey Chaucer, John Lydgate, and Robert Henryson.

My second assumption in confronting my topic is that formalist definitions of fable as genre (some of which I will discuss in Chapter 1) are superfluous to a historicized understanding of the medieval phenomenon of the elegiac Romulus collection. In spite of the varying nature of the tales in the collection, medieval readers accepted them as fables, largely because the collection was associated with the name of the first fabulist, Aesop. For these readers, the form of the fable was more accidental than essential, subject to the whim of the teller, but fable's function was of primary importance. Function was determined partly by external circumstances: texts brought to bear upon the fable, political situations in which it was recounted, and the degree to which it communicated morality within a particular context. All-encompassing formal definitions tell us more about our own desires to master fable than medieval reception of the literary form.

My third assumption is based upon the second: Aesopic fable is best approached not as a literary genre but as a mode of discourse, a set of rhetorical practices that lies as much in the control of the teller as in the inherited narrative per se. The most standard of these practices is to attribute a fable to Aesop in order to give it added authority. Another standard practice is to point out a particular moral application for the narrative, whether that moral is stated explicitly or, as in the instance recounted above, merely implied. Other standard practices favor the use of animal characters and brevity instead of prolixity. Nevertheless, many so-called fables, including several in the elegiac Romulus collection, flout one or more of these discursive practices while remaining identifiably fables. By considering fable not as a genre but simply as a mode of discourse, we allow it the wide variety of forms which it has always encompassed. That variety is apparent in the widely varying uses of the terms "fable" and "fabular" in the twentieth century, when the flat morality inherent in this discursive mode is considered its least attractive feature. More importantly for this study, such a broadening of definition in relation to medieval literature helps to allow the Latin term *fabula* more of the range of meanings which it had in the Middle Ages: it was "fiction" as well as "fable."

The relative freedom with which fable could be adapted leads me to another assumption, one which flies in the face of much of the critical work on fable in the past century, notably that undertaken by such scholars as

Klaus Grubmüller and Hans Robert Jauss. I assume that most of the readers of the elegiac Romulus—and certainly most schoolboys—were not interested in the collection's sources and background. For medieval readers the collection simply represented the most widely accepted redaction of Aesop. Instead of exploring the collection's past, readers were interested in guaranteeing it a future by making the fables their own.

My final assumption may seem obvious, but it bears some emphasis: no one need adhere faithfully to a single interpretation of an Aesopic fable, even in the centuries under examination in this book. A fable's value as a mode of discourse lies in its adaptability to different discursive situations and registers. To believe that a fable is best interpreted in one particular way suggests an entrenched dogmatism which the later Middle Ages did not espouse.

In Chapter 1, I will examine the slippery nature of fable as a so-called literary genre and its representation in the equally slippery figure of Aesop in the Middle Ages. The indeterminacy of his history over several centuries gave fabulists a range of choices about the aspects of the authorial persona to emphasize in order to determine a particular reception for their fables. Chapter 2 presents an overview of the literary-critical texts most influential in determining the medieval reception and use of fable. In Chapter 3, I will summarize a body of evidence from manuscripts and incunables that has received little attention: the commentary tradition and pedagogical practices associated with the elegiac Romulus collection as a curricular—indeed, a canonical—text. The final half of this book will bring the material from the first half to bear upon the "translated" fables written by three medieval British vernacular writers: Geoffrey Chaucer, John Lydgate, and Robert Henryson. As former students of curricular fable, these writers (like both Patavino and his "educated man") molded their material according to their classroom experience of the literary form, its history, and the most common hermeneutic practices associated with it. Curricular accoutrements as much as the earlier fable texts themselves determined the nature of the British vernacular translations.

Figuring the Fable and Its Father

As modern readers, we need to take our first step toward understanding Aesopic fable by confronting the difficulty of defining it as a genre; attempts to delineate the generic rules of fable reveal distinct shortcomings in relation to nearly all classical and medieval fable collections. I intend to offer a critique of some of these definitions and then cite and elaborate upon the work of theorist Jean-Marie Schaeffer. Although Schaeffer's notions about fable as a mode of discourse fit all Aesopic fable, we need not cast our nets so widely as to cover the entire corpus of that literature. We have the relative luxury of concentrating upon only the sixty fables of the elegiac Romulus collection in relation to available discursive and generic theories in order to judge which ones might most closely have approximated the views of the generations of readers for whom this collection was the authoritative Aesopic text. Schaeffer's theories will then lead us to examine the biography of Aesop as it survived in the Middle Ages.

Most modern scholars, inheritors of "scientific" approaches to the classification and interpretation of literature, long for fable to adhere to strictly definable generic limitations and for its father, Aesop, to be a historically verifiable person about whom something—anything—definite can be said. Needless to say, such concerns with literary taxonomy and historical veracity did not interest medieval readers of fable. In fact, the very indeterminacy of fable's form and the fragmented biographical material on its founding father that discomfit modern scholars served medieval readers and revisers of fable as an open field of opportunity for appropriation and translation of fable (and to some extent, of Aesop himself). Poststructuralist literary theory can help us bridge the gap between the modern desire to over-determine and the medieval imperative to diversify and displace.

Philologist Ben Edwin Perry's editions of both Latin and Greek fables have guaranteed him a lasting place in the study of Aesopic literature; as Morten Nøjgaard has stated, Perry was "the first to base his work upon a truly exhaustive documentation [of fable literature]."[1] Standing as a monument to Perry's exhaustive research is his "Analytical Survey of Greek and Latin Fables in the Aesopic Tradition," the appendix of 725 titles that appears in *Babrius and Phaedrus*.[2] While his introduction to that book includes ruminations about fable and its nature, his article entitled simply "Fable"[3] gives his most succinct attempt to define the literary form. There he asserts that what defines a "genre" or "form" in literature is "its mechanical structure as narrative which alone remains constant throughout all the particulars and is unmistakeable [*sic*]." As the basis for his discussion of the "form" of fable, he then makes the apparently unremarkable assertion that "A fable is a story." In spite of its simplicity, however, such a definition must lead Perry to dissatisfaction with the body of literature which he will be forced to discuss (and, in relation to this study, with several of the fables in the elegiac Romulus): "The materials contained in our ancient and medieval collections of fables ascribed to Aesop, and in other collections which belong to the same tradition, are so varied in kind that no conceivable definition of fable, however broadly it might be formulated, could apply to all of them. Some of them are not even stories, but similes or allegorical descriptions, which fall outside the fundamental form-pattern of narrative."[4] Among other non-narrative fables in the elegiac Romulus are Fable 25, "De terra et mure," an expanded version of Horace's metaphor of the mountain giving birth to a mouse, and Fable 49, "De Thaida et Damasio," a dialogue between a prostitute and a young man.

After citing some examples of the variety of texts associated with the formal label "fable," Perry posits what he considers a sound basis for classifying the form:

> So many different kinds of story have been brought into fable-books, or otherwise associated with Aesop, that they cannot be comprehended under a single definition. We can only describe the principal types of narrative which we find in the corpus of our fables and decide which type among them is predominate [*sic*], in theory as well as in practice, and how its limits should be defined. The class of stories will constitute a large central core, marked off from the whole by subjective limitations which cannot be exact and will always be subject to doubt or dispute in their application to particular cases. To this class we may apply, more appropriately than to anything else, the name "fable" or "Aesopic fable" in a technical sense; but we must keep in mind the fact that this central type is surrounded by other types of narrative which often pass under the name of fable, because the connotation of this word has been so general and so vague.

In spite of Perry's caveats, he posits a tautological, essentialist notion of what constitutes this "genre": fables are those texts which are most fable-like. In exclusionary language that mirrors social structures, Perry personifies the "central core" of fables that both exemplify and enforce the standards that allow entrance into their "class," but nonstandard texts, even though they may "pass" as fable, are consigned to perpetual marginality.

When we confront the elegiac Romulus fables, a historically predetermined group of *fabulae* which circulated as a collection, Perry's defining criteria appear more misleading than instructive. No attempts to define all of a fable's formal characteristics remain from the Middle Ages, and one must doubt whether definitions of this type ever existed. In the case of the elegiac Romulus, the collection's association not only with the name of Aesop but also with the imprimatur of its legendary imperial translator Romulus meant that the collection had *auctoritas,* and the perception of the text's historical authority outweighed interest in its components' form.

Perry's assertions in this article and in the introduction to his edition of the fables of Babrius and Phaedrus are summarized and commented upon by Jan M. Ziolkowski in "The Form and Spirit of the Beast Fable."[5] The title of this article implies both an interest in formal definitions and an acknowledgment that such definitions must remain to some degree inadequate unless supplemented by other considerations. Although Ziolkowski's project is to define "beast fable," initially he turns his attention to defining fable more broadly. He concedes that his goal represents a modern preoccupation with which earlier receivers of fable would have had little sympathy:

> Medieval fabulists were even likelier than their ancient predecessors to include extraneous material in their fable collections. . . . Because fabulists were indiscriminate about their material, adopting modern principles [of definition] puts us in the awkward position of rejecting from the corpus of genuine fables items that seem chronologically close to Aesop himself and that were deemed by ancient fabulists to have been fables. Nonetheless, the risks of such exclusion seem less hazardous than the confusion of leaving fable amorphous. (8)

Just what these risks might be, Ziolkowski does not elaborate, but once again the variety in fable collections becomes a liability due to the "extraneous material" adopted by "indiscriminate" fabulists.

Ziolkowski distills Perry's criteria for the fable into four "rules":

1. Fables must be fictitious.
2. Fables must record a single action, short chain of actions, or

speech that took place once in the past. This criterion facilitates separating fables from proverbs, which are not restricted to "once in the past."

3. A fable [must] relate the actions of specific characters. Although a fable illustrates a general truth, the characters in fable do not merely embody abstract concepts (as is the case in personification allegory).

4. The fourth, and most important, of Perry's criteria is that a fable at least pretends to be told for the sake of a moral, not merely for entertainment.[6]

The first three of these rules contradict themselves. "Speech that took place once in the past" must imply either historical truth, a definition that flies in the face of the etymology of the word *fabula* (and the first rule above), or the use of the past tense in constructing fables. The elegiac Romulus and its commentaries flout both senses of the clause. Most of the collection's fables are written in the present tense, perhaps because the elegiac Romulus author planned to use them as curricular texts for students whose Latin was still inexpert; this verb tense, along with the fables' generality, leaves them in an atemporal limbo, not a clear historical moment. Furthermore, while most readers would not doubt that nearly all fables in the elegiac Romulus are fictitious, modern readers might find that some tales with only human characters could have actually occurred (for example, the aforementioned dialogue between a prostitute and a potential client, "De Thaida et Damasio"), and some medieval commentators felt it their duty to point out "true" fables in the collection. For example, the commentator whose work appears in Heinrich Quentell's edition of the *Esopus moralizatus* takes great pains to tell his readers that one of the fables in the verse Romulus does not appear to be a fable ("non praetendit fabulam");[7] that text, sometimes entitled "De Leone et Pastore" in medieval books, is commonly known to modern audiences as "Androcles and the Lion," a narrative not currently prized for its verisimilitude. The fact that this tale, in which an animal and a human interact, should be judged historically plausible must indicate the subjectivity of such judgments and therefore one of the weaknesses of the rule given above.

Ziolkowski uses Perry's fourfold description of fable to make short work of defining a subcategory of fabular literature, the beast fable: "a beast fable is a fable in which the principal actors are animals. In other words, a beast fable must both satisfy the four criteria established by Perry and feature animals as its protagonists." In describing the "spirit" of this form of literature, Ziolkowski turns to a number of qualities relevant to the verse Romulus as curricular text: the literature's appeal to a broad audience, its use as satire (especially by those of lower status to ridicule those of higher rank—and often by slaves to criticize masters), and its value as a testing ground for a variety of literary styles and discursive registers. Finally, Ziolkowski argues for the use of a literary category of "beast literature," in which "beast fable is and probably always will be preeminent."[8]

Ziolkowski's focus upon beast fable overlooks Libyan or Libistican fables, those populated partly or entirely by human characters. They appear in the earliest extant fable collections, and no evidence suggests that they have not always served the same discursive function as fables whose characters are beasts. In most collections (including the elegiac Romulus), Libistican fables effectively prevent the reader from perceiving any comforting allegorical barriers between humans and beasts: people in fables act in beastly ways, and beasts sometimes behave more morally than human characters. Ziolkowski's division of types of fable is suggested by no classical or medieval collection that we have inherited and apparently works against the precepts held by compilers of those collections.

These critics' attempts to define fable by form and content deprive collections such as the verse Romulus of their full variety, deprivation which medieval students would not have comprehended. Perry and Ziolkowski imply a belief in a Platonic idea of fable, before indiscriminate compilers allowed their collections to become adulterated with non-fabular material, a golden age when real fable defined itself clearly and exclusively. Genre theorist Jean-Marie Schaeffer has described the pitfalls of this approach: "For a Platonist, the genre is to the individual text what the idea is to the phenomenal object—its timeless model, its *eidos*. Genre not only 'is' but, for that matter, it alone 'is'; the empirical texts are only realizations more or less in accordance with this abstract essence."[9] My subject in the current study, however, is an "adulterated" collection, a fallen representative of a Platonic idea according to the standards set by formalists, so we must look elsewhere for critical approaches that will not delimit fable beyond the relatively generous classical and medieval outlines exemplified in the verse Romulus.

Some students of fable in recent years have not attempted to fit this varied literature into restrictively unitary definitions. In *The Fable as Literature*, H. J. Blackham falls back on some formal criteria (for example, that "fable is narrative fiction in the past tense"),[10] but then he turns, hesitantly, to a very different kind of formalism: "A formal definition [of fable] might be: a narrative device, to provoke and aid concrete thinking, focused on some general matter of concern."[11] He then lists ways in which fable's function, not its form, determines its nature. The German scholars who have contributed most to the discussion of fable in the Middle Ages, Hans Robert Jauss and Klaus Grubmüller, define fable in relation to a spectrum of similar types of literature with animal characters. The title of Jauss's book, *Untersuchungen zur Mittelalterlichen Tierdichtung*,[12] demonstrates his interest in placing fable in a larger context of beast literature, which includes beast epic and fairy tales acted out by animals; however, this classification of literature by "characters" alone excludes Libistican fable, as Ziolkowski's definition does. Grubmüller duplicates some of Jauss's subgeneric interests while shifting his taxonomy from structure to function. In *Meister Esopus* Grubmüller considers the fable first as situationally specific (drawing on the writings of Jacob Grimm and Karl Meuli), and then as exemplum and allegory.[13] The rhetorical functions of beast fable, which cross the subgeneric boundaries described by Jauss, seem closer in spirit to a medieval understanding of fable than flat formalist definitions.

But the very title of Grubmüller's book provides a fruitful critical framework for beginning to think about fable in the classroom. One of the constants of fable in the surviving classical and medieval collections (as well as in later ones) is the necessary association of the name of Aesop with this mode of discourse; the authors of the earliest extant Latin collections, Phaedrus and Avianus, invoke the founding father's name in their respective prologues, and Phaedrus writes several fables in which Aesop plays a central role. In spite of the fact that the medieval Romulus collections are now identified as often by the name of their legendary translator as by Aesop's, the standard introductory text for these collections, which takes the form of an epistle from Romulus to his son, credits Aesop with the invention of fable, and in the Middle Ages these collections were nearly always labeled with Aesop's name. While resorting to a description of fable collections as Aesopic would not satisfy Perry in his search for a "mechanical structure" inherent in individual fable narratives, working to define the Aesopic fable as a textual representative of its author figure seems preferable to excluding from consideration as fable some texts which Phaedrus and Avianus, our earliest Latin fabulists, considered fabular; we thereby avoid engaging in exclusionary judgments which would have struck classical and medieval readers as hair-splitting.

The most helpful description of fable as a literary construct reliant upon the name of Aesop appears in another article by Jean-Marie Schaeffer, "*Aesopus auctor inventus*: Naissance d'un genre: La fable ésopique."[14] While the essay is less than forthcoming about its considerable debt to

Michel Foucault's essay "What Is an Author?" and the concept of the author-function, it helps twentieth-century readers make the imaginative leap
necessary to reconsider fable as a literary form capable of revivification, the
attitude held by classical and medieval authors. Schaeffer tacitly rejects
formal critical projects like those of Perry and Ziolkowski; in his view, the
concept of fable in the European tradition is and always has been too closely
bound up with the name of Aesop to have an independent formal essence of
its own. This view approximates that of medieval students of fable as well:
the elegiac Romulus was studied not in order to teach correct and incorrect
fable form, but because it represented the available Aesop, an *auctor*.

Schaeffer asserts that the association of the fable with Aesop served to
legitimate the mode of discourse by providing it with a point of origin in
antiquity; however, the name also serves other functions. (Since no English
translation of Schaeffer's work is available, I include lengthy translated
excerpts here.)

> If "Aesop" seems to us the origin of the fable, it is not because he
> actually constitutes the historic locus of the birth of fable, but because
> he has been cast as founding father by the generic tradition of fable, in
> the first place by Phaedrus, who in this respect can be considered the
> real birthplace of the genre.
>
> Initially we should note that the proper name "Aesop" means a
> multiplicity of things: one can distinguish three different figures.
>
> (a) "Aesop" as a proper name coupled with a textual collection, or
> rather with different textual collections in different eras. Thus our
> contemporary textual "Aesop" is actually a collection going back to
> at least the first century A.D. and which is identified as the
> "Augustana."[15] Actually, the collection that fulfills the function of
> textual origin can be different according to the era. However, it will
> always be traced to "Aesop." We see that "Aesop" can't be the textual
> origin of the genre for the very simple reason that this proper name
> designates very different hypotexts in different eras.
>
> (b) "Aesop" as a proper name mentioned by the ensemble of fabu-
> lists and constituted by them as origin and/or hypotext, but also as
> narrated character.
>
> (c) "Aesop" as a quasi-mythical character moving across antique
> and post-antique literature, and also doubtless across popular imagi-
> nation. He was made concrete as a literary character as early as the
> first century in a "Life of Aesop. . . ."
>
> We can therefore say that if "Aesop" has become the origin of the

fable, that is due to a projection of the origin that constitutes one of the constant traits of the genre. But one would be guilty of misinterpretation in identifying a specific, constant hypotext with this name. In fact, the origin is a textual result of the generic tradition. If we now read the anonymous collection, the "Augustana," as the work of Aesop, we have to see such a reading as essentially an effect of the generic tradition (instituted by Phaedrus) . . .

Inasmuch as the origin is the effect of a retrospective projection, it always exists as explicit generic consciousness. It does not grow from the actual birth of the genre, which can easily be ignored by the textual tradition (ignoring that renders the recourse to an imaginary generic legitimation all the more tempting). Ancient literature knew two processes of generic legitimation: reference to an inventor, or the postulation of a mythological origin. At the time of the birth of Aesopic fable, both devices are found: Phaedrus chooses legitimation through the inventor "Aesop," while Babrius prefers mythological legitimation which takes the birth of fable back to the golden age. If we say that Phaedrus rather than Babrius constitutes the locus of the birth of the literary genre, it is not just because he precedes Babrius chronologically, but above all because fabulists on the whole have followed the example of the projection of the origin instituted by Phaedrus, a type that has become a rule of the genre: the fable will be Aesopic or it will not be.[16]

The first figure of Aesop that Schaeffer describes—the texts representing the author—is, for our purposes, the elegiac Romulus. Schaeffer's second figuration of Aesop as originary function is represented in the epistolary preface to the elegiac Romulus, but Aesop as a narrated character does not appear in the collection; even so, this absence did not deter Robert Henryson from creating a character named Aesop in his seventh fable, so we should assume that the concept of stories about Aesop was not incomprehensible in the Middle Ages. Schaeffer's third Aesop, the one associated with the "Life," will be discussed in the next section of this chapter.

These specific functions of the name of Aesop in relation to the discourse that is fable can also be inferred from Foucault's more general discussion of an author's name: his ideas about nineteenth- and twentieth-century novelists apply with equal validity to the father of the fable:

An author's name is not simply an element of speech (as a subject, a complement, or an element that could be replaced by a pronoun or other parts of speech). Its presence is functional in that it serves as a means of classification. A name can group together a number of texts and thus differentiate them from others. A name also establishes different forms of relationships among texts. Neither Hermes [Trismegistus] nor Hippocrates existed in the sense that we can say Balzac existed, but the fact that a number of texts were attached to a single name implies that relationships of homogeneity, filiation, reciprocal explanation, authentication, or of common utilization were established among them. Finally, the author's name characterizes a particular manner of existence of discourse. Discourse that possesses an author's name is not to be immediately assumed and forgotten; neither is it accorded the momentary attention given to ordinary, fleeting words. Rather, its status and its manner of reception are regulated by the culture in which it circulates.[17]

Aesop belongs alongside Hermes Trismegistus and Hippocrates as legendary authors whose names have helped to unify an amorphous textual tradition and determine its reception. Among the relationships of the texts united under the name of Aesop, common utilization is surely the most significant for our study. While the variety of types of narrative called "Aesopic fable" bothers formal critics attempting to describe the literary form divorced from its author figure, inheritors of the elegiac Romulus as a curricular Aesopic collection were comfortable with its heterogeneity; certainly the variety in the collection did not interfere with its common use in the curriculum. Foucault's claim that an author's name brings greater attention to a text is mirrored in Schaeffer's assertion that fable needs the historical legitimation provided by the name of Aesop (lest it be mistaken for mere anecdote or folktale, a fable teller's worst fear).

The rhetorical place of Aesop in relation to fable inscribes both the discursive mode's history and the act of appropriation of the later reviser: while Schaeffer's argument that a fable must be Aesopic carries some validity, I would add that it is equally important that a fable text can never truly be Aesop's. In other words, the act of writing a fable necessitates the author's admission of debt to an absent father, appropriation of his literary offspring, and the implicit understanding that the text then stands to be retold by later authors. Such retelling is not generally undertaken in the name of the intermediary appropriating author (that is, an author would probably not choose to describe his project as revisions of fables by Marie de France or Odo of Cheriton), but in the name of the father, Aesop.

Again borrowing from Foucault's criticism, Schaeffer contrasts fable as discursive practice and fable as genre:

The fable as discursive practice can be defined as a narration with an obligatory transcendent interpretation. It is a story which stands for "something else," implying that the level of the fiction ought to be translated into a transcendent semantic range. The fable as a possible literary genre is circumscribed by discursive practice inasmuch as it reveals the fundamental rule that the literary practice ought to employ, lest it leave not only the genre, but also the discursive practice. In this sense the genre of fable (or the genres of fable, if one distinguishes the Aesopic fable from the Asian fable, as it would be helpful to do) possesses a very special characteristic: the limits of other genres are far from always coinciding with the limits of a specific discursive practice.[18]

The sketchiness of Schaeffer's definitions of these criteria tacitly demonstrates his willingness to allow fable to take on different appearances and valences in different historical periods. His only formal criterion for fable— its obligatory transcendent interpretation—reflects the standard defining criterion that a fable have a moral, though even this notion leaves open the possibility that the interpretation might be applied by the reader rather than inherent in the text.

Finally, Schaeffer describes fable's adaptability, using terminology reminiscent of Karl Meuli's notions of fable's "situational reference" (*Situationsbezug*):[19] "As discursive practice (for example, as an orator's device) the fable in its individuality is always tied to a situational context which at the same time motivates its narration and constitutes the parameters of the transcendent translation. In the fable as literary genre, such a context is missing: this poses problems at the level of transcendent translation. If an authorial context is missing, it is a case not of narrated fables, but of fables to narrate: they are waiting for their narrator who will deliver them from their 'inertia.'"[20] Here is perhaps another of the incentives for adherence to the practice of revising fable in the classroom. The "literary" fables of the elegiac Romulus require vivification through contextualization, whether rhetorical (implying a degree of intellectual artifice), moral, or most likely a combination of the two. If extant scholastic commentaries represent a contextualization of fable considered sufficient by the medieval educational system, then schoolchildren and teachers had a number of artificial situational options from which to choose, ranging from spiritual allegory to simple social figuration to perhaps even classroom satire.[21] But further situational contexts in which both fable narrative and interpretation would be relevant, such as the political situation in Padua in 1249, surely remained immanent.

Schaeffer summarizes his argument by focusing more upon Aesopic text than upon the author-function:

There are three essential rules for the generic play "Aesopic fable." These are the projection of its origin as generic—and finally ideological—legitimation, as well as two rules determining the textual relation that is established between the text of the fabulist and his "Aesopic" model.

(a) The "Aesopic" text functions as hypotext in the strict sense of the term, and the hypertext defines itself by the formal transformations that it causes this text to undergo. Numerous transformations are possible. Besides basic linguistic translation we should add the transformation from prose to verse (and vice versa) as well as the transformations already enumerated by classical rhetoricians: one can tell the fable directly, one can attribute it to another person, one can insert it in a narrative, one can amplify or abbreviate it, or further, one can bind it to an explicit moral (if that is missing in the hypotext, etc.)

(b) The "Aesopic" text functions as a model from which to take the prescription of writing for the invention of new stories functioning as fables. Rhetoricians thus proposed taking off from an "Aesopic" moral and inventing from that moral a new fable. Given the variability of the hermeneutic bond between the fable and its transcendent translation (i.e., the high degree of indeterminacy of the moral), the invention of new fables obviously risks introducing a certain thematic dispersion, with the same moral capable of referring to numbers of subjects or to highly diverse values, according to the era.[22]

Nearly every type of textual transformation listed by Schaeffer is represented in the history of the reception of the elegiac Romulus collection. Linguistic translation is inscribed in the introductory epistle, with Romulus's claim to have translated the text from Greek; this in turn sanctions the translation of the fables from Latin into other languages, the project undertaken by Lydgate and Henryson. The rhetorical manipulations of a fable text that Schaeffer cites were part and parcel of its reason for inclusion in the school curriculum, and as we will see, these modifications strongly influenced the forms that the curricular fables took in vernacular translations.

Schaeffer's notion that fables provide formal and thematic models for further fabulation is clearly illustrated in curricular commentary on the elegiac Romulus, where commentators use fables to gloss and explicate other fables. Such a practice is also woven into Chaucer's *Nun's Priest's Tale,* notably in Chauntecleer's series of exempla supporting the prophetic force of dreams, and in the thematic links among Henryson's *Moral Fables.* And these fabulists also made rhetorical use of what Schaeffer calls "the variability of the hermeneutic bond" between the fable and its moral, Chaucer by overloading his fable with morals and Henryson (and even Lydgate) by using the multiplicity of fables within their collections as a basis for exploring hermeneutic variables between narratives and their "transcendent" meanings.

Foucault's "What Is an Author?" gives a broader context to Schaeffer's specific ideas. Foucault writes that "the 'author-function' is tied to the legal and institutional systems that circumscribe, determine, and articulate the realm of discourses."[23] During the centuries when the best-known textual embodiment of Aesop was the elegiac Romulus, the primary institutional systems controlling that text and its reception were the Church and the educational system which it created and administered in order to validate its principles. This institutionalization of fable is also reinforced by our vernacular fabulists: Chaucer chose the Nun's Priest to narrate his fable, Lydgate himself was a monk, and Henryson, evidently schoolmaster at the abbey school of Dunfermline, leaves all of the elegiac Romulus fables that he does not revise "vnto the freiris" [to the friars].

Searching for the Runaway Slave, Finding the Father of Fable

While the name of Aesop serves to legitimate fable as an ancient, authoritative literary form, its use is problematic inasmuch as it calls upon the user to imagine the signified behind the sign. Biographical information about the father of the fable was sketchy in the Middle Ages, at least until the advent of printing. Then the textual Aesop embodied in the verse Romulus had competition from another Aesop, an expanded fable corpus prefaced by a biography. We will begin our discussion of the father of fable with this *Life of Aesop,* supposedly an early- fourteenth-century import to Europe from Byzantium, because the unified narrative that it presents will help us make sense of the fragments of the fabulist's "biography" that are scattered through a number of texts written or available in the earlier Middle Ages. As a group, these texts present a surprisingly unified picture of Aesop that served to delineate models of appropriation of his textual offspring.

In the second half of the fifteenth century, when printing presses were becoming active across Europe, the elegiac Romulus was printed at least fifty times in France, Germany, Italy, and the Netherlands; it had to wait until 1502 to appear in England at the press of Richard Pynson, and the following year it was printed in the competing establishment of William Caxton's successor, Wynkyn de Worde.[24] Nearly all of these printings paired scholastic commentaries with the fables, and many included vocabulary glosses, indicating that the books were meant for classroom use.[25]

The popularity of the Latin elegiac Romulus collection probably contributed to the popularity of another Aesopic collection in vernacular languages. Compiled by Heinrich Steinhöwel and first published in a bilingual Latin-German edition by Johann Zainer in Ulm in 1476–77, it was prefaced by a *Life of Aesop* and comprised most of the elegiac Romulus, Greek fables translated by Rinuccio d'Arezzo, the fables of Avianus, the *Disciplina Clericalis* of Petrus Alphonsus, and tales from Poggio Bracciolini's *Facetiae*.[26]

The translation and publication record of Steinhöwel's compilation in the first fifteen years of its history rivals that of the elegiac Romulus in its curricular form. In 1478 in Augsburg Günther Zainer reprinted the German text, and in 1479 and 1480 in the same city Anton Sorg printed one Latin and two German editions. An Augustinian monk, Julien Macho, translated the collection into French, and it appeared in 1480 in Lyon (where the *Auctores octo* curricular collection, including the verse Romulus, was enjoying a healthy popularity in at least six editions by five printers before 1500).[27] William Caxton's English translation of Macho's text appeared in 1484,[28] and a Dutch translation produced in Gouda reached the market in 1485.[29] The year 1488 saw the publication of Macho's translation of his own French version into Spanish in Toulouse,[30] and a Czech version was published in Prague by J. Kamp.[31] In 1489 the German printer Johann or Hans Hurus published yet another Spanish version of the text, this one translated from a German edition and produced in Saragossa.[32] A Colognish edition appeared in the same year.[33] A Low German translation was published in Magdeburg in 1492; Catalan[34] and Danish translations were not forthcoming until the mid-sixteenth century.[35]

A number of factors guaranteed the remarkable popularity of Steinhöwel's compilation. Clearly its use of German inspired translators working in other languages to add Aesop to their "national" literatures, and book buyers readily responded. The collection's encyclopedic scope, the broadest of its day, must have contributed to its success as well. However, broadening the parameters of the fifteenth-century textual Aesop had less lasting influence upon the Aesopic tradition than the Steinhöwel compilation's dissemination of the *Life of Aesop*, the earliest versions of which were written between 100 B.C. and A.D. 200.[36] According to Perry, this "biography" was reborn in an eleventh-century Byzantine recension and probably initially reached medieval Europe through the thirteenth-century monk Maximus Planudes, "one of the very few Byzantines of his day who had any acquaintance with Latin or with the culture of the West." In 1296 he served as an emissary to Italy, and Perry dates the arrival of Planudes's version of the *Life of Aesop* in Europe at the beginning of the fourteenth century.[37] One fourteenth-century Latin manuscript of the Planudean *Life* survives as MS 26 in the Biblioteca Lolliniana in Belluno,[38] but it is assumed to have had little influence. Indeed, Perry determined that the Planudean branch of the *Life of Aesop* was unrelated to the branch from which Rinuccio d'Arezzo made the Latin translation that appeared in Steinhöwel's Aesop.[39]

Unlike modern scholars, late medieval readers were not concerned about the provenance and history of this text; it consistently reappears in the fifteenth century and later with no explanation of its background, but this absence did not slow its dissemination along with the fables. The reason for its immediate, widespread, and long-lasting popularity is not far to seek: it has no small entertainment value, a quality intensified by its frequent publication across Europe with woodcuts related to those published in the first German edition. Even so, at least the first third of this text presents our *auctor* in a less-than-favorable light: he is a malformed, disabled slave who vomits publicly, discusses urine and excrement with his master, bares his sleeping mistress's buttocks to a group of dinner guests, and nearly brings about the ruin of the couple's marriage. And in the Lolliana manuscript (as in the Greek versions of the text), Aesop is found masturbating by his mistress, who is so excited by the size of his penis that she promises him a shirt if he will make love to her ten times consecutively. In these and other episodes, Aesop is hardly the type of *auctor* that medieval schoolmasters would have wanted to hold up to their pupils as a moral model, or modeler of morals; rather, he is a stereotypical folkloric trickster who often goes unpunished for improprieties. Not only does he avoid punishment, but the same wit that causes so much trouble in the first half of the book earns him important, respectable rewards later: he gains his freedom from slavery by means of his cleverness and then becomes a diplomat whose fable telling wins him international notoriety and even a golden monument in his image. In short, the *Life of Aesop* does not show wickedness punished and virtue rewarded in the standard pattern of moral literature, and thus it must have presented a challenge to those touting Aesop's fables as inherently moral.[40]

The trickster-slave Aesop has proven a terrible embarrassment to subsequent generations as well, most notably those writers and scholars who have taken fable seriously. In the early 1630s a revisionist *Vie d'Aesope* was written by Claude-Gaspar Bachet, sieur de Méziriac, who turned to classical authors, especially Herodotus and Plutarch, to produce a biography that effaced the trickster and emphasized Aesop's rise to political power.[41] Although La Fontaine's version allows Aesop some of the trickery in the Planudean *Life,* the French fabulist erases most of the early episodes mentioned above.[42] In Victorian England fable historian and editor Joseph Jacobs called the Planudean *Life* "Noodle literature"; he claims to have sacrificed reprinting the relatively brief *Life* because of lack of space, even though his work stretched to two volumes.[43] In this century Ben Edwin Perry damns the *Life* with faint praise, even as he begins an exhaustive textual history of it: "The *Life of Aesop* belongs to a species of folk literature of which very little has survived. . . . [I]t is a naive, popular, and anonymous book, composed for the entertainment and education of the common people rather than for educated men, and making little or no pretense to historical accuracy or literary elegance."[44] Perry claims that the *Life* deserves attention mainly as "one of the few genuinely popular books that have come down from ancient times."[45]

Although late medieval educators as perpetuators of the Aesopic tradition may have viewed the *Life of Aesop* with the embarrassment later felt by Bachet, La Fontaine, and Jacobs, the text could not have been received with such overwhelming international enthusiasm if it had not been valued by an educated, book-buying public. Were educated readers, then, willing to sacrifice the idea of an authoritative Aesop, father of moral fables, for an Aesop who was a physically malformed, tricky, and sometimes purposefully malicious slave? Such a radical change of viewpoint seems unlikely, and its unlikeliness raises the possibility that the fifteenth-century appearance of the scurrilous trickster in the *Life* might not have signaled a complete rupture in the Aesopic tradition. Indeed, above and beyond the survival of the Lolliana manuscript mentioned earlier, fragments of "biographical" material about Aesop appear in works by a number of learned writers in both Latin and vernacular languages (and allusions to it have been perceived in Chaucer's work).[46] On the whole, these fragments duplicate or resemble episodes of the *Life of Aesop,* and even when they do not, they generally augment rather than contradict the "biography."

Even if we ignore the existence of two textual branches of the *Life* in fourteenth-century Italy, the evidence about Aesop that survives in other medieval documents, when taken collectively, provides a synopsis of the most important aspects of his life: he was an uneducated slave, but nevertheless he was ingenious, and ultimately a monument was built in his honor.

But the medieval writers who mention Aesop's life use the aspects that they reproduce primarily in order to validate their individual rhetorical projects. Citations of Aesop's life tend to become entangled with authors' attitudes toward their own Aesopic texts, as the roughly chronological presentation of such instances below demonstrates.

The most concentrated textual evidence that Aesop was known as a trickster slave in Latinate Europe appears in the fables of Phaedrus, the Roman writer whose collection was, at several removes, the source for the medieval elegiac Romulus. In the only surviving manuscript of Phaedrus's fables, the ninth-century Codex Pithoeanus now housed in the Pierpont Morgan Library, the heading of the collection characterizes the fabulist as *Augusti liberti,* the freed slave of the emperor Augustus. This description indicates why Phaedrus, inheritor and perpetuator of the Aesopic tradition, would have been interested in the status of Aesop as a slave who earns his freedom.

Phaedrus recounts several fables in which Aesop as slave plays a central role. In Fable 19 of Book 3, Aesop is called "domino solus ... familia," "the only servant (or slave) his master had."[47] Indebted to the legend of Diogenes, the fable tells of Aesop searching through town for fire to cook an early dinner for his master. While returning home, he is asked why he has his lamp lit in broad daylight; he replies that he is searching for a true man. This witty, cynical Aesop resembles the trickster character central to the *Life.*

More significant and influential than this tale is Phaedrus's homage to the father of the fable, grudging though his praise may be:

> Aesopi ingenio statuam posuere Attici,
> servumque collocarunt aeterna in basi,
> patere honori scirent ut cuncti viam
> nec generi tribui sed uirtuti gloriam.
> quoniam occuparat alter ut primus foret,
> ne solus esset, studui, quod superfuit.
> nec haec invidia, verum est aemulatio.
> quodsi labori faverit Latium neo,
> plures habebit quos opponat Graeciae.

> [The Athenians set up a statue in honor of the gifted Aesop, and by so doing placed a slave on a pedestal of everlasting fame, that all men might know that the path of honour lies open and that glory is awarded not according to birth, but according to merit. Since another had forestalled me from being first in this field, I did my best to keep him from being the unique representative as well as the first, the only

thing left that I could do. This is not envy, but emulation. Now if Latium shall look with favour upon my work she will have more authors to set against those of Greece.][48]

Phaedrus may have learned of this monument from a version of the *Life of Aesop*. In the text as we now know it, the King of Babylon, in gratitude for Aesop's service as an emissary to Egypt, orders that a gold statue of the fabulist should be erected in a public square;[49] only the location of the monument differs in Phaedrus's poem. But if Phaedrus knew the Aesopic biography, he chose to ignore Aesop's final career as diplomat, and even his status as freedman. His interest in the monument grows out of Aesop's originary status, not his final attainments, and this attitude belies a certain condescension: although Aesop earned a monument, he was basically only a slave who had made good. Phaedrus's condescension is all the more evident inasmuch as his own history as a slave is marginalized in the heading to his collection, not woven into his fables, a telling silence about Phaedrus's former status.

Further glimpses of Aesop as both slave and trickster appear in an appendix to the Phaedrus collection (preserved in Bibliothèque Nationale MS IV F 58), copied by Nicolo Perotti in the fifteenth century from a lost manuscript of fables attributed to the Roman fabulist. In spite of the varying quality of its Latin and its wide-ranging subject matter, Perotti's appendix has generally been attributed to Phaedrus.[50] For this study, the pedigree of the appendix is far less important than its very existence: it provides evidence that other manuscripts of work identified as Phaedrus's existed in the late Middle Ages, that those manuscripts received some attention from scholars, and that stories about Aesop's life were circulating with them.

The seventeenth fable in the appendix describes an Aesop in the service of an unattractive mistress given to wearing thick makeup in a perpetually unsuccessful attempt to attract men. Aesop is brutally frank about the reason for her romantic failures, and she orders him flogged for his honesty. Later, when some of her jewelry disappears, she summons the household and threatens to have all of the servants whipped unless someone identifies the true thief. Aesop responds that the threat means little to him, as only a short time earlier his mistress had him whipped for telling her the truth.

Other fables in the collection do not rely so heavily on Aesop's slavery, but they show him reacting with sympathy to slaves and serfs. For example, in Fable 20 of the appendix, a slave running away from his master describes to Aesop the horrors of his former situation; Aesop replies that those horrors will pale in comparison to those he will suffer as a runaway—and the slave returns to his master. (While modern readers do not find Aesop's response sympathetic, Phaedrus considered it wise, as his promyth shows: "Non esse malo addendum malum" [One should not add trouble to trouble].) Although Aesop's own servitude is not emphasized here, the fable shows the character's cynical understanding of the condition of slavery.

Revisers of the fables of Phaedrus produced collections substantially different from his in tone and content. Gone is the cynical, personal narratorial tone, as is the implicit identification of the freed Roman slave-fabulist with his freed Greek predecessor. Oddly, the only fable about Aesop himself that survives in a number of manuscripts is the description of the monument built in his memory by the Athenians.[51] The location of the monument in Athens rather than in Babylon indicates that the early fabulists in this branch of Aesopic literature had Phaedrus rather than the *Life of Aesop* as their source for this fable; if so, the fabulists have excised Phaedrus's mention of Aesop's slavery.

A clearer survival from the *Life of Aesop* appears in several of the manuscripts that include the fable of the statue. The effacement of the narratorial voice of Phaedrus from these collections leaves a void which allows the reentry of the presence of an Aesop in a dedicatory epistle at either the beginning or the end of several collections.[52] Here Aesop dedicates the collection to a certain "Rufus," a precise translation of the Greek "Xanthus," meaning "red." Xanthus is the name of Aesop's second master in the *Life*, the philosopher who is the butt of the majority of Aesop's tricks but who ultimately frees the slave.[53] (Interestingly, these dedicatory letters do not characterize Aesop as a slave.)

Vincent of Beauvais knew at least some of the particulars of the death of Aesop as it is recounted in the *Life:* Vincent begins and ends his fable collection in the *Speculum historiale* with references to the time and place of the fabulist's death. He opens his prologue to the fables by declaring that Aesop was killed at Delphi in the first year of the reign of Cyrus ("Anno regni Cyri primo Hesopus a Delphis interimitur").[54] While the *Life* neither mentions Cyrus nor attempts to date Aesop's death, it describes his murder at Delphi at the hands of a crowd that has framed him for the theft of a gold chalice.[55]

In his epilogue, Vincent states that he has learned about the death of Aesop from Eusebius,[56] but oddly, Vincent's certainty about Aesop's death apparently eroded during the writing of his brief collection of twenty-nine Phaedrian fables. At the end of his epilogue, which appears under the term "actor," he writes: "utrum Hesopus iste sit ille quem Eusebius a Delphis anno primo Cyri peremptum esse testatur, an forsitan alius, incertum habeo."[57] [I consider it uncertain whether this Aesop or perhaps another is the one whom Eusebius declared to have been slain at Delphi in the first year (of the reign) of Cyrus.] Vincent reserves the use of the heading *actor* for modern opinions, whether his own or those of other "modern doctors";[58] here he apparently expresses his own doubts. Vincent's shift from certainty about an event in the life of Aesop in his prologue to uncertainty about it in his epilogue seems an odd change of opinion to commit to the page, unless it is read in light of his appropriation of Aesopic fable. True to Schaeffer's assertion, Vincent invokes the name of Aesop as originary function for the literary form to be reproduced, but even then, it is the death of the author that he cites, thus creating a void that the new fabulist can fill. When Vincent has written his fables and has become the Aesop of the moment, certainties about the historical Aesop become less important, because the texts with which his name is associated are rewritten yet again. Since his textual relics—the primary evidence of his existence—have been revivified, the reconstruction of Aesop's personal history becomes less necessary. In effect, his history is recast as his reception, but this reception allows Vincent at least temporarily to take on Aesop's role of *auctor*.

Perhaps the most significant evidence that Aesop's identity as a slave survived in the Middle Ages lies in the prologue to the *Fables* of Marie de France. As if emphasizing her knowledge of the background of her source text, Marie states twice in twenty-five lines the original situation in which the fables were recounted, but the first of the "ancient fathers" of fable that she names is not Aesop.

> Romulus, ki fu emperere,
> a sun fiz escrit, si manda
> e par essample li mustra
> cum il se deust cuntreguaiter
> que hum nel peu[s]t enginner.
> Esop[es] escrit a sun mestre
> que bien cunust lui e sun estre,
> unes fables ke ot trovees,
> de griu en latin translatees. (12–20)

[Romulus, who was an emperor, wrote to his son, describing for him and showing him by example how he ought to guard himself so that no one could deceive him. Aesop wrote for his master, whose personality and thought he knew well, some fables that he had created and translated from Greek to Latin.]

[S]i comencerai la premere

des fables ke Esopus escrist,
que a sun mestre manda e dist. (38–40)[59]

[I will begin the first of the fables that Aesop wrote, which he recounted for and presented to his master.]

In the carefully stratified and codified society that Marie's work embodies,
the existence of a *mestre* implies the existence of a slave. The word does not
appear elsewhere in the fables; in order to describe a person of relatively
high social status who does not have proprietorship of his social inferiors,
she always uses the word *seigneur.*[60]

In the forty-line prologue to a collection noted for its economy, Marie's
double emphasis on Aesop's slavery seems redundant, but the two passages
serve different rhetorical purposes. The poet's first citation of Aesop's status
occurs in the middle of the prologue, as part of a history of the discursive
mode that includes the work of Romulus; thus Marie nods to conventional
scholastic prologues, which require a description of the text's *causa
efficiens*—that is, the author.[61] It is noteworthy that in Marie's discussion of
this history, Romulus takes precedence over Aesop; thus Marie has already
effected a substitution of translator for *auctor*—the very substitution which
she intends to reenact—and of emperor for slave. Marie further validates
translation by characterizing Aesop as both the first writer and the first
translator of fable; thus the birth of fable prefigures the project at hand.
Having thus recreated the history of fable as one of substitution and translation, Marie returns to Aesop's slavery in the final lines of the prologue to
describe her own project: "*I* will begin the first fable that Aesop wrote [for
his master]." Here is a new beginning with a new authority figure at the
helm; in order to reduce Aesop's stature while she raises her own, the narrator reemphasizes the old authority figure's low status and replaces him
with the newly authoritative "*I*" of the translator/redactor.

Concomitant with Marie's appropriation of Aesop's history and texts is
the acknowledgment that her own fables may be appropriated by others. In
her collection's epilogue she attempts to guarantee that her accomplishments retain their association with her name.

Al finement de cest escrit
que en romanz ai treité e dit,
me numerai pur remembrance:
Marie ai nun, si sui de France.
Put cel estre que clerc plusur
prendereient sur eus mun labur,
ne voil que nul sur li le die;

cil fet que fol ki sei ublie.
Pur amur le cunte Willame
le plus vaillant de nul realme,
m'entremis de cest livre feire
e de l'engleis en romanze treire.
Esopë apel'um cest livre,
qu'il translata e fist escrire.
del griu en latin le turna. (lines 1–15)

[At the end of this work, which I have treated and narrated in Romance language, I will name myself as a remembrance: Marie is my name, I am from France. It may be that many clerks will appropriate my work as their own, but I want no one else to claim it for himself. He who lets himself be forgotten commits folly. For the love of Count William, the most valiant of any realm, I undertook the writing of this book, and translating it from English into Romance. This book is called Aesop, because he translated it and had it written down; from Greek he put it into Latin.]

In the large, widely circulated canon of Marie's work, she identifies herself only three times,[62] but this instance is the most self-conscious, lengthy, and emphatic of the three, doubtless because she understands fable to be one of the most easily appropriated types of discourse. If her concern partly grows from the fear that her unique accomplishments as a woman writer will be co-opted by male clerks, hers is also a fear that would have been shared by any medieval fabulist, regardless of gender.

The structure of the epilogue echoes that of the prologue: as Romulus's responsibility for the perpetuation of fable took precedence over Aesop's creation and translation of it in the prologue, here Marie describes her own perpetuation of the literary form before she turns to Aesop. Furthermore, she recasts herself in the Aesopic role of having a *mestre* in Count William, her patron. Having taken upon herself the trappings of the *auctor* whose role she is assuming, Marie then reduces Aesop from historical figure to text: he *is* the book that he translated: "Esopë apel'um cest livre."

Editors of Marie's text in the last two centuries have not commented upon where she might have learned of Aesop's slavery. The *Fables*' most recent editor, Charles Brucker, chose to emphasize the shortcomings of medieval literary historiography instead of searching for Marie's source. Defining the Aesop mentioned in line 17, Brucker writes: "Personnage fictif qui, pour les auteurs du moyen âge, représente la tradition ésopique dans son ensemble; il ne s'agit pas d'Esope, auteur grec des Fables, tel que nous l'entendons aujourd'hui."[63] [Fictitious character who, for medieval authors, represented the Aesopic tradition in its entirety; he has nothing to do with Aesop, Greek author of fables, as we understand him today.] In his German translation of Marie's work, Hans Ulrich Gumbert carries this non-medieval distinction a step further, providing this note to the prologue: "Um eine Differenz zwischen dem vermutlichen Autor der berümten griechischen Fabeln und der 'kontaminierten' Gestalt zu setzen, die nach mittelalterlicher Überzeugung die Fabeltradition begründete, steht an dieser Stelle nicht die übliche deutsche Graphie, 'Äsop.'"[64] [In order to establish a difference between the supposed author of the renowned Greek fables and the "contaminated" character who founded the fable tradition according to medieval belief, the normal German spelling, "Äsop," is not used at this point.] By depriving Marie's Aesop of the prize of standard German orthography, Gumbert apologizes to his audience for the "contamination" of Marie's understanding of the authorial figure, as if she had been free to choose between pristine veracity and sullied legend. Perry and Ziolkowski's longing for the formally pure fable of a lost golden age—Aesop as (edited) text— is echoed in Brucker and Gumbert's desire for a historically pure Aesop, a father of the fable cleansed of accretion; the slippery, nonauthoritative slave Aesop continues to be an embarrassment.

Marie apparently took her fables from an English translation of the *Romulus Nilantii* that does not survive;[65] in lines 16–17 of her fable collection's epilogue, Marie attributes this translation to King Alfred. Since the extant version of the *Romulus Nilantii* does not mention Aesop's slavery, we are left with the likelihood that the absent English text gave Marie this information. Or could she have had it from some other source? This possibility deserves consideration particularly in light of the fact that Marie, as a woman, could have been closer to (and less embarrassed by) marginalized, orally transmitted literature than male redactors of fables as representatives of institutionalized education would have been. The story of Aesop's slavery could have survived in the oral tradition, as Perry implies when he calls the *Life* "folk literature."[66] Beyond this putative source lies the equally plausible possibility that as a poet of the Anglo-Norman aristocracy, Marie had access not only to a lost English translation of the *Romulus Nilantii* but also other lost Aesopic literature, and perhaps even a *Life of Aesop*.

The survival of Marie's fable collection in twenty-three manuscripts, mainly from the thirteenth and fourteenth centuries, bears witness to the text's popularity.[67] Among other would-be fabulists whose attention it reached were two of the British authors discussed later in this book: Geoffrey Chaucer, whose *Nun's Priest's Tale* is partly based on Marie's "Del coq et del goupil," and John Lydgate, whose *Isopes Fabules* is probably a translation of the first seven of Marie's fables. Marie's work also exerted considerable influence on the scholastic commentary tradition that grew out of the elegiac Romulus: the standard Latin source for prose plot summaries of the fables, the so-called Romulus LBG, is indebted to Marie's fables in both style and narrative detail.[68] The Romulus LBG prologue, one of two that became standard in the fifteenth century ("Grecia, disciplinarum mater . . ."; see Appendix 2, p. 204), follows Marie's precedent by invoking the name of Aesop as father of the genre but gives equal attention to the emperor Romulus as Latin translator and Alfred as English translator. Whether by an accident of textual transmission or the design of the redactor of the Romulus L B G, Aesop's slavery is not mentioned here.

The aspects of the life of Aesop that survived from the classical era demonstrate two methods of remembering Aesop as the originary function of fable. In the collections by authors whose names we know, Aesop's absence tends to be emphasized, whether that absence is constructed as physical (his death) or social (his status as slave). His literary relics therefore need to be revived and to have their status raised by revisers of fable. Although these fabulists may openly acknowledge a rivalry between themselves and Aesop (for example, Phaedrus and Marie de France), they triumph against their ancient rival simply by creating a fable collection not only dominated by their own names and voices, thereby clearly displacing Aesop, but also recast as teaching truths about contemporaneous social or religious concerns. Modern editors perpetuate a variation on this act of naming: in such titles as "Steinhöwel's *Aesop*" and "Caxton's *Aesop*," they transfer ownership of the textual Aesop to his translators.

At the opposite end of the spectrum are those collections which do not name their narrators, or which pretend to be narrated by Aesop himself as represented in the letter to Xanthus. These collections generally emphasize the Aesop of the monument, the man whose memory is glorified by the Athenians. The fable about the monument validates the view of fable *as* cultural monument: the literary form belongs to Aesop, and it does not require further validation through association with any other name. As Rita Copeland has pointed out, "Where translation is theorized strictly as access to a textual legacy, it is not theorized as appropriation."[69] In these collections "truth" lies not in the adaptation of fable to fit contemporary concerns, but rather, in literary history itself. Twentieth-century scholars hoping either to recreate formal purity in fable or to tease the real Aesop out of the legends surrounding him apparently identify with this group of fabulists, as servants of the "true" Aesop whose textual legacy they hope to revive.

Here then are two opposing paradigms for the perpetuation of fable in Aesop's name. The self-conscious fabulist substitutes himself for the absent Aesop (and masters the slave narratives), while the anonymous fabulist sacrifices his identity to the idolized Aesop and adds his project to the monumental body of work that bears the founding father's name. While curricular practices keep students of fable within the latter paradigm, vernacular fabulists clearly align themselves with the former.

I would like to leave this discussion of the Aesop(s) of the Middle Ages with a suggestion that combines both the ideas of Jean-Marie Schaeffer and the biography of the father of fable. Schaeffer's assertion that the name "Aesop" represents both a text and a historical (or at least legendary) person holds as true for the Middle Ages as it does for the present day. Inasmuch as Aesop's text was constructed as the proper site for appropriation, and inasmuch as he is conflated with his text, we cannot discount the possibility that medieval readers transferred the appropriation of the author's textual relics to the life of the author himself, especially given the fragmentary nature of material about him. Just as a medieval reader could choose a relevant fable and reconstruct it in a particularly relevant form, so he could also construct an Aesop that would serve his particular purposes.

Lest this suggestion seem too hypothetical, let us take as a microcosm of Aesopic history the nineteenth- and twentieth-century attempts to identify the medieval "Aesop" whose work we are studying, the author of the elegiac Romulus. French scholar Léopold Hervieux claimed to have identified the author of the collection, a discovery described in a chapter of *Les Fabulistes Latins* entitled "Dissertation sur le véritable auteur des fables en vers élegiaques."[70] He puts his faith in a number of manuscripts and incunables that name the author as Walter the Englishman, whom Hervieux identifies as chaplain of Henry II, the Anglo-Norman king whose court elevated French culture over indigenous English culture. German critics, including the redoubtable Klaus Grubmüller, have chosen to identify the collection with Isaac Nevelet, its early seventeenth-century editor whose *Mythologia Aesopica* was published in Frankfurt in 1610;[71] thus a German claim to an important moment in the collection's history comes to the forefront. Italy, too, pretends to authorship of the collection. In 1961 a ceremony at the Palatine Library in Parma marked the donation to the library's collection of the only known copy of the 1481 edition of the *Esopus moralizatus* printed by Andrea Portilia in Parma. The speaker, one Dr. Ciavarella, raised an authorial specter that Hervieux had hoped to exorcise: that the verse Romulus was the work of one Salo or Salon of Parma, whose name, like Walter's, is cited in several early manuscripts.[72] These attempts to identify the fabulist as closely as possible with one's own national identity remind us that no appropriation of the Aesopic—nor of Aesop himself, if we should feel so self-confident—is politically neutral. These scholars share with medieval readers the desire to appropriate the Aesopic for their own purposes, and such desires, always based upon selectively chosen documentation, can never call themselves anything but truth.

2

Theories of Fable

Telling Truth, Fearing Falsehood

In our examination of what the phrase "Aesopic fable" might have meant to medieval readers, we have seen that in relation to the term "Aesopic," biographical material was scarce though relatively consistent in its portrait of the father of fable. The medieval uses of the word "fable," however, are neither scarce nor consistent, for in its Latin form, *fabula,* this term signified all types of fiction, not simply the mode of discourse that concerns this study, and attitudes about its value varied widely.

The standard definition of *fabula* supplied by medieval grammarians, according to Paule Demats, was "Fabula est quod neque gestum est nec geri potuit."[1] [Fiction is that which has not been done nor can be done.] Such a category represents an enormous body of textual material ranging from the relatively benign but palpably false Aesopic fable to the licentious *fabulae* in Ovid's *Metamorphoses;* indeed, Peter Dronke asserts that in certain twelfth-century writings, *fabula* was used to mean "myth" specifically, though in general it could retain the meanings of "fiction" and "beast fable."[2]

Any text labeled *fabula* was suspect in medieval Christian ideology, in which only Scripture was beyond suspicion. In Dronke's words, for medieval readers, "The makers of fabled images are untrustworthy: they can deceive themselves and others by thinking fabled images are truth."[3] Therefore, defining the term in the Middle Ages presented a challenge, and most medieval literary theorists responded by dividing the broad term in one way or another, defending types of *fabula* that either communicated truth or could be made to do so through certain types of interpretation. Nevertheless, there remained some doubt among grammarians and philosophers about whether a narrative like Aesopic fable that was not based on truth could teach truth, and we see these writers expressing a remarkable variety of opinions about the value of this mode of discourse.

Even so, Päivi Mehtonen had shown that in the later Middle Ages the trichotomy of literary types—*historia* (roughly, "history"), *argumentum* (plausible fictions, narratives that could have happened but did not), and *fabula*—did not divide into categories as neatly as we might anticipate, since all were meant to be read for ethical edification.[4] The need for litera-ture with ethical content opened the possibility of fable being read seriously, in the manner that Augustine suggested in the passage quoted in the intro-duction to this book. We will see that attitudes toward fable moved gener-ally toward greater respect over the course of roughly a millennium.

Because many literary theorists posited a subdivision of *fabula* attrib-uted specifically to Aesop (or, more rarely, to the Roman fabulist Avianus, who acknowledged his debt to Aesop), I will not consider the full breadth of meaning of the term *fabula* in this chapter. In effect, the theorists who mention Aesop engage in the same rhetorical gesture as the fabulists who use his name to indicate the pedigree of their fables: the name gives the literature historical weight and authority. However, it is important to note that even the staunchest believers in Aesopic *fabula* as a valuable mode of discourse knew that they were called upon to define and defend it against the types of *fabula* that were sometimes thought to be immoral or amoral in nature, and simply conjuring the authoritative name of Aesop was not a strong enough defense.

In this chapter's consideration of the inherited texts that helped to deter-mine the reception of Aesopic fable, I have grouped their authors in histori-cal groups which were meaningful to medieval readers: first the *auctores,* both pagan and Christian authority figures whose writings contributed to the educational heritage which the Church sanctioned in the Middle Ages, and then the medieval inheritors and adapters of those ideas (some of whom had also gained the status of *auctores* by the fourteenth and fifteenth cen-turies). A few of these critics attribute no particular truth telling or moral value to fable itself, although they extol its utility as a rhetorical tool and a vehicle for entertainment. More often, however, writers espouse fable as a moral form of literature, a view which does not preclude its usefulness in pedagogy and as entertainment. Believers in the moral value of fable gener-ally locate that morality in one of two sites: either in the moral truism attached externally to the fable plot, a truth detachable from and indepen-dent of the narrative, or in a truth veiled figuratively or allegorically by the narrative, of which the moral is only an ostensible facet. In either of these cases, the narrative shell enclosing the truth is discountenanced, and for that reason it can become the site of rhetorical free-play, whether in Latin prose paraphrases or vernacular translations. Furthermore, the variety of opinion among the critics discussed here allowed adapters of Aesopic fable to play not only with the plot but also with the location of "truth"; will it reside in an appended moral, or the reader's externally applied allegorical interpretation? Can fable be written so that some kind of truth inhabits the false narrative itself, or can there be truth in any part of fable at all? The opinions about fable in this chapter cover a spectrum of discursive positions from which fabulists could choose in order to add further inventive dimensions to their literary products.

Classical and Early Medieval *Auctores:* Defining the Discursive Field

During the centuries when the verse Romulus was most popular, fables were subjected to the inherited classical curricular practice of the *progymnasmata,* described by Quintilian (A.D. c. 35–100) in the *Institutio Oratoria* and further codified by the fourth-century grammarian Priscian in the *Praeexercitamina.* Charting the best course of study for schoolboys in lower levels of elementary education, Quintilian writes:

> Igitur Aesopi fabellas, quae fabulis nutricularum proxime succedunt, narrare sermone puro et nihil ne supra modum extollente, deinde eandem gracilitatem stilo exigere condiscant; uersus primo solvere, mox mutatis verbis interpretari, tum paraphrasi audacius vertere, qua et breviare quaedam et exornare saluo modo poetae sensu permittitur. Quod opus, etiam consummatis professoribus difficile, qui commode tractauerit cuicumque discendo sufficiet.

> [Therefore let pupils learn to paraphrase fables of the Aesopic sort, which follow closely upon the stories of the nursery, in plain and unexcessive language; and thereafter to effect the same simplicity of style in writing. (Let them learn) to resolve metrical verses into prose, and then to reshape it more freely in a paraphrase; in this it is permitted both to abridge and to elaborate, so long as the poet's meaning remains intact. This task is difficult even for polished instructors, and the person who handles it well will be qualified to learn anything.][5]

Quintilian's suggestion reinscribes the traditional literary activity of appropriating fables, not only for children but also for adults—even schoolteachers. However, Quintilian's interest in fable is purely pedagogical, not explicitly moral (partly because, in Quintilian's view, the good rhetorician is inherently moral). For Quintilian, fable's primary value lies in its simplicity: later in the book he asserts that this discursive mode is appropriate entertainment for simple minds, both children's and peasants'.[6] In a sense, Quintilian's lack of direct attention to morality in relation to fable made his work easier for Christian writers to adopt; his otherwise unexceptionable claims needed only the addition of the veneer of Christianized morality that was always provided for pagan *auctores*. Quintilian's work influenced such prominent medieval educators and thinkers as Alcuin of York, John of Salisbury, and Vincent of Beauvais.[7]

Priscian's *Praeexercitamina,* a translation of a Greek grammar treatise by Hermogenes, became a standard guide for medieval education. The discussion of fables appears early in his book, reflecting the place of fables early in the curriculum. Because Priscian describes both the nature of fables and related classroom methodology, I will quote from his work at some length.

> Fabula est oratio ficta verisimili dispositione imaginem exhibens veritatis. Ideo autem hanc primam tradere pueris solent oratores, quia animas eorum adhuc molles ad meliores facile vias instituunt vitae. Usi sunt tamen ea vetustissimi quoque auctores, ut Hesiodus Archilochus Horatius, Hesiodus quidem lusciniae, Archilochus autem vulpis, Horatius muris. Nominantur autem ab inventoribus fabularum aliae Cypriae, aliae Libycae, aliae Sybariticae, omnes autem communiter Aesopiae, quoniam in conventibus frequenter solebat Aesopus fabulis uti. Et pertinet ad vitae utilitatem et fit verisimilis si res, quae subiectis accidunt personis, apte reddantur, ut puta: de pulchritudine aliquis certat, pavo hic supponatur: oportet alicui astutiam tribuere, vulpecula est subicienda: imitatores aliquos hominum volumus ostendere, hic simiis est locus.
>
> Oportet igitur modo breviter, modo latius eas disserere. Quomodo autem hoc fiat? Si nunc narratione simplici proferantur, nunc etiam sermo inductis fingatur personis. Exempli causa: "Simiae convenerunt et consilium habebant de urbe condenda et, quia placuit illis, paratae erant incipere aedificationem; sed vetus inter eas prohibuit ab incepto eas docens quod facile capiantur si intra muros concludantur." Sic breviter dices. Si velis producere, sic: "Simiae convenerunt. Consiliabantur de urbe condenda. Quarum una in medium veniens contionata est, quia oportet ipsas quoque civitatem habere. Videtis enim, aiebat, quod civitates habendo homines habent etiam domos singuli et contionem universi, et in theatrum ascendentes delectant animos spectationibus et auditionibus variis." Et sic proferes orationem morando dicens, quod et plebiscitum scriptum est, et finges etiam orationem veteris simiae.
>
> Expositio autem fabularum vult circuitionibus carere et iucundior esse. Sed oratio qua utilitas fabulae retegitur, quam epimythion vocant, quod nos affabulationem possumus dicere, a quibusdam prima,

sed a plerisque rationabilius postrema ponitur. Sciendum vero, quod
etiam oratores inter exempla solent fabulis uti.

[A fable is a composition made up to resemble life, projecting an
image of truth in its structure. This is what orators first offer to children, because thus they can easily introduce impressionable young
minds to the better things. The great authors of antiquity also used
fables, men like Hesiod, Archilochus, Horace. Hesiod used the fable
of the nightingale, Archilochus that of the fox, Horace that of the
mouse. Some stories are called Cyprian by their inventors, some
Libyan, some Sybaritic, but all have in common the label Aesopian,
because Aesop was accustomed to use fables frequently among
groups. This technique applies to the needs of life and becomes real-
istic if the things which happen to the subject are then related to the
experiences of real men. For example, when one wants to talk about
beauty, a peacock may be brought in; if it is one's purpose to treat of
cleverness, let him tell about a little fox; if he wants to show how
human beings are imitators, let that be the place for apes. Now it is
also important to tell the story succinctly in some cases, at greater
length in others. How can that be done? By telling a simple story one
time, then at another giving speech to participants, as for example:
"The apes came together to discuss building a city, and agreed that
they should start construction. But one old ape in the group prevented
them from beginning by pointing out that they could be easily captured if they were hemmed in by walls." That is the succinct form. But
if you want to develop it more, then do this: "The apes came together
and had a council meeting about establishing a city. One of them
stood before the group and proclaimed that it was important for them
to have a city. 'For you see,' he said, 'that men who have cities have
individual homes and an assembly hall for the whole tribe, they go to
theaters where they enjoy themselves in pleasant sights and sounds of
all kinds.'" And you may draw out the oration in this way by lingering
over details, telling how the written vote was taken, and developing in
the same way the speech of the old ape. In developing the fable, one
should avoid circumlocutions and be more informal. But the statement which points out the moral of the fable, which we call
epimythion (and which we can also call the *affabulation*) is placed at
the beginning by some authors, but by most (and more reasonably) at
the end. Be sure that you note how orators frequently use fables
among their examples.][8]

Priscian apparently took for granted that fable served as useful rhetorical modeling clay for children, but to this idea he adds a number of other observations about fable as curricular text. The treatise distinguishes between *expositio* and *oratio,* the former informal or perhaps even humorous (*iocundior*) and the latter purposeful; *expositio* avoids circumlocution, presumably in order to expedite the appearance of the *oratio,* which is built around the fable's *epimythion* or *promythion.* Although such verbal economy typified medieval Latin fable paraphrases, it was to become the exception in vernacular fables.

Tacitly suggesting that a fable's narrative is based upon falsehood, Priscian emphasizes that any truth in a fable resides in the way that its structure (*dispositio*) reflects real life: the successful teller relates his fable to "the experiences of real men," and thus the fable "project[s] an image of truth," though not truth per se. In a curricular context, with pupils revising fables in the enclosed, artificial environment of the classroom, such experience probably remained at a level of considerable generality. Specificity, however, could apply outside the classroom: the fable quoted by Patavino's "educated man" was clearly linked to the experiential "truth" of its hearers, even of Ezelino. Priscian's ideas about fable are more detailed inasmuch as they espouse situational specificity as an integral part of mastering this mode of discourse, but this prescription eschews generic rules for discursive ones.

Priscian's and Quintilian's texts function similarly in two important ways. First, they both cite Aesop as the originary name associated with fable, thus giving the literature the authority associated with an already classicized past (though Priscian takes the significant step of listing literary fable tellers and their fables in order to highlight the mode's subsequent authoritative pedigree). On the other hand, both theorists also state that schoolmasters should require pupils to challenge the classical authority of the texts by making the fables their own through rhetorical revision in the classroom. These seemingly contradictory views epitomize an essential paradox in Aesopic fable: it must draw its authority from its father figure Aesop, lest it be mistaken for a mere spontaneous anecdote, but that authority can be only literary-historical, never actual. To the current teller go the spoils (or, in thirteenth-century Padua, the spoliation) of the telling.

That this pedagogical advice was followed in the millennium between Quintilian's era and the fourteenth and fifteenth centuries is evidenced in literally hundreds of documents;[9] these include the commentaries discussed at length in Chapter 3. Most clearly indebted to progymnasmatic principles is Alexander Neckham's *Novus Avianus,* a late-twelfth or early-thirteenth-century adaptation of the Roman fable collection which was the standard curricular choice in Europe until the thirteenth century. Neckham retells Avianus's second fable, "De Aquila et Testudine," in three forms: *copiose, compendiose,* and *subcincte*— that is, first practicing *amplificatio,* then rewriting the fable without appreciably adding to or subtracting from it, and finally practicing *abbreviatio.*[10]

One of the few *auctores* to include Aesopic fables in a hierarchical taxonomy of fictional forms was Macrobius (fl. c. 400). Although the literary categories in his *Commentarii in Somnium Scipionis* are well known, the definition of *fabula* bears repeating here as a source for many later commentators on literary genre. After defining *fabula* as fiction generally, he divides it into specific categories.

> Fabulae, quarum nomen indicat falsi professionem, aut tantum conciliandae auribus voluptatis aut adhortationis quoque in bonam frugem gratia repertae sunt, auditum mulcent: velut comoediae, quales Menander eiusque imitatores agendas dederunt: vel argumenta fictis casibus amatorum referta; quibus vel multum se [Petronius] Arbiter exercuit, vel Apuleium nonnunquam lusisse miramur. Hoc totum fabularum genus, quod solas aurium delicias profitetur e sacrario suo in nutricum cunas sapientiae tractatus eliminat. Ex his autem, quae ad quamdam virtutis speciem intellectum legentis hortantur, sit secunda discretio, in quibusdam enim et argumentum ex ficto locatur et per mendacia ipse relationis ordo contexitur: ut sunt illae Aesopi fabulae elegantia fictionis illustres. . . . Ex hac ergo (secunda) divisione, quam diximus, a philosophiae libris prior species, quae concepta de falso per falsum narratur, aliena est.

> [Fables—the very name acknowledges their falsity—serve two purposes: either merely to gratify the ear or to encourage the reader to good works. They delight the ear as do the comedies of Menander and his imitators, or the narratives replete with imaginary doings of lovers in which Petronius Arbiter so freely indulged and with which Apuleius, astonishingly, sometimes amused himself. This whole category of fables which promise only to gratify the ear a philosophical treatise avoids and relegates to children's nurseries. The other group, those that draw the reader's attention to certain kinds of virtue, are divided into two types. In the first both the setting and the plot are fictitious, as in the fables of Aesop, famous for his exquisite imagination. . . . Of the second main group, which we have just mentioned, the first type, with both setting and plot fictitious, is also inappropriate to philosophical treatises.][11]

Macrobius judges fables unfit for philosophical discourse, paradoxically because the moral truth that can be drawn from them cannot compensate for the fact that no historical truth has gone into them. This attitude is all the more striking—and inconsistent—in light of his espousal of allegorical interpretation of the stories of the pagan gods, which were also *fabulae* though of a different category (I.ii.11). While his ideas about the interpretation of mythology were celebrated, his banishment of fables was not; instead, he became the theorist whom later critics had to refute. In spite of his general lack of enthusiasm about fable, Macrobius grants the literary form a certain weak agency: it "draws a reader's attention to virtue," presumably an allusion to its entertaining narrative surface. What Macrobius leaves unstated is that fable cannot truly teach virtue; only philosophy can.

Ironically, patristic philosophers seemed less concerned about the inherently false nature of fable narrative than Macrobius did. In the passage from *Contra Mendacium* quoted in the introduction, St. Augustine defends fictitious narratives that conceal true meanings:

In quo genere fingendi humana etiam facta vel dicta irrationalibus animantibus et rebus sensu carentibus homines addiderunt, ut eius modi fictis narrationibus, sed veracibus significationibus, quod vellent commendatius intimarent. Nec apud auctores tantum saecularium litterarum, ut apud Horatium, mus loquitur muri, et mustela vulpeculae, ut per narrationem fictam ad id, quod agitur, vera significatio referatur; unde et Aesopi tales fabulas ad eum finem relatas, nullus tam ineruditus fuit, qui putaret appellanda mendacia: sed in Litteris quoque sacris, sicut in Libro Judicum ligna sibi regem requirunt, et loquuntur ad oleam, et ad ficum, et ad vitem, et ad rubum. Quod tutum utique fingitur, ut ad rem quae intenditur, ficta quidem narratione, non mendaci tamen, sed veraci significatione veniantur.

[In (this) sort of fiction, men have put even human deeds or words to irrational animals and things without sense, that by this sort of feigned narrations but true significations, they might in more winning manner intimate the things which they wished. Nor is it only in authors of secular letters, as in Horace, that mouse speaks to mouse, and weasel to fox, that through a fictitious narration a true signification may be referred to the matter in hand; whence the like fables of Aesop being referred to the same end, there is no man so untaught as to think they ought to be called lies: but in Holy Writ also, as in the book of Judges, the trees seek them a king, and speak to the olive, to the fig, to the vine, and to the bramble. Which, in any wise, is all feigned, with intent that one may get to the thing which is intended, by a feigned narration indeed, yet not a lying one, but with a truthful signification.][12]

Here Augustine is not defending fiction for its own sake; rather, he believes that it is valuable only insofar as it represents truth behind a surface of apparent falsehood. While emphasizing the representational aspect of fiction, Augustine stresses a similarity between the secular fable and the fable in the book of Judges, thus casting Aesopic fable in a favorable light. This is the most straightforward Christian defense of the genre likely to be found in patristic writing.

A passage from Augustine's *Quaestiones evangeliorum* provides a helpful gloss on what Augustine might mean by a lying fiction. Here he asserts that not everything that is fabricated is necessarily a lie:

Non enim omne quod fingimus mendacium est; sed quando id fingimus quod nichil significat, tunc est mendacium. Cum autem fictio nostra refertur ad aliquam signficationem, non est mendacium, sed aliqua figura veritatis. . . . Fictio igitur quae ad aliquam veritatem refertur figura est, quae non refertur mendacium est.

[Not everything we make up is a lie. When we make up something that does not signify anything, there we have a lie. However, when our fiction refers to a certain meaning, it is not a lie, but a figure of truth. Therefore, fiction is a figure if it is used with reference to some truth. On the other hand, fiction is a lie, if the reference is lacking.][13]

Although this passage does not mention Aesopic fable, it helps to define the terms used in the discussion of Aesopic fable in *Contra Mendacium*. The differential element between a lying fiction and an acceptable one is figural reference. In relation to fable, as we have seen, the truth to which the narrative refers can be located in the moral, in a scholastic comment, or in the situation for which the fable is tailored. Whatever the ultimate truth, Augustine is careful not to align it with authorial intention: the responsibility for locating it belongs as much to the reader as to the author, since the reader brings a frame of reference to the work.

Obviously familiar with Augustine's *Contra Mendacium*, Isidore of Seville may also have been influenced by Macrobius, if only in his desire to categorize fiction in terms of what it communicates. In the *Etymologiae* he defines fables as follows: "Fabulas poetae a fando nominaverunt, quia non sunt res factae, sed tantum loquendo fictae." [Poets have named "fables" from "speaking" (*fando*), since they are not things that happened (*res factae*) but only fictions by speaking (*loquendo fictae*).][14]

Here all of fiction is categorized as a discursive act, since fiction, which describes events that have not taken place in history, exists only as speech.

In his subdivisions of fiction, Isidore divides fables into two types: the Aesopic, in which no humans are present, and the Libistican, in which they are. He also states that a fable has one of three goals: "Fabulas poetae quasdam delectandi causa finxerunt, quasdam ad naturam rerum, nonnullas ad mores hominum interpretati sunt." [Poets have invented some fables for the sake of pleasing, some according to the nature of things, and some are interpreted according to human character.][15] Isidore sees a clear division between purely delightful fictions and instructive fable. Entertaining plots ("quasdam delectandi causa finxerunt") such as were written by Plautus and Terence carry no implicit truth. On the other hand morally instructive tales belong to a different category, the description of which is taken almost verbatim from Augustine's *Contra Mendacium* as quoted above. The verb "interpretati sunt" clearly sets these narratives apart as having a figurative meaning which the reader must actively seek; Isidore contrasts this with the pleasure with which poets imbue certain fictions, an aesthetic characteristic that remains within the artist's purview. But if, as Martin Irvine has stated, Isidore's goal in this book is to make a distinction between *fabula* and *historia,* he "leaves the status of literary fiction unresolved,"[16] not least because he does not fully define how to distinguish between these two major categories; his subdivisions of fiction are more precise.

Later Medieval Fable Theorists: Toward Christianizing the Fable

The writers described above present a wider variety of ideas about the nature and function of fable than their later medieval counterparts do; to the later writers fell the task of revising the ideas of earlier *auctores* to justify the place of fable in the Christian curriculum.

A practical, school-oriented discussion of fables appears in the *Accessus ad Auctores,* an early-twelfth-century manual giving brief critical introductions to classical texts. For the purposes of this book, it is noteworthy that the *Accessus* author chose to organize his discussion by author rather than by the generic or discursive function of each author's text. The very presence of the fourth-century fabulist Avianus is also significant, since most of the authors here (Prudentius, Homer, and Ovid, for example) would seem to demand much more complex interpretative methodology than the fabulist. In the section of his treatise on Avianus, he draws upon the distinction made by Isidore between Aesopic and Libistican fables but concentrates upon a more academic definition of the discursive mode than Isidore's:

Iste liber intitulatur *Avianus,* et fuit Romanus civis, quem rogavit quidam Theodosius nobilis romanus ut scriberet sibi aliquas fabulas, in quibus delectaretur. Cuius rogatui Avianus satisfaciens scripsit ei quasdam fabulas, in quibus non solum valuit delectari, verum etiam allegoricum sensum in singulis notare, quoniam habet unaquaeque fabula suam intentionem et suam moralitatem. . . . Materia eius sunt ipsae fabulae et commune proficuum allegoriae, intentio eius est delectare nos in fabulis et prodesse in correctione morum, utilitas eius est delectatio poematis et correctio morum. Ethicae subponitur, quia tractat de correctione morum.[17]

[This book is called *Avianus,* and he was a Roman citizen whom a certain renowned Roman, Theodosius, asked to write for him some fables in which he might take delight. Satisfying his request, Avianus wrote certain fables for him in which he was able not only to take delight but also to observe allegorical meaning in each one, because each fable has its own intention and its own moral. . . . His matter is these fables, and allegories for the common good; his intent is to delight us with these fables and to be profitable in the correction of morals; his utility is the delight of a poem and the correction of morals. Ethics is underlying, because (the book) treats of the correction of morals.]

Using the standard categories for scholastic introductions of his era,[18] this commentator emphasizes the way in which the fabulist altered his patron's commission by pairing simple delight with instruction, both of which feature in the intention described here. Fable's delightful exterior and its allegorical mode are given equal weight as parts of Avianus's subject matter ("non solum valuit delectari, verum etiam allegoricum sensum in singulis notare"). Thus the author of this treatise ensures that fable readers will look for instruction, because reading only for delight contravenes the author's explicit intention. Perhaps because this writer is addressing the work of only one author rather than attempting to define fable generally, he locates "truth" in the authorial intention for each fable; however, when he states that "each fable has its own intention and its own moral," he tacitly opens the troubling possibility that a fabulist may include contradictory fables within a single collection. Thus "truth" becomes situational in a slightly different sense than we have seen before.

Following the paragraph quoted above is the subheading "Misterium fabularum Aviani" (*misterium,* according to Niermeyer, meaning "hidden thing" or "allegorical sign," terminology often used in scriptural exegesis), under which a brief interpretation of each of Avianus's forty-two fables is given. A single example will serve to demonstrate what qualified as interpretation. The first fable in the collection, "De nutrice et infante," tells of a nurse whose charge so consistently refuses to sleep that she threatens to throw him to the wolves outside. A wolf at the door hears the threat and anticipates a tasty meal, but the child soon falls asleep. The wolf then retreats to complain to a friend that he has been tricked by the nurse. In the illogical moral, the narrator tells anyone tempted to believe a woman's sincerity to take the lesson of the fable to heart. The *Accessus* writer gives the following interpretation: "Hic hortatur nos ne temere credamus omni promittenti, ne dampnum incurramus ut lupus seductus a femina" (22). [Here (the author) urges that we not rashly believe everything that has been promised, lest we incur loss, like the wolf led astray by the woman.] This *misterium* is remarkably similar to Avianus's own *moralitas*, "Haec sibi dicta putet seque hac sciat arte notari, feminem quisquis credidit esse fidem." [Let anyone who believes in a woman's sincerity reflect that to him these words are spoken and that it is he whom this lesson censures (Duff 684–85).] The commentator does not view the text objectively enough to avoid the obvious logical fallacy presented in the original moral, that the nurse did not unconditionally promise the child to the wolf. Indeed, the major difference between Avianus's *moralitas* and the *Accessus* comment is the use of the first person instead of the original, rather formal third person singular: this fable is being told for us, and we are to apply the moral to ourselves. This, evidently, passes for instruction and perhaps even for the fable's "allegorical sense." While it is significant that the weak gestures of interpretation in the *Accessus* were considered adequate in the Middle Ages, the text is more interesting simply for its inclusion of fable in the literary canon and its commentator's use of a validating metalanguage for the interpretation of fables, even if his terminology strikes modern readers as too high-flown for the hermeneutic process that it describes.

Also during the twelfth century, the *Commentarii in Somnium Scipionis* itself became the subject for a commentary by the Chartrian scholar William of Conches, whose interpretation of Macrobius allegorizes the allegorizer. Judging all types of fiction to be greater than simply meaningless entertainment, William borrows the images of the nursery with which Macrobius had dismissed fable, elaborating upon them to show that the foundation of learning can be laid there: "Cunas nutricum vocat scolas poetarum, quia ut corpora puerorum in cunis lacte nutriuntur, ita anima poetarum edificantur in scolis, vel ita minus periti in eis auctoribus, scilicet levioribus sententiis habent instrui." [He calls the literary authors "children's nurseries": for as the nurse nurtures the infant in the cradle on lighter foods, so is the student nurtured on matter from the lighter authors; this is also for the sake of practice, so that he may more easily understand the heavier ones.][19] William also remedies his source's neglect of the allegorical nature of the fable.

> Per fabulas enim, quas ille [Aesop] composuit, ad aliquam morum instructionem exortamur, et tamen per eas nichil veri significatur, ut-pote est illud, quod refert de vulpe et corvo. . . . Per hanc igitur fabu-lam, etsi veri nichil significet, per eam tamen innuit hanc moralitatem, quod multociens id, quod aliquis clauso habet ore, aperto amittit.

> [By Aesop's fables we are brought to some insight into behavior, and yet they signify nothing true. . . . Consider for instance the fox and the crow. . . . Even if it (the fable) signifies nothing true, by way of it Aesop is able to suggest a moral point: often what someone has if he keeps his mouth shut is lost if he opens it.][20]

In his discussion of fable William attempts to bring Macrobian fable theory into line with contemporary educational practice. In doing so, he echoes (perhaps only by chance) Quintilian's assumption of kinship between fables and the stories which have been told to children by their nurses (I.ix.2). William's imagery also recalls New Testament passages in which newly converted Christians are compared to unweaned infants who are not ready for solid food.[21]

William's gloss on the *Commentarii* involves him in some careful seman-tic shifting: falsity, mentioned very clearly three times in Macrobius, is euphemized to an ambiguous "nothing of truth is signified" (nichil veri significatur). Nevertheless, William sees value in a fable's moral and its extraliterary application; although no univalent moral is necessarily "signi-fied" in the fable narrative, a lesson can be extrapolated from it, and it seems related to authorial agency, since Aesop "suggests" a specific moral point. William effectively inverts Macrobius's dismissal of the fable by im-plying that authorial intention lead the reader out of the falseness of the narrative to a general truth.

A lengthy and detailed discussion of the fables of both Aesop and Avianus occurs in the *Dialogus super Auctores* by Conrad of Hirsau (c. 1070–c. 1150), who used Isidore as a primary source but also knew the *Accessus ad Auctores* and possibly the work of his contemporary, William of Conches. The opening section of the dialogue in which the *magister* and his *discipulus* discuss Aesop is taken directly from Isidore of Seville and includes not only his definitions of Aesopic versus Libistican fables but also the three possible goals for fables: merely to delight, to explain the nature of things, or to provide a moral lesson. After the *magister* gives a brief interpretation of the fable of the wolf and the lamb at the river, in which rapists, thieves, and heretics are compared to wolves and innocents to lambs, the pupil poses a theoretical question alluded to in the *Accessus ad Auctores:* does the teacher take the meaning from the author's subject matter or from his intention? The master replies that Aesop took his subject matter from base and corruptible human nature, through which man makes himself similar to beasts, birds, stones, or trees. Something similar is used in the pages of Scripture, says the teacher, who cites the fable in Judges. The teacher adds: "Ex ipse materia patet auctoris intentio, quia per hoc opus variis compactum figmentis voluit et delectare hominumque naturam quasi rationis expertem ex brutorum animantium collatione ad se revocare. Causa finalis lectionis fructus est." [The author's intention is clearly seen from his choice of subject matter. For through this work, assembled as it is from various invented stories, he wanted to delight and also to recall irrational human nature to its true self by a comparison with brute beasts. The final cause is the profit (*fructus*) to be derived from reading the book.][22] Conrad proposes that by corrupting proper human nature, people transform themselves—make themselves what they are not—and therefore the purpose of fables is to call them back to themselves ("ad se revocare"). The degradation of sinful men to the status of beasts, taken from 2 Peter 2:10–12 or Jude 10, was also a commonplace in expositions of the *Metamorphoses,* but the idea that proper interpretation of fables reverses this debasement seems to be Conrad's alone. By implication, Conrad sees one type of falseness—fiction, in which animals speak—mirroring another type, when humans are false to the divine truth which created them. In other words, fables are essentially negative examples, embarrassing readers into moral behavior by depicting animals who appear too human for our comfort.

A discussion of Avianus follows immediately, for reasons explained by the master: "Sequitur Avianus in ascensu parvulorum et velut in gradu lactentis infantiae positus eorum, qui solidum cibum nondum possunt capere nec adhuc disciplinis validioribus auctorum maiorum operam dare." [Avianus is the next stage in the ascent of the young (to knowledge). He comes at the stage when they are not yet weaned, still cannot take solid food or give their attentions to the sterner discipline of more important authors.][23] Both the weaning metaphor and the usefulness of these fables for early study are carried through the dialogue. Avianus is a step higher than Aesop both because the Roman was a Catholic (according to Conrad) and because his fables, unlike Aesop's, are in verse.[24] In addition, Avianus supplies direct moral statements before or after his fables, thus clarifying their meaning and value ("sensum et fructum").[25]

At the end of this elaborate defense of fables, the master confuses his student by reinforcing the Macrobian notion that fables actually signify nothing. When the student points out that the teacher has contradicted himself ("numquam enim ad mores hominum fabulas suas poetae referrent, nisi per eas aliquid significarent"),[26] the teacher defines what is significant and what is not.

> Aliud enim sunt poemata et in his vulgaria proverbia nihil ponderis habentia, utpote quasi sonus levis transeuntia, aliud divina eloquia, quae fundata et aeterna sunt spiritali intelligentia; et verba, immo literae simplices et nudae, signa quaedam sensus latentis sunt: putasne, cum *caelum et terra transibunt,* hesopicae fabulae durabunt? Verum *verba* domini *non transibunt.*

> [For poems, and among them common proverbs which have no weight, are one and the same thing, for they are transient, like a slight sound that is heard, but God-inspired sayings, which are founded in and made eternal by their spiritual meaning, are quite different. Words, or rather simple unadorned letters, are outward indications of a hidden meaning (*sensus*), but are quite different from the eternal, unchanging Word. Do you think that when "heaven and earth shall pass away" (Mark 13:31) the fables of Aesop will endure? But "the words of the Lord will not pass away" (Luke 21:22).][27]

There is nothing surprising in the master's tirade against secular literature; this philosophy was common even beyond the age of Chaucer. But though Conrad's retraction may consign the fables of Aesop and Avianus to meaningless transience, the fable of the trees in Judges prevents him from rejecting fable as a mode of discourse. Logically, if the study of secular fables can provide a basis for understanding the fable in Judges, then such study must be worthwhile, for it leads to the ultimate truth inherent in Scripture, as Augustine implies.[28]

John of Garland, who wrote in the first half of the thirteenth century, espoused the view that fable could and should be used to cloak the truth. To describe this use of fable in the *Parisiana Poetria,* he employs one of the conventional metaphors for allegory in the Middle Ages (and one favored earlier by William of Conches),[29] the "integument" or "veil" behind which higher truths are disguised:

> Si narratio fuerit obscura, per fabulam appositam uel per appologum clarificetur, per integumentum quod est veritas in specie fabule palliata. Et notandum quod omnis appologus est fabula, sed non conuertitur. Est enim apologus sermo brutorum animalium ad nostram instructionem, ut in Aviano et in Esopo.

> [If a whole narrative is obscure, it may be made plain by means of a suitable story or fable, through the device known as integument, which is a truth cloaked in the outward form of a story. And notice that every apologue is a fiction (*fabula*), but not vice versa. For in an apologue dumb animals are made to speak for our edification, as in Avianus and Aesop.][30]

John takes the important step of defining apologue as a subcategory of *fabula*, thus alleviating some of the confusion surrounding the Latin meaning of the more inclusive term. He emphasizes intertextuality in his explanation of the nature of apologue: it both conceals and clarifies the truth to which it is applied, whether that truth be an inherited moral or a political situation (as in the terrorized court of Ezelino da Romano) or simply a moral truism. Although John assumes that apologue will rhetorically clarify the truth, his concomitant assertion that fable can *hide* the truth is both an overstatement and a medieval commonplace. The claim that fable innately or artificially "hides" the truth makes the interpretation of a fable appear more challenging than it really is, perhaps in order to give young readers the impression that they are moving curricular mountains rather than laboring to bring forth hermeneutic mice.

In 1256 Hermann the German completed his translation of the *Middle Commentary on the Poetics* by the Arab scholar Averroes; it, in turn, was a translation of Aristotle's *Poetics*. Its popularity was limited, partly because current discussions of imagery and symbolic language were dominated by pseudo-Dionysian thought which this work reinforced but did not radically alter.[31] The treatise's ideas about fable contradict the most popular interpretive trends of the era during which Hermann lived:

> Dixit [Aristotiles]. Et patet etiam ex hiis que dicta sunt de intentione sermonum poeticorum, quoniam representationes que fiunt per figmenta mendosa adinventitia non sunt de opere poete. Et sunt ea que nominantur proverbia et exempla, ut ea que sunt in libro Esopi et

consimilibus fabulosis conscriptionibus. Ideo poete non pertinet loqui nisi in rebus que sunt aut quas possibile est esse. . . . Compositorum vero fabularum et proverbiorum opus non est opus poetarum, quamvis huiusmodi proverbia et fabulas adinventicias componant sermone metrico; quamvis enim in metro communicent, tamen alterius eorum completur operatio intenta per fabulas etiam si sit absque metro; et est instructio quedam prudentialis que acquiritur per tales adinventicias fabulas. Poeta vero non pertingit ad complementum propositi sui per ymaginativas commotiones nisi per metrum. Fictor ergo proverbiorum adinventiciorum et fabularum adinvenit seu fingit individua que penitus non habent existentiam in re, et ponit eis nomina. Poete vero ponunt nomina rebus existentibus, et fortassis loquuntur in universalibus; ideoque ars poetrie propinquior est philosophie quam sit ars adinventicia proverbiorum.

[Aristotle says: It is clear from what has been said about the purpose of poetic discourse that representations arrived at by means of false and invented fictions are not part of the work of the poet. These are what are called proverbs and exemplary tales (*exempla*), like those in Aesop and similar fabulous writings. So, it is not a poet's business to speak other than in terms of objects which exist or which can exist. . . . The task of composing proverbs and fables is not the same as that of a poet, although men compose proverbs and invented fables of this sort in metre. For, although they both use metre, the purpose of proverbs and fables is achieved through the stories themselves, and would be achieved even if metre were absent. It is a kind of instruction in prudence which is acquired through such invented stories. But it is only through metre that the poet attains his end by imaginative stimulation. Thus, the writer who makes up invented proverbs and fables invents or imagines individual things which do not exist at all in reality, and gives them names. But the poet gives names only to those things which already exist. And perhaps poets speak in universal terms. Therefore, the art of poetry is closer to philosophy than is the art of inventing proverbs.][32]

This curious passage resembles Macrobius's *Commentarii* in its refusal to allow fable to enter the halls of the discourse which the author defines—in Macrobius's case, philosophy, and here, poetry (which this work characterizes as philosophical). Furthermore, Macrobius's belief that fables were meaningless because they were based on no literal truth is echoed in this passage: a poet's work must be based upon reality, but fables by nature are not, and therefore they do not qualify as poetry. Regardless of their true philosophical import, however, fables in Aristotle's formulation are clearly educational, and the faint praise with which they are described ("a kind of instruction in prudence") reflects one of their curricular functions in Hermann's day.

A later inheritor of the Macrobian tradition of generic classification was Giovanni Boccaccio, whose *De genealogia deorum gentilium* attempted to justify nearly all types of literature in terms of their ability to communicate truth through allegory. In Book XIV, Chapter 9, which is entitled "It Is Rather Useful than Damnable to Compose Stories," the writer's classifications of fiction closely parallel those found in Macrobius, but Boccaccio shunts "old wives' tales," which even he cannot defend, to an isolated fourth position. His first classification is the fable, which "superficially lacks all appearance of truth; for example, when brutes or inanimate things converse. Aesop, an ancient Greek, grave and venerable, was past master in this form; and though it is a common and popular form both in city and country, yet Aristotle, chief of the Peripatetics, and a man of divine intellect, did not scorn to use it in his books."[33] In asserting that fable only apparently and superficially lacks truth, Boccaccio acknowledges earlier criticism that fable is completely false, but he inherently criticizes his predecessors as bad readers. Like Priscian, he cites not only the creator of fable but also one of its most authoritative perpetuators, Aristotle. As he continues to defend this mode of discourse, Boccaccio shows a debt to Augustine or Isidore in citing the fable in the book of Judges as justification for studying Aesopic literature.[34]

Of particular relevance to this study is an anecdote that Boccaccio writes about the uses of fiction in education. Robert, son of King Charles of Sicily and later king himself, was uninterested in his studies until his master "lured his mind with the fables of Aesop into so grand a passion for study and knowledge, that in a brief time he not only learned the liberal arts familiar to Italy, but entered with wonderful keenness of mind into the very inner mysteries of sacred philosophy."[35] In Boccaccio's formulation, the apparent falseness and rhetorical sweetness of fable become lures to draw unwitting—and even unwilling—readers into the "inner mysteries of sacred philosophy." The last phrase in this description takes aim at Macrobius, whose work Boccaccio knew: even if fable was deemed inappropriate for philosophical discourse by the earlier writer, Boccaccio finds it a sufficient route for reaching that inner sanctum.

In Book XV Boccaccio discusses the manner in which pagan poets' stories should be interpreted. In Chapter 8, entitled "The Pagan Poets of Mythology Are Theologians," he cites the three types of theological interpretation which Augustine took from Varro: mythical, physical, and civil.

Boccaccio writes that physical theology is "natural and moral," and that it is found often among the great poets, who "clothe many a physical and moral truth in their inventions." He concludes this passage with the same biblical example used above: "Nor let my pious critics be offended to hear the poets sometimes called even sacred theologians. In like manner sacred theologians turn physical when occasion demands; if in no other way, at least they prove themselves physical theologians as well as sacred when they express truth by the fable of the trees choosing a king."[36] Again, figurative discourse is emphasized here, and Boccaccio repeats Augustine's association of Aesop with the fable in Judges. Boccaccio's work gives evidence that by the later Middle Ages, readers could openly acknowledge a connection between the lowly figuration of the fable and higher theological allegorical interpretation. These ideas represent an important change in fable theory from the time of Macrobius; whereas the earlier writer espoused the need for external truth even in fictions, the later one stresses that truth in all fictions must be found through allegory.

The views of fable detailed above represent the genre's theoretical tradition up to and beyond the era in which the elegiac Romulus was written. The wide variety of theories about the genre—that it signified nothing or that its only value was in signification, that it required no interpretation or that its interpretation was more important than the text itself, that it was readily accessible to children or that it shared formal complexities with Scripture— must have been partially familiar to the Latin fabulist. We would do a disservice to both that writer and his community of readers if we attempted to synthesize the views above into a comprehensive, cohesive theory of Aesopic fable over all of the centuries that we call the Middle Ages. However, a few general similarities unite the work of the later writers: they believed that fable was worth reading and studying and that it communicated a moral truth of some kind in spite of (or perhaps even because of) the falseness of its entertaining exterior. The obvious truth of fable lay in its moral, a proverbial distillation of a generalized truth, but another current idea, traceable to Augustine through Boccaccio, held that the narrative concealed a truth of its own, only partially manifested in any moral truism.

At the heart of both views of fable is relative uninterest in the narrative, the fable plot. In the former view, while the plot serves as a means to an end, only the end is worth retaining in memory, and readers remember it in order to enact it in the ethical decisions of day-to-day life. In the latter view, the plot is to be challenged by various hermeneutic practices, which historically included allegoresis, so that the beastly exterior will fall away from a truth that has structured the fable. Because both of these views stress moral interpretation as fable's raison d'être, they allow fable tellers greater freedom in adapting, amplifying, and abbreviating fable: while the rhetorical vehicle must ultimately reach its destination, it may take any number of routes there, some of those quite circuitous, as scholastic fable commentary demonstrates.

What the material in this chapter should also show us is that when medieval vernacular fabulists expressed doubts about the legitimacy of their literary pursuits, they were necessarily engaged in more serious self-examination than was implied by the conventional modesty topos, in which authors forewarn of their own ignorance and rhetorical weaknesses. For no matter how favorable an author's attitude toward fable, he could not control that of his readers, who may well have been more suspicious of the value of fable than of other modes of discourse and genres. And the vernacular fabulist's task became all the more difficult when this suspicion was compounded by the fact that many medieval readers would already have mastered fable through curricular practices relating to the elegiac Romulus and might not think they have much left to learn from the childish fable. The ways that they achieved curricular mastery of this mode of discourse are the subject of the next chapter.

3

Toward a Grammar of Medieval Fable Reading in Its Pedagogical Context

This chapter studies the intersection between our two earlier topics, the medieval understanding of Aesop as father of fable and of fable as a fictitious discursive mode, and the uniquely medieval practices of scholastic commenting on "classical" texts that gives detailed evidence of how readers responded to curricular Aesopic fables in the fourteenth and fifteenth centuries. Extant manuscripts and incunables bear witness to many pedagogical and interpretive practices associated with the elegiac Romulus, ranging from the rudiments of language acquisition that are still at the heart of teaching Latin today to techniques of intertextual elaboration and allegorization that challenge the modern understanding of fable. My goal here is to describe and analyze the pedagogical uses and significance of the full range of scholastic practices associated with fable, for these served as the lenses through which medieval readers, including Chaucer, Lydgate, and Henryson, viewed fable. It is important to confront this variety, because a number of modern critics, looking at medieval vernacular fable in light of modern attitudes toward it as a humble, simple genre for children, have misperceived aspects of the works of these poets as humorous, indecorous, inappropriate, or willfully arbitrary, though medieval readers would probably have seen only variations on familiar curricular practices associated with fable. As modern readers of medieval vernacular texts, we need to accustom ourselves to the impressive number of curricular addenda and interpretive options available to medieval fable readers, so that we can more fully appreciate the interests and accomplishments of vernacular fabulists as they incorporate those elements into their translations.

The teaching and learning of fable texts and authorized methods of interpretation were the province of clerical culture, a culture like every other in its desire to perpetuate a normative body of knowledge that gained its bearer entry into that culture. Pierre Bourdieu has written extensively about the multifaceted process of reinforcing "legitimate language" in the academy. His work focuses upon modern France, where shades of correctness of vocabulary and grammar are adjudged by the Académie Française, the historically sanctioned arbiters of language, but the Académie's role in relation to French is not unlike the medieval church's role as perpetuator of the Latin tradition and arbiter of the Latin grammar and rhetoric taught to medieval schoolboys. Indeed, the power dynamic which Bourdieu describes in an essay reproduced in *Language and Symbolic Power* parallels that in medieval pedagogy. Here Bourdieu writes of how literature both reifies the "legitimate language" and reinforces belief in its legitimacy: "It is not a question of the symbolic power which writers, grammarians, or teachers may exert over the language in their personal capacity, and which is no doubt much more limited than the power they can exert over culture. . . . Rather, it is a question of the contribution they make, independently of any intentional pursuit of distinction, to the production, consecration, and imposition of a distinct and distinctive language [i]n the collective labour which is pursued through the struggles for what Horace called *arbitrium et jus et norma loquendi.*"[1] It is surely no coincidence that Bourdieu resorts to Latin in order to describe the process of learning legitimate language; he goes on to describe how grammarians have labored to extract rules "from the practice of the professionals of written expression (from the past), by a process of retrospective formulation and codification."[2] Such was also the work of medieval grammarians of Latin, and the rules of proper Latin were communicated through texts such as the elegiac Romulus.

Bourdieu summarizes the inculcation of legitimate language in relation to institutionalized education: "legitimate language is a semi-artificial language which has to be sustained by both a permanent effort of correction, a task which falls both to institutions specially designed for this purpose and to individual speakers. Through its grammarians, who fix and codify legitimate usage, and its teachers who impose and inculcate it through innumerable acts of correction, the educational system tends, in this area as well as elsewhere, to produce the need for its own services and its own products, i.e., the labour and instruments of correction."[3] Bourdieu's description of legitimate language extends far beyond modern France. The medieval church, keeper of the Latin tradition, had a strong interest in using its political power to reinforce continually the centrality of Latin in learned discourse, thereby keeping alive the need for its own schools and universities.

The legitimation of grammatical rules represented only one part of the educational process that schoolboys underwent (and of course this process extended to texts beyond fable, texts both earlier and later in a pupil's course of study). Other aspects of learning unique to fable contributed to a pupil's education, specifically to what Bourdieu labels the linguistic "habitus," the field of discursive possibilities in which the speaker undertakes linguistic exchanges in order to reap profit, whether social, political, or financial. If learning Latin represents one goal of the study of fable, others (discussed earlier in this book) include the understanding of acceptable attitudes toward the use of fable in one's discourse as a kind of basic intertextual reference, along with proper acknowledgment of the fable's originator, Aesop. Thus the habitus of the medieval Latin speaker was defined not only by grammatically correct Latin but also by a set of standard practices for legitimating the authoritative texts that he cited.

In order to define the ways that this canonical fable collection helped to establish a part of the linguistic "habitus" of educated Europeans over two centuries, this chapter unavoidably runs the risk of recasting manuscript and printed evidence from two centuries and several countries as a monolithic, univalent body of pedagogical and interpretive approaches; such was not the case, however. Not all of the teaching and reading methodologies exemplified in extant fable manuscripts were available to all fable readers—especially schoolboys—between 1300 and 1500. Even so, the literary canon of any educational system is normative, exemplifying and reinforcing the literary and thereby the social values of its audience. While the teaching material associated with the fables was not so restrictive as to suggest that fables could bear only one kind of meaning, the range of approaches to both instruction in Latin and the interpretation of fable text remains quite limited; on the other hand, the modes of instruction and explication seem less mutually exclusive than accretive, offering a range of acceptable discursive and interpretive strategies. Furthermore, these methodologies are largely consistent with approaches taken to other classical Latin texts, although they represent only a subset of the interpretive strategies in commentaries on lengthier, more difficult classical texts.

The strongest historical reason for the cohesion in types of pedagogy surrounding the elegiac Romulus was that these pedagogical methods historically preceded the very composition of the elegiac Romulus, having developed over the previous millennium (as Martin Irvine has expertly described). Indeed, the displacement from the grammar-school curriculum of the fables of Avianus in the eleventh and twelfth centuries by the elegiac Romulus in the thirteenth century may have been a function of the fact that the author of the elegiac Romulus, educated in the grammatical precepts popular in the twelfth century, expressly incorporated many of these precepts into his work. So the elegiac Romulus could well have been one of the earliest texts written specifically for the medieval grammar-school curriculum, resulting in a more popular teaching text than the more literary tales by the fourth-century writer Avianus.

Since much of the evidence cited below comes from outside Britain and postdates Chaucer and often Lydgate, it may initially seem irrelevant to a discussion of these authors. However, by comparing extant fourteenth- and fifteenth-century fable interpretation with earlier commentaries on other texts, I hope to make clear that no form of interpretation need have been invented specifically for association with fable: medieval exegetical practices had been largely standardized by Chaucer's day, and the elegiac Romulus collection, as a "classical" text, came under their purview.

And just as temporal considerations need not render later manuscript evidence irrelevant to our discussion of earlier authors, so geographical distance need not hinder speculation about association of commentaries (and even manuscripts) from the continent with fabulists in Britain. William J. Courtenay and other historians of education have shown that numerous English students attended continental universities.[4] One such student, Robert Waldeby O.E.S.A., earned his doctorate at Toulouse and then became the tutor of Richard II. Many continental students also traveled to England, generally to attend Oxford; the largest group of these during the second half of the fourteenth century were Franciscans from Italy. It is logical that they would have brought with them canonical texts from their earlier education, including copies of the elegiac Romulus. Nicholas Orme has also cited several examples of English grammar-school teachers holding posts in three or four different schools during their careers. One of the best-known English grammarians of the fourteenth century, William Wheatley (b. ca. 1280), apparently undertook his university studies in Paris but then returned to England to hold successive posts as schoolmaster in Sulham (Berkshire) in 1305, Stamford in 1308, and Lincoln by 1316, finally becoming rector of Yatesbury (Wiltshire) in 1317.[5] Although Orme points out that evidence about the lives of schoolmasters is relatively scarce, much of what remains shows that mobility among this group was, if not the norm, at least a distinct possibility.[6]

Although I will provide dates and provenances for the manuscripts cited here whenever possible, I will not attempt to create a Lachmannian stemma of familial relations among them.[7] This would be a futile task for "canonical" commentaries by well-known figures like Arnulf of Orleans, for even when the author of a commentary was known and respected, his work could undergo radical revision as it was transmitted from teacher to pupil.

In relation to the Ovidian tradition, Ralph J. Hexter writes of the relaxed attitude toward commentaries in the medieval academy, in which schoolmasters and other scribes freely adapted the non-authoritative scholia that they inherited.[8] Hexter finds relative stability among only the commentaries bearing the name of a renowned scholar, such as the *Ars Amatoria* commentary by Arnulf of Orleans.[9] However, Berthe Marti asserts that the tendency to preserve Arnulf's commentaries did not extend to his work on Lucan's *Pharsalia:*

> Every *magister* who used or copied Arnulf's commentary felt free to alter it by drawing upon the information which had been accumulated by succeeding generations of interpreters, and by them added to the common body of glosses found in the margins of most texts of the poem. He would modify the length and content of the scholia to suit his own purposes. As is the case with most similar compilations, Arnulf's commentary is found in various forms, some fuller than others. It is impossible to establish with any certainty which ones, among the manuscripts copied almost during his lifetime, may represent the original text, and whether the apparently interpolated texts correspond to revisions made by the author in the course of his teaching career, or again whether other *magistri* or students or scribes are responsible for the additions and omissions.[10]

If the transmission of a commentary by a scholastic authority of Arnulf's stature was handled with the degree of freedom described by Marti, then anonymous commentaries on more easily interpreted texts must have been modified even more freely. All extant fable commentaries are indeed anonymous, unless the names in the colophons in a handful of manuscripts belong to actual commentators rather than scribes; this information, however, cannot be retrieved from surviving materials. In this tradition we know the name of only one commentator (discussed at the beginning of the next chapter), but either his fable commentary no longer exists, or, if it does, his name has been dissociated from it.

The most helpful approach to individual commentary manuscripts treats them as textual representatives of individual readings. Indeed, the variety of reader response available in manuscripts has prompted a reappraisal of how scholars studying medieval literature should use these texts. One of the most eloquent recent defenders of the study of manuscripts as individual readings is John Dagenais, who has studied the manuscripts of the fifteenth-century Spanish *Book of Good Love*, a lengthy poem which includes translations of eight fables from the elegiac Romulus. In *The Ethics of Reading in Manuscript Culture: Glossing the "Libro de Buen Amor,"* Dagenais negotiates between old philological practice and poststructuralist literary theory in order to focus attention upon individual manuscripts; these he characterizes not as more or less skillful and precise copies of previously existing works of literature but as examples of readers' responses. While Dagenais acknowledges that Roland Barthes's ideas of endless interpretive play (*"jouissance"*) and deconstructionist challenges to the authority of the text can be applied fruitfully to the medieval practice of glossing, he counterbalances those theories, adopted wholeheartedly by the so-called New Medievalists,[11] with the necessary historicizing assertion that, regardless of the variety of forms and patterns used by glossators, readings were not undertaken in the spirit of textual play but in order to lead to ethical behavior in the reader/glossator.[12] As a name for the negotiations between reader and text, Dagenais borrows from the friar in Chaucer's *Summoner's Tale* the term "glosynge," glossing in its broad medieval sense. Dagenais later lays out some of the difficulties in the study of this multifarious medieval practice:

> it is clear that no dictionary of "standard" or "commonplace" medieval symbology or allegory could ever hope to account for all the readings we observe. . . . Though there were surely certain patterns, most of them strongly influenced by the practices of biblical exegesis and the mythographic tradition, which both writers and readers might invoke, the glossator's goal in "glosynge" his source (the description fits most, if not all, medieval "creative" activity) was not to plug in a specific symbolic code that readers could decipher using the same key. It is true that many medieval readers would have seen a potential for Christ or the devil behind a reference to "lion." But what were the rules that permitted medieval readers to determine, at a given moment of reading, that "lion" meant "Christ" and not "the devil"? The key, then, lies not in a dictionary or code book . . . , however complete, but in a grammar of medieval reading. As Honorius of Autun put it in his commentary on the Psalms, "Carmen huius libri . . . est convertibile ad omnem sensum cuiuslibet intentionis" (*PL* 172:274: "The song of this book can be converted to any sense of any intention whatsoever").[13]

Honorius of Autun anticipated by several centuries the infinite play of signifiers beloved of postmodern readers, but in relation to fable commentators writing for or as grammar-school pupils, the virtually infinite interpretive range of biblical exegesis may not have been permissible. Fable commentary represents only the fundamentals of what Dagenais labels "a grammar of medieval reading," the mere rudiments of exegetical practice that provided the foundation for learning other, more complex ways of reading.

This chapter aims to construct such a grammar using the relatively limited field of interpretive possibility occupied by scholastic fable. Even within this clearly defined range of texts, however, this chapter is neither an exhaustive grammar nor a history of the scholastic reception of the elegiac Romulus, since such a study would require a book unto itself. No one medieval pupil of fable could have come in contact with the variety of pedagogical approaches described below; rather, this evidence merely gives an idea of the richness of the discursive practices determining the very understanding of fable.

All of the activities of reading, teaching, and transmitting fable text that are outlined here play a part in the concept of "grammatica" as broadly defined by Martin Irvine:

> *Grammatica,* a Latinized Greek term, was also called *litteratura,* the discipline of the written, and one who was grammatically educated was a *litteratus,* competent in reading and interpreting Latin writings. As a discipline sustained by the dominant social and political institutions of medieval Europe, *grammatica* functioned to perpetuate and reproduce the most fundamental conditions for textual culture, providing the discursive rules and interpretive strategies that constructed certain texts as repositories of authority and value. In its foundational role, *grammatica* also created a special kind of literate subjectivity, an identity and social position for *litterati* which were consistently gendered as masculine and socially empowered.[14]

This chapter roughly follows the paradigm of Irvine's description. It begins with manuscript evidence of how the fables helped pupils to gain competence in the reading and interpreting of the Latin language. The second section of the chapter is devoted to the "discursive rules and interpretive strategies" described in the scholastic prologues and commentaries to the elegiac Romulus, and the final portion of the chapter will examine the evidence of how readers—adults and schoolboys—positioned themselves in relation to the elegiac Romulus, a text at one remove (at least as far as medieval readers were concerned) from its *auctor,* Aesop.

Pedagogical Practices for the Elegiac Romulus

The extant manuscripts of the elegiac Romulus, numerous though they are in comparison to surviving copies of some other medieval texts, represent only a small fraction of the copies that were made in the fourteenth and fifteenth centuries. Furthermore, the number of copies made on parchment and/or paper during those centuries must have been small in comparison to the number of copies made on the schoolboy's standard writing surface, the wax tablet, a board covered with a thin layer of wax to be inscribed with a stylus.[15] As teachers dictated, students took down a text in order to commit it to memory, after which they could smooth the surface of the tablet for later use. Thus the vast majority of copies of fables from the elegiac Romulus were effaced within days if not hours of the time that they were transcribed.

Some students procured scraps of paper and parchment on which to copy the fables, and a few examples of these inelegant products have survived. Perhaps the effort of a student, Bodleian MS Can. lat. 128, a four-teenth-century manuscript comprising both paper and parchment pages, was later bound with other texts. More representative of the form and format of school texts is Munich BS MS 22906.1, a thirteenth- or early-fourteenth-century octavo copy of only nine of the fables. Presently lacking a cover of any kind, this worn, water-stained, largely illegible pamphlet apparently had a number of successive owners. It shows additions by hands other than that of the fables' original scribe, marginalia which crowd the pages, filling available space up to the fold. The placement of these crowded addenda clearly indicates that the pamphlet circulated in its present, un-bound form, as it would have been impossible for anyone to write in the inner margins, close to the fold in a bound volume (and once this marginalia was added, it would have become impossible to read if the manuscript had been bound). Many similarly illegible, well-worn pamphlets were doubtless discarded not only during the era when the texts were part of the curriculum but also in subsequent centuries when the fables had fallen out of fashion.[16]

As material for pupils at the beginning of their grammar-school educa-tion, the fables were often copied with enough space between lines to allow for the insertion of vocabulary glosses; these could be Latin synonyms (by far the most common type of gloss), vernacular translations, or a combina-tion of the two. In *Teaching and Learning Latin in Thirteenth-Century England,* Tony Hunt has reproduced the Latin lemmata and vernacular glosses from an early-fifteenth-century English manuscript of the elegiac Romulus, British Library MS Add. 10089.[17] Vernacular glosses in several other European languages are represented in extant manuscripts of the fables. For example, interlinear Spanish glosses appear in Lambeth Palace MS 431, and Italian glosses in Bib. Laurentiana MS Strozzi 80, Biblioteca Marciana 4615, Parma Biblioteca Palatina MS 686, and Bib. Riccardiana MS 350. German glosses are used in Basel MSS A.N. II.42 and F.VII, and in Wolfenbüttel MS 81.16 Aug. fol., which carries vernacular glossing to its logical conclusion by also providing German rather than Latin plot summaries for the fables.[18] These represent the beginnings of rhetorical invention in the vernacular.

Vertical vocabulary expansion between languages was augmented by horizontal expansion in Latin through the use of the rhetorical device *derivatio,* in which several words based upon the same root appear close enough to each other to invite comparison.[19] One need not venture far into the elegiac Romulus in order to find examples of this device: the moral of the second fable, "The Wolf and the Lamb," reads:

> Sic nocet innocuo nocuus, causamque nocendi
> Invenit. Hii regnant qualibet urbe lupi.[20]

> [Thus a harmful one harms a harmless one and finds a reason for harming. Such wolves as these rule in any city.]

In this sentence alone, pupils could analyze the verb *noceo* in a present active form, as a gerundive, and then in both positive and negative forms of the substantive adjective *nocuus.* In the final four lines of the next fable, "The Frog and the Mouse," pupils must negotiate among three verb forms based on the verb "to be": *adesse* (to be present), *prodesse* (to be helpful), and *obesse* (to injure). Examples of *derivatio,* which are too numerous in this collection to bear listing here, were, of course, far more important as a pedagogical tool for Latin grammar in the original text than in later translations, where they were unlikely to be translatable.

Beyond broadening vocabulary, the fables served as exemplars for the examination of the grammar and rhetoric of the ancient language. Biblioteca Marciana MS 4658, which appears to have been a teacher's manual for the elegiac Romulus,[21] lacks the fables themselves but gives plot summaries, interpretive comments, and elaborate, detailed *constructiones* for all of the fables. The *constructiones,* which also generally appear in printed editions of the fables, analyze the fable phrase by phrase, often changing the difficult poetic syntax into standard prose word order and then providing Latin synonyms, and matching antecedents with far-flung pronouns; this practice places the words in what grammarians called the *ordo naturalis,* and it represents a significant grammatical exercise in and of itself. As Suzanne Reynolds has said, "[O]rdo naturalis is what exposition (as opposed to composition) must use; the order of *expositio* (a grammatical activity) is not the same as the order of the text under scrutiny (a rhetorical product)."[22]

At certain points the teacher who wrote MS Marciana 4658 added further grammatical explication to the *constructiones,* almost always in relation to verbs. For example, the verb "fatur," which appears in line 19 of

Fable 12, "De duobus muribus," exacts the following explanation: "Nota quod 'fatur' declinatur 'farii' vel 'fare,' 'fatur,' et caret prima persona quae non invenitur, 'for,' sicut nec 'dor' nec 'scior.' Unde dicitur 'dor,' 'for,' sive 'scior' praesens non continet usus" (f. 9r). [Note that "fatur" is declined "farii" or "fare," "fatur" and lacks the first person which is not found, "for," as is neither "dor" nor "scior." Therefore it is said that (in) "dor," "for," nor "scior," present use does not apply.]

In Fable 33, "De vulpe et ciconia," the appearance of the verb "*caveto*" in the promyth prompts the scribe to give not only three definitions but also a mnemonic distich:

> Nota quod hoc verbum "caveo,-es" habet tria significata. Primo idem est quod "vito,-as," ut "Cave malas societas"; id est vita. Secundo idem est quod "observo,-as," ut "Cave mandata dei"; id est "observa." Tertio idem est quod adhibere cautellam ut "Cave tibi a mulieribus," et iste modo est absolutum. In aliis duabus significationibus, est transitum. Unde versus:

> > Hoc verbum caveo sibi vult tria vira tenere:
> > Vitat et observat, cautellam vult adhibere. (ff. 23v–24r)

[Note that this verb "caveo,-es" had three meanings. The first is the same as "vito,-as," as in "Beware evil associations; that [meaning] is "avoid." The second is the same as "observo,-as," as in "Beware the laws of God"; that (meaning) is "observe." The third is the same as to apply caution, as in "Beware of women," and that sense is intransitive. In the other two meanings, it is transitive. Thus the verses:

This verb "caveo" chooses to maintain three strengths for itself: it avoids, it observes, and it chooses to apply caution.]

The Marciana manuscript shows that students had attained only middling grammatical skills before studying the elegiac Romulus, and those skills must have been strained to the limit as they simultaneously began learning definitions of the rhetorical devices in the elegiac Romulus. Even in the first fable, the commentator names the rhetorical device associated with the noun *nitor* (brilliance), which describes the jewel in the dung-heap, as follows: "'Nitor,' id est 'pulchritudo,' id est lapis preciosus: est hic color rethoricus qui dicitur 'intellectio,' quae fit quando ponitur pars pro toto, scilicet 'nitor' pro toto iaspide dicitur" (f. 2r). ["Brilliance," that is "beauty," that is the precious stone: this is a rhetorical color which is called "*intellectio*," which is created when the part is used for the whole, as when "brilliance" is said for the entire jasp.] By the time the teacher had led his pupils through the first twenty fables, they would have identified examples of and rehearsed definitions for the rhetorical figures of *pleonasmus, hendiadys, interpretatio* (thrice), *denominatio, translatio, circutio* (twice), *antithesis,* and *intellectio* yet again. Other rhetorical figures appear later in the collection.

The scribe of Siena MS J.IX.1 simply assumes that his reader has a working knowledge of rhetoric. In the margins of the manuscript are seven citations of five rhetorical devices, including *topografia, pleonasmus,* and *auferesis* in "De Lupo et Agno" alone (f. 64v). These labels, the marginality of which only loosely associate them with the ornaments that they name, call upon the reader to identify the phrases exemplifying them; such tests of identification could have been duplicated orally in the classroom, with the teacher naming a rhetorical device for students to find.

Fable Commentary: The Pedagogy of Appropriate Appropriations

In spite of its widespread use in the medieval grammar-school curriculum, scholastic fable commentary has received little attention from modern scholars, for a number of reasons. The most important of these is doubtless fable's low place on the twentieth century's literary totem pole, particularly in the English-speaking world, which lacks a "high culture" fable collection of the stature of La Fontaine's or Lessing's. Within the academy, scholars gravitate toward medieval commentaries treating more elevated classical literature such as Ovid's *Metamorphoses,* Virgil's *Aeneid,* or Horace's *Satires,* commentaries which are sometimes identified by the names of their authors (Pierre Bersuire, Arnulf of Orleans, Bernardus Silvestris) and which exerted palpable influence upon medieval writers dominating the twentieth-century canon, especially Chaucer. Furthermore, some of the best-known commentaries of the so-called twelfth-century Renaissance have been edited and/or translated, allowing a wider audience to study them.[23]

Fable commentary, especially that associated with the elegiac Romulus, has remained far less accessible. The manuscripts that contain these commentaries, many of them nearly illegible classroom texts, remain unpublished in libraries across Europe. Although commentaries appeared in the *Esopus moralizatus* and the *Auctores octo,* the early printed textbooks that included the elegiac Romulus (and those books are both more legible and more numerous than manuscripts), they represent only the final, fossilized form of what had earlier been a dynamic interpretive tradition: further reader response of the type in which medieval scribes engaged, that is, marginalia, remains largely absent from printed editions that contained their own commentaries.

Students of German literature have given the greatest attention to these commentaries, partly because most of the extant commentary manuscripts were produced in Germany in the fifteenth century and are housed in libraries in Germany and Poland. Also, commentaries are closely related to several important German fable collections, including the first German vernacular printed book, *Der Edelstein* by Ulrich Boner. Those German scholars who have begun discussion of fable commentary have done so resolutely in terms of old philological practices: much of their work is descriptive, falling generally into the categories of source studies for particular fable collections or diachronic studies of single fables.[24] In both groups, the emphasis is placed firmly upon textual transmission, and although all of these studies identify the schoolroom as the likeliest site of that transmission, they do not discuss the politics and significance of the age-old practice of mastering fables.

Nor do these studies contextualize commentary within a broader discussion of commentaries on Virgil, Ovid, and other writers, although the commentaries relating to those authors' works historically preceded the appearance of allegorized fables in the curriculum. Their precedence is clear for a number of reasons. First, while fables in the Middle Ages were categorized as either "moral" literature or meaningless literary fluff, other pagan literature prompted very different responses. The *Metamorphoses* in particular—a florilegium of murder, rape, incest, adultery, and homosexuality—requires radical allegorical treatment in order to make it espouse Christian morality. The squeaky classical text requires the allegorical grease first, as manuscript history bears out. The Christianizing commentaries on the *Metamorphoses* that survive today are fully a century older than our earliest allegorizing commentary on the elegiac Romulus. We should bear in mind, too, that the elegiac Romulus was evidently written by a near-contemporary of Arnulf and Bernard, after which it would have needed to earn canonical status before being deemed worthy of a commentary. At that point, canonical commenting procedures would have been transferred to it from other texts.

Thus the fable commentary tradition cannot claim to have broken literary-historical ground in the forms and patterns of allegory which it comprises; those came from more "adult" texts. But if the availability of standard forms of scholastic commenting elsewhere seemingly diminishes the importance of their application to fable, these commentaries deserve study for no other reason than that the vernacular authors who wrote fable collections in the fourteenth and fifteenth centuries could well have encountered these interpretive techniques first in the classrooms where they studied the elegiac Romulus.

The "Romulus" Epistle: Canonizing Translation

Helping to determine appropriate interpretive responses to the elegiac Romulus was the prefatory epistle universally associated with it. Although written in the Middle Ages, the letter purports to be from the Roman emperor Romulus to his son, Tiberinus (or a variant thereof):

> Romulus Tiberino filio! de civitate attica Aesopus quidam, homo graecus et ingeniosus, famulos suos docet, quid homines observare debeant. Verum ut vitam hominum et mores ostenderet, inducit aves, arbores, et bestias et pecora loquentes probanda cuiuslibet fabulae. Ut noverint homines fabularum cur sit inventum genus, aperte et breviter narravit. Apposuit vera malis, composuit integra bonis, scripsit calumpnias malorum, argumenta improborum, docens infirmos esse humilis, verba blanda potius cavere et cetera multa et miserias his exemplis scriptis. Id ego Romulus transtuli de graeco (sermone) in latinum. Si autem legeris, Tiberine fili, et pleno animo advertas, invenies apposita ioca, quae tibi multiplicent risum et acuant satis ingenium.[25]

> [From Romulus to his son, Tiberinus: a certain Aesop, of Athenian citizenship, an ingenious Greek man, taught his household what men ought to attend to. In order to show truth as well as the life and mores of people, he introduced birds, trees, beasts, and cattle speaking, as things to be recommended as good in every fable. In order for men to know why the genre of fable had been invented, he narrated clearly and briefly. He added true things for bad people, he composed pure things for good people; he wrote the lies of evil people, the arguments of wicked people, teaching the weak to be humble, and especially to beware of flattering words and afflictions and many other things by offering these examples in writing. I, Romulus, have translated these from the Greek language into Latin. If you read them, Tiberinus my son, and turn toward them whole-heartedly, you will discover appropriate jests that will increase your laughter and duly sharpen your character.]

As Österley has pointed out, the letter seems indebted to Phaedrus's picture of Aesop as Athenian and as "*ingeniosus*,"[26] but these details could have come from any of the monument fables cited above. Emphasizing the discursive nature of fable rather than its pedigree, the letter devotes some attention to Aesop and his literary accomplishments but then consigns him to a secondary position in order to highlight Romulus's own translation project for his son. In other words, the absent father of the genre is displaced by a literal father for this particular collection, and the reader is implied by the son, Tiberinus, the "you" about to begin studying the collection.

The imperial example of textual appropriation is thus immediately set out for the reader. This appropriation via translation would have had a twofold significance for medieval readers: it creates an authorizing history for the text by embodying both the *translatio studii,* the "carrying across" of learning from the ancients to the moderns (that is, from the Greeks to the contemporaries of "Romulus") through the supposed translation of this collection directly from Greek,[27] and the *translatio imperii,* the relocation of political and cultural ascendancy from its Hellenic seat in the time of Aesop to the Roman—and specifically Romulan—imperial court.[28]

Both of these "translations" could be replicated at one historical remove by medieval readers of the fables. In the medieval classroom the *translatio studii* could involve the change from poetic syntax to prose summary, as in scholastic commentaries, or from Latin to vernacular, a translation analogous to Romulus's from an ancient literary language to a modern spoken one. Evidence of the latter practice exists in a number of manuscripts with vernacular glosses listed below. The *translatio imperii* operated at a different figurative level, appropriating texts from the pagan kingdom of Rome for use in the kingdom that medieval Europeans believed to be the seat of the world's power, the realm of Christendom. Medieval Christians had to reinvent fable just as Romans had.

The *Accessus:* Categorizing the Text

Although any discussion of the scholia for a canonical text should begin with an examination of the *accessus* to the text under consideration, these scholastic introductions raise special questions in relation to fable as a low-level curricular text. Copies of the elegiac Romulus that begin with an *accessus* are less numerous than those which use as a preface only the Romulus epistle. While *accessus* generally introduce the copies of the fables made in Germany in the fifteenth century, and they often appear in incunables of the elegiac Romulus, they do not unite any readily identifiable group of fourteenth-century manuscripts. Indeed, their absence rather than their presence defines one group of school texts of the elegiac Romulus: Paul Gehl finds no *accessus* at all among the trecento Tuscan school manuscripts that he studies.[29]

The absence of *accessus* from the majority of extant manuscripts probably indicates that they were not always part of the classroom activity associated with fable. Some schoolmasters might not have known any *accessus*. Others could have used an *accessus* to aid only their own understanding of the text at hand without presenting it to pupils with very limited Latin skills. Or, in order to avoid this problem, schoolmasters could simply have summarized the salient points of an *accessus* orally in class, perhaps in a vernacular language, without requiring students to copy the text.

A. J. Minnis and others see the *accessus* as theoretical guides to reading the texts which they introduce, but the *accessus* to Walter's fables show a variety of notions of where the collection originated, what fables can mean, and how they can be read. Minnis's implicit suggestion that *accessus* can be to some degree dated according to their differing lists of literary categories is irrelevant to the elegiac Romulus, since the greatest shift in categorical paradigms in *accessus* took place around the beginning of the thirteenth century, contemporaneously with the incipient popularity of the elegiac Romulus as a curricular text. Although some commentaries originated as scholia to the prose collection that gave rise to the elegiac Romulus,[30] the *accessus* could be changed and updated at the whim of its copier, or conversely, a new commentary could be introduced by an older *accessus*. Therefore, as with the fable commentaries themselves, the precise dating of any particular *accessus* must be left to conjecture, as all of the literary categories that they list were already in use in *accessus* to other texts by the time that the elegiac Romulus was written.

Using the prologue categories created by R. W. Hunt, Minnis suggests that the "type C" form of prologue, which gained considerable popularity as an introduction to *auctores* in the twelfth century, might be traced to Boethius's commentary on Porphyry's *Isagoge*, in which the commentator gave six headings to be discussed in any work of philosophy. This form of prologue, "refined by generations of scholars and to some extent modified through the influence of other types of prologue,"[31] generally included the following headings: "*titulus libri*," "*nomen auctoris*," "*intentio auctoris*," "*materia libri*," "*modus agendi*," "*ordo libri*," "*utilitas*," and "*cui parti philosophiae supponitur*." These terms are the basis for the *accessus* to a thirteenth-century manuscript of our fable collection which, to borrow a phrase, provides a textbook example of a "type C" prologue. However, British Library MS Add. 33780, an early-fourteenth-century manuscript, clouds the issue of authorship with the introduction of a certain "Salon" as the fabulist responsible for the collection (see Appendix 4, p. 218).[32] Although this manuscript is among the older extant copies of the elegiac Romulus fables accompanied by a detailed commentary, its commentator's views on the interpretation of fables resemble those of humanist scholars more closely than those of medieval allegorizers. According to this writer, fables teach readers ethics or morality, instructing souls how to live well. Although the very mention of the word *animus* gives the prologue a religious dimension, its overwhelming purport remains moral and earthly; the commentator implies that while fables can teach souls to spend their time on earth well, readers must look elsewhere for true religious instruction. Horace's requirements for literature, *prodesse* and *delectare,* are attributed to the pagan author and are left on a more literal level than they are in the fable collection's prologue.

The relative absence of religious doctrine in this *accessus* reflects a similar absence in earlier scholastic introductions to Ovid as described by Hexter, who cites and reproduces several manuscripts containing "type C" *accessus* like that in MS Add. 33780.[33] He writes, "The earlier, mostly neglected texts are surprising in the relative scarcity—in fact, considering the texts discussed in (these) pages, the total absence—of allegorizing and Christianizing comment."[34] He concludes his study by reiterating that while the later, heavily allegorized Ovidian commentaries legitimately represent one "medieval Ovid," earlier school commentaries show "the desire of . . . commentators to explicate Ovid, that is, to explain him to their students as best they could on his own terms."[35] Certainly the MS Add. 33780 *accessus* characterizes the elegiac Romulus in the terms of ethical and moral instruction that had been the standard domain of fables before the twelfth century.

At least one extant "type C" *accessus,* however, links the fables to religious discourse: this introduction appears in Biblioteca Marciana MS 4018, a fourteenth-century "Liber Catonianus" which Hervieux identifies by its former shelf mark, MS LXXXVIII, Class. XI.[36] Because this *accessus* to the elegiac Romulus differs appreciably from most other scholastic introductions, Hervieux reproduced it in his catalogue of manuscripts. It begins with the same "type C" categories as above (*"materia," "intentio," "utilitas," "cui parti phylosophye supponatur,"* and *"titulus"*), but after rehearsing these, the commentator takes an unusual turn by quoting a distich related to biblical exegesis:

> Lictera gesta refert, quod credas aligoria
> Moralis quod agas, quod speres anagogia. no[ta][37]

Quattuor sunt expositiones sacre sancte scripture, una storialis, alie tres spirituales: prima allegorica, secunda moralis siue tropologi[c]a, tertia anagogica. Sicut sunt quatuor doctores, ita sunt quatuor expositiones. Primo exposuit beatus Jeronimus, secundo beatus Ambrosius, tertio beatus Gregorius, quarto beatissimus Augustinus. Storia dicitur ab *storin* quod est lictera, scilicet licteralis sensus. Allegorica dicitur

ab *aleon,* quod est alienum, et *gogos,* quod est ductio, id est aliena
ductio. Moralis dicitur, siue tripologiscus [*sic*] sensus dicitur a *tropos,*
quod est conuersio [et *logos* quod est sermo. Anagogica dicitur ab *ana*
quod est super] et *gogos* quod est ductio, id est superna ductio, id est
quando inferiora ad superiora, diuina gratia, reducuntur. Et dicitur
quatuor. Istis moralibus tractat esopus in libro suo et ponit duos
tantum: ponit licteralem et allegoricum sensum. Licteralem ponit in
versibus qui continent fabulas; allegoricum ponit in notabilibus
versibus et illis quod credere non debemus.[38]

[The literal presents the acts, the allegorical that which you ought to
believe, the moral what you ought to do, the anagogical what you
ought to hope.

There are four meanings of sacred holy scripture, one historical, the
other three spiritual: the first allegorical, the second moral or
tropological, the third anagogical. Just as there are four doctors, so
there are four meanings. First blessed Jerome explained, then blessed
Ambrosius, then blessed Gregory, then most blessed Augustine. The
historical is said from "*storin,*" which is the letter, namely the literal
sense. The allegorical is said from "*aleon,*" which is "other," and
"*gogos,*" which is "conveying," that is, "conveying other things."
The moral or tropological sense is said from "*tropos,*" which is
"change," and "*logos,*" which is "speech." Anagogical is said from
"*ana,*" which is "above," and "*gogos,*" which is "conveying," that is
"conveying celestial things," which is when inferior things are drawn
back to superior ones through divine grace. And four things are said.
Aesop treats of these morals in his book and presents only two: the
literal and the allegorical senses. He presents the literal in the verses
that contain the fables, the allegorical in the notable verses and in
those about what we ought not to believe.]

While the writer of this *accessus* does not state explicitly that the reading of
fables resembles the reading of Scripture in all aspects, he implies that since
two of the levels of reading, literal and allegorical, are common to both, the
understanding of fables and Scripture is based on the same foundation.
Allegorical meaning, which represents the real goal of learning from fables,
lies in the noteworthy verses, presumably the *moralitates* and other distichs
quotable out of their narrative contexts, and in the interpretive activity
through which readers come to terms with those things in which they should
not believe. The noteworthy verses—the detachable *moralitates* which are
a primary difference between the elegiac Romulus and the previously ca-

nonical fables of Avianus—earn this commentator's approbation, as they did many readers'. This high praise for fable reflects not only the ideas of Augustine but also those of Boccaccio, who probably lived before or during the time that the manuscript was copied.

"Type C" *accessus* with differing emphases appear in several fifteenth-century German manuscripts. Freiburg Universitätsbibliothek MS 21, for example, introduces its list of four literary topics with a brief excursus on the figure of Aesop that amplifies the description in the Romulus epistle (Appendix 5, p. 223). In spite of the change of roles (and even orthography) for Tiberinus and Romulus from the standard prefatory epistle, this literary history serves largely the same purpose as the fictional letter from the emperor to his son: it inscribes the *translatio imperii* and *translatio studii* from Greece to Rome, even though the dissipation of public cares does not credit the fables with any value as moral instruction. The *accessus* then lists four topics which it defines: the *materia,* which are the fables themselves; the *intentio auctoris,* which is to exhort people to read the book; the *utilitas,* which is that by reading we may know how the author composed the work (*exposuit*); and *cui parti philosophie ponitur,* which as usual, is ethics. Although this *accessus* writer does not deem the book's title worthy of inclusion in the list of goals that he sets out for himself, he nonetheless mentions it as "Incipit Esopus," but he adds, "Esopus non est nomine autoris sed galtherus. Vt autem suus liber recipere honestius hoc nomine intitulatur . . . esopos . . . nomen est cuiusdam herbe. Sicut isopus bonos et varios dat odores sic ille liber vtilitates" (f. 1v). [Aesop is not the name of the author, but rather, Walter; in order, then, to receive his book honestly, it should be called by that name . . . "Esopus" . . . is the name of a certain herb. Just as hyssop gives off good, varied odors, so this book (gives) useful things.] Thus the issue of the author's identity is raised yet again, with Aesop becoming the founding father and "Galtherus" the inheritor. What this *accessus* suggests that most others lack is the notion that the horticultural imagery in the prologue of the elegiac Romulus allegorizes Aesop himself: the founding father is represented in the sweet-smelling, useful vegetation.

Munich Bayerische Staatsbibliothek MS Clm. 16213 gives another variation upon the list of categories in the "type C" *accessus* (Appendix 5, p. 223). Here the literary history is embellished with another stage in the transmission and translation of the fables: after Romulus translated the fables into Latin, an English king is responsible for bringing them into his language ("Deinde rex anglie afferens in anglicam lingwam transferri precepit" [f. 292r]). For our purposes it is noteworthy that this detail, which also appears in the Romulus L B G, borrowed from Marie de France's epilogue to her fables, credits the first vernacular translation to an English translator.[39]

According to Minnis, the introduction of Latin translations of Aristotle into the curriculum of the thirteenth century resulted in the appearance of the so-called Aristotelian prologue. Although this prologue paradigm addresses largely the same topics as the "type C" *accessus*, it names them *causae*, a term borrowed from the philosopher's *Physics* and *Metaphysics*.[40] A work's author was described as the "*causa efficiens*"; the old "*materia libri*" became the new "*causa materialis*"; the "*causa formalis*" examined the form of the work in both the aesthetic and organizational senses of the word; and the "*causa finalis*" was the writer's objective in undertaking his project.

While extant *accessus* include categories labeled *causae* more frequently than categories from the "type C" *accessus*, these texts suggest less of a shift from one paradigm to another than the simultaneous existence of the two forms of *accessus*, with scholars at liberty to borrow from either set of categories. Knowledge of Aristotle does not necessarily predispose an *accessus* writer to choose Aristotelian causes, as demonstrated by the *accessus* writer in the Munich manuscript above, who quotes from the philosopher but adheres to "type C" categories. By the same token, writers who knew the definitions of the *causae* did not feel constrained to reject the old literary categories, as a number of "hybrid" *accessus* show.

One type of hybrid is represented by Biblioteca Ambrosiana MS Trotti 161, an Italian copy of a commentary unaccompanied by fable texts, completed on December 12, 1404 (f. 97r). The *accessus* is introduced by the incipit of the elegiac Romulus prologue, giving the scholastic introduction the appearance of a comment upon that prologue rather than a separate introduction to the entire collection:

> "Ut iuvet et prosit," etc. In principio istius libri, sicut in principio aliorum, sex requiruntur per ordinem. Primo que sit causa efficiens huius libri. Secundo que sit materia praesentis operis. Tertio que sit intentio auctoris. Quarto que vtilitas ex hic opere reportetur. Quinto quis sit libri titulus. Sexto et ultimo cui parti philosophie supponatur. Quantum ad primum dico quod causa efficiens huius libri est duplex, quia quedam est propinqua et quedam est remota. Causa efficiens remota fuit esopus, grecus a cuius dictis extractus fuit libellus iste. Causa efficiens propinqua fuit quidam Romanus nobilis (genere) Romulus nomine qui composuit hunc librum extrahendo a dictis esopi ut dixi ad instructionem iuvenum ut eis darentur bonum [exemplum?]. (f. 92r)

["In order to please, in order to profit," etc. In the beginning of this book, as in the beginning of others, six things are required regarding the arrangement. First, what is the efficient cause of this book. Second, what is the material of the present work. Third, what is the intention of the author. Fourth, what use ought to be derived from this work. Fifth, what is the title of the book. Sixth and last, which part of philosophy does it belong under. As for the first, I say that the efficient cause of this book is twofold, because a certain one is near and another remote. The remote efficient cause was Aesop, a Greek from whose sayings this book was extracted. The near efficient cause was a certain Roman of noble birth named Romulus who composed this book by extracting from the sayings of Aesop, as I said, for the instruction of youth in order that they be given good examples.]

This commentator sees value in the possibility of dividing the *causa efficiens,* a division which is not logical under the heading of "*nomen auctoris*"; thus he is able to discuss the "remote" and the "near" authors, implying that authors who are nearer still may also engage in similar translations. He also indicates that Romulus selected his fables from a larger body of work, the process of selection that vernacular authors later applied to the elegiac Romulus. This *accessus* gestures toward the combination of prologue types that informs most of the extant scholastic introductions.

A relatively common hybrid gave almost equal attention to both the older categories and the newer ones. Such an *accessus* appears in Munich Staatsbibliothek MSS 14703, 19667, and 7680, as well as Wrocław Biblioteka Uniwersytecka MS IV.Qu.81 and Prague Statni Knihovna MS I.C.26; all of these copies date from the mid-fifteenth century and were penned in Germany. Although the *accessus,* with the Aristotelian incipit "Quod est mirabile est dilectabile," is too lengthy to merit reproduction in its entirety here, a summary of its structure will be worthwhile.[41]

This lengthy description of fable leads the commentator into lists of both some "type C" categories and the four *causae.* The fables' *utilitas* is "correctio vitiorum et delectatio morum," while their *titulus,* as usual, is "Incipit esopus." The intention of the book is "diversarum fabularum iocundarum cum suis moralitatibus introductio," and the philosophical category to which the book belongs is the sermon, due to the "duo versus morales" which conclude each fable. Having covered these points, the commentator rehearses the *causae,* in spite of a good deal of repetition between this list and the previous one. The "*causa materialis,*" which the commentator points out coincides with the subject, is once again "correctio vitiorum et inductio morum." The "*causa formalis*" is subdivided into two categories, the "*forma tractatus*" and the "*forma tractandi.*" "Causa efficiens dicitur fuisse magister esopus," the commentator writes, dutifully acknowledging the father of fable as the mode of discourse requires but also leaving room for doubt about the true authorship of this particular work. Lastly, the "*causa finalis*" corresponds with the "*utilitas.*" This unusually prolix *accessus* seems to have been written in order to guide readers through the terminology of both standard *accessus* paradigms, showing how they overlap. Such repetition would have been helpful to students, who needed to understand definitions of all of these terms and also the relations between them.

An Aristotelian prologue with the incipit "Grecia disciplinarum mater," which can be traced back at least to the Romulus L B G, appears in fourteenth- and fifteenth-century manuscripts,[42] but it gained its widest audience when it was used as *accessus* to editions of the *Esopus moralizatus*. In Appendix 2 (pp. 204–11), it is reproduced from Heinrich Quentell's edition of 1489. The *Esopus moralizatus accessus* may have developed into the introduction of the later *Auctores octo*. Not only does the latter represent an interesting hybrid of the Aristotelian prologue and the "type C" *accessus*, but also through the commentator's care in defining each term it gives a strong sense of the intended audience, evidently a group whose familiarity with these concepts could not be taken for granted. This *accessus* writer devotes nearly as much effort to defining the scholastic terminology in the prologue as to filling those categories in relation to the fables. The text in Appendix 3 (p. 212) is taken from the "Fabularum Esopi" section of the unpaginated *Auctores octo* printed in Lyons by Jehan de Vingle in 1495. For the purposes of this discussion the *Auctores octo accessus* is also important for its classification of fables as allegorical, defining this mode of discourse as "ut id quod minus videtur inesse inest et id quod magis." This prologue prepares the reader for the relatively systematic allegorical approach which characterizes the commentary as a whole.

The apparent delight that *accessus* writers took in subdividing the Aristotelian *causae* is manifested clearly in a manuscript roughly contemporary with these printed editions. Bibliothèque Nationale MS Lat. 8023 examines the four causes, the title of the work, and the subdivision of philosophy to which it belongs. The efficient cause is divided again along literary-historical lines, attributing the elegiac Romulus fables to a poet whose name is clearly a variant of the "Gualterus" cited by Hervieux; this description, however, shows more than a passing interest in the figure of Aesop: "Causa efficiens sit magister garritus qui composuit istum librum, et non ysopus, ut dicunt quidam, sed quia ysopus erat honeste vite immo istum librum sub nomine eius intitulant, quia vir erat autentique et sciens. Alii dicunt quod ysopus fecit istum librum qui cognomine vocabatur garritus" (f. 63r). [The efficient cause is Master "Garritus" who composed this book, and not Aesop, as some say, but because Aesop led an honest life indeed, they call this book by his name, because he was an original and wise man. Others say that an Aesop who was called by the family name "Garritus" wrote this book.]

The "*causa materialis*" is "*scientia moralis*" again, especially due to the proverbial verses at the end of each fable. Following a definition of fable indebted to Isidore's, the *accessus* writer repeats Isidore's division of fables into the Aesopic ("esopice sunt animalia quando bruta finguntur inter se vel rebus inanimatis") and Libistican ("libistice sunt res inanimate quando finguntur loqui cum hominibus vel [equaliter] dicuntur libistice quia in libia fuerunt reperte").

The "*causa formalis*" labeled "*modus metrica,*" is subdivided as usual into the "*modus tractatus,*" here interpreted as the verse prologue, and the "*modus tractandus,*" the fables themselves. Each fable, too, must be subdivided into its two sections, the narrative (*exposicione*) and the moral (*versus proverbiales*).

The "*causa finalis*" undergoes the most rigorous subdivisions. The category itself is divided into the public (*communis*) and private (*privatis*). The latter cause is again subdivided into two categories: so that the author can have fame after death ("ut fama posset acquirere in mortalem"), while the other motivation seems more Christian: "ut posset se in aliquo opere executare quod tangitur in prohemio, cum dicitur ne mihi torpentem, etc." [so that it can have executed upon itself in every instance that which is touched upon in the prologue, i.e, as when it is said: "Ne mihi torpentem"].

The public cause is also binary, divided into the immediate (*propinqua*) and the remote (*remota*). The immediate cause can be divided into Horace's requirements for literature, "*delectatio*" and "*fructus,*" the profit once again linked with the "*versus proverbiales.*" In subdividing the remote public cause, our indefatigable *accessus* writer reaches the point of exhaustion: "Sed remota est triplex, scilicet remota, remotior, remotissima, sicut in libris." Beyond giving student readers examples of the three grammatical degrees of an adjective, this sentence seems nonsensical, unless the *accessus* writer is alluding to the fact that the sixty fables are often divided into three books of twenty fables each, a structure inherited from the prose Romulus tradition.

This *accessus* writer apparently revels in the adaptability of the Aristotelian prologue form, but his subdivisions describe a number of attitudes toward fable which are not communicated elsewhere. Here readers are told that Aesop was an honest man, and that fable is valuable enough as a literary form to have earned him lasting fame. Although the full significance of Aesop as warp of weaving ("ysopus stamine tectus") remains unelaborated, it is presumably related to the etymology of the word *textus,* which comes from the verb *texere,* "to weave." This *accessus* takes us some distance from the early medieval suspicion that fable's literary and ethical importance is negligible; "*scientia moralis*" implies far greater import.

One more type of *accessus* deserves attention, even though it is not widely represented among extant manuscripts. This introduction loosely resembles Minnis's category of the "extrinsic" *accessus,* in contrast to the intrinsic introductions discussed above. In an extrinsic *accessus,* the writer systematically described the academic discipline to which the text belonged. Minnis writes, "[T]he medieval distinction between extrinsic and intrinsic analysis hinged on a difference in the object or analysis rather than differences of vocabulary or ideology: the former concerned an art or science, while the latter concerned a text."[43]

As is true with other *accessus* to the elegiac Romulus, the examples of this category of introduction are not as free from the influence of other prologue types as examples that Minnis finds in other texts, but these *accessus,* again from mid- to late-fifteenth-century exemplars, define the disciplinary heading under which fable can be considered. The *accessus* of Wolfenbüttel Herzog August Bibliothek MS Helmstedter 185 (Appendix 5, pp. 224–25) judges fable's value in relation to rhetoric, and especially the metaphor as a rhetorical ornament which has its main appeal in delighting its audience. This *accessus* author, like others, plays with the gardening imagery of the prologue, thereby suggesting that the metaphorical significance of a fable must germinate and grow in the mind of its reader.[44]

A final type of Aristotelian *accessus* can be identified by an incipit which sets a very different tone in its definition of fable: "Homo indiget recreatione propter multos labores." This *accessus,* which appears in Trier Stadtbibliothek MS 132 and Stuttgart Württembergische Landesbibliothek MS HB.I.27,[45] cites a number of *auctoritates* from the *Ethics* of Aristotle and an unidentified work of Seneca, both of which emphasize the mental fatigue that comes with the use of reason and the necessity of such recreation as fables can provide. The *accessus* then defines the four standard causes comprising the Aristotelian prologue. This *accessus* is interesting largely because it amplifies the *prodesse et delectare* aspects of literature inherent in the verse prologue, but it emphasizes the delightful—perhaps even the ludic—over the profitable. Fable's association with play features in marginal comments in a number of manuscripts described below, but generally at the end of copies of the fables; this *accessus* writer is willing to allow his readers to engage with the notion of play much earlier in their reading of the elegiac Romulus. Even so, the commentaries which follow in these manuscripts approach the fables with conventional seriousness, bringing to bear upon them only the standard varieties of allegory and nothing identifiably humorous.

It is noteworthy that no single *accessus* dominates at any point in the textual history of the elegiac Romulus, even after the advent of print culture, for the "Grecia, disciplinarum mater" *accessus* shared the scholastic market with the "In principio huius libri" introduction. These two texts were printed repeatedly in the same quarter-century that the group of five similar German manuscripts mentioned above was copied with an entirely different *accessus* from the incunables.

If any generalization can emerge from this overview of the various elegiac Romulus *accessus,* it must be limited to the assertion that these fables were held in the same esteem as other "classical" texts introduced by the same kind of material. The very presence of an *accessus* seems as likely an influence on a reader's attitude as the definitions given in it. In a broader context, these *accessus* are simply part of the metalanguage that validates the study of the text they introduce. Indeed, learning competent use of this metalanguage may have been the primary reason for the inclusion of *accessus* in those settings where they appeared, allowing students to take those terms with them from the elegiac Romulus to the study of other texts. Certainly none of the interpretive terminology used in the *accessus* is carried forth in the commentaries following them (if commentaries follow at all, for some *accessus* precede uncommented texts). However, some of this terminology is echoed in the vernacular fables examined in subsequent chapters, and insofar as fable readers were familiar with the authorizing terminology of *accessus,* it would have contributed to the authority with which they regarded the work of the vernacular authors.

The Commentaries

In the groups of *accessus* described above we find some basic structural similarities—for example, the terms requiring definition and elaboration—but then we also find a variety of definitions for those terms, as well as varying degrees of connection to the text which they purport to explicate. On the whole, only this degree of structural similarity informs the commentaries: only a certain number of types of interpretive activities appear to have been sanctioned in the centuries which we are examining, fewer in number than the forms of interpretation brought to bear upon lengthier, more challenging texts.

The basis of fable commentary is paraphrase, and some commentaries do not move beyond it. In some instances the paraphrase represents little more than a "translation" of the Latin from poetic syntax into more easily comprehensible word order. This kind of commentary privileges fable plot and moral above all else. Simple paraphrases appear at least as a part of almost every commentary, for such paraphrase was the prerequisite for types of comment that manipulated the fable texts more actively.

Every comment in British Library MS Harley 2745 exemplifies paraphrase at its simplest; one example will suffice. For the first fable, here entitled "De jaspide et gallo," the commentator writes the following summary:

> In hoc apologo ostendit autor quod stultus non debet vilipendere sapientiam et hoc ostendit per quendam gallum qui invenit jaspidem quandam in fimo, cui dixit gallus, "O jaspis, non es mihi utilis, nec curo de te. Plus vere amarem ego malum frumentum quam te." Per gallum intellige stultum, per jaspidem sapientiam. Iuxta illud stultus villipendit sapientiam. (f. 137r)

> [In this apologue the author shows that a fool ought not to despise wisdom, and he shows this through a certain cock that discovers a jacinth in a dung-heap, to which the cock says, "O jacinth, you are not useful to me, nor do I care for you. I would really have loved bad grain more than you." By the cock, understand a fool; by the jacinth, wisdom. In a similar manner, a fool despises wisdom.]

Since this comment is more a passive redaction than an active interpretation, its writer must have aimed only at making the narrative more easily readable. Even in simplifying the text, however, the writer has brought some small knowledge of Latin to bear upon it by adding a few synonyms for words in the text (for example, "*vilipendere*" and "*frumentum*") and employing a verb tense which does not appear in the original, the subjunctive imperfect ("*amarem*").

The position of this comment, too, is significant: while most comments follow or appear in margins alongside the fables, this one is written partly between the rubricated title and the text of the fable, although in a hand smaller than the text hand. Its position effectively discourages the manuscript reader from beginning the verse fable before looking at the prose summary. This scribe, then, has manipulated not only the *littera* of the text but also its physical position in relation to the fable text.

This type of flat summary represents a pupil's (and commentator's) first step toward freeing the text from the rhetorical trappings of its poetic form, stripping it down to its "true" meaning.[46] While these summaries do not include the specific interpretive readings that we find in the heavily allegorized commentaries that became the hallmark of the later Middle Ages, they show medieval readers' initial confrontation of the text. Rita Copeland has described the practice at length: "Paraphrase is the most obvious feature of *ennaratio* in classical and medieval practice; its pedagogical value is also self-evident. Perhaps for this reason its hermeneutical status is less understood or recognized. It is through the mechanics of paraphrase that the text truly becomes the property of the commentator. . . . Through paraphrase the commentary becomes container of, no longer supplement to, the original text, at least in terms of graphic, formal disposition."[47] As much as transference from Latin to a vernacular language, the change from verse to prose represents translation.[48] In relation to classroom study of fable texts, such translation corresponds with the moment at which the rhetorical figures of *abbreviatio* and *amplificatio* could come into play, and pupils can engage imaginatively with the material before them. Vernacular translators inevitably favored amplification over abbreviation, partly because of the incorporation of scholastic commentary and commenting techniques into the translated texts.

Very few commentators, however, were content to rely exclusively upon paraphrase of the fables. These readers eschewed homogeneity by engaging in more active interpretation, elaborating upon the ethical lesson that the fable moral states flatly and succinctly, although fable commentators did not employ so many forms of interpretation as to tax young readers unduly. In order to simplify my discussion, I will use the following categories to describe the most common types of interpretation in fable commentaries.

¶ Simple allegory: The standard, classical form of reading associated with Aesopic fables, in which the actions of the fable characters are to be translated into morally marked human terms. Generally the fable *moralitas* itself is based upon simple allegory. I include in this category the commentary *moralitates* which give the broadest, most basic moral judgments about the characters: the good person, the bad person, the foolish person, the wise person, and so forth. As is the case with the jewel above, objects may be made to represent abstract qualities (for example, the jewel as wisdom in the first fable). This type of reading differs from paraphrase only inasmuch as it makes the moral somewhat more precise and directed.

¶ Allegory with social roles: simple figuration augmented by specific mention of the social hierarchy and power structures, the basis of which is generally the natural chain of order in the animal kingdom. Here the commentary *moralitas* generally mentions the rich, the poor, rulers, peasants, and so on.

¶ Allegory with religious roles: simple figuration augmented by religious roles played out in social life. Although a subcategory of figuration with social roles, this type deserves separate examination because it bridges the gap between simple figuration and spiritual allegory. Here one character represents a religious person and another represents a lay person. The commentator may also explain the role which God or the devil plays in the situation, but divine power has no direct allegorical representative in the fable. In other words, the basic action of the fable is still interpreted as social and earthly, but metaphysical ramifications of the action are usually brought into play.

¶ Spiritual allegory: Interpretation of a fable whereby social and/or metaphysical roles are given for the characters, and the action of the fable must then be completely reinterpreted on a metaphysical level. Such reinterpretation of action in commentaries ranges from the straightforward (that is, a bad fable character represents the body and a good one the soul, a bad character is read as the devil and a good one a Christian, etc.) to the unexpected (that is, reinterpreting an evil action by means of allegory so that the fable is read *in bono*).

¶ Natural allegory: An intertextual form of allegory derived from bestiaries and lapidaries in which the natural properties of an animal or stone appear in the commentary. Commentators often cite their source texts, but even when they do not, this type of allegory identifies itself by reifying the object in the fable which it describes, instead of requiring readers to allegorize that object as something else. Natural allegory does not usually engage with the plot of the fable, since the properties discussed in the encyclopedic texts rarely coincide with those mentioned in the narrative.

¶ Exegetical allegory: A form of interpretation in which the action of a fable is read so as to mirror an event or episode from the Bible. This form of allegory clearly demonstrates the way that the study of fables was connected to biblical allegoresis, since the interpretive task here is identical to typological interpretation of Old Testament stories as adumbrations of New Testament events: structural and conflictual similarities between scriptural and fabular events are emphasized so as to make the narratives parallel each other.

Simple fable allegory needs little explanation, as it coincides closely with the modern—which is to say both the classical and the humanist—method of fable reading. It is adequately represented by the text from the Harley manuscript given above, and by a number of readings in the appendices.[49] In curricular practice, this simple type of reading was conjoined with paraphrase; the instructional emphasis was apparently on the mechanics of Latin composition rather than interpretive strategies.

Allegory with social roles requires little more interpretive effort than simple allegory, but its emphasis upon social class clearly caught the attention of Lydgate and Henryson. Furthermore, class concerns are already inscribed in a number of fables from the elegiac Romulus, notably those in which characters ask for and/or are persecuted by leaders. British Library MS Add. 33780 includes allegory with social roles in two different power relations. The manuscript indicates its primary audience in the following allegory of Fable 51, entitled "De Patre Monente Filium" in this manuscript. The fable describes a father telling his ill-behaved son the story of an ox which teaches a calf to stop struggling and submit to the yoke. Following the plot summary for the fable, the commentator in this manuscript writes, "Per patrem sive per antiquum bovem intelligi sapiens dominus vel sapiens magister, qui servos vel scolares suos verbis et exemplis sine magna lesione curialiter cor[r]igit, quod satis declaratur par versus notabiles" (f. 25v). [By the father or the old ox, understand a wise lord or wise teacher, who carefully corrects his servants or students with words and examples, without great harm, which is declared sufficiently by the notable verses.] This comment encodes a double social lesson: lords are to servants as masters are to schoolboys, and verbal reprimands are the most effective weapons of men in these positions of power. Implicit in this reinforcement of social hierarchy is the suggestion that schoolboys must learn grammar in order to administer verbal lashings to their social inferiors and thereby rise to positions of authority.[50]

In Basel Öffentliche Bibliothek der Üniversität MS F.IV.50, similarly structured allegory is applied to Fable 4, "De Cane et Ove," one of the fables translated by both Lydgate and Henryson. Here, after the plot paraphrase, the commentator writes, "Allegoria: per canem intelligitur fallax homo vel mercator aut alius mercenarius gaudens semper de fraude contra suos debitores miseros, petens eos magis aggravare" (f. 139v). [Allegory: the dog is understood as a deceitful man or a merchant or another mercenary, always rejoicing from the fraud against his poor debtors, seeking greatly to aggravate them.] Stereotypical false men here flesh out the general term.

Allegory with social roles takes on slightly greater specificity when religious roles are applied. To some degree these readings necessarily work

against social readings, instead emphasizing the power of the clergy over
the laity, even lay people with greater worldly power than clerics. Although
characters representing religious men cannot completely overturn social
hierarchies, they can point out to their social superiors that their earthly
actions, especially evil ones, have heavenly repercussions.[51] For an example
of this type of allegory we can return to Fable 51, the fable of the father and
the son, as it is interpreted in the *Esopus moralizatus*. After the paraphrase
of the plot, the commentator writes:

> Allegorice per filium rebellem patri possunt intelligi peccatores non
> obedientes preceptis dei, et sic etiam per patrem intelliguntur spiritu-
> ales instructores, scilicet predicatores verbi divini qui debent precedere
> peccatores virtuosis exemplis et doctrinis, proponendo etiam vitam et
> exempla seculorum, ut ipsi peccatores sic exemplis virtutum attracti
> vitam postponant erroneam. (n.p.)

> [Allegorically, by the son rebelling against his father, sinners disobey-
> ing the precepts of God can be understood, and thus by the father,
> spiritual instructors are also understood, namely preachers of the di-
> vine word who ought to go before sinners with virtuous examples and
> teaching, setting forth also the life and the example of the times, so
> that these sinners, thus drawn in by examples of virtue, set aside their
> erring life.]

A variant upon this type of reading appears in British Library MS Add.
11897, in the allegory for "De milvo egrotante et penitentiam agente," the
fable of the dying kite repenting of his sinful life before his mother. The
penitent kite is given the role of a dying person, but the mother is allegorized
at the conclusion of the comment as "ecclesiam, que dicat vilibus raptoribus
et usurarios, 'Mi nate,' ut in littera mater dixit ad milvum natum eius" (f.
8v) [the church, which says to vile robbers and usurers, "My child," as in
the text the mother says to her child, the kite]. Although this interpretation
synecdochically substitutes the personified whole (the church) for the literal
part (the clergy, the voice of the church), its allegorization of religious roles
on earth remains clear. This allegorical role was already in circulation in
several well-known sources, perhaps most widely from Augustine's reading
of the Song of Songs, but also in Bersuire's allegorization of Ovid. That
commentator gives the role of the Christian church to the wife of the pagan
king of heaven: "Iuno uxor Iovis signat ecclesiam uxorem Christi." [Juno,
the wife of Jove, represents the church, the wife of Christ.][52]

Spiritual allegory is a logical extension of allegory with religious roles,
for in the allegory described above, when a sinner is chastised and educated,

the commentator's ethical goal is to chastise him not only as a social entity but also as a religious being—that is, as a soul with aspirations toward heaven. Erich Seeman provides a standard type of spiritual allegory in his discussion of the history of fable commentary as represented in fifteenth-century German manuscripts. This comment is taken from Munich Bayerische Staatsbibliothek MS Clm. 14529, a copy of the fables and commentary completed on September 23, 1465. After its plot summary, the fifteenth fable in the collection, that of the fox winning a crow's stolen cheese by praising the bird until it sings, is allegorized as follows:

> Moraliter: per coruum intellige quemlibet hominem, per caseum bona opera, per wlpem astuciam demonis. Dyabolus enim semper laudat hominem et incendit ipsum per superbiam in tantum, quod superbiens ex laude ista omittat graciam, extra quam non est salus. Doctrina ergo fabule talis est: Non semper debemus credere dulcibus verbis illorum, qui nobis ascribunt laudem et gloriam indecentem, sed transeundum est ad conscienciam, considerando vtrum bona vel mala intencione hoc fiat, ne nobis contingat ut corvo, etc. (f. 83v)[53]

> [Morally: by the crow understand any man, by the cheese good works, by the fox the astuteness of a demon. The devil certainly always praises a man and excites him so much through pride that, priding himself in this praise, he lays aside grace, outside of which there is no health. Therefore the teaching of this fable is of such a sort: we ought not to believe always in the sweet words of those who attribute unseemly praise and glory to us, but it ought to be turned over to the conscience for considering whether it is done with a good or bad intention, lest it affect us as it did the crow.]

This comment is more detailed than many: it not only gives allegorical roles for the characters but also leads the reader through the plot a second time, reiterating the action of praising and the consequent sin of pride that are at the heart of the fable.

The interpretive template that dominates spiritual allegory in fable commentaries places the body or soul of a Christian in conflict with the devil. This type of allegorization was favored in the *Auctores octo;* fully a third of the fables prompt the commentator to reproduce this reading.[54] One such comment relies partially on the conflict between devil and Christian while fully elucidating the arbitrary nature of allegorical roles in the fable commentary tradition. In Fable 40, "De Rustico et Mustella," a rustic captures and kills a weasel that has been killing mice in his house; the *Auctores octo* commentator states that the rustic can be interpreted as "deum vel dyabolum" (n.p.) (God or the devil). By allowing the rustic to play either of the two most powerful and antagonistic roles in Christian allegory, the commentator creates two very different readings at the same time, and he also clearly implies that allegorical rethinking—the creation and internalization of a germane ethical lesson—is as much the province of the reader as of the commentator. Honorius of Autun had anticipated this kind of bipolar interpretation, as had Bersuire, who sees a similar duality in the role of Apollo in Book I of the *Metamorphoses*. In this context the god can represent "virum iustum . . . vel dice contrarie quod iste signat malos prelatos et tirannos" [a just man . . . or say on the contrary that he stands for bad prelates and tyrants].[55]

Another common pair of opponents in spiritual allegory are the body and the soul, which the *Auctores octo* commentary brings to bear upon Fable 58, entitled "De Negociatore et Asello" in Hervieux's edition. An ass, beaten and overworked by his merchant owner, looks forward to the release that death will provide, but after dying he is flayed and his skin is crafted into tabors that continue to receive beatings. In the *Auctores octo* the commentator summarizes the plot and then allegorizes it as follows: "Allegoria: quod tu debes melius affectare vivere in patientia et virtutibus adherere, quam appetere mortem iniuste. Per asinum [intellige] corpus cuiuslibet hominis, per institorem animam quae stimulat ut bene faciat" (n.p.). [Allegory: you should always strive better to live in patience and to adhere to virtues than to seek death unjustly. By the ass, understand the body of any man, by the pedlar the soul that goads it to do well.] Here the soul dominates, urging the body to follow Christian precepts, but just as often in spiritual allegory, the body drags the soul to perdition, as in the allegories of "De Mure et Rana," Fable 3 in Appendices 2 and 3.

One instance of body/soul allegory in the elegiac Romulus commentaries deserves particular attention; it is consistently applied to the most threatening, least juvenile fable in the collection. Hervieux's base text entitles the forty-eighth fable "De Viro et Uxore,"[56] but to modern readers of classical literature it it best known as the story of the widow of Ephesus from Petronius Arbiter's *Satyricon*.[57] A woman, renowned for her fidelity and virtue, suddenly finds herself widowed. She is disconsolate, refusing not only to leave her husband's tomb but also to eat. In the vicinity is a soldier guarding the bodies of thieves hanging from crosses. The king has ordered that the disappearance of any of the bodies will mean death for the guard. The guard hears the widow's laments, leaves his post, and attempts to comfort and feed her. He succeeds on both counts. The soldier then returns to his duty, only to find that one of the bodies has been stolen. He goes back to the woman and bemoans his fate, to which she replies, "Better to hang a dead man than kill a living one." At her insistence, they take her husband's corpse from his tomb and hang it on the cross. The fable's moral is flatly misogynistic: "Sola premit uiuosque metu penaque sepultos / Femina: femineum non bene finit opus." [Only a woman oppresses the living with fear and the entombed with punishment; feminine work does not end well.]

The bad end of womanly work is exemplified not only in the action of the fable but also in its structure. The central character of the fable offends against medieval sensibilities in at least three ways: she drastically abbreviates her period of mourning by becoming involved with the guard, she allows her husband's corpse to be mutilated, and, perhaps most disruptively, she gets away with her actions, leaving the tale without the clear moral closure that punishment would have provided. This is not, then, a moral fable, and because of its "openness," it required a different allegorical approach in order to give it closure and make it more appropriate as a teaching text.

That closure took the form of allegory which inverts character type and motivation, an *in bono* reading of a narrative which provides no positive role models for its readers. The *Esopus moralizatus,* which only rarely employs allegorical readings, interprets the fable as follows:

> Allegorice per mulierem potest intelligi anima rationalis et per virum ipsum corpus castum sive mundum. Tandem venit mors, id est delectatio mundi, et capit, id est ducit hominem ad peccata et trahit carnem ad vanitates. Sed mulier, id est anima, residens circa tumulum, plorat et flet in nocte, id est in conscientia occulta. Tandem custos furis, id est bonus angelus, visitat illum locum attendens illam contritionem et tandem ipsam animam trahit in coniugem, id est in eternam beatitudinem.

> [Allegorically, by the woman the soul of a rational person can be understood, and by the man the chaste body itself or the world. At last comes death, that is the delight in the world, and captures (them), that is leads the man to sins and pulls the flesh to vanities. But the woman, that is the soul remaining around the grave, laments and weeps in the night, that is in hidden conscience. Then the guard of the thief, that is a good angel, visits that place, directing his attention to that contrite one, and then he leads that soul into marriage, that is into eternal blessedness.][58]

An atypical fable—one populated with characters who are both human and ostensibly immoral—requires atypical allegorization, treatment radical enough to transform it into a beautifully orchestrated episode of spiritual transcendence. Strongly reminiscent of certain allegorical interpretations of Ovid's poetry, this allegory shares with Ovidian commentaries the technique of reading against a narrative in which no positive ethical examples appear—in other words, offering an *in bono* reading of a work that might otherwise teach a sinful lesson. The fable allegory has a parallel in Bersuire's *Ovidius moralizatus* in the allegorization of the Myrrha's incestuous relationship with her father, Cinyras, in Book X of the *Metamorphoses*. Bersuire writes that Myrrha represents the good Christian, because the act of embracing her father, who represents God, symbolizes receiving the sacraments.[59] In both of these readings, illicit sexual intercourse becomes the beginning of eternal glory for the soul. The allegorization of this fable, then, would expose children to the standard technique of reading against the narrative grain, but because this fable is the only literally "immoral" one in the collection, such allegory does not need to be employed again.[60]

While exegetical allegory shares with spiritual allegory the goal of teaching a religious lesson, spiritual allegory requires individual praxis whereby the reader should carry over or "translate" the lesson from the fable text into the spiritual text which he is playing out in life; this translation is at the heart of the ethical reading discussed by John Dagenais, Judson B. Allen, and others. Exegetical allegory requires the reader to conceive of a connection not between text and life but between text and text, specifically between fable and Scripture. A commentator creates this conjunction by highlighting parallels in action or symbolism between a fable and a biblical narrative.

The most common exegetical reading found in extant documents is associated with the second fable in the elegiac Romulus, "De Lupo et Agno." It appears most frequently in fifteenth-century manuscripts, especially those of German provenance. In the fable, a wolf unjustly accuses a lamb first of muddying his drinking water and then of being disrespectful; finally the wolf kills the lamb. Stuttgart Württembergische Landesbibliothek MS HB. XII.4 gives both social and exegetical readings for the fable:

> Per lupum intelliguntur oppressores sive calumniatores. Per agnum vero innocens, quia iste lupi [*sic*] innocentem agnum devoravit. Sic oppressores innocentes ubique locorum opprimunt. Vel aliter per agnum Christus et per lupum Synagoga qui dicebant "Destruis nostram legem." (f. 330r)

> [By the wolf oppressors or false accusers are understood. By the lamb an innocent person is understood, because these wolves devour the

innocent lamb. Thus oppressors oppress innocent people everywhere. Or otherwise by the lamb Christ (is understood), and by the wolf Judaism, which says "You are destroying our law."]

The second interpretation recasts the fable as an allegory of the episode central to anti-Semitic teaching in the Middle Ages, the Jews' supposed crucifixion of Christ. Furthermore, the double reading of the fable unites Jews, liars, and oppressors as allegorical significations for the wolf, thus implicitly adding yet another dimension to the anti-Semitism.[61]

The most detailed exegetical allegory appears in British Library MS 11897, a late-fourteenth- or early-fifteenth-century German copy of the elegiac Romulus with a marginal commentary in a miniscule gloss hand. Although this commentary favors spiritual allegory over other types of reading, it brings exegetical allegory to bear upon its Fable 45, entitled "De Quadrupedibus et Avibus" in the manuscript reproduced by Hervieux.[62] Here the bat becomes a traitor to the birds while they are at war with the quadrupeds, but the birds finally win. The bat is then denuded and forced to fly only at night. The second half of the moral alludes to Scripture ("Vtiliter seruit nemo duobus heris" [No one usefully serves two masters], a paraphrase of the first sentence of Matthew 6:24), but the commentator draws closer ties between the fable and the gospels. According to him, the birds represent Christians and the quadrupeds gentiles or Jews. He then adds:

> Per vespertilionem ipsam Judam foediorem qui, relicta fide et societate christianorum, scilicet apostolorum, transtulit se in societatem infidelium iudeorum, tradendo eis sanguinem innocentem, scilicet christi, dicens, "Quid vultis mihi dare, et ego eum vobis tradam." Unde exutus vellere, id est veste innocentie transfugus, arripuit pennam vento agitabilem, id est vile precium et transitorium XXX denariorum, quo sibi voluit querere laudem. Et ideo edictum subiit ne nisi nocte volet, id est laqueo se suspendens, evisceratus in tormentis tenebrosis iugeat, et de pena in penam vadat. (f. 18v)

> [By the bat (understand) that very foul Judas, who, having abandoned faith and the society of Christians (namely the apostles), he crossed over into the society of Jewish infidels, handing over to them innocent blood, namely that of Christ, saying, "What do you want to give to me if I hand him over to you?" Whence stripped of his pelt, that is, deserted by the clothing of innocence, he took flight, moving by the wind, that is, the worthless value of thirty transitory pieces of silver, with which he wanted to seek praise for himself. And on that account

he suffered the edict that unless he flew at night, that is, hanged himself in a noose, he would be bound and eviscerated in dark torments, and from one punishment to another he would go.]

This comment, the most detailed allegorical parallel between biblical history and fable narrative that I have seen, has an analogue in the *Ovidius moralizatus*, where Bersuire writes that Peleus and Thetis, representing Adam and Eve, were ancestors of Achilles, representing Christ.[63] In another example of this type of reading that appears in a commentary on the *Aeneid* tentatively attributed to Anselm of Laon, the commentator points out that Augustine believed that the fall of Troy was contemporaneous with Moses leading the Israelites across the Red Sea; thus the pagan Aeneas becomes a figure for the biblical Moses, since both led their people to promised lands.[64] All of these examples of exegetical allegory are exercises in typological interpretation. A commentator who could successfully find reflections of a biblical story in a pagan fable would be well on the way to discovering structural similarities between events in the Old Testament and stories that mirror them in the New Testament.

The final type of allegory that we should examine in relation to curricular fable is also intertextual. Natural allegory focuses upon an animal or object in a fable and describes it with textual material borrowed from etiological literature. A lengthy example of natural allegory appears in Bibliothèque Nationale MS Lat. 8023 after the third fable, "De Mure et Rana." Making no effort to link the interpretation to the fable beyond the fact that both texts concern mice, the commentator writes:

> Nota quod mus secundum ysodorus [*sic*] est animal pusillum. Ab humo dicitur quia ab humo nascitur. Unde mus humidus est quam terra. Unde nota quod mus habet talem proprietatem quod dum luna est plenilius tunc eius iecur crescit et dum luna minuit, sic similiter eius iecur minuit similimodo. (f. 65v)

> [Note that a mouse, according to Isidore (of Seville) is an insignificant animal; from the soil it is said (to come) because it is born out of the soil, whence the mouse is moist like the earth. Note that the mouse has such a property that when the moon is very full, then its liver grows, and when the moon diminishes, similarly his liver diminishes.][65]

The commentary goes on to describe the mouse's unclean urine, its venomous bite, and its tendency to gather winter provisions during the summer. Thus the appearance of the mouse in "De Mure et Rana" becomes the occasion for reproducing a good deal of material ostensibly unrelated to this fable; if appropriate anywhere in the elegiac Romulus, these etiological descriptions fit the fable of the city mouse and country mouse more closely. Implicit in the use of this type of comment early in the collection is the commentator's invitation to employ it later: a reader who learns to use natural allegory in Fable 3 of the elegiac Romulus will find it useful again before he finishes studying the collection.

The comment above stands in relation to the bestiary tradition as a marginal comment in British Library MS Add. 11897 stands in relation to the tradition of lapidaries, the compendia which explain the special natures of precious and semiprecious stones. In the manuscript, to the left of the first fable, the following fragment is written separately from the comment but in the same miniscule hand: "In lapidaris dicitur jaspidis esse decem species septemque feruntur. Caste portatus fugat et febres et iidropes. Optimus in viridi translucentique colore" (f. 2r). [There are ten species of jacinth recorded, and seven are recorded here. When chastely carried, it drives out both fever and dropsy. The best is of green and translucent color.] Although the scribe has not written the passage in verse form, it comprises lines 1, 6, and 4 of the "De iaspide" section of the verse lapidary *De Gemmis,* ascribed to Evax, King of Arabia. We will return to this lapidary in relation to John Lydgate's version of the fable, but in relation to this manuscript the passage is significant for providing a link between the fables and the system of natural allegory upon which lapidaries are based.

The examples of fable commentary given above represent the forms of reading that I have found in roughly one hundred manuscripts and some incunables. While I would hesitate to assert that these must represent all the types of fable reading undertaken in the Middle Ages, the fact that these forms dominate is surely significant. The range of allegorical tropes here is quite limited, more circumscribed than the kinds of reading that appear in commentaries on Ovid and Virgil, for example. The limited number of allegorical types and patterns found in extant medieval documents relating to the elegiac Romulus suggests that educators probably wanted to familiarize their students with only a few allegorical tools before exposing them to the more complex allegorical readings in lengthier pagan texts. If, in the course of studying the elegiac Romulus, students could learn how to handle these few methods of reading, they would have accomplished enough.

It is also noteworthy that because the fables in the elegiac Romulus were obviously not meant to be taken literally, their literal level could not be misinterpreted so as to lead the proverbial ignorant reader into sinful responses. Simple allegory could be understood and practiced by even the most jejune reader. Only the more complex story of the widow of Ephesus requires forceful allegorical intervention, for in the other fables in this collection, misinterpretation is not an issue.

Evidence from fable commentaries in manuscripts and incunables indicates that on the whole, commentaries were organized so as to expose students to the full variety of commenting practices early in their study of the collection. The appendices amply demonstrate that within the first seven fables, readers could have learned several approaches to reading, any one of which they could have chosen to apply to any of the later fables. (Again the fable of the widow of Ephesus is an exception because of its marked difference from all other fables in the collection.) Two or more forms of reading in a comment upon a single fable indicate that commentators, perhaps of all ages, were free to experiment with multiple views of texts. By extension, then, manuscripts that give full comments for the early fables but leave many or most of the later ones uncommented need not indicate that only a handful of fables received full interpretation; rather, they may signal that a pupil wrote only enough comments to satisfy himself (or his instructor) that he had internalized an adequate range of comment types, after which he could have continued to apply those types to fables orally in the classroom.[66]

Exegetical and natural allegory are not the only forms of intertextuality to be practiced upon fable: the use of *auctoritates*, a standard medieval commenting practice, often adds another dimension to fable commentary. They provide ethical (and canonical) reinforcement for comments, helping readers to draw connections between the moral message of the fable and other texts, but they engage with the narrative only conceptually, not as a story to be allegorized. Indeed, *auctoritates* generally present only a gloss upon the fable's *moralitas,* a thematic reading. The two authoritative texts which are quoted most frequently in fable commentary are the Bible and the *Disticha Catonis.* That verses from Scripture should function as *auctoritates* is not surprising in a text meant to teach ethics, and the frequent recourse to the *Distichs of Cato* is also sensible as a gesture of canonical reinforcement: all pupils studying the fables had already studied Cato as the first text in the grammar-school curriculum, so schoolmasters could reasonably expect their pupils to remember apothegms apposite to particular apologues.

Most commentaries use *auctoritates* sparingly, if at all. Those which provide only prose paraphrases of fable plots generally do not add authoritative quotations to those summaries. The *Esopus moralizatus* cites only three *auctoritates:* Psalms in relation to Fable 3 (see Appendix 2, p. 208); Matthew 7:15 ("Adtendite a falsis prophetis") in relation to Fable 26, "De Agno et Lupo"; and Seneca's *De Beneficiis* ("Oblivisci beneficii accepti est animi malignantis")[67] in relation to Fable 42, "De Leone et Pastore." The *Auctores octo* commentary limits itself to a few quotations of or allusions to the Bible, and a quotation from "Salo" which I have been unable to identify.[68] British Library MS Add. 11897 has recourse to *auctoritates* with far greater frequency than most commentaries. The *Disticha Catonis* is quoted fifteen times, the Bible six. MS Add. 11897 also reproduces quotations from the following writers and texts: Boethius's *De Consolatione Philosophiae*, Geoffrey of Vinsauf's *Poetria Nova* (five times), Gregory the Great, Ovid, Aristotle (thrice), and the *Novus Cato*. The commentator also quotes one vernacular and several Latin proverbs.[69]

The elegiac Romulus made reciprocal contributions to the play of proverbial intertextuality: unlike the fables of Avianus, which had fulfilled the need for fables in the grammar-school curriculum before the twelfth century, the elegiac Romulus fables had fully detachable *moralitates,* useful as maxims on their own or in relation to other texts. The writer of these fables alluded to the special nature of his collection's *moralitates* in the distich which usually appears after the sixtieth fable: "Fine fruor versu gemino, quod cogitat omnis / Fabula declarat datque quid intus habet." [I derive advantage from the end with the double line, wherein all people think (that) a fable declares and gives forth what it has within.] This distich functions as a meta-moral, the two lines that pinpoint the locus of ethical meaning for the collection in its entirety. Bibliothèque Nationale MS Lat. 8023 explicates the distich thus: "'Fine,' etc., id est, dat intellectum suum, etc. Hoc est dictum quod in toto isto libro in qualibet fabula in fine germino versu declaratur quod debet omnis homo cogitare et quem fructus habet intus, id est quem fructum in se continet" (f. 101r). ["The end," etc., that is, he gives his understanding, etc. By this it is said that in this entire book in any fable there is declared at the end, in paired verses, that which all people ought to think, and the fruit that the fable has inside, that is, whatever fruit it contains in itself.]

The value of the *moralitates* as detachable units is mentioned in several manuscripts, with Munich Bayerische Staatsbibliothek MS Clm. 19667 providing one of the lengthiest and clearest defenses. It appears after the distich above and concludes the fables: "finaliter concludendo librum suum ipse ponit modum inquirendi fructum unuscuiusque fabuli. Hoc est quod ipsa docet referri ad mortalitatem et applicare ad vitam nostram, [licet] vult tamen quod fructus uniuscuisque fabule comprehenditur in duobus versibus in ultimo loco eiusdem fabule positus (f. 99r). [Finally in concluding his book, he sets out the means of seeking the fruit of every fable. That is what it teaches to be conferred on human nature and to apply to our life, namely, he wants the fruit of every fable to be understood in the two verses put at the end of that fable.] The commentator goes on to discuss at length two reasons for the value of the two-verse *moralitates*. The first is that after the author's play in each fable, he shows the real value of the narrative.[70] The other reason is their brevity, which makes them easier to remember than longer texts treating morality. To support his ideas about the *moralitates,* the commentator quotes Cicero's *Topics,* Boethius's *De Consolatione Philosophiae,* and Aristotle's *Rhetoric* and *De Anima.*

The detachment of the distichs from their fable narratives is exemplified in manuscripts from three centuries in which the fable morals are simply listed on their own, in a manner very similar to the way that the *Disticha Catonis* were copied.[71] The existence of these manuscripts raises the possibility that the *moralitates* were in active use as proverbs separate from the fables. Perhaps in some instances the distichs were not even identified with the verse fables (although the anonymity of the proverb would have resulted in its loss of the *auctoritas* associated with Aesop). British Library MS Harley 5751, a crudely produced schoolbook, uses *moralitates* and other distichs from the elegiac Romulus in two settings: first, in a list of *auctoritates* from Ovid, Alain de Lille, Boethius, Juvenal, John of Garland, and others, two *moralitates* and distichs from the elegiac Romulus appear, labeled "Esopus" or "Ysopus." Then the young scribe produces a six-page list of twenty-seven *moralitates* and nine internal distichs from the fables, each preceded by a general subject heading; for example, the moral of the fable of the city mouse and the country mouse is labeled "Paupertas" (f. 261r), the moral of the lion and the mouse is headed "Misericordia pauperum" (f. 262r), and the moral of the swallow and the flax is marked "Utile consilium" (f. 262r).[72] The categorization of moralizing distichs under simple rubrics may have been yet another school exercise, the ultimate type of progymnasmatic *abbreviatio.*

Moralitates also appear scribbled on flyleaves and as pen tests. On the back flyleaf of Bodleian MS Can. lat. 127, which contains an unglossed copy of the elegiac Romulus, I have found the epimyths of four fables;[73] these appear amidst various other maxims, proverbs, and scribbling. Cambridge University Library MS Add. 6676, copied by a student in Leipzig in 1410, reproduces only the first thirty-seven elegiac Romulus fables, but with consummate attention the copyist (or perhaps a later reader) has reproduced as a pen test the *moralitas* to Fable 10; ironically, these are among the most legible lines in the very lengthy schoolbook. Other *moralitates* from the elegiac Romulus probably appear in equally isolated, mundane surroundings in extant manuscripts not necessarily including the fables, but they are likely to remain unidentified as belonging to the elegiac Romulus.

The frequent use of *auctoritates* in fable commentaries is integral to the fable "translations" produced by Chaucer, Lydgate, and Henryson. All three of these authors understood that fable was an acceptable site of intertextual exploration, and all three exploited this knowledge, though to very different ends: Chaucer satirically, Lydgate unquestioningly, and Henryson in a variety of ways.

In sum, these manuscripts amply demonstrate that a limited number of allegorical patterns were made available to pupils and older readers of fable in scholastic commentaries and that even though a handful of fables had specific readings which followed them across Europe over centuries, any fable could be interpreted according to any allegorical form, at the whim of the reader, or perhaps at the behest of a teacher. The set of allegorical patterns described here became as manipulable and interchangeable as fables themselves, and they should suggest to us yet another dimension of intertextuality: a reader familiar with these scholastic interpretations might begin with an allegory in mind and remember fables to which it could apply. And when pupils finished the study of the elegiac Romulus, remembering the allegorical patterns and how to apply them was surely at least as important as remembering the fables themselves, for the curriculum demanded that students make their way through more complex classical texts demanding allegorical interpretation.

Free-Play in the Margins: Ludic Elements in Elegiac Romulus Manuscripts

In the manuscript tradition of the elegiac Romulus, a number of marginal comments not directly related to scholastic commentary show readers' attitudes toward the text that they are reading and studying. I call these "ludic" elements because they engage in play with the text, its author, or its classroom presentation, but like most examples of "play" in the Middle Ages, they are fraught with seriousness.[74] Although this marginalia is not commentary per se, it teaches us how fable readers positioned themselves in relation not only to the canonical text but also the canon-building environment of the classroom.

The elegiac Romulus was a likely text for marginal "playfulness" inasmuch as it occupied a special place in the curriculum. As Gehl states in *A Moral Art,* "The stylistic wordplay of [the fables] was reinforced by the genre itself; in fable, all these sobering lessons were put in the mouths of talking animals. The power of fables for schoolchildren resided in their combination of charming rural settings and urbane play of language. Moreover, they were the only straightforwardly narrative text in the Florentine elementary curriculum."[75] What is true for the Florentine curriculum generally holds true across Europe in the fourteenth and fifteenth centuries. The young students studying the elegiac Romulus may have been likelier than their older counterparts to engage shamelessly in textual playfulness and to leave evidence of it behind.

The most common playful element to be added to these manuscripts is wordplay based upon the similarity between the name of the *auctor* and that of the herb hyssop, *ysopus* in Latin. It seems likely that this pun first appeared as a distinction between the fabulist, Esopus, and the plant, *ysopus,* as it is reproduced in Bibliothèque Nationale MS Lat. 8509 and other manuscripts: "Ysopus est herba, sed esopus dat bona verba." [Hyssop is an herb, but Aesop gives good words.][76] In some manuscripts, however, the conjunction *sed* falls away, leaving only "Ysopus est herba, esopus dat bona verba."[77] Here the relationship between the two clauses is unclear: do the clauses contrast, or is the healing nature of the herb hyssop comparable to the healing ethical effect of fable? So thought a few scribes. As we saw above in the *accessus* to the Freiburg fable manuscript, the writer elaborates upon the similarity between the names: he etymologizes the author's name, writing that it comes "from hyssop, which is the name of a certain herb. As hyssop [has] good and varied odors, thus this book [has] usefulness" ("ab esopo, quod nomen est cuiusdam herbe. Sicut isopus bonos et varios odores, sic ille liber utilitates" [f. 1r]). The fables in Milan Biblioteca Nazionale Braidense MS AD.10.42, n.2 open with a sentence explaining that hyssop is suitable for purging the lungs.

The full conflation of the names of plant and fabulist appears in Bodleian MS Can. lat. 128: "Exopus est herba, exopus dat bona verba," and in two other manuscripts.[78] Such identification of Aesop with hyssop was evidently common enough to annoy some students of fable, who correct this misunderstanding in their work. For example, the fables in Stuttgart Württembergische Landesbibliothek HB.I.127 conclude with the following two lines: "Explicit Esopus. Peccat qui dicat ysopus. Ysopus est herba, esopus dat bona verba" (f. 196v). [Here ends Aesop. He who says "hyssop" errs. Hyssop is an herb, Aesop gives good words.]

If the catchphrase about Aesop and hyssop were mere nonsense, surely it would not have had such long, widespread popularity. But if these lines were originally meant as an orthographic mnemonic to help pupils distinguish between Aesop and hyssop, why did they continue to circulate when distinction had become conflation? Aside from the metaphorical link between the salubrious nature of medicine and morality, the conjunction of

Aesop and hyssop could reflect the well-known metaphor of *ruminatio,* one of the central practices of medieval reading. Mary Carruthers has described it as follows: "The ruminant image is basic to understanding what was involved in *memoria* as well as *meditatio,* the two being understood as the agent and its activity. . . . *Ruminatio* is an image of regurgitation, quite literally intended; the memory is the stomach, the stored texts are the sweet-smelling cud originally drawn from the meadows of books (or lecture).[79] Carruthers cites the centrality of this metaphor to acts of composition as well, since a writer relies upon the memory of what he has read in order to compose. In this sense, hyssop, a health-giving plant, is to be ingested, ruminated, and regurgitated in context, a model which resembles Meuli's generic definition of fable according to context (*"Situationsbezug"*).[80] At the risk of overextending the metaphor, I might also point out that *ruminatio* is particularly appropriate to fable inasmuch as it is based upon connecting animal and human behavior, one of the interpretive fundamentals of fable. It also asks the reader to think of the corpus of Aesop, whether that of the imagined author or merely his work, as related to lowly vegetation; it is as common as grass, though more valuable.[81]

Petrarch linked the practice of *ruminatio* and a fable from the elegiac Romulus in a letter to Boccaccio in 1359, in which he discusses the texts he learned as a schoolboy:

> I ate in the morning what I would digest in the evening; I swallowed as a boy what I would ruminate upon as an older man. I have thoroughly absorbed these writings, implanting them not only in my memory but in my marrow. . . . But sometimes I may forget the author, since through long usage and continual possession I may adopt them and for some time regard them as my own; and beseiged by the mass of such writings, forget whose they are, and whether they are mine or others'. . . . I grant that I like to embellish my life with sayings and admonitions from others, but not my writings, unless I acknowledge the author or make some significant change in arriving at my own concept from many and varied sources in imitation of the bees. . . . I much prefer that my style be my own, uncultivated and rude, but made to fit, as a garment, to the measure of my mind rather than to someone else's . . . each [writer] must develop and keep his own style lest by dressing grotesquely in others' clothes . . . we may be ridiculed like the crow.[82]

At the end of this passage Petrarch alludes to the fable of the crow in peacock feathers, one of the elegiac Romulus fables; it appears as Fable 35, "De

Cornicula et Pavone," in Hervieux's edition. The Italian author has indeed mastered the hyssopian and the Aesopian, ruminating upon the texts until they become a part of his own corpus. Regardless of whether Petrarch knew the metaphorical conjunction of Aesop and hyssop, he has clearly shown how the metaphor might be internalized and ruminated upon; it goes beyond the merely playful.[83]

A simile relating to Aesop's name appears in at least two manuscripts. Berlin Lat. Qu. 18. concludes, "Explicit hoc opus quod splendet velud peropus. Ysopus est herba sed esopus dat bona verba" (f. 218v). [Here ends this work that shines like bronze. Hyssop is an herb, but Aesop gives good words.] *Peropus,* a variant of *pyropus* (bronze) is defined in a marginal comment on the first page of the elegiac Romulus in British Library MS Add. 11897, along with an *auctoritas* from Ovid ("Flamasque imitante piropo" from *Metamorphoses* II.1–2). The original writer of this simile may have associated Aesop and bronze as an allusion to the literary age which preceded the golden and silver ages of classicism; if so, his classification was unique.[84]

Other ludic phrases capitalize upon the concept of play. One appears in Wrocław Biblioteka Uniwersyteka MS IV.Qu.64, in its explicit (which also includes the Aesop/hyssop wordplay): "Explicit expliceat, ludere scriptor eat" (f. 46v). This jussive subjunctive seems to be addressed to the teacher: the pupil, having finished his work, demands a recess. The type of play demanded by pupils takes on a carnivalesque aspect in the explicit to Lambeth Palace MS 431, which begins with the *ysopus* conflation. This young scribe writes: "Finito libro, frangamus ossa magistro" (f. 136v). [Having finished this book, let us break the bones of the master.] Both of these lines indicate that the play in and with the texts extended beyond the boundaries of study into the world of the school. One kind of play leads to another, as the playfulness of the genre of fable leads to the allegorical free-play of various interpretations. V. A. Kolve describes several children's beating games in the Middle Ages in relation to the buffeting of Christ in the medieval cycle drama (185–86); these may also inform the quotation above. The carnivalesque inversion of power in the buffeting plays is duplicated in the schoolboy's threat to break the bones of his master, a threat that both mimics and mocks the physical violence that informs many fables.

Lengthy though this discussion of curricular fable manuscripts has been, it merely summarizes a body of literature worthy of a book-length study of its own. However, this chapter provides at least an overview of the variety of discursive practices associated with fable for roughly two hundred years. It also hints at the possibility of rich, multilayered readings of fable that might strike modern readers as odd, inconsistent, and poorly organized. But manuscripts show that medieval commentators engaged in just such reading, as Christopher Baswell has pointed out in relation to a late-fourteenth-century commentator on Virgil's *Aeneid*, whom Baswell calls the Norwich commentator. In this description he typifies many fable commentators, too: "He is certainly a wayward reader and unsystematic commentator, his attention shifting from one topic and approach to another, making much of an occasional obscure point, ignoring another which seemed important to other medieval readers, and switching from one emphasis and format to another. And he is not altogether persistent, his notes breaking off suddenly. . . . But above all his very waywardness provides traces of an enthusiastic reader and re-reader."[85] Baswell has described a man involved in what John Dagenais has called "the particular texture of medieval reading, its starts and stops and bumps and skips."[86] But if the field of discursive practices relating to fable and other classical texts is bumpy, it is also remarkably expansive.

And surely part of the bumpiness of the commentary on the elegiac Romulus has to do with the nature of the text itself, for it is, after all, a compilation of short, separate narratives that ask to be considered individually. Because some are deeply serious while others are humorously light, they ostensibly demand different interpretive treatments according to tone, for the collection need not have an overarching thematic or structural cohesion into which disparate treatments must fit (even though they must all lead to ethical behavior). The curricular fables therefore offer a far more fertile field for experimentation with widely varying types of interpretation than does a work unified in narrative and tone, such as the *Aeneid*.

And this brings us to another important reason that fable occupied a place early in the grammar-school curriculum: its short narratives *are* separate and treatable individually. The collection implicitly teaches young commentators that they must proceed episode by episode through their text, commenting upon manageable pieces of narrative. In this collection, which was probably the first curricular text in which pupils had to comment upon plots, the division of the text is done for them; it prepares them to undertake *divisio* of lengthier texts later. One of the most frequently commented works, Ovid's *Metamorphoses*, partakes of the episodic nature of a fable collection in spite of its overall coherence, so it might not have presented as many problems to medieval readers as the *Aeneid*. This text gave headaches to the Norwich commentator, whose "tendency to take the epic to pieces, both by the provision of topic headings and in local allegorization . . . can be seen as a kind of breakdown of Virgilian reading."[87] So when adult authors returned to infinitely malleable, structurally simple fable, they may have been demonstrating a nostalgia for the breadth of interpretive choices available to them, each relatively independent of the next—but ironically, their first impulse as translators was to make those narratives more complex through rhetorical strategies borrowed from curricular practice.

Although the manuscript evidence of scholastic fable commentary (like the Aesopic tradition in general) resists orderly classification according to time and, to some extent, place, it sketches for us the literary macrocosm within which Chaucer, Lydgate, and Henryson penned microcosmic masterings of Aesop. The scholastic fable tradition challenges the uncertainties about this mode of discourse that we saw expressed in the previous chapter by classical and patristic writers: in spite of those writers' divergent attitudes, the critical apparatus that fables received, somewhat more limited than but otherwise identical to that which was supplied for pagan texts held in the highest regard, raises them to something approaching the same high authoritative status. Therefore it is not surprising that vernacular writers who experimented with translations of other classical texts should turn to fables for rhetorical experimentation. And now we turn to them.

4

Commentary Displacing Text

The Nun's Priest's Tale and the Process
of Reading Curricular Fable

As a preamble to my discussion of Geoffrey Chaucer's *Nun's Priest's Tale,* we should note that the only Aesopic fable commentator from medieval England whose name we know was a contemporary of Chaucer, and the outline of the commentator's life, from Carmelite prior at Oxford, to confessor to Henry V, to bishop of Chichester, is well documented.

Stephen Patrington was a native of Yorkshire but studied at Oxford, where he became a Carmelite before 1366;[1] he was the prior of the order's convent there by 1373 and held that position at least until 1382. Patrington became one of the leading voices to denounce the Lollards at Oxford, and in February 1382 he bore to John of Gaunt the letter written by the friars of that city denouncing Wyclif and his followers. By 1390 Patrington had earned the degree of doctor of divinity. In 1397 Patrington was granted an annuity of £10 by John of Gaunt, and that grant was confirmed on Christmas Eve of that year by the noble who would soon become King Henry IV. In 1399 Patrington became Prior Provincial of his order in England, and on Christmas Day in 1401, he preached before the king. Henry V made Patrington his confessor in 1413 and raised his annuity to £69.10s.6d. An active anti-Lollard campaigner at Oxford in 1414, he was appointed and consecrated bishop of St. David's in 1415, and the following year he received custody of the temporalities of Chichester. He died in 1417.

William of Walsingham described Patrington as learned in the trivium and the quadrivium, and certainly his expertise in the former is evidenced in the commentary attributed to him on the *Ecloga* of Theodulus, another curricular text. Although Patrington's fable commentary does not survive (or survives dissociated from his name), his authorship of such a work gives us a clear idea of the degree of learning of at least one fable commentator, and the fact that this attribution survives at all demonstrates that writing such a commentary was not considered demeaning in any way.

Because Patrington was in London in the 1390s and perhaps even frequented the court of King Henry IV soon after his accession to the throne, the Carmelite may have crossed paths with a petitioner for royal favor there, Geoffrey Chaucer.

In a period when a bishop and confessor to the king was identified as a commentator upon Aesopic fable, who or what was the Aesop of vernacular poet Geoffrey Chaucer? Did Chaucer study the elegiac Romulus as a child? What was Chaucer's attitude toward *fabula* in both the narrower sense addressed in this book and the broader sense of fiction generally? Although the historical evidence that would definitively answer the first two questions has not survived, Chaucer's interest in fable and its father surfaces repeatedly in his oeuvre.

In spite of the fact that Chaucer was familiar with misgivings about *fabula* among patristic writers, grammarians, and rhetoricians, and although he understood that Latin was the language of authoritative texts in his day, *The Canterbury Tales* stands as the first great collection of *fabulae* in English, several of them having their roots in Latin clerical culture. Furthermore, the very structure of the compilation, with the portraits of the pilgrims in the General Prologue followed by a series of tales that they tell, may remind us of the scholastic practice of introducing the author of a *fabula* so as to allow us to judge his or her work in relation to that author's life; at the very least Chaucer invites us to engage with the *accessus* category of *intentio auctoris* as we read the tales, thus contextualizing the tales' fiction, in this case within another fiction where its efficacy can be judged. Such dramatic readings of the tales still dominate the study of the tales today.

Beyond *The Nun's Priest's Tale*, the other story most often placed in the modern category of fable is *The Manciple's Tale*, a categorization based mainly upon its talking animal and its moralizing conclusion. But although this tale seems Aesopic, it belongs to a different medieval category of *fabula*, the Ovidian, having been drawn from the *Metamorphoses*. Even so, as we have seen in previous chapters, common methodologies united commentary on Ovid and Aesop, and Chaucer seems to have taken advantage of these similarities: he recasts the Ovidian fable as an Aesopic fable, with a heavy dose of moralizing at the end, giving the tale an overall structure akin to scholastic fable followed by amplified moralizing commentary, even if the moral gives itself the lie by asserting in a verbosely repetitive fashion that one should hold one's tongue. It will be useful for us to keep the conventional fable structure of *The Manciple's Tale* in mind as we approach Chaucer's unconventionally structured *Nun's Priest's Tale*, where Chaucer creates a different type of relationship between text and commentary.

Elsewhere in *The Canterbury Tales* Chaucer mentions Aesop by name in the *Tale of Melibee*, but in this instance he is simply following the text that he is translating, Renaud de Louens's *Livre de Melibée et de la Dame Prudence*, itself a translation of Albertanus of Brescia's *Liber consolationis et consilii*. In one of her many lengthy speeches comprising numerous *auctoritates*, Prudence counsels Melibee, "And Isope seith, 'Ne trust nat to hem to whiche thou hast some tyme werre or enemytee, ne telle hem nat thy conseil'" (1183). The proverb attributed to Aesop in the Latin, French, and English versions of the story is not drawn from the elegiac Romulus, but from another Latin Aesopic collection.[2] However, a distich from the elegiac Romulus appears twice in the *Liber consolationis et consilii*, though it is not identified with Aesop; these lines, from Fable 35, "De Cornicula et Pavone,"[3] appear in passages of the Latin book untranslated by Renaud, whose work is only about two-thirds the length of the original. Since no evidence indicates that Chaucer knew Albertanus's Latin text,[4] the fabular material is absent from the *Melibee*. The tale shows only that Chaucer was as comfortable as Renaud had been to list Aesop among the plethora of authoritative figures cited by Prudence; the citation shows no direct knowledge of the elegiac Romulus.

Suggesting that Chaucer had some knowledge of the figure of Aesop, Nicolai von Kreisler has found in Chaucer's work a likely allusion to an episode in the *Vita Aesopi*. In an article entitled "An Aesopic Allusion in the *Merchant's Tale*,"[5] von Kreisler focuses on Januarie's response to his brother Justinus's rhetorically elevated advice not to marry:

"Straw for thy Senek and for thy proverbes!
I counte nat a panyer ful of herbes
Of scole-termes." (1567–69)

Pointing out that in Chaucer's day a pannier of herbs would have been valuable property, von Kreisler relates these lines to a scene from the *Life of Aesop*, in which the slave, carrying a pannier to fill with herbs, goes out to the garden with his master, the philosopher Exantus. There the gardener asks why weeds grow better than cultivated plants, a question which Exantus cannot answer. Aesop, however, responds that the earth is mother to weeds which she nurtures naturally, but only stepmother to plants cultivated by humans. Von Kreisler writes, "[T]his anecdote of how a servant bests his master with clever repartee illustrates the popular belief that the abstract philosophy of the learned cannot supplant the wisdom of the commonfolk, or, more concisely, that book-learning is no substitute for common sense."[6] By relating the lines from Chaucer's tale to the episode from the *Life*, von Kreisler asserts that the irony of Januarie's position in the argument is heightened, since he refuses to recognize the common sense in Justinus's advice.

Citing only oral tradition rather than a likely written source from which Chaucer might have learned the story, von Kreisler was apparently unaware of the existence of the Lolliniana manuscript,[7] which could have supported his argument more convincingly. Even so, the article raises the possibility that Chaucer (and presumably his contemporaries, if this allusion was to have been appreciated) might have known the *Life of Aesop* in one form or another.[8]

This possibility should lead us to consider parallels between Aesop and the fabulist whom Chaucer created in the Nun's Priest. The cleric is participating in the pilgrimage to Canterbury largely in order to minister to the spiritual needs of the Prioress. While she is the object of considerable admiration from the narrator of the General Prologue, the Nun's Priest is hardly a presence at all but merely one of the "preestes thre" mentioned cursorily at the end of the forty-five lines devoted to the Prioress (164). In the view of Chaucer the pilgrim, he is her servant, not so different in status from Aesop, who had to create an identity and freedom for himself through his storytelling. The Aesop who told tales for his master is mentioned in the fables of Marie de France, one of which served as a source for this fable; the Nun's Priest tells his fable in a similarly unbalanced power relationship with the Prioress.

But if the view of the Nun's Priest as servant represents one possibility for placing him in a literary-historical context, an equally likely one (and one which Chaucer knew that all of his readers could understand) springs from the Nun's Priest's relative anonymity. A shadowy figure generating fable, his lack of identity problematizes the authority behind his text, and that ambiguity further problematizes the fable's lack of moral closure. The "dramatic" reading of the Nun's Priest in the shadow of the Prioress cannot inform our reading of the fable text as fully as the "absence" of the fabulist can.

Although *The Nun's Priest's Tale* is one of the best-known beast fables in European literature,[9] its structure threatens to preclude it from a genre known primarily for its brevity and simplicity. The fabular part of the tale—the fox's capture and release of the cock Chauntecleer—occupies less than half of the tale, while the first three-fifths are devoted largely to the description of the old woman, her rooster, his dream, and the debate surrounding its interpretation. Why is the conventional fable narrative sequestered in the final half of the work? Would Chaucer's medieval audience have been able to make more of the overall structure of the tale than we can? One explanation for this structure lies in scholastic fable commentary and the way that it taught medieval pupils the processes of reading fable. To understand how this process is exemplified in *The Nun's Priest's Tale,* we must first understand the way that Chaucer manipulated his sources in order to construct the tale.

In a two-part article in *Speculum,* Robert A. Pratt found that the fable itself is closely related to one of Marie de France's popular fables, "Del cok e del gupil," while the earlier portions of the tale come largely from the fourteenth-century *Roman de Renart le Contrefait* and Branch II of the *Roman de Renart.*[10] Amid numerous similarities to these sources, many significant differences also emerge, three of which provide a starting point for this examination of the tale.

1. In both sources, the fox has entered the farmyard before Chauntecleer's dream, thus showing the reader that even as the dream occurs, it is in the process of coming true. In *The Nun's Priest's Tale* the fox first appears after the dream and the chickens' debate.

2. Only in *The Nun's Priest's Tale* does Chauntecleer alone recount his dream; in both Reynardian texts, the narrator recounts it (though in the *Roman de Renart* Chauntecleer later repeats it to his wife, Pinte).[11]

3. In the beast epics, the main conflict unfolds between the cock and the fox, but in *The Nun's Priest's Tale,* Chaucer "has made the rivalry of the cock and hen more important than the rivalry of cock and fox," according to Pratt.[12]

These three differences between the sources and Chaucer's tale intensify the focus upon Chauntecleer's dream, not as the narrator's exploration of a gallinaceous psyche but as a textual paraphrase of a dream which is "written" by a rooster and denied the authority granted it by the narratorial voice in the French text. The dream-text itself, not the early arrival of the fox described in the sources, raises the specter of the predator in Chaucer's tale. Ultimately, the lengthy interpretation of the dream distracts both the characters and the readers from the threat of the fox, at least until the fox begins to act upon that threat.

Alongside Pratt's examination of *The Nun's Priest's Tale*'s fabular and beast-epic source history, some scholars have taken steps toward providing a historical contextualization of the tale as a beast fable; it has been both compared to patristic definitions of fable and examined in relation to aspects of rhetoric generally learned by medieval students.[13] In addition, Peter W. Travis has studied how the fable exemplifies some standard medieval curricular principles in his article "*The Nun's Priest's Tale* as Grammar-School Primer." Of the tale's compendious nature, Travis writes, "Chaucer has designed *The Nun's Priest's Tale* as a palimpsestuous text comprising dozens of schoolboy assignments—not only reading assignments, but translations, paraphrasings, glosses, applications, imitations, and themes amplifying and defending truths discovered in the master text."[14] While Travis correctly asserts that Chaucer relies upon "his audience's collective memory, the key to which is old books and old assignments"[15] in order to understand the tale fully, Travis sees the "dozens of schoolboy assignments" as randomly drawn from standard rhetorical and grammatical practices in the grammar-school classroom, resulting in "apothegm, *sententia,* exemplum, and proverb tussl[ing] with fable, history, allegory and riddle for the admonitory center of the literary stage."[16] This chapter will show that *The Nun's Priest's Tale* is less a literary wrestling match among assignments than a fully exploited curricular fable whose unique structure, as anatomized by Pratt, resembles a fourteenth-century model for the presentation of fable in the classroom. The tale re-presents a curricular process of *narratio* and *enarratio,* narration and interpretation, which encompasses the tale in its entirety. Furthermore, Chaucer could have looked no further than curricular practices relating to Aesopic fable as inspiration for many of the apparently "palimpsestuous" elements in the tale.

As delineated in the description of commentaries in the previous chapter, scribes and printers not only had some degree of choice about what commentary to reproduce but also more than one acceptable format for presenting fable text and commentary on a page. In most copies of commented fables the plot summary and commentary occupy space either beside or beneath each fable, as a kind of extended footnote, kissing the foot of the text that they serve. But when confronting syntactically tortuous Latin verse fables, would medieval schoolboys have turned to a plot summary only *after* reading a fable text? It seems much more logical that in presenting a text to lower-level Latin students, a schoolteacher would have used the plot summary and commentary to introduce the fable. Such an introduction would have then allowed pupils not only to devote less mental energy to plot structure but also to pay more attention to the intricacies of grammar, for which the elegiac Romulus was considered a model.[17]

The notion that plot summary and commentary should precede the fable text both temporally in classroom study and spatially on the page is supported by the *ordinatio,* or page layout, of some manuscripts and early books that aped those manuscripts. The early exemplars of the elegiac Romulus fables and their commentaries include a few variations on the theme of physical displacement of text by commentary, the most striking in manuscripts that do not reproduce the fable collection at all but merely provide pages full of plot paraphrases and commentary.[18]

More similar to *The Nun's Priest's Tale*, however, are the books in which scribes or printers have given the plot summary and commentary visual priority over the fables. For example, the scribe of British Library MS Harley 2745 first copied the title of a fable, then immediately beneath it he wrote four or five lines of commentary in a small gloss hand, and just below the last full line of commentary, he began the fable text. Depending upon the length of the comment, the scribe sometimes completed it in the margin alongside the fable, thus wrapping two sides of the text in commentary. A less conciliatory arrangement of fable text and commentary appears in Milan Biblioteca Ambrosiana MS I. 85 supra. Dated July 1415, the manuscript was copied by Johannis Brixianus (that is, of Brescia in northern Italy). He first copied the incipit of each fable, then the fairly lengthy plot summary and its allegorical meanings, and then the fable itself. This page format was popular enough to have been employed in other manuscripts[19] and at least two incunables, one printed by Jean Bouyer in Poitiers in 1490 and one printed by Bernardinus de Nusintiis in Naples in 1497. In these books, academic plot summaries and commentaries command the attention of the reader by fully displacing the fable texts; the marginal has become both spatially and phenomenologically central.

In the scholastic fable commentaries described above, the progression from the non-authoritative plot summary to scholastic interpretation(s) to the fable itself bears a striking resemblance to the order of the Nun's Priest's material in his story, a resemblance further strengthened by the changes that Chaucer wrought upon his sources. The dream-text serves as both a paraphrase of Chauntecleer's nightmare and a summary of the fable to come, but, unlike its Reynardian predecessors, it is not recounted in the authoritative narratorial voice which will later tell the fable. Rather, Chaucer textualizes it in the voice of a "reader" within the tale, the cock, who, like a school pupil required to make sense of unfamiliar material, needs help if he is to understand it. The birds' commentary on the abbreviated plot summary both drains authority from the specific dream-text by discussing dreams generally and displaces the fable, pushing it into the final half of the tale. In spite of these gestures of displacement, experienced readers and, to some extent, Chauntecleer himself know that his dream will ineluctably come true. Chauntecleer implies this knowledge in his exempla about the validity of premonitory dreams, while readers bring the same knowledge to the tale not only because of the laws of nature but also because of the laws of literature: for all its amplifications and embellishments, this tale is recognizably a fable, and members of the audience know that it must follow its preordained course.

The phenomenon of commenting voices moving from the margins into the narrative of the master text has been expertly described by Christopher Baswell in "Talking Back to the Text: Marginal Voices in Medieval Secular Literature." Baswell cites a commentary on Ovid's *Heroides 7*, Dido's letter to Aeneas, which was written in the voice of the letter writer herself, "virtually a second, marginal narrative in the voice of Dido."[20] An extension of this type of character-voiced commentary is exemplified in two commentaries on the *Aeneid* copied during Chaucer's lifetime; these commentaries "paraphrase in the voices of the characters but also invent new speeches for them, to explain apparent gaps in the logic of the center text, and thus actually take on the role of the *auctor*."[21] As we will see below, many of the standard commenting practices associated with scholastic fable are voiced in the *Nun's Priest's Tale* by Chauntecleer himself, and his lengthy comments threaten to displace the fable text from a position of centrality to one of marginality.

The scholastically sanctioned displacement of text in favor of commentary could have alerted medieval readers to other aspects of scholastic glossing and curricular practice with which Chaucer constructed his tale as he revised his sources. Some borrowings from the classroom are used parodically, some straightforwardly, and others ambiguously, but Chaucer's intentions do not disguise the curricular motifs themselves. Studying these markers can help us understand how Chaucer exploits tension between his contemporaries' expectations about when and how the fable plot would unfold and the displacement of the plot by delaying the action in order to comment upon it. Even the brief plot is full of what John Dagenais calls the starts and stops, references and expansions which typify the process of medieval reading.

The first "stop" in the text occurs before readers can identify the tale as a beast fable, when they meet the old woman who owns the cock and who initially attracts the Nun's Priest's attention so completely that he claims to be telling a tale about her ("This wydwe, of which I telle yow my tale").[22] The peasant who owns the Chantecler in *Le Roman de Renart,* Constans de Noes, is introduced in a manner similar to that used by Chaucer in introducing the widow,[23] but in retrospect, medieval readers might also have recognized the presence of an animal's owner as an element of scholastic fable commentary. Some prose plot summaries embellish the fables by providing human owners for the animal characters, even though no humans are mentioned in the original Latin texts. In an Italian manuscript of the elegiac *Romulus*, for example, the commentator tells us that the rooster in the first fable is owned by "quidam nobilis homo in quodam rure vel in quadam villa," and that the lamb in the second fable belonged to "quidam pastor nomine Sachomano."[24] Not only are these humans entirely absent from the fable text, but also they fail to resurface in the commentator's plot summaries. Their presence is meant to serve the same function as that of the widow in the Nun's Priest's story: to validate the life (and in some cases, the death) of the animal by implying that it would have resonance in the world of humans.

I believe that the passage also serves to literalize one of the negative attitudes toward Aesopic fable that Chaucer certainly knew: that fable is based upon falsity or is itself false. By stating that the tale will focus on the widow, the Nun's Priest makes the rest of the fable a lie in terms of the oral contract he has made with his listeners, but his lie is not immediately apparent to the Canterbury pilgrims, who must educate themselves about the subject matter, moving beyond this self-consciously false "surface" to a different level of meaning. (By the time the Nun's Priest revises the description of his subject matter by stating, "My tale is of a cok, as ye may heere" [3252], the listener/reader fully understands what the tale is about; into this revision Chaucer has structured a significant shift from what the authorial "I" tells—a lie—to what the listening "you" hears—a truth, of sorts.)

When we reach the description of the hero of this fable, we find it constructed so as to place Chauntecleer solidly in the realm of medieval education.

> In al the land, of crowing nas his peer.
> His voys was murier than the murie orgon
> On messe-dayes that in the chirche gon.
> Wel sikerer was his crowyng in his logge
> Than is a clokke or an abbey orlogge.
> By nature he knew ech ascencioun
> Of the equynoxial in thilke toun;
> For whan degrees fiftene weren ascended,
> Thanne crew he, that it myghte nat been amended.
> His coomb was redder than the fyn coral,
> And battailled as it were a castel wal . . . (4040–50)

This is a most quadrivial bird. Here we find metaphorical representations of all four of the nonverbal liberal arts exemplified: music in his talent for singing, arithmetic in his infallible calculations of divisions of time, astronomy in his understanding of each town's location in relation to the equinoctial circle, and geometry in his architectonic comb (geometry being the architect's principal *modus operandi*).[25] Chauntecleer both knows and embodies these disciplines; whether he will measure up in the verbal arts of the trivium remains to be seen.

The plot of Chaucer's tale begins with Chauntecleer groaning and waking from a dream to provide a suggestive but incomplete picture of a menacing fox. Interpretation immediately becomes central to the tale as Pertelote asks what her husband's groan signifies ("What eyleth yow, to grone in this manere?" [4080]). He replies with the summary of his dream:

> "Now God," quod he, "my swevene recche aright,
> And kepe my body out of foul prisoun!
> Me mette how that I romed up and doun
> Withinne our yeerd, wheer as I saugh a beest[26]
> Was lyk an hound, and wolde han made areest
> Upon my body, and wolde han had me deed.
> His colour was bitwixe yelow and reed,
> And tipped was his tayl and bothe his eeris
> With blak, unlyk the remenant of his heeris;
> His snowte small, with glowynge eyen tweye.
> Yet of his look for feer almoost I deye." (4086–96)

Chauntecleer prefaces his dream-text with a clear indication that it exists in order to be interpreted ("my swevene recche aright!"). Of course this adumbration of the subsequent conflict, a miniature of the fable, does not provide a full account of what will happen; Chauntecleer does not even elaborate upon how this unidentifiable animal signaled that he wanted the bird dead. The narrative's brevity is typical of scholastic plot summaries, in which most commentators sketched a fable in no more than two sentences. Chauntecleer's recitation of his fable could have reminded Chaucer's early audiences of how the very act of academic paraphrase is bound to result in an abortive version of a text that must necessarily lack not only the authority but also much of the substance of the original.

Significantly Chaucer has not provided us with a gallinaceous dream-vision: as mentioned above, *The Nun's Priest's Tale* differs from its sources in that the dream here is recounted only in the voice of the dreamer, not in the voice of the tale's narrator. Readers are not invited into the rooster's dream for a less mediated description of what happens, as they are in

Chaucer's other poems in which the characters dream (for example, Troilus's and Criseyde's dreams [II.925–31, V.1233–43] and, more appositely, Cresus's dream of the tree in the final section of *The Monk's Tale,* which directly precedes the Nun's Priest's fable). Rather, the dream is summarized by Chauntecleer and thus taken from the realm of "reality" into textuality. Chauntecleer's dream-text is to his dream as *The Nun's Priest's Tale* is to its sources, since both re-present earlier texts. For us, as for Pertelote, the dream only exists as a textual artifact representing another text which Chaucer has chosen to displace. Rita Copeland has stated that by means of paraphrase, "the commentary becomes container of, no longer supplement to, the original text,"[27] and Chauntecleer's recitation of the dream accomplishes such containment, effectively distancing the authority of not only the dream-text but also of the Old French texts which Chaucer is translating.

The skewed double interpretation of Chauntecleer's dream-text that follows illustrates Copeland's assertion that the goal of exegesis is to "achieve a certain difference with the source" (103). Even the dullest grammar-school pupil could interpret this text readily: the red, hound-like animal is a fox, and since foxes want chickens dead, Chauntecleer instinctively fears the beast and should continue to do so. However, Pertelote and Chauntecleer are engaged in *hermeneia,* achieving a difference with the source text by interpreting, in this case, not what the dream means, but whether it can mean anything at all.

As some scholars have pointed out, Pertelote is apparently familiar with Macrobius's *Commentarii in Somnium Scipionis,* for she reads the dream as a manifestation of the imbalance of Chauntecleer's humours.[28] In her learned opinion, the dream is an *insomnium* or nightmare, a classification that Macrobius calls "not worthy of interpreting, since [it has] no prophetic significance."[29] If we also read the dream as beast fable in miniature, we are reminded that Macrobius is equally dismissive of this genre: he writes that Aesopic fables are "inappropriate to philosophical treatises,"[30] simply because a text based entirely upon falsity cannot be interpreted. In light of the scholastic tradition, then, Pertelote implies that fables are the insomnia of literature; although all readers have to live through them, they should move beyond them as quickly as possible into other kinds of reading.[31] For Pertelote, the content of the dream-text itself cannot directly teach any great truth, but it is symptomatic of the truth—that Chauntecleer needs a laxative.

In defense of her interpretation she cites one of the *Disticha Catonis,* the Distichs of Cato, the lengthy compilation of proverbs that were the first

canonical Latin text that medieval European schoolboys studied.[32] Like the
fable plot in the dream-text, the distich is drastically abbreviated: Pertelote's
paraphrase of the distich achieves a clear difference with its source text.
Although she quotes only half of the distich (and thus substantially mis-
quotes it), her incomplete presentation remains unchallenged by Chauntecleer, implying a tacit acceptance that such difference from one's scholastic source is inevitable.

Chauntecleer counters by pointing out Cato's low status among authority figures, perhaps directly attributable to his low place in the curriculum.
The cock says:

> . . . as touching daun Catoun,
> That hath of wysdom swich a greet renoun,
> Though that he bad no dremes for to drede,
> By God, men may in olde bookes rede
> Of many a man moore of auctorite
> Than evere Caton was, so moot I thee,
> That al the revers seyn of this sentence,
> And han wel founden by experience
> That dremes been significaciouns
> As wel of joye as of tribulaciouns
> That folk enduren in this lif present. (4161–71)

In order to prove that experience shows dreams can come true,
Chauntecleer provides a veritable collection of fabulistic exempla in which
dream-texts are validated by later (textual) reality. Oddly, he refuses to
name the author of these exempla, which can be traced back to both Cicero
and Valerius Maximus. Instead, he simply credits the stories to "oon of the
gretteste auctor that men rede" (4174). Chauntecleer thereby constructs a
disputation between *auctores*—his against Pertelote's—but then he will not
disclose the identity of his chosen authoritative ally, in spite of his later
ability to cite not only Macrobius and Daniel specifically but also
hagiography and Trojan history more generally. His reticence to name his
source may represent a misused principle of scholastic commentary: in
nearly all fable commentaries Aesop is repeatedly mentioned not by name
but simply as *auctor,* nomenclature which negates the author's identity but
adds prestige to his text. In compiling a suitable collection of authoritative
exempla, Chauntecleer is attempting to displace one authoritative figure
with a "greater" one, as the progression through the medieval curriculum
did, but his argument is substantially weakened by his substitution of the
author's status for his identity, when typically the latter corroborates the

former. On the other hand, by leaving the *auctor* unidentified, Chauntecleer forces us as readers to focus on the exempla themselves rather than their author, and he denies Pertelote the opportunity of rebutting his evidence with a figure of even greater authority.

Two of the tales that the cock relates to the dream are longer than the text they purport to interpret, their very length serving to displace both the dream-text in the past and the fable in the future. In the first, one of two pilgrims is murdered by men who hide his body in a dung-cart; his ghost, appearing to the other pilgrim, tells him where to find the corpse. The other story develops from a premonitory dream of a shipwreck. Pratt has convincingly argued that the exempla were drawn mainly from Robert Holkot's *Super Sapientiam Salomonis,* a commentary on the biblical Book of Wisdom, though Chaucer may first have known them in Cicero's *De divinatione.*[33] If we look at these possible sources in light of the scholastic background provided by the elegiac Romulus collection, we can see more clearly the significance of the texts as fables brought by Chaucer into the service of his larger fable.

The first exemplum differs from its textual predecessors not only in some general embellishments but also in the conclusion given to the tale. Earlier versions of the story have the living pilgrim finding the dead one in the dung-cart, but Chaucer revises the climactic discovery, having Chauntecleer call attention to it as he does so:

What sholde I moore unto this tale sayn?
The peple out sterte and caste the cart to grounde,
And in the mydel of the dong they founde
The dede man, that mordred was al newe. (4236–39)

The added concluding action of dumping out the contents of the dung-cart (displacement of both the corpse and the authority of the original tale) may indicate a more direct link between Chaucer's tale and the fables of the Romulan tradition than we have hitherto seen: this exemplum parodies the first tale in the Romulus collection and most of the collections related to it, including that by Marie de France. These begin with the well-known fable of a cock searching for food by scratching in a dung-heap; there he finds a jewel, which, according to the moral, represents the gift of wisdom buried in fables (see Appendix 1, p. 196). Chaucer effectively turns this story upside down: the scholastic fabulist was a man telling a fable of a cock scratching in a dung-heap, but here is a cock telling a fable of humans searching through a dung-heap, specially and rather self-consciously created only in Chaucer's version of this exemplum. Both the searching cock in the Latin fable and the searching man in the vernacular exemplum find something that represents wisdom, since in effect the presence of the corpse in the dung-heap represents the wisdom inherent in taking dreams seriously; ironically, both creatures also find something that they would rather not find. This reworked tale of Chauntecleer's becomes the parodic jewel in the midst of the heap of authoritative texts that shape *The Nun's Priest's Tale*.[34]

Chauntecleer closes the first exemplum with a conventional marker of scholastic interpretation in the verse, "Heere may men seen that dremes ben to drede" (4253).[35] The formulaic use of the Latin word *hic* (here) signals the moment of transition from a text to the commentator's version of its meaning. In the *Esopus moralizatus,* for example, every comment begins with the phrase "Hic auctor ponit aliam fabulam cuius documentum est," after which the commentator paraphrases the moral (see Appendix 2). The fourteenth-century *Auctores octo* commentary (Appendix 3) uses such phrases as "Hic auctor dicit quod," while Biblioteca Comunale MS 156 in Treviso has frequent recourse to "Hic est duplex moralitas" (f. 61r) and similar markers. As a well-read student of literature, Chauntecleer has apparently learned that the end of each fable requires this type of clearly marked moralizing statement. What escapes his notice is that all of his exempla could conclude with the same aphorism (and indeed, the second story closes with much the same statement in two slightly different versions [4296–4499]). Of course the "moral" needs no such reiteration, but his amplifying repetition satisfies the rhetorical requirement that a moral follow a fabular narrative. Medieval audiences familiar with scholastic practice would have seen here that Chauntecleer, a fable character somewhat too big for his tale, was bound to express himself using the fabulistic terms and structures that validate his textual existence: he works naturally within the parameters of the discursive mode in which he exists. Ultimately the cock's inability to effect a structural synthesis among the exempla here is less important than his inability to synthesize the dream-text and his future, but the problem is the same in both instances.

Although Chauntecleer's exempla demonstrate that dreams can portend terrible mishaps, his final statement about his own nightmare implies a different relationship between dream and subsequent experience. He tells Pertelote, "Shortly I seye, as for conclusioun, / That I shal han of this avisioun / Adversitee..." (4341–43). Chauntecleer's unusual turn of phrase indicates the relationship between a commentary's plot summary and the fable to follow: the earlier text is inexorably acted out in the later one. In the larger framework of the Aesopic tradition as a whole, such inexorability is the lot of every fable character, destined to repeat the same actions every time a fable is retold.[36]

Medieval readers would have been struck by the parodic intent of the particular tales that Chauntecleer chose as glosses for the dream-text, and by the absurdity of a beast telling fables about humans: here are two distinct achievements in Chaucer's tale. However, material from the curricular fable tradition shows that the tale's medieval audience would not necessarily have been surprised that a tale or two were used to explicate another, for this practice occurred in the scholastic setting. Fable manuscripts include a very similar kind of commentary based upon constructing loose relationships between short narratives and one of the curricular fables. For example, Fable 21 of the elegiac Romulus ("Fabula nata sequi," ff. 15r–16v), which tells of the Athenians searching for a king, prompted a commentator to write two fables into his commentary, now Biblioteca Marciana MS 4658. These stories, of some foxes trying to keep flies off their meat, and an unreasonable stag attempting to chase a horse out of his pasture, both reflect the verse fable's central theme of government in the way that Chauntecleer's exempla represent the theme of portentous dreams of death that his dream-text supposedly exemplifies.

Pertelote's and Chauntecleer's textual interpretations fall into the two most common binary categories of medieval fable interpretation (and indeed, the interpretation of nearly all medieval fiction): the earthly and the spiritual. Pertelote's reading of the text is as mundane as it can be. In her opinion, the text was created by a creature on earth, and it only has meaning for creatures on earth who find themselves in certain unfortunate earthly situations. For Chauntecleer, this dream-text and others, if interpreted correctly, represent supernatural intervention which will help earth-bound creatures through potential misfortunes. Two-part, mutually exclusive interpretations like these, in which the secular appears alongside the spiritual, are scattered through numerous fable manuscripts and incunables, but the taxonomy for the two types of moral in Biblioteca Ambrosiana MS I. 85 supra reflects the interpretive division in *The Nun's Priest's Tale*. In each fable comment the commentator calls the social interpretation of fables "*humanum*" and the spiritual readings "*divinum*." Pertelote's reading of the dream-text is distinctly human (despite the fact that she is not), while Chauntecleer's concentrates on the divine intervention at work in certain dreams.

In their fervor to strike different interpretive postures, each avian commentator erases the fact that the dream is really about a fox, and thus each commentary substitutes itself for the text. The chickens' comments, although marginal to the real import of the dream, have become new centers of attention for us as readers. Furthermore, because the two commentaries are so closely paired, by the time we have read through the coupled interpretations, the dream-text is thoroughly displaced. The real *coup de grace,* however, occurs when the coupling of interpretations is literalized in the coupling of the interpreters: Chauntecleer "feathered Pertelote twenty tyme, / And trad hire eke as ofte, er it was pryme" (4367–68). Even this carnality is significantly bipartite—first feathering as foreplay, and then treading as fulfillment. The action utterly displaces the dream-text, causing the commentators themselves to lose sight of it. Thus the commentary ends, the dream is all but forgotten, and we are finally ready for the fable text.

That the dream-text is so thoroughly displaced as to be driven from Chauntecleer's memory would have made the tale more humorous for Chaucer's early readers, since the medieval curriculum stressed memorization. Indeed, the British vernacular fabulists whose work is discussed in the next two chapters emphasize the place of the Aesopic fable in the storehouse of memory. In *Isopes Fabules,* John Lydgate's Middle English renderings of seven of the elegiac Romulus fables,[37] the poet twice connects Aesop's authorial intention with memory ("myn auctour remembreth by wrytyng" [102] and "Isophus . . . / This fable wrote for a memoryalle" [827–28]); these lines suggest that although writing ensures a fable's survival, its proper site is in human memory.[38] The suitability of fable for storage in the memory was made more explicit in Robert Henryson's *Morall Fabillis,*[39] in which Fable 6, "The Sheep and the Dog," is introduced with the phrase, "Esope ane taill puttis in memorie" (1146). Although readers of Chaucer's fable may keep Chauntecleer's dream-text in their memories, the cock does not—and he forgets it at his peril.

In forgetting the primary import of the text requiring interpretation, Chauntecleer is guilty of bad reading, and for medieval readers such misreading had ethical implications. The "translation" of texts into ethical behavior was one of the purposes of reading in the Middle Ages; this goal has been explored at length by Judson Boyce Allen[40] and, more recently, John Dagenais. His paraphrase (and displacement) of Allen provides a guide to how Chauntecleer has misread his dream-text: "According to Allen, the medieval text must be viewed not as verbal icon, not as Letter alone, but as an 'event' that actualizes the ethical behavior of a reader, absorbs the reader into its own ethical system, and stimulates, among other ethical acts, its own reenactment (and, I would add, its own retelling and recopying)."[41] Neither the dream-text nor the exempla that Chauntecleer recounts stimulate him to action; rather, the exempla displace the dream-text, since

Chauntecleer treats them only as the verbal icons representing one of the greatest authors, authoritative texts whose message Chauntecleer can recite but cannot internalize. Although Chauntecleer initially gives voice to his fear of the red creature in the dream, his reenactment of the dream-text shows him overcoming that fear in order to enjoy the fox's flattery. Proper behavior—in this case, simple self-preservation—will fall prey to the vice of pride.

The conclusion of the chickens' commentary liberates the commenting voice of the Nun's Priest himself, and he shapes the fable with references to authoritative writers or works of literature apparently meant to help the audience to understand the action of the fable. Among these are Augustine, Boethius, Bishop Bradwardine, *Physiologus*, Geoffrey of Vinsauf, Virgil's *Aeneid*, Saint Paul, and the Bible. Yoking this highly authoritative literature to a beast fable might strike modern readers as only one more aspect of the Nun's Priest's satirical strategy or perhaps of Chaucer's satire of the Nun's Priest; however, we should rule out the latter possibility, because the use of such *auctoritates* was not at all uncommon in fourteenth- and fifteenth-century fable commentaries. Nearly every commentary draws in one or two authoritative texts, and the most learned manuscripts of the elegiac Romulus fables include no fewer than ten *auctoritates,* several of which are cited in more than one comment. A late-fourteenth- or early-fifteenth-century German manuscript in the British Library (MS Add. 11897) glosses the fables with references to Bernard of Clairvaux, Gregory the Great, Horace, Ovid, Aristotle, Henricus Septimellensis, and others. Like the Nun's Priest, this commentator also refers to the Bible, Boethius, and Geoffrey of Vinsauf, but the commentator's favorite, most frequently mentioned *auctor* is Cato, to whom Pertelote and Chauntecleer themselves refer.[42] So while the specific phraseology and context of each *auctoritas* in Chaucer's tale may provide a satirical dimension, the mere presence of most of them in proximity to a fable would not have bespoken satire to an educated medieval audience.

One of the Nun's Priest's most outlandish comments is prompted by the appearance of the fox in the yard, which evokes comparisons from scripture and epic:

> O false mordrour, lurkynge in thy den!
> O newe Scariot, newe Genylon,
> False dissymulour, o Greek Synon,
> That broughtest Troye al outrely to sorwe! (4416–19)

The Nun's Priest's metaphor comparing the fox to Judas Iscariot brings from the margins the comparison made between the traitorous bat and

Judas in the exegetical comment on Fable 45 in MS Add. 11897, a manuscript roughly contemporaneous with Chaucer.[43] However, as did Chauntecleer in his list of *auctores,* the Nun's Priest moves from Christian to pagan writings, thus glossing a fable with other narratives yet again. This shift might well have been disconcertingly humorous for Chaucer's audience, partly because it further negates the human/animal dichotomy that should separate narrator and beastly subject; Chauntecleer and the Nun's Priest follow the same order of *auctoritas* in their glossing, initially citing the biblical but saving for last what they believe to be their strongest suit, the classical. While the narrator may well bemoan the traitorous nature of a Ganelon or a Sinon, men who chose to turn against their allies, rationally he cannot castigate the fox for being true to its nature in chasing fowl. Thus the humor lies not in the choice of text cited by the narrator, but in his misappropriation of it (along with the overly elevated tone of his anguished apostrophes).

If we look at this passage in light of the comparison of the fox to Judas, Ganelon, and Sinon, it becomes apparent that even in the Nun's Priest's vilification of the fox, there is a certain felicity in the determinism of the narratives which he cites. Although Judas was a traitor to Christ, he also had to set in motion the events leading to Christ's resurrection and the salvation of humanity. Ganelon was a traitor to Roland, but after his death Roland was revered as a saint.[44] While Sinon's treachery resulted in the destruction of Troy, that destruction, according to the legend current in fourteenth-century England, resulted in Brutus's founding of the Britain in which the Canterbury pilgrims lived. These comparisons remind us that events that seem tragic in the short run may have positive results.

Several authority figures are cited in the Nun's Priest's lengthy digression on God's foreknowledge; its position just after the description of the fox entering the farmyard, when the attack upon Chauntecleer is clearly at hand, is an obvious displacement of the inevitable. The first lines of this digression are particularly significant in the context of scholastic commentary displacing the texts that they interpret; they address larger philosophical issues which both foreshadow and delay the conflict of cock and fox.

> O Chauntecler, acursed be that morwe
> That thou into the yerd flaugh fro the bemys!
> Thow were ful wel ywarned by thy dremys
> That thilke day was perilous to thee.
> But what that God forwoot moot nedes be,
> After the opynyoun of certeyn clerkis.
> Witnesse on hym that any parfit clerk is

That in scole is gret altercacioun
In this matere and gret disputisoun
And hath ben of an hundred thousand men. (4420-29)

The clause questioning whether God's foreknowledge predicates events stands in a purposefully ambiguous relationship to the phrase "after the opynyoun of certeyn clerkis." These lines state literally that according to the opinions of certain clerks, what God foreknows must take place. However, within the world of this text, the lines ask to be read differently: what is foreknown about Chauntecleer's future cannot take place until after the clerk who is the Nun's Priest has aired his "opynyoun" about divine prescience and a variety of other subjects. Text will follow commentary.

In the passage above, the Nun's Priest places an odd emphasis upon the cock's cataclysmic decision to fly down from the beams on this fateful day, as if the narrator believes that roosters might naturally spend full days on their perches. The narrator's extraneous attention to flying from the beams, which does not appear in any of the known source material for this tale, is apparently a detail added by Chaucer. It was also sometimes a detail added to plot paraphrases in scholastic commentaries on the fable of the cock and jewel, mentioned above. Although the curricular Latin fable takes place only in the dung-heap, a commentator whose work survives in a handful of fable manuscripts engaged in amplification of the plot by introducing his paraphrase as follows: "Gallus sollicitus de dape mane descendit de trabe et incepit vertere fimum pedibus et rostro."[45] [A cock desiring a meal early in the morning descended from a beam and began to turn up a dung-heap with his claws and beak.] As the fable commentator has rhetorically displaced his source text by adding his own details, Chaucer has taken an available naturalistic detail—that cocks perch on beams and sometimes leave them—and made it central to the "tragedy" which is about to unfold. In making a minor etiological observation the immediate cause of an apocalyptic event, Chaucer's parodic intent is as clear to modern readers as it would have been to their medieval counterparts, but Chaucer's readers in the Middle Ages would have understood that Chaucer was also parodying the rhetorical practice of *amplificatio*, which could clutter the narrative landscape with minutiae that threaten to take on narrative lives of their own.

The Nun's Priest concludes his diversion with an intermediate, anti-feminist *moralitas* of sorts:

I wol nat han to do of swich mateere;
My tale is of a cok, as ye may heere,
That tok his conseil of his wyf, with sorwe,

> To walken in the yerd upon that morwe
> That he hadde met that dreem that I yow tolde.
> Wommennes conseils been ful ofte colde;
> Wommannes conseil broghte us first to wo,
> And made Adam fro Paradys to go,
> Ther as he was ful myrie and wel at ese.
> But for I noot to whom it myght displese,
> If I conseil of wommen wolde blame,
> Passe over, for I seyde it in my game.
> Rede auctors, where they trete of swich mateere,
> And what they seyn of wommen ye may heere.
> Thise been the cokkes wordes, and nat myne;
> I kan noon harm of no womman divyne. (4441–56)

If fable strikes us as an unlikely discursive mode to serve as a vehicle for anti-feminism, we need only remember the two anti-feminist fables in the elegiac Romulus collection, Fable 48, "De Viro et Uxore," and Fable 49, "De Thaida et Damasio." But more importantly, we should note that here, at one of the most dangerous moments in his relationship to his audience, the Nun's Priest's reference to *auctoritas* is diplomatically bereft of both name and content; again he mimics Chauntecleer's rhetorical strategy of refusing to name the relevant authorities.

Then, after much displacement, we finally reach the fable—the "destinee that [may] nat been eschewed" (4528).

Among the best-known and apparently least fabular passages in the tale is one describing the cacophony of the farm animals and owners as they race after Russell and Chauntecleer:

> So hydous was the noyse—a, benedicitee!—
> Certes, he Jakke Straw and his meynee
> Ne made nevere shoutes half so shrille
> Whan that they wolden any Flemyng kille,
> As thilke day was maad upon the fox. (3393–97)

These lines, which refer to one of the leaders of the Peasants' Revolt of 1381 and a brutal attack that he led against foreign traders during the uprising, represent the only mention of a political event from Chaucer's lifetime to appear in *The Canterbury Tales*. To my knowledge, scholastic curricular fable commentators did not use contemporary politics to gloss their fables, for inasmuch as many of the commentators were schoolboys, they would not always have had such information at their fingertips (and also their commenting practices were meant to draw connections among authoritative texts, not ancient fables and current events). Although Patavino's chronicle shows that a fable could comment upon a political development, evidently the opposite did not hold true.

Interestingly, however, the reader of the *Aeneid* whom Christopher Baswell has dubbed the Norwich commentator cited the Peasants' Revolt when he commented upon the epic simile describing a traitorous, riotous crowd in Book 1 of Virgil's epic. The comment simply mentions the names of two men, John Latimer and "Horyn," probably the John Horn who was widely believed to have encouraged the participants in the revolt.[46] Thus we have evidence that the use of recent history in a comment was not beyond the realm of possibility generally, even if such comments are not associated with fable specifically.

The Nun's Priest's allusion within a fable to a political event from the lifetime of most of Chaucer's original readers may have struck that audience as odd and unsettling. But this comment invites us to think back over the fable to other "historicizing" elements in it, details that do not fit the medieval understanding(s) of fable as the mode of discourse. Why, for example, does the Nun's Priest provide a date upon which the action occurs, probably May 3 (3187–90)? And why is that date then linked with a day of the week, Friday, about which the Nun's Priest holds forth for more than ten lines (3341–52)? If we considered these two details in conjunction, we could even establish the two or three specific years in the late fourteenth century when May 3 fell on a Friday—but for my purposes it is more helpful to focus on the function of this date within the narrative. Even though fables conventionally take place in general, universalized time, the Nun's Priest attempts to place the action on a specific day, just as the massacre of Flemish wool merchants by Jack Straw's gang took place on a specific day in recent English history.

The presence of the date, along with several other telling details, functions to push the fable from the realm of the ahistorical into history itself, and in light of the fable theory discussed in Chapter 2, we can see that this unique detail, more than any other rhetorical gesture, betrays the Nun's Priest's desire to raise the status of fable: it changes from being a story that did not and could not happen to one that definitely occurred, occupying a place in the continuum of time that we also inhabit. The Nun's Priest communicates his ambitions for the fable most clearly when describing the activity of the rhetor who might set down the inevitability of unhappiness:

> For evere the latter ende of joye is wo.
> God woot that worldly joye is soone ago;
> And if a rethor koude faire endite,

He in a cronycle saufly myghte it write
As for a sovereyn notabilitee. (3205-9)

In spite of the fact that the subject of human misery might be appropriately examined in several types of text, the Nun's Priest recommends that a rhetor should examine it in chronicle, the genre most closely associated with history. Since the fall from joy to woe is the very trajectory that the Nun's Priest is about to chart in his tale, he implicitly associates his tale with the truth of history rather than the falsehood of *fabula*.

This detail should cause us to examine the story yet again in comparison to a text important to the history of England, Virgil's *Aeneid*. Indeed, the Nun's Priest himself invites this comparison by alluding to the epic several times,[47] and many perceptive critics have accepted the invitation to read *The Nun's Priest's Tale* through the *Aeneid* in order to reveal its mock-epic tone.[48] Although I would not go so far as to argue against calling this tale a mock epic, I believe that the study of commenting techniques for Aesopic fable and the *Aeneid* may lead us to a revised understanding of this nomenclature. As students of hierarchical generic theories, we see lowly fable as far removed from lofty epic, and therefore when we see Chaucer associating the *Aeneid* with beast fable, we use these generic hierarchies to focus on rhetorical disjuncture between genres, and in that disjuncture we see parody. However, scholastic commentary shows that medieval readers did not perceive this generic disjuncture as insuperable, for they used Virgilian *auctoritates* to comment upon fable: both were authoritative, classical rhetorical products that could comment effectively upon each other, thus emphasizing moral and rhetorical similarities between the texts.

However, one insuperable difference separated these texts for medieval readers: the *Aeneid* could be read as history (and not just any history, but one with direct links to the founding of Britain), while Aesopic fables were read as events which could not have happened. Baswell has pointed out that one of the consistent strains of commentary on the Aeneid is historicizing comment, notes that help to place the beliefs and practices of the epic characters in a historical context that would help medieval readers understand them better.[49] Clearly this kind of commenting practice had no place in relation to fable, which is by nature not history. But this is the very type of connection that the Nun's Priest wants to emphasize: the connection between the newly historicized chronicle of Chauntecleer and earlier histories, including texts such as the Bible and *The Song of Roland*, and incorporating allusions to Richard I and Jack Straw. (Of course such connections do not preclude commentary-style intertextual linkages between this tale and *fabulae* such as "Daun Burnel the Asse" and others, but those comments do not "de-historicize" the history of Chauntecleer.)

So for medieval readers, the humorous conjunction of dissimilar discourses would not have been that between Aesopic fable and epic, but between palpably false *fabula* and "true" history. This connection makes itself apparent only accretively as one reads the fable, with the Nun's Priest engaging in ever-broader and more eloquent connections between epic and fable; indeed, the movement in midstream away from *fabula* toward history should remind us of the change in *The Manciple's Tale* from immoral Ovidian fable to moral fable resembling the Aesopic variety. In both the Manciple's and Nun's Priest's narratives, a classical type of narrative that raised suspicions among some medieval readers tries to ascend the discursive ladder.

The Nun's Priest's attempt to shift from fabular to historical discourse may provide another reason for the absence of Aesop from this beast fable—the author of greatest authority in relation to this mode of discourse remains unnamed because though he seems to be Aesop, he is displaced by Virgil and others—fable threatens to be displaced by epic. And it is via connections through scholastic commentary that this kind of displacement can slip up on the unknowing reader: the familiar forms of displacement in curricular commenting practices only gradually reveal the radical metamorphosis of the narrative to which they contribute.[50]

In spite of the Nun's Priest's ambitions, he returns to the realm of fabular discourse at the end of his tale, where proverbial morals displace each other repeatedly, leaving none to dominate. Chauntecleer generalizes about his experience in one couplet ("For he that wynketh, whan he sholde see, / Ay wilfully, God lat him nevere thee!" [4621–22]), and Russell the fox follows suit ("Nay," quod the fox, "but God yeve hym meschaunce, / That is so undiscreet of governaunce / That jangleth whan he sholde holde his pees" [4623–25]). As if unable to allow the beasts the last word, the Nun's Priest himself adds, "Lo, swich it is for to be recchelees / And necligent, and truste on flaterye" (4626–27).[51] This tripartite moral mirrors the structure of the end of Marie de France's fable; there as here, any one of these morals might suffice as an interpretive gesture to sum up the fable, but instead, no single voice gains dominance.

Although the Nun's Priest gives himself the last word, he finally displaces his own authority, and in so doing he mimics a scholastic practice by raising the possibility of a divine reading after the three earthly, social ones:

But ye that holden this tale a folye,

As of a fox, or of a cok and hen,
Taketh the moralite, goode men.
For Seint Paul seith that al that writen is,
To our doctrine it is ywrite, ywis;
Taketh the fruyt, and lat the chaf be stille. (4628–33)

The Nun's Priest calls attention to the need to interpret this text, to find its real meaning, as Chauntecleer hoped to do with his dream-text. In asking for interpretation, he unnecessarily raises the Macrobian notion that the fable might be thought meaningless—"a folye," which Pertelote believes Chauntecleer's dream-text to be, in effect if not in cause. Like the dream-text within it, this tale will prompt its interpreters to react either like a Pertelote, holding the fable mere folly, or like a Chauntecleer, scratching away at the text to find its transcendent significance.

The closing lines of *The Nun's Priest's Tale* demand another commentary, and in some manuscripts of *The Canterbury Tales,* the fable receives one from the Host (whom we do not assume to represent an educated reader):

"Sire Nonnes Preest," oure Hoost seide anoon,
"I-blessed be thy breche, and every stoon!
This was a murie tale of Chauntecleer.
But by my trouthe, if thou were seculer,
Thou woldest ben a trede-foul aright.
For if thou have corage as thou hast myght,
Thee were nede of hennes, as I wene,
Ya, moo than seven tymes seventene.
See, whiche braunes hath this gentil preest,
So gret a nekke, and swich a large breest!
He loketh as a sperhauk with his yen." (4637–47)

Achieving a difference with his source text, the Host comments not upon the fable itself but upon its relation to its narrator; this is a painfully inappropriate "dramatic" reading of the tale. The Host has heard Chauntecleer textualize his dream for his audience, Pertelote, in order to say something about himself and to ask for commentary, so likewise the Host assumes that the Nun's Priest has textualized himself in his tale for his audience of pilgrims (an assumption perhaps exacerbated by the Nun's Priest's duplication of several of Chauntecleer's own rhetorical strategies). The hen responds to Chauntecleer that his dream-text represented little of value; by calling the Nun's Priest's fable only "a murie tale," the Host expresses a similar unwillingness to read significance into it. Pertelote stated that the dream-text's only real significance was in relation to the body of its narrator, a cock; the Host finds the fable's significance in relation to the Nun's Priest's body, whose physical attributes metaphorically transform him in the Host's eyes to a "trede-foul" or a "sperhauk." In Pertelote's interpretation, the dream-text signified Chauntecleer's need for intestinal catharsis; the Host's reading of the tale leads him to speculate about the Nun's Priest's need for sexual catharsis.

In a reading that is finally neither *humanum* nor *divinum,* the Host fails to interpret the animals in the fable as representative of humans so as to glean a human, moral lesson from the fable; rather, he reads the body of the human before him as an animal's, and he fantasizes that body back into a fabular setting, where it can abandon morality in pursuit of more than one hundred females. This is a completely inverted reading of the fable—and we should allow the inversion its full range of meanings, including its archaic connotation of homosexuality, for the Host's blessing of the Nun's Priest's "family jewels" and his appreciative gaze upon the man's body have strong homoerotic implications.

But the Host's Pertelotish response to the fable is also quite conventional in terms of scholastic commentary, inasmuch as it threatens to recreate exactly the kind of dialogue of displacing comments that occurred between Pertelote and Chauntecleer in the tale, particularly if the Nun's Priest were subsequently to insist upon the divine reading that his citation of St. Paul in the tale's final lines requires. Not surprisingly, no such comment from the Nun's Priest has come down to us, and the Host turns away from the priest in search of a tale from another pilgrim (4651–52).

In relation to the paradigms for elevating or effacing Aesop that are outlined in Chapter 1, *The Nun's Priest's Tale* strikes a balance, the fulcrum of which is the narrative framework of *The Canterbury Tales.* The tale obviously cannot recreate a verbal monument to the *auctor* Aesop—his name never crosses the Nun's Priest's lips. Even so, the repeated references by both the cock and the Nun's Priest to unnamed but great authors and authoritative texts create a vacuum that asks to be filled by the figure of Aesop. But any conjuring of Aesop by the relatively anonymous fabulist telling this tale must be subsumed in the *Canterbury Tales* as a whole, a "fable" collection (at least in the sense of "fiction") dominated by the name of Geoffrey Chaucer, both in its early history and now. In this instance the father of fable would only have been subservient to the so-called father of English literature.

Because Chaucer elsewhere shows interest in structuring tales around both commentaries and their concomitant gestures of displacement, we might be tempted to see *The Nun's Priest's Tale* as offering only one more instance of a favorite authorial technique. Even if we disregard several prologues, which comment upon the narratives that follow but are separable from them, ostensibly scholastic commentary introduces (and temporally displaces the plots of) other tales. Perhaps the most obvious instance of this structure has already been examined in a different context in this chapter. *The Merchant's Tale* begins with the narrator discussing marriage and then passing the discussion to January's brothers, Placebo and Justinus: the argument becomes such a scholarly disputation that January derides Justinus's opinions as "scole-termes" (1568). Also related to scholastic commentary, the Pardoner's rhetorical divisions of the sins to be examined in his tale represent the conventional religious variation upon the same commenting procedure.

I would argue, however, that in *The Nun's Priest's Tale* Chaucer's use of an overall structure closely akin to that which framed scholastic fable commentary in the classroom and sometimes on the page has a very different effect from the introductory commentaries that he uses elsewhere. In aforementioned tales in which commentary precedes plot, the commentary sketches some possibilities for the tale, but because those tales do not begin with a "master" text to be interpreted, the issues discussed remain more abstract. No other tale begins with a textualized summary of the subsequent conflict provided by one of the characters who will participate in that conflict. As I have suggested, that text, brought to Chauntecleer by some external force, assumes a certain causality in the cock's mind, prescribing rather than describing events in the future: it predetermines what will become his "history."

But if Chaucer's emphasis on the dream-text molds expectations that the dream will come true in the plot, the tale's own history as well as the history of its discursive mode are equally forceful in creating reader expectation. Manuscript evidence such as that cited above shows some important aspects of the interpretive framework within which medieval readers received and situated fable, and Chaucer exploited a number of possibilities in that framework without ultimately privileging any one of them.

The unification of commentary and plot within the fable is only one of several unifying gestures in the tale. In the medieval classroom, the fable's summarizer, its commentator, and its animal characters were two or three separate entities. Not so for Chauntecleer, who is envisioner of his story, commentator upon it, and participant in it; for medieval readers as for modern ones, such a conflation of roles adds humor to the tale. Significantly, this triad of roles is also played out by "Chaucers" in relation to *The Canterbury Tales:* he is envisioner of a collection of tales mostly inherited from other sources, commentator upon it (particularly at its inception), and participant in it.[52]

If we look at the shape of *The Nun's Priest's Tale* in light of the tripartite nature of the fictionalized Chaucer in his work, we might see the poet Chaucer reacting to the larger question of how a writer can give an inherited text authority and what can deprive it of that status. Obviously mere age and repetition cannot make a text authoritative; rather, the greatest validator of *auctoritas* is experience, as Chauntecleer himself says (4168), and one's experience becomes personal history. But for educated medieval readers, the tale parodied their experience of canonical authority in education and the practices which it employed, simultaneously showing them that they were ineluctably bound to negotiate within the structures and strictures of education in order to master experience as it attacked them outside the classroom: their world was as defined and delimited by their epistemologies as ours is for us. Chaucer tacitly suggests that all readers need to learn to negotiate between text and commentary, experience and education, in order to overcome the tendency to allow one to displace the other. Chauntecleer's negotiations nearly fail, but the rest of us readers continue to try.

5

John Lydgate's *Isopes Fabules*
Appropriation through Amplification

The John Lydgate who translated *Isopes Fabules* into English had not yet become the Lydgate who has received the lion's share of critical attention during the past decade: the poet-apologist for Henry V and exemplar of the Lancastrian policies for the advancement of the English language.[1] If John Shirley's marginalia in MS Ashmole 59 is reliable, the Lydgate who wrote the fables was only another cleric at Oxford, where he lived from roughly 1405 to 1410, before the second decade of the century brought him notoriety in the form of important commissions from Prince Henry, later Henry V.[2] The propagandistic prince-pleasing of *The Troy Book* is entirely absent from *Isopes Fabules;* indeed, Lydgate's political sympathies seem more closely aligned with his own peasant background than with the interests of an aristocratic or royal patron. The collection espouses the economic state of "suffisaunce" for the lowest levels of society while railing against the more powerful who would oppress the lower classes either through misapplication of law or through tyranny. *Isopes Fabules,* the earliest extant collection of fables in English and perhaps the earliest extant work of poetry by Lydgate, may show the author being truer to his own interests than he would be when writing for patrons later.

In these seven tales we may also see Lydgate remaining true to the understanding of fable as discursive mode that he had learned in the grammar-school curriculum at the Benedictine abbey of Bury St. Edmunds, which he had entered by 1385, when he was about fifteen years old. The adult Lydgate, never known as a radical poetic innovator (beyond his innovations as Lancastrian propagandist),[3] is not attempting to redefine the nature of fable, in spite of (or perhaps because of) his apparent familiarity with Chaucer's remarkably innovative *Nun's Priest's Tale* when he embarked on his translation. *Isopes Fabules* does not explore any rhetorical terrain that had not already been mapped in Lydgate's sources, including scholastic fable and commentary; in fact, the poet is reticent to transgress the tonal and structural boundaries which he clearly understood as defining fable.

But for literary historians the very value of these fables may lie in their conservatism, for in them we can see commenting practice translated into vernacular literature in a relatively straightforward form.

What *Isopes Fabules* suggests most strongly is that much of the act of commenting upon a medieval text lay in the process of amplification, the classroom practice recommended by Priscian and others. In Lydgate's project, amplification is conjoined with translation and compilation, creating difficulties for scholars attempting to unravel the threads of this collection's literary history; nevertheless, in several passages that Lydgate himself added to the fables, amplification in and of itself becomes a rhetorical gesture of appropriation in which the amplifier's voice mingles with and ultimately subsumes the voice of his *auctor,* whether Aesop or another authority figure.[4]

Sources and Manuscript History

In Lydgate's prologue, if it may be called that (for in manuscripts it is not separated from the fable of the cock and the jacinth), the poet admits that he is doing more than a simple translation; he is also compiling. He asks that his readers look favorably upon his "compilacion" (41), which he "compyle[s] . . . for a remembraunce" (54). This relatively unusual nomenclature suggests either that Lydgate was acknowledging the use of different sources compiled within each fable or that he hoped to draw moral tales from a number of Aesopic (and perhaps other) sources.

In the compilation Lydgate used at least three texts other than the verse Romulus: Marie de France's *Fables* (which was evidently his primary source),[5] Chaucer's *Nun's Priest's Tale,* and the verse Romulus with a scholastic commentary. The verbal parallels with Marie's collection are so close that Lydgate could have had a copy of the work before him as he wrote; the echoes of the other texts, which occur at a conceptual and structural level, allow for the possibility that Lydgate worked from memory to bring their influence to bear upon the fables. In addition he ornaments his text with some of the same *auctoritates* that we have seen in the scholastic commentaries, although many of these were such medieval commonplaces that he need not have taken all of them directly from the fable commentary tradition.

I will not reproduce Paul Sauerstein's substantial list of similarities between Marie's and Lydgate's fables, but I would like to discuss the important resemblances between Lydgate's prologue and parts of Marie's collection, since both show us how the authors position themselves in relation to their projects of appropriation and translation. Lydgate's debt to Marie de

France is apparent in the opening stanza of his collection, written entirely in rhyme royal:

> Wisdom ys more in prise þen gold in cofers
>> To hem, þat have savour in lettrure.
> Olde examples of prudent philosophers
>> Moche auaylyd to folke þat dyd her cure
>> To serche out lykenes in nature,
> In whyche men myght conceue & clerely see
> Notable sentence of gret moralyte. (1–7)[6]

The stanza translates Marie's first ten verses quite closely:

> Cil ki seivent de lettruure,
> Devreient bien mettre cure
> Es bons livres e escriz
> E a [es]samples e as diz
> Ke li philosophe troverent
> E escristrent e remembrerent
> Par moralité escriveient
> Les bons proverbes qu'il oieient,
> Que cil amender se peüssent
> Ki lur entente en bien eüssent.

Lydgate uses a number of English cognates in translating the passage ("lettrure," *"lettruure"*; "examples," *"essamples"*; "philosophers," *"philosophe"*; "cure," *"cure"*). He also duplicates Marie's interest in the classical background of the genre (discussed in Chapter 1), although his notion that a Roman Aesop wrote his fables to please the senate is unique in the fable tradition and quite different from Marie's description of the fabulist writing for his master.

> Vnto purpos þe poete laureate
>> Callyd Isopus dyd hym occupy
> Whylom in Rome to plese þe senate,
>> Fonde out fables, þat men myght hem apply
>> To sondry matyrs, yche man for hys party,
> Aftyr þeyr lust, to conclude in substaunce,
> Dyuerse moralytees set out to þeyr plesaunce. (8–14)

Sauerstein has suggested that Lydgate may have confused the Greek Aesop with the Roman fabulist Phaedrus (27), but given the paucity of extant medieval evidence of Phaedrus's work, it seems more plausible that Lydgate conflated Aesop with the Romulus of the relatively widely known introductory epistle discussed in Chapter 3. Whatever the poet's source, this biographical sketch of Aesop as writing for the senate serves as an *a priori* justification for Lydgate's concern with the concept of law in the fables.

Another important aspect of *Isopes Fabules* which Lydgate borrowed from Marie is his identification of himself by name in his collection:

> For whyche I cast to folow þys poete
>> And hys fables in Englyssh to translate,
> And, þough I haue no rethoryk swete,
>> Haue me excusyd: I was born in Lydgate;
>> Of Tullius gardeyn I passyd nat þe gate,
> And cause why: I had no lycence
> There to gadyr floures of elloquence. (29–35)

By effacing not only the role played by an intermediary fable collection—in this case, Marie's—but also the initial stage of textual transmission and translation of fable from Greek to Latin, Lydgate has claimed for himself the authority of directly translating the work of an *auctor* from Latin into English. He then enhances his authority by naming himself while simultaneously making use of the modesty topos of rhetorical ineptitude. This topos is double-edged, as it is also an allusion to the conventional garden imagery which the verse Romulus fabulist himself used in his prologue (Appendix 1, p. 195). Thus Lydgate inscribes a complicated series of appropriations and acknowledgments with remarkable economy, showing that even early in his career he was working to guarantee a name for himself as a poet.

A subtle lesson that Lydgate may have learned from Marie's fables is that identification of one's authorship at the end of a collection is less forceful than similar self-advertisement as an integral part of a prologue (especially when the author can make his name a rhyme word at the center of a tightly structured, familiar stanzaic form). The placement of this authorial identification may also indicate that, unlike Marie, Lydgate did not begin his work with a view toward translating all of her fables and tying them off nicely with an epilogue similar to hers; his compilation was open-ended from its earliest stages.[7]

Regardless of Lydgate's ambitions for *Isopes Fabules,* the extant manuscript evidence does not attest to wide circulation of the work in the fifteenth century. Only MS Harley 2251 contains all seven fables; MS Trinity College Camb. R.3.19 reproduces roughly five and one half of them, divided around some two hundred other folia of Lydgate's poetry. And the fable of the dog and the cheese, the briefest in the collection, appears on its own in MS Ashmole 59. Even in the Harley and Trinity College manuscripts, the order of the fables differs, and neither order follows that of the verse Romulus, Marie, or any other known fable collection. In the two manuscripts, the fables appear as follows:

MS Trin Coll. Camb R.3.19	MS Harley 2251
I. The Cock and the Jewel	I. The Cock and the Jewel
II. The Wolf and the Lamb	II. The Wolf and the Lamb
III. The Frog and the Mouse	III. The Dog and the Sheep
IV. The Dog and the Sheep	IV. The Wolf and the Crane
V. The Wolf and the Crane	V. The Frog and the Mouse
VI. The Dog and the Cheese	VI. The Marriage of the Sun
	VII. The Dog and the Cheese[8]

In the Trinity College manuscript the first three fables and the first three stanzas of the fourth are written together on ff. 12–16; most of the fourth fable is absent. The last two fables appear toward the end of the manuscript (ff. 236–37), and the fable of the marriage of the sun is entirely missing. The inclusion of that fable in MS Harley 2251 brings Lydgate's work a step closer to Marie's collection, for these are also her first seven fables, though presented in a different order.

Although I disagree with Derek Pearsall about the content and order of the two major manuscripts, the inference that he draws from the two exemplars is certainly plausible: "One might conclude that the *Fabules* were a task that Lydgate returned to at odd times, and that their unity in the two complete manuscripts is scribal."[9] But neither the collection's genesis nor its unimpressive manuscript tradition should blind us to the possibility that Lydgate wrote into the collection a certain thematic unity—or more precisely, a thematic progression through social concerns about self-governance and larger issues of government. Since Lydgate's fables have received very little critical attention as a group,[10] I will examine them first as a collection before discussing their relation to scholastic fable. In the case of *Isopes Fabules* this double examination is instructive inasmuch as it demonstrates how Lydgate accomplished his thematic manipulations of the tales without relying on scholastic commenting techniques. He brings commentary to bear much more superficially, using it to ornament and, above all, to amplify. In other words, Lydgate does not effect a synthesis between his special thematic interests and his rhetorical embellishments of and elaborations upon the fables; these aspects of his project remain almost as separable from each other as fable text and commentary in schoolbooks.

"Suffisaunce," Law, and Tyranny in *Isopes Fabules*

After defining his poetic project in the prologue discussed above, Lydgate radically reshapes the fable of the cock and the jewel. As in Marie's fable and its Romulan predecessors, the cock finds a jewel in a dung-heap, where he is laboring as he has been "taught by nature" (113); as we would expect, the cock has no use for the jewel and leaves it lying where he has found it. However, in a speech describing the different qualities and desires which nature has given to minerals and animals, he explains that the rejection is due not to ignorance but to the fact that the jacinth represents something too far above his social station, a station determined by nature. He says:

> "Precyous stones longen to iewellers
>   And to princes, when þey lyst wel be seyn:
> To me more deynte in bernes or garners
>   A lytell rewarde of corn or good greyn.
>   To take þys stone to me hit were but veyn:
> Set more store (I have hit of nature)
> Among rude chaffe to shrape for my pasture." (169–75)

In the moral, labeled "Lenvoy" in the Trinity College manuscript, the narrator justifies the cock's decision in terms of Christian theology:

> The cok demyd, to hym hit was more dew
>   Small simple grayne, þen stones of hygh renoun,
>   Of all tresour chief possessioun.
> Suche as God sent, eche man take at gre,
> Nat prowde with ryches nor groge with pouerte.
>
> The worldly man laboreth for rychesse,
>   And on þe worlde he set all hys intent.
> The vertuos man to auoyde all ydelnesse
>   With suffisaunce hold hymself content. (213–21)

The cock's industry, a natural virtue, and his contentment with "suffisaunce" are read by Lydgate as admirable. Indeed, Lydgate, who has already identified himself as the narrator (32), has asked God and grace for "suffysaunce" in compiling his book, and thus he links himself with the virtuous cock.

Because of Lydgate's modification of the verse Romulus's and Marie's *moralitates*, the vernacular fable collection opens with the positive example of natural wisdom and contentment with one's lot in life, rather than a pejorative view of self-satisfied ignorance. While this change completely inverts the moral of the earlier versions of the fable, such inversion was not unknown in the Middle Ages, as scholastic commentaries have shown us.[11] Lydgate has simply offered an *in bono* reading of a fable originally *in malo*. But the change represents something far more clever in relation to Lydgate's compilation as a whole. Instead of giving his readers a translation of a fable about interpretation and wisdom, a fable that a reader must understand before confronting other fables, Lydgate assumes that his audience already knows how to read this mode of discourse; even so, he takes his cue from earlier Romulan collections by using the first fable to provide a point of reference for reading the subsequent ones. For Lydgate's collection that point of reference is natural allegory, that is, allegorizing according to natural properties. Lydgate employs this kind of interpretation in his bestiary-like description of the cock (56–98), and in turn the cock borrows natural allegory from lapidaries in listing the virtues of the jewel he finds (148–61). But a similar allegorical system cannot unite what nature has put asunder: the cock has no use for the jewel because of their respective places in the natural order, and the natural order is mirrored by the social order, as Lydgate makes clear in lines 213–17 above. Lydgate's first fable, then, exemplifies a standard of virtue against which we must judge the other fable characters, instead of ignorance that we must eschew.

The fable of the cock and the jewel involves only one animate character, but when two are involved, we see strict divisions between vices and virtues, as Lydgate tells us at the beginning of the next fable, that of the lamb and the wolf (225–26, 232–33). The emphasis on nature continues through this fable: the animals are "contrary of nature" (246), the river cannot flow uphill "ageyn nature" (275), the wolf has a "naturall haterede" (286) of the lamb, who has a "naturall mekenes" (356). By the standard which Lydgate has set for the first fable—that living according to one's nature is good—the wolf would not be entirely reprehensible in eating the lamb, and we would not have much of a fable. However, after the animals discuss whether the lamb, standing downstream, could be muddying the wolf's water, Lydgate introduces the social construct of law into the natural conflict. The action of the fable closes in a mere three verses, the first spoken by the wolf.

> "The lawe shall part vs, whyche of vs haþ ryght."
> But he no lenger on þe lawe abood,
> Deuouryd þe lambe & aftyr soke hys blood.
>
> The lambe was sleyn, for he seyd soþ.
>   Thus was law tornyd to rauyne,
> Dome execute by þe wolfis tothe. (292–97)

Here Lydgate deftly changes the basis for judgment from natural to social: in the natural order the wolf's destruction of the lamb may not be pleasant, but it is not morally objectionable. However, when the wolf invokes the law but then kills the lamb in spite of the invocation, the reader's moral judgment is called into play. If the case is whether the lamb is muddying the wolf's water, we know that legally the lamb would be judged innocent, so the wolf's "dome" is wrong. Significantly, this initial mention of the concept of law as something separate from nature comes from the mouth of a lying, ravenous creature. In a sense, it represents a fall: the complete understanding of nature in the first fable has been corrupted by misapplied law in the second.

"Nature's law" sets the tone for the next fable, the frog and the mouse, in its first line, and Lydgate broadens the moral picture from the simple opposition of good and evil in the second fable to a more complex picture here. While the wolf's intent was clearly to kill the lamb, the frog, representing those whose "naturall disposicions" (372) are fraudulent, is "dowble of entent" (385) in deceiving the mouse: the frog will appear friendly while plotting violence. The mouse, however, is true to his nature in desiring only "suffisaunce," as he explains while showing his house to the frog:

"See," quoth þe mowse, "þys ys a mery lyfe.
　Here ys my lordshyp & dominacion.
I lyue here esyly out of noyse & stryfe.
　Thys cloos all hoole ys in my subieccion.
　　Suffisaunce ys my possessione." (400–404).

Later, having mentioned Cresus and Midas and having cited Solomon, the mouse says, "Nature ys content with full lytell þyng" (432) in contrast to the unnatural desires of tyrants (435–41), a comparison that initially strikes readers as irrelevant but that anticipates Lydgate's later concerns.

In Lydgate's fable, the kite who snatches the swimming opponents from the river eats the frog "because of hys fatnes" (499), but the mouse, "sklender and lene" (498), falls unharmed to the ground. The mouse's slenderness embodies his natural preference for simple "suffisaunce" over riches and excess.

The last line of this stanza returns to the early fables' principal concepts: "Lawe & nature pleynyn on folke vnkynde" (504). Although the role of law in the fable is unclear, we are apparently meant to understand that lying, one half of the unnatural frog's "dowble entent," represents an offense against both society and nature. Here as elsewhere, Lydgate puns on the word "kynde"; the frog is unkind in what has become the modern sense of the word because he wants to kill the mouse, but in a larger sense he is "unkynde" because of his unnatural desires—he cannot benefit directly from the murder of the animal.

After this point in the fable collection, nature falls from the spotlight: the word is used only by deceitful characters when constructing lies (for example, 596–97 below). Instead, "law" becomes the central concept of the fourth fable, and misused law there ushers in the illegal, unnatural evil of tyrannical rule in the last three fables, where law is silenced. In the second half of his collection Lydgate devotes the greater part of his attention to the characters who are self-serving, obstreperous liars.

The fourth fable, the story of the dog who takes a sheep to court, examines the corruption of law. The judge seems to protest a bit too much in presenting himself as irrefutable representative of the law:

> Quod the iuge: "The lawe thow must abide,
>   Til ther be yoven sentence of iugement;
> I may no favour do to nowther side,
>   But atwene both stande indifferent,
>   As rightful iuge of hert and hole intent,
> Til I may se by lawe to make me strong,
> Whiche of the partyes have right or wrong.
>
> "The lawe, first founde on a triewe grounde,
>   May nat declyne from his stabilnesse." (575–83)[12]

Taking his vocabulary from the judge's declamation, the dog calls his cause "iust and triewe" (589), and to prove this assertion he formally introduces his false witnesses, the wolf and the kite:

> "To offende trewth the wolf doth gretly drede,
>   He is so stidefast and triew of his nature;
> The gentil kyte hath refused al falshede,
>   He had lever grete hunger to endure,
>   Lovyng no raveyne vnto his pasture,
> Thanne take a chykken, by record of writyng,
> To his repast, or any goselyng." (596–602)

By painting pictures of the wolf and kite as genteel but false to their own natures, the dog's lies betray the overall falseness of his witnesses, but nevertheless the sheep is judged to be in debt to the dog. The narrator says that "the lawe" compelled the sheep to sell his fleece (622–23); the sheep dies of cold and the other animals eat him, providing yet another example of how "poore folk be devoured alwey by the riche" (637), and of how falseness in law is brought about by falseness to one's nature.

Lydgate revises the fable of the wolf and crane to emphasize the wolf's natural disposition to lie.[13] In earlier recensions of the fable the wolf's decision not to reward the crane is economically described, as if such despotic decisions were so much a matter of course that they needed no elaboration; in the Middle English version, however, the poet carefully describes the wolf's falseness:

> The wolffe denyed that he had be-hyte,
>> Sowght a-gayne hym froward occacion,
> Seyd, he had don hym grete wn-ryght,
>> And hym deseyvyd by fals colusion. . . . (778–81)

It is this lie that Lydgate elaborates upon later in the fable:

> And semblably, makyng a fals excuse
>> To pay theyr dewte wnto the poraile,
> Takynge ther service & labour to ther vse,
>> [Gverdounles] to make them to travayle
> Yf they aught ax, tyrauntes them assayle,
> And of malys constreyne them so for drede,
> They not so hardy of them to ax ther mede. (799–805)

Lydgate finds this situation particularly unjust since tyrants have "possescions and riches" while the poor must labor for what he elsewhere calls "suffisaunce"—their meat, drink, and food (806–807). The five-stanza moral also addresses the impossibility of poor people receiving just rewards from tyrants. In this fable we have moved so far into the territory of tyranny that the concepts of law and nature no longer apply; Lydgate simply throws up his hands and tells his readers, "Fly from daunger, yf ye may askape" (843).

And the concern with tyranny is to continue in the fable of the sun's marriage, the first line of which echoes the previous fable by promising to address "the vice also of tiranny" (848). In this case, the fable does not really suit the moral which Lydgate tacks onto it. The fable characters are concerned that if the sun marries and procreates, too many suns will burn up the earth, but of course even very limited natural experience tells readers that there is only one sun; nevertheless, Lydgate feels obliged to ruminate at some length (stanzas 129–33) upon the topic of a tyrant passing on his tyrannical ways to his heirs.

The poet seems pressed to wrap up his compilation with the fable of the dog and the cheese, which he dispatches in four stanzas. Here, in elaborating upon the dog's "covetyce" of the cheese that he has seen in the water, Lydgate unites the major thematic concerns discussed above:

> By whiche exsample men may conceyve & lere,
> >   By experience prevyd in many place,
> Who all covetythe, faylyth offt in fere,
> >   One man allone may not all purchace,
> >   Nor in armys all the worlde enbrace.
> A meane is best withe good governaunce,
> To them that be content withe suffisaunce. (946–52)

In a sense, the fable represents nature's revenge: by a trick of nature, that is, the reflection of the cheese in the water, the dog loses all he has, and "all" is the word with which Lydgate broadens the focus from the cheese to the world (948), keeping us mindful of tyrannical greed. Between the extremes of total loss and tyrannical proprietorship lies the natural mean of "suffisaunce."

The appearance of the cheese in the water may not be the only reflection inherent in this fable. This fable, moved from fourth place in the Latin collection to last in both extant manuscripts of *Isopes Fabules,* provides a mirror image of the first fable, whose theme is also "suffisaunce." Each tale involves only one animal and an inanimate object. In each narrative the animal must confront its own nature in determining what represents "suffisaunce." The cock's decision is admirable, providing a positive example against which other animals can be judged. The dog's is not, but in the final couplet, "Lyke as the hownd, not content withe one chese / Desyryd tweyne, bothe he dyd lese" (958–59), Lydgate reminds us that covetousness destroys contentment, reminding us further of the contented beast with which the collection opens.

But is this suggestion of symmetry evident in other aspects of the collection? Possibly, but because of the differences in fable order in the manuscripts, my claims here must remain largely speculative. The first three of *Isopes Fabules,* if they are presented in the Romulan order as they are in the Trinity College manuscript, celebrate the virtues of three creatures true to their natures: the cock, the lamb, and the mouse. The narrator praises each of these genuinely virtuous characters at some length.[14] The fable of the dog and the sheep balances vice against virtue, and when vice wins the trial, the scales are tipped in its direction. Thereafter, the fables concentrate on the tyrannical, unnatural behavior of vicious, covetous characters.

Structural questions aside, this summary of Lydgate's fables shows that his thematic concerns were on one level largely social but that both the natural and social orders textualize the divine order on earth. The concept of natural law covered a multitude of topics in the later Middle Ages, but it was based upon the belief that "God had implanted in the very nature of things, and especially in the nature of man, norms of conduct that were more binding than any mere human laws."[15] According to one of the most important and popular medieval texts on the concept of natural law, Gratian's *Decretum,* "Natural law holds primacy over all others in time and dignity, for it commenced from the beginning of rational creatures, nor does it vary with time, but remains immutable."[16] Such a formulation of natural law appropriately includes the beasts that populate fable, both in themselves and as they allegorically represent humans. However, while Lydgate invokes natural law in social struggles, he cannot suggest religious solutions for social ills. The poor are not encouraged to seek justice from a God who will defend them against the rich; instead, they must learn to be content with "suffisaunce," or, when all else fails, to flee tyranny.

If one attempted to historicize this example of Lydgate's early poetry as his other works have been historicized recently, one would be left with the conclusion that Lydgate's political sympathies after the dethronement of Richard II were not innately Lancastrian. Indeed, in the first decade of the fifteenth century in England, raising the issues of breaking natural law and imposing tyrannical rule must have seemed nothing less than pointing a finger at the new occupant of the throne, a man who had not chosen the quietism of mere aristocratic "suffisaunce." But if *Isopes Fabules* betrays a Lydgate disenchanted with Henry IV, the poet himself revised his own persona to the degree that such biographical reading seems nearly impossible.

Scholastic Fable Commentary and *Isopes Fabules:* Amplification and Ornamentation

A large number of details points to Lydgate's use of the elegiac Romulus and scholastic fable commentary in his compilation, but the details that he borrowed are not preserved in any single commentary. The task of separating conventional commenting techniques applicable to any pagan literature from specific references to fable commentary therefore becomes difficult. Even so, those aspects of Lydgate's fables which are most clearly indebted to the scholastic commentary tradition show that Lydgate could only approach this poetic project as an extension of the curricular practices that he had internalized in relation to fable, in spite of the fact that few of these scholastic influences are traceable in Marie de France's work.

The greatest impact of scholastic fable commenting practices upon *Isopes Fabules* is apparent in the structure of each of Lydgate's fables, structure very different from that of Marie's fables, which generally open with the narrative and conclude with the *moralitas*. Each of Lydgate's fables is introduced by a summary of its moral lesson; this promythion may be as short as four lines or as long as several stanzas. Lydgate's inspiration for this kind of introductory material probably came from a scholastic commentary such as the *Esopus moralizatus* or *Auctores octo* commentary, in which comments provide a paraphrase of each fable's *moralitas* before the summary of the fable plot. Like Chaucer, Lydgate knew the value of commentary introducing text, but unlike the *Nun's Priest's Tale,* none of Lydgate's fables problematizes the relationship between commentary and text. Furthermore, Lydgate is entirely uninterested (or patently unsuccessful) in exploiting that relationship for its humor: rather, the summary and moralization are presented in the prosaic voice of the Lydgatian narrator, who is striving for maximum moral import in each fable, both before and after its plot.

In the preface to the tale of the cock and the jewel, Lydgate makes use of natural allegory from the bestiary tradition in his description of the cock's habits; although the scholastic commentaries that I have studied do not apply this kind of allegory to this particular bird, the *Esopus moralizatus* version of Fable 20, "De Yrundine et Lino," elaborates upon the pact between the swallow and humans in a manner strongly reminiscent of the bestiary tradition (Appendix 2, p. 211). BN Lat. 8023 also makes use of this tradition. However, the description of the cock is indebted to more than bestiaries; in line 93, a simile comparing the bird to a lion ("In vertu strong & hardy as a lyon") echoes the same comparison in the *Nun's Priest's Tale,* in which Chauntecleer, basking in post-coital contentment, "looketh as it were a grym leoun" (3179). This nod to Chaucer becomes a deep bow when Lydgate tells us that the cock "ys of poettis callyd Chauncecleer" (101), and that the particular bird in this fable has "hys wyues about hym euerychone" (107); Lydgate's fable requires neither of these details. Even at this early stage in his career, Lydgate turns to Chaucer as *auctor* of an authoritative text as a gloss on his own.

Yet another similarity between the cock in *Isopes Fabules* and Chaucer's fable hero is their ability to cite *auctores.* Lydgate's bird cannot complete a stanza before showing the breadth of his knowledge as he addresses the jewel:

"Euax to the yeveþ praysyng manyfolde,
Whos lapydary bereþ opynly wytnesse,
Geyn sorow & woe þou bryngest in gladnesse.

The best iacyncte in Ethiope ys founde

> And ys of colour lyke the saphyre ynde,
> Comforteþ men, þat ly in prison bounde,
>   Makeþ men strong & hardy of hys kynde,
>   Contract synewes þe iacyncte doþ unbynde. . . ." (152–59)

These lines loosely resemble parts of Evax's "De Iaspide," the fourth description in his lapidary:

> Iaspidis esse decem species septemque feruntur
> Hic et multorum cognoscitur esse color[u]m
> Et multi nasci perhibetur partibus orbis.
> Optimus est viridi translucentique colore,
> Et qui plus soleat virtut[i]s habere probatur.
> Caste portatus fugat et febres et hydropem
> Apposit[e]que iuvat mulierem parturientem,
> Et tutamentum portanti creditur esse.
> Nam consecratus gratum facit, atque potentem.
> Et sicut perhibent, phantasmata noxia pellit
> Cuius in argento vis fortior esse putatur.[17]

[There are ten species of jacinth recorded, and seven are recorded here, and it is known to be of many colors, and it is said to be native to parts of much of the world. The best is of green and translucent color, and it is the one that proves to have the most strength. When chastely carried, it drives out both fevers and dropsy, and it appropriately helps a woman giving birth. And it is believed to be a protection to the one who carries it. A consecrated one makes him pleasing and powerful. And as people say, the one whose power is thought to be stronger (mounted) in silver drives away noxious visions.]

Lydgate's interest in the jewel's place of origin and color derives from Evax, and the Middle English poet may have translated help for women in labor as the less detailed unbinding of contracted sinews, perhaps in order to make this virtue more appropriate to a clerical audience. Later, as the cock closes his praise of the gem with the line, "Double of vertu þe saphyr in gold closyd" (198), he echoes the final line of the Latin poem, different though the precious stones and metals are.

While Lydgate on his own might have turned to a lapidary in search of material for amplifying this fable, it is also possible that he had seen this fable glossed with similar information. In British Library MS Add. 11897, a German manuscript apparently written during Lydgate's lifetime, lines 1, 4, and 6 of Evax's poem are included in the marginalia associated with the fable of the cock and the jewel (f. 2r). If such glossing was common, the cock's quotation of an *auctor* not only indicates a general debt to Chaucer's well-versed rooster but also gives an example of how nicely "educated" he is; some of Lydgate's readers could have appreciated not only the gloss itself but also the fact that the bird remembered a scholastic comment conventionally related to the fable.

In the following fable, that of the lamb and the wolf, the wolf makes a startling reference to the law as he is about to kill the lamb, but he immediately overrides legality with physical force:

> "The lawe shall part vs, whyche of vs haþ ryght."
> But he no lenger on the lawe abood,
> Deuouryd þe lambe & aftyr soke hys blood. (292–94)

This incongruity, absent from Marie's version of the fable, is brought out forcefully in the *Auctores octo* commentary, in which the commentator interrupts the fable's plot summary to insert a brief but clear moral judgment against the attacking wolf: "Apprehenso eo contra iusticiam, devoravit" (Appendix 3, p. 213). Only this type of precedence for the wolf's mention of legal justice in Lydgate's fable can make sense of the poet's attention to law at this point, for natural law has given the wolf physical dominion over the lamb.

After the wolf has slain his prey, we find the first of many biblical references in Lydgate's fables:

> Thus was law tornyd to rauyne,
> Dome execute by þe wolfis tothe;
> By whyche lawe Naboth lost hys vyne,
> Whylom commaundyd by law, whyche ys dyuyne,
> No ravenous beste (þe Byble doþ deuyse)
> Shuld be offred to God in sacryfyse. (296–301)

The story of Naboth from III Kings 28 and the mention of animal sacrifice may have been meant to serve as a transition to a moralizing detail, tangential to the fable:

> The[i] dey[e] boþe: þe wolfe may nat auayle
> Be hit for houndis caren most corumpable,
> The lambe vp seruyd at þe kyngis table. (341–43)

The wolf's sinfulness corrupts him physically, depriving him of the ultimate reward of presentation to the king. But even though Lydgate tries to prepare his reader for this moralization, based on no action in the fable, it remains only barely connected to the tale that it purports to moralize. It makes use of an interpretive context self-consciously created by the fabulist himself specifically for moralizing. This odd figurative structure is similar to the etymology of the word "*diabolus*" in the *Esopus moralizatus* allegorization of Fable 3, "De Mure et Rana" (Appendix 2, p. 206): the writer of the commentary plot summary glosses one of his own comments, not part of the fable itself. Similarly, Lydgate draws the detail about the king's table from an example of *auctoritas* with which he has glossed the fable, not an incident integral to the narrative. This odd glossing technique gives a new meaning to Barthes' endless play of signifiers: for Lydgate, who seems unwilling to give multiple independent meanings to a fable character, one signification must be linked to another, creating a linear series of glosses that moves away from the authoritative fable text but can be retraced to it.

Lydgate's version of the fable of the mouse and the frog is the amplified version probably first written by Marie de France and reproduced in the Romulus L B G[18] and the *Esopus moralizatus*. That Lydgate was translating Marie's work is apparent at the beginning of the mouse's speech of welcome to the frog. Marie writes:

La suriz li respunt, "Amie,
Pieca k'en oi la seignurie.
Bien est en ma subectiun
Quant es pertuz tut envirun." (15–18)

After rendering these lines in English, Lydgate begins his own amplification of the speech by turning immediately to one of his primary thematic concerns in line 404:

"See," quoth þe mowse, "þys ys a mery lyfe.
   Here ys my lordshyp & dominacion.
I lyue here esyly out of noyse & stryfe.
   Thys cloos all hoole ys in my subieccion.
      Suffisaunce ys my possessione." (400–404)

The mouse's exemplary citations of Cresus (420), Midas (421), Solomon (428), Diogenes (437), Alexander (438), and Priam (441) owe nothing to Marie, whose fable characters never speak of literary or historical figures; rather, the mouse's knowledge bears further witness to the influence of *auctoritas*-laden scholastic commentary (or the well-read commentator Chauntecleer from the *Nun's Priest's Tale*). Central in this list of kings is Solomon, the biblical figure whose work is most often quoted in fable commentaries. Lydgate greatly amplifies Proverbs 17:1, "Melior est buccella sicca cum gaudio, quam domus plena victimis cum jurgio."

Salomon wryteþ, howe hit ys bet by halfe
   A lompe of brede with reioysyng,
Then at festis to haue a rostyd calfe
   With heuy chere, frownyng or grogyng. (428–31)

The changes made by the poet here hint at his general method of modifying his sources, giving them greater specificity and detail.

In the fable of the dog and the sheep, the transition from promythion to fable closely resembles that employed in scholastic commentaries. After Lydgate prepares his readers for the subject matter of the narrative by castigating witnesses who perjure themselves, he writes:

Whych þyng to preue by exsamples full notable
Of olde Isopus whylom wrote þys fable.

Hauyng thys conceyte, set hit for a ground;
   By maner lyknes rehersyng in sentence,
He wrete þer was whylom a gret hounde. . . . (538–42)

The *Auctores octo* commentary on "De Cane et Ove" begins as follows: "Hic auctor dicit quod non faciamus alicui misero nec procuremus damnum, et hoc probat per litteram, dicens quod quidam canis calumniosus pascebat panem ab ove . . ." (Appendix 3, p. 214). Lydgate clarifies the purpose of the scholastic form of introduction which he adopts: the fable is meant to prove a moral truth (a direct translation of the verb *probat*, used in many scholastic comments), and it was written by Aesop (the *auctor* mentioned at the beginning of each comment). Furthermore, Lydgate explains the reason that promythia are provided: they serve as a "grounde," a basis for better understanding of the fable to follow.

Moralizing after the fable, Lydgate again had recourse to the proverbs of Solomon, the very author quoted in the *Auctores octo* comment on this fable (Appendix 3, p. 214). But while the quotation in the scholastic commentary is difficult to relate to this fable (and may have been meant for the fable of the dog and the meat), Lydgate elaborates upon Proverbs 25:18, a verse more clearly relevant to his tale ("Jaculum et gladius et sagitta acuta, homo qui loquitur contra proximum suum falsum testimonium"). Here the poet seems intent upon blurring the distinction between what is his and what is Solomon's.

To a false witnesse, record in Salamon,
   Proverbiorum, .iij. thynges bien compared
A shrew[e]d dart, an hoked arow is oon,
   Al for the werre as it is declarid,

Yit vnder trety somtyme they be spared;
But a false witnesse hath this avauntage
With mowth infect alwey to do damage.

Agayne sharpe quarels helpith a pavice,
    Agayne arowes may be made defence,
And though a swerd be riche and of grete price,
    Somtyme he sparith for to do offence;
    But a false iurrour, by mortal violence,
Nat only causith men her bloode to shede,
But makith hem lese theyr lyf and goode for meede. (659–72)

This passage shows Lydgate concerned less with setting a parallel *auctoritas* alongside his fable than with recasting Solomon's words to suit his own interests. Only a reader familiar with the verse from Proverbs would discern which things are being compared to a false witness, so intertwined are Lydgate's amplification and Solomon's list. The simple juxtaposition in Proverbs 25:18 is teased into sermonic comparisons of Lydgate's own, amplified with images of ruthlessness and violence. Because the poet uses Solomon more as a rhetorical ornament than as an *auctor,* the authoritative statement has become a slave to, rather than a reinforcement of, the message of the appropriating author.

Lydgate then calls upon the English commentator on Solomon, Robert Holkot, to continue the diatribe against false witnesses:

It is remembred by record of auctours,
    As writeth Holcot vpon sapience,
How ther folwith .iij. incomoditees
    Of false forsweryng ageyn conscience:
    First, rehersith this auctour in sentence,
Vpon a booke whan a false iurrour
Forswerith hym-self, he is to God a traytour.

There-vpon, this matier to conclude,
    That false forsweryng is to God treason,
First he makyth this simylitude:
    That if a man withyn a regioun
    Wold countrefete, by false collusioun,
The kynges seale, the people to begile,
What were he worthy to deye by civile?

And semblably, who can considre wele,
    The name of God, ordeyned to impresse,

Is the signacle of the celestial seale,
    Yoven to al Cristen of trowth to bere witnesse,
    And who that euer mysvsith it in falsenesse,
Holcot affermyth it, for short conclusion,
That he to God doth opinly treason. (680–700)

Paul Sauerstein located the source of this passage in Lectio 167 B of *Super Libros Sapientiae:*

> Circa perjurium est notandum. Pro perjurus est multipliciter detestandus et specialiter propter tria. Est enim perjurus prodiciousus per infidelitatem quo ad deum. Injuriosus per falsitatem quo ad proximum et perniciosus per iniquitatem quo ad seipsum. Primo igitur perjurus est prodiciosus per infidelitatem quo ad deum. Proditio foret magna si ille qui haberet custodiam sigilli regii sigillaret literam pactionis quam rex maxime detestaretur et si hoc faceret de sigillo pape esset excommunicatus ipso facto brachio seculari tradendus. Nomen dei est nomen comissum nobis quasi quoddam sigillum ad testificandum veritatem et confirmandum etc.[19]

> [About perjury this ought to be noted. A perjurer ought to be despised for numerous reasons, but especially because of three. Truly, the perjured person is unnatural for infidelity toward God. (He is) unjust through falsity toward his neighbor and pernicious through his iniquity toward himself. It is a great betrayal if he who has custody of the seal of the king seals a letter of agreement that the king has greatly detested, and if he did this with the seal of the pope, he would be excommunicated for having done it, to be turned over to the secular arm. The name of God is a name committed to us like a certain seal for attesting to and confirming the truth.]

Considering Lydgate's work in light of its source, we can see even more clearly the poet's desire to focus solely upon secular miscarriages of justice: he translates Holkot's passage on counterfeiting the king's seal but ignores Holkot's equal emphasis on misuse of the pope's seal.

Lydgate translates some of Holkot's other ideas in stanzas 101–103 before finally reaching the second and third "incoditees of false forsweryng."

For the iurrours first disseyvith the iuge,
    Causith his neyghburgh for to lese his right,
    His conscience hurt, of grace blent the light,

As a renegat, that hath the Lord forsake,
Lyke to be dampned, but he amendis make. (724–28)

This is the true lesson of Lydgate's fable: the false witness will suffer eternal damnation unless he makes amends. In spite of the fact that this threat has meaning only on a spiritual level, Lydgate does not transform it into spiritual allegory: because his target is clearly false witnesses on earth, he concludes the stanza with the specific exhortation that they change their ways rather than the generalized spiritual threat of hell. The totalizing interpretive gesture of spiritual allegory would close off the opportunity for further amplification about the sinful nature of false witnesses.

In his fable's penultimate stanza Lydgate credits Aesop with comparing false witnesses to harpies, a comparison for which I have found no source in any text that the poet might have attributed to "Isopos."

Isopos iurrours doth discryve,
    Callith theym Arpies, houndes infernal,
With ravenous feete, wynged to flee blyve . . . (729–31)

This metaphor may also have been borrowed from Holkot's commentary on the Books of Wisdom. In Lectio CLIII Holkot writes of three groups of sinners who deny knowledge of God: "periuri, maliciosi, et fallaces, cuiusmodi sunt falsi testes et falsi advocati et falsi iudices qui scienter veritatem negant"; he contrasts these with the truth that is Christ. Later in the *lectio,* Holkot draws upon the *auctoritas* of Sidonius:

De istis loquens Sidonius in quadam epistola sic eos describit: "Hi sunt in convivis scurre, in exactionibus arpyie; in collocutionibus bestie; in questionibus statue; ad intelligendum saxie; ad iudicandum ligne; ad ignoscendum ferrei, ad iniurias pardi, ad facecias ursi; ad fallendum vulpes; ad superbiendum thauri; et ad consummandum minotauri."[20]

[Speaking about these in a certain letter, Sidonius describes them thus: "They are buffoons at feasts, harpies in the collection of debts, beasts in conversation, statues in investigations; they are stones to understand, wood to judge, iron to pardon; panthers toward injury, bears toward humor; foxes for driving away, bulls for taking pride, and minotaurs to sum up."]

The fable text, which survives in only the MS Harley 2251 exemplar, may be corrupt in the first line of this stanza: the name "Sidonius," substituted for "Isopos" in line 729, would result in a more metrically regular line. At any rate, Lydgate's choice of a mythical creature that was half human and half beast suits fable nicely, situating the sub-humans between the human world of the English legal system and the animalistic world of beast fable.

Lydgate's citation of Holkot as *auctor* resembles his use of Solomon earlier: the narrator's sermonic amplification overwhelms the *auctoritas* to the degree that it becomes merely the occasion for Lydgate's preaching more than a reinforcement of the fable's message. If Lydgate props up his project with Holkot's authority, he also displaces it with his lengthy tirade; Holkot himself is irretrievable.

The fable of the wolf and the crane has several elements in common with the *Esopus moralizatus*, the first in its opening stanza:

> In Isopus forther to proced,
>> Towchynge the vyce of wnkyndenesse,
> In this tretes a lytyll fabill I rede
>> Of engratytude, ioynyd to falsenesse. . . . (750–53)

Like line 753, the commentary promythion focuses on two of the sins of bad people: they are "ingrati et beneficiorum immemores" (Appendix 2, p. 209). Lydgate uses the nominal form of the English cognate for the substantive adjective *ingrati*, but he changes the second quality to "falsenesse," reflecting the changes he makes in the plot itself. In the elegiac Romulus fable and comments upon it, the wolf's refusal of the reward to the bird is mere tyrannical caprice, while in Marie's version the wolf claims that the crane's reemergence from the wolf's jaws constitutes reward enough. Lydgate's wolf lies when claiming that he never offered his healer a reward (778–81, 799ff.).

Lydgate also removes his beast fable from the undefined territory where these tales usually take place, mentioning in passing that when the wolf is stricken at a feast, doctors for him were sought "thorow all the cort" (764). Although this location, absent from Marie's fable, might provide evidence of an anti-Lancastrian bent in Lydgate's fables, Lydgate could have borrowed the detail from the *Esopus moralizatus* commentator, who also associates the wolf with a court; the animal is "potens in curia leonis regis ut summus prepositus regis" (Appendix 2, p. 209). The wolf's residence at court helps to justify Lydgate's moralization about tyranny:

> The tyraunt hathe possescions and riches,
>> The poure travelythe for meate, drynke, & fode,
> The ryche dothe the laborar oppresse,
>> For his labour denyethe hym hys lyflode,
>>> The lambe must suffre, the wolffes bene so wode. (806–10)

POCKET NOVEL MYSTERY, PRE-CD RELEASE
'EIGHT DAYS IN THE LIFE OF GRACE'
W/ THE COLD AFTER AND THE CLOSE AT THE
BETA BAR, 9:30 SAT. SEPT. 20, 2003

FOR MORE INFO VISIT
THEBETABAR.COM OR
POCKETNOVELMYSTERY.COM

This social moralization closely resembles the epimythion in the *Esopus moralizatus:* "Moraliter, per gruem intelliguntur pauperes et impotentes qui sunt sub potentioribus. Videtur enim potentioribus quod pauperes sufficientem mercedem recipiunt pro suis laboribus in hoc quod eos vivere promittunt et bona residua que [potentes] habent, [pauperes] non usurpant" (Appendix 2, p. 209). [Morally by the crane poor and powerless people who are under the powerful are understood. It seems to powerful people that poor people receive adequate reward for their labors in what they promise them for living, and the remaining goods that the powerful have, the poor do not lay claim to.] The Middle English poet's view of the desperate situation of the poor is considerably darker than that of his source. In Lydgatian terminology, the commentator tells us that the rich think that the poor have "suffisaunce," while the poet says that the oppressed are denied their livelihood. Although these situations are not mutually exclusive, Lydgate draws a sharper picture of political impotence than earlier fabulists had.

In rewriting Marie's fable of the sun who wished to wed, Lydgate follows her lead by ignoring the verse Romulus's framing narrative of the wise man using the fable of the sun's marriage to warn the guests at a thief's wedding about possible future troubles. He gives a scholarly cast to the fable by assigning mythological names to the characters whom Marie has identified generally, the sun and Destiny. The sun is Phoebus, and Destiny, a single figure in Marie's fable, becomes "Parchas sustren, that in the nombre three / Ben callid of poetis spynners of destyne" (874–75). These characters are joined in their judgment against the sun's marriage by "Theofrast, a manne ronne ferre in age" (881), and "The Romayn poete Cocus Marcial" (886). The former *auctor* is Theofrastus, author of the *Liber de Nuptiis,* the work quoted extensively by Chaucer's Wife of Bath and read by her uncooperative husband Jankyn (Prologue, 235–47, 248–75, 670ff.). "Cocus Marcial," a variant of the Latin *coquus* (cook), was the common medieval name for the Latin epigrammatist Martial, though both its origin and meaning remain obscure.[21]

This odd group of mythological figures, a patristic writer, and a classical poet can only strike the modern reader, if not the medieval one, as a bizarre mixed metaphor of a jury, a melange more suitable to dream-vision than to fable. However, British Library MS Add. 11897 and other fable commentaries rely on a similarly mixed group of pagan and Christian *auctores* for proverbial glosses for the verse Romulus. Lydgate's inclusion of the two writers here again represents an encroachment of marginalia upon text, an example of the way in which authorities who should be passive, external commentators are called upon to play active roles in the plot of the fable, in

spite of a certain incongruity in placing them alongside mythological characters. Here Lydgate's tendency to cite *auctores* only to sweep them away in
a flood of amplification is carried to a logical (though non-amplificatory)
conclusion: these authority figures do not speak for themselves at all. Their
authority remains simply nominal, with no proverbial wisdom undergirding
it. They are purely rhetorical ornament.

When the jury's decision has been handed down, Lydgate makes the
connection between the heat of the sun and the cruelty of a tyrant, whose
heirs are bound to be as bad as he:

> If he have eyres for to succede,
>   Folowe theyr fader in successioun,
> By tirauntry, then are they more to drede
>   In theyr ravyne and extorcioun,
>   By theyr counseil and false convencioun;
> For multitude of robbers, where they gon,
> Doth more damage, sothly, than doth oon.
>
> Men may at the ie se a pref
>   Of this matere, old and yong of age,
> Lasse is to drede the malice of oo thief,
>   So sayne merchauntis, ridyng in theyr viage,
>   But wher many on awaytith on the passage,
> Ther standith the parell, as it is often sene,
> By whiche example ye wote what I mene.
>
> Oon ageyn oon may make resistence,
>   Oon ageyn many, the conquest is vnkowth;
> Nombre of tirauntis thurgh theyr violence
>   Pursweth the pore, both est and sowth;
>   Gredy wolfis, that comyn with open mowth,
> Vpon a folde theyr nature can declare
>   By experience, whether they wil hurt or spare. (904–24)

In the discussion of thievery in lines 911–17, Lydgate steps back beyond
Marie's unframed version of the tale to the Latin version, in which the wise
man tells the story about the sun in order to persuade the wedding guests to
stop the proceedings so that the thief will not have evil children. But the
procreation of thieves is not Lydgate's primary concern; tyranny is, and in
order to keep it at the forefront of his moralization, he reduces the reason
for the elegiac Romulus's framing narrative to little more than a metaphor
for tyranny—a comment upon it.

Bringing *Isopes Fabules* to a swift close, Lydgate was willing to sacrifice a multivalent narrative and *moralitas* for the sake of brevity in the fable of the dog and the cheese; indeed, in comparison to the other extensively amplified fables, it seems an exercise in *abbreviatio*. None of the moral material here can be identified with any source but Lydgate himself, who may have envisioned the tale as a summary of the collection's moral concerns in the manner described earlier in this chapter.

Why Lydgate wrote many of his short poems remains a mystery, and his intention in writing *Isopes Fabules* is not fully clear either. If the work were a full translation, its existence could be explained by the popularity of both its French and its Latin sources, but because it purports to be Lydgate's own compilation, that explanation is only partially satisfactory. If in compiling the fables Lydgate drew from scholastic commentaries containing religious allegory (available sparingly in the *Esopus moralizatus* and more readily in the *Auctores octo* commentary), he rejected that kind of elaboration upon the fables. His concerns were primarily social, and within that general realm, his clearest goal was to decry injustice as represented by liars and tyrants. Only through a close comparison with possible sources can we see the degree to which he threw this problem into relief in *Isopes Fabules*. In fact, his target is so clear and his anger so pronounced that I believe it very possible that he wrote the fables to commemorate a specific miscarriage of justice in which he found himself, a patron, or a friend on the losing side of a judgment. Indeed, the introduction tells us that he is compiling his book as a "remembraunce" (54), and he could be commemorating just such an event. If so, the legal terminology and imagery found at unexpected moments in the text (126, 325–26, 330–31, 831, 851) may have made more sense to the informed medieval reader than they do to us. These suggestions, however, can only lead to biographical or historical questions that are not within the purview of this study.

What this chapter has shown, I hope, is that Lydgate understood the curricular fable tradition, and that he worked to bring aspects of curricular practice to bear upon his translation. Among those aspects, amplification dominates, exerting a rhetorical tyranny over Lydgate's sources and *auctoritates* by co-opting them and embellishing them almost beyond recognition; they become enslaved by Lydgate's pedanticism. If Lydgate appreciated Chaucer's satirical use of amplification in the *Nun's Priest's Tale,* he did not choose to emulate it. Here amplification is the rhetorical vehicle for moral instruction, as it was in medieval classrooms.

It is also apparent that Lydgate did not fully understand the strategies for appropriating fabular discourse that Marie and other sources had employed. Although Lydgate's prologue shows that he wanted to create a fable collection that would identify itself as a part of his own literary corpus, he also mentions Aesop as *auctor* at the beginning of each fable, as if he is in some sense unwilling to appropriate the authority of the father of fable. (This repetition starkly contrasts Marie's general reticence to mention Aesop's name beyond the prologue and epilogue of her collection.) Lydgate's attempt to share authority with Aesop may betray his discomfort with the fact that his primary source is not an authoritative Aesopic text, but a vernacular one whose authority he cannot co-opt. Instead, he must use the materials provided by a vernacular collection to conjure an Aesop to whom he can point as his *auctor* and source. As much as the incompleteness of the collection, Lydgate's unwillingness to commit to a clear strategy of appropriation contributes to the sense of unfinished business that characterizes *Isopes Fabules*.

Robert Henryson's *Morall Fabillis*

Reading, Enacting, and Appropriating

Middle Scots poet Robert Henryson's *Morall Fabillis* is a unique work in the history of medieval vernacular fable, not only because of its lengthy, detailed allegorical *moralitates,* but also because of its innovative inclusion of episodes from beast epic alongside curricular fables. By bringing into the realm of moral fable the Old French Reynardian literature, previously re-garded as entertainment rather than moral edification, Henryson tacitly reminds his readers of the Pauline notion that concludes Chaucer's beast-epic–beast-fable hybrid, *The Nun's Priest's Tale:* "[A]l that writen is, / To oure doctrine it is ywrite" (4631–32). Furthermore, Henryson only slightly favors the morality inherent in fable over that which he unearths in beast epic: his collection comprises seven fables from the elegiac Romulus and six beast-epic episodes, symmetrically structured around a fable told by Aesop in a dream-vision.[1]

In spite of the modern acceptance of the notion that Henryson was a schoolmaster writing during the final quarter of the fifteenth century, when published fable commentaries were available, Henryson's *Morall Fabillis* have not yet been studied fully in relation to curricular fable texts. While his use of the elegiac Romulus as a source text is clearly indicated by a Latin quotation in the prologue to the collection, modern scholars have generally been content to base their source studies on modern editions of the Latin fables, not medieval ones. Only Douglas Gray moved beyond this level of generality to suggest connections between some of Henryson's fables and the allegories in the *Esopus moralizatus* and *Auctores octo;* Gray, however, devotes only three pages of his book to discussing similarities in subject matter.[2] In this chapter I will examine the Prologue, *moralitates,* and some structural principles of the Aesopic fables in Henryson's *Morall Fabillis* in relation to the scholastic language, pedagogical practices, and allegories in fable manuscripts and books available in the late fifteenth century. Many of the comparisons here are based on the *Esopus moralizatus* and *Auctores octo* commentaries, but I will also cite similarities between the Middle Scots fables and commentaries found only in manuscripts, especially British Library MS Add. 11897, the commentary of which resembles much of Henryson's work.

Henryson's project is the most scholarly vernacular fable collection to emerge during the Middle Ages. *The Moral Fables* is a compendium of approaches and attitudes toward fable, here expanded to include the sister genre of beast epic. However, the variety of subject matter and interpretive technique has proved disconcerting to critics unfamiliar with the diversity that typifies the scholastic fable tradition. A substantial number of critics in the 1950s, 1960s, and even the 1970s found Henryson's changes of interpretive mode so opaque that they chose not to read the narratives and *moralitates* as integrated,[3] a baby-and-bathwater rejection that neither elucidates Henryson's work nor shows an understanding of medieval fable as both a canonical text and a popular mode of discourse. Wisely, most Henryson critics in the past three decades have followed Denton Fox's advice that the two parts of each fable should be considered together and that the collection should be viewed as a unified work of literature rather than a random compilation.[4] Nevertheless, curiosity and uncertainty about Henryson's moral messages remain, even in the work of the sensitive critic Douglas Gray, who calls the *moralitates* "selective and arbitrary" (124). On one level, this judgment is irrefutable: Henryson's choice to apply one *moralitas* and not another to a certain fable was entirely his own. By comparing his work to scholastic fable commentaries, however, we can see clearly that Henryson viewed his own work as part of a tradition (even though the very tradition had long been based on selectivity and arbitrariness). Henryson himself would probably have called the collection a full exploitation of the variety inherent in the treatment of this mode of discourse in the Middle Ages.

But Henryson adds significantly to discursive conventions by creating an impressively wide variety of relationships between narrator and fable narrative, between fable and moral, and between Aesop and the appropriating author. These innovations create a progression that spans the fables: we begin with a timorous narrator who seems hesitant to take full control of his subject matter, but he actually begins to live the fables that he tells, thus giving him the authority to confront the father of fable himself, Aesop. After this meeting, he gains enough confidence to adopt the voice of the father himself, moralizing with greater authority, and attributing to him fables that were not actually his. Unlike Lydgate's compilation, Henryson's makes use of a narrator who learns as he compiles: unlike Chauntecleer, he both knows the fables and fully understands what they mean. The narrator thus provides readers with an example of how to use curricular practice to internalize fable, but as he gains authority, he himself changes in both his perception of his audience and the manner in which he addresses them.

The Prologue and the Construction of Narratorial Authority

In the Prologue to the *Morall Fabillis* Henryson draws upon two parts of the standard Latin fable curriculum: the verse prologue of the elegiac Romulus and several of the *accessus,* or scholastic introductions, which accompanied the Latin collection in manuscripts and books. These sources are combined with common fable theory in such a way that Henryson prepares his audience for a vernacular collection of broader concern than any of its sources.

The tone of Henryson's prologue is instructive, seeking to justify the project in terms of scholastic endeavor:

> Thocht feinȝeit fabils of ald poetre
> Be not al grunded vpon truth, yit than,
> Thair polite termes of sweit rhetore
> Richt plesand ar vnto the eir of man;
> And als the caus quhy thay first began
> Wes to repreif the of thi misleuing,
> O man, be figure of ane vther thing. (1–7)[5]

Here Henryson's narrator acknowledges the conventional criticism of fables because of their basic falseness, a criticism that could have reached him through the writings of Augustine or Macrobius,[6] but he immediately negates that criticism by emphasizing the importance of figuration. The word "caus" in line 5 would have reminded Henryson's contemporaries of the Aristotelian form of scholastic introduction;[7] indeed, this stanza may represent an adaptation of the *causa materialis* which the *accessus* to the *Esopus moralizatus* gives for the elegiac Romulus collection, "Causa materialis vel subiectum huius libri est sermo fabulosus in respectu ad vertutes morales."

Although the horticultural imagery in the Prologue's second stanza is taken directly from the Latin prologue (Appendix 1, p. 195), the Latin narrator speaks metaphorically of himself as a gardener tending the growth of his rhetorical flowers, while Henryson's narrator distances himself from verbal horticulture through a simile; poetry, "in lyke maner" (8) to a garden bringing forth flowers and grain, has "ane morall sweit sentence" (12). The shift from first-person metaphor to depersonalized simile serves two purposes. First, it separates Henryson's own poetic activity from that of the original cultivator, Aesop, and his Latin translator. Our narrator can compare himself to the *auctor* but at this point cannot presume to play the same part as the master of the discursive mode. Second, this distancing simile frees our narrator for another role, as we shall see.

The next stanza, a justification for mixing pleasure and instruction which is as indebted to the elegiac Romulus as it is to Horace, closes with Henryson's quotation of the second line of the Latin prologue, "Dulcius arrident seria picta iocis" (28). To educated medieval readers who would have memorized the prologue in school, this verse was doubtless familiar enough to serve as a clear identifier of the collection that Henryson was translating. The line presents one of the Latin fabulist's justifications for writing fables, but Henryson apparently places it here in order to prepare his audience for what is to follow: a citation of the "serious things" inherent in a traditional modesty topos, but adorned with the pleasantries of some unexpected role-playing on the part of the narrator. This passage initially appears to be a light-hearted, satirical depiction of the traditional scholastic use of fables in a quasi-scholastic setting with the readers serving as "maisteris," but comparison with scholastic texts brings out its darker aspects. The poet writes of Aesop:

> Of this poete, my maisteris, with ȝour leif,
> Submitting me to ȝour correctioun,
> In mother toung, of Latyng, I wald preif
> To mak ane maner of translatioun—
> Nocht of my self, for vane presumptioun,
> Bot be requeist and precept of ane lord,
> Of quhome the name it neidis not record. (29–35)

Superficially Henryson's modesty topos seems quite conventional, but a closer examination of the stanza reveals unique aspects of the author's narratorial self-creation. One change is signaled by the word "maisteris," a term appropriate to the classroom.[8] In asking leave of his masters to begin his translation, the narrator places himself in the role of a student speaking to his teachers. While the translation of fables was an age-old classroom exercise, the satirical edge of this passage becomes clearer in light of the translation myths that were also part of the standard scholastic introductions to the elegiac Romulus fables. In not only the Romulus epistle but also the *Esopus moralizatus* and the *Auctores octo accessus*, for example, great care is taken to mention the name of the patron who has requested the translation, so that his commission will redound eternally to his greater glory. Henryson, on the other hand, leaves his readers doubting whether his narrator really has been commissioned, for surely someone submitting his

work for the consideration of "maisteris" would not be qualified to undertake a translation for a lord.

But we should examine the passage yet again. Henryson's narrator
brings into play a sin, "vane presumptioun," which will not taint his translation, and then tells us that he need not name the lord by whose precept he
is working. Henryson here could be hinting at the ways in which his Christian fable collection will differ from earlier texts: his work need not glorify
an earthly lord, because it is written to glorify the spiritual one. Through
this calculated ambiguity, Henryson prepares his readers for the fact that
his collection will examine both the relationship between earthly nobles
and their subjects, and that between the heavenly lord and his creatures.
This ambiguity also prepares the reader for the spiritual allegory that will
inform several of the fable *moralitates*; earthly power relations anticipate
and allegorically represent more important spiritual ones.

The narrator further derides his own ability in lines 36–42, which on
their own seem a wholly conventional disclaimer of verbal skills:

> In hamelie language and in termes rude
> Me neidis wryte, for quhy of eloquence
> Nor rethorike, I never vnderstude.
> Thairfoir meiklie I pray your reuerence,
> Gif ye find ocht that throw my negligence
> Be deminute, or yit superfluous,
> Correct it at your willis gratious. 36–42

Here Henryson satirizes both the dictates of Priscian's *Praeexercitamina*
and his own narrator. The narrator's self- declared lack of rhetorical talent
directly contradicts the generic requirement of fable cited in the prologue's
first stanza, providing further evidence that he is ill-qualified for the task.
Rhetorical sweetness, the genre's primary raison d'être, must pave the way
if instruction in proper living is to follow. Furthermore, to adhere to
Priscian's pedagogical model, a student was required to make a fable either
"deminute" or "superfluous"; the narrator's request for correction expresses fears based upon scholastic practice, though even at the outset of his
project, Henryson must have known that the "superfluities" added to the
original fables would be his stamp upon them.

Of course Henryson gives his narrator the lie in relation to his rhetorical
weakness, not only by means of his elegant rhyme royal stanzaic form but
also in the very terms expressing inarticulateness: this stanza includes no
fewer than seven latinisms, betokening an elevated rhetorical style. Indeed,
Bengt Ellenberger has pointed out, perhaps somewhat too mathematically,

that the prologue contains 2.6 times the average number of latinisms per line of the *Morall Fabillis* as a whole.[9] Thus Henryson paints the narrator as a man who is classically educated, as any fabulist should be, but who wears his learning lightly.

In the next two stanzas, Henryson clarifies the balance that he is attempting to strike between the fables' classroom role and their value as exempla. The narrator attributes to his *auctor* a far more ambitious agenda for fables than the source itself posits:

> My author in his fabillis tellis how
> That brutal beistis spak and vnderstude,
> And to gude purpois dispute and argow,
> Ane sillogisme propone, and eik conclude;
> Putting exempill and similitude
> How mony men in operatioun
> Ar like to beistis in conditioun. (43–49)

Here Henryson plays upon Priscian's dictates that fables be rhetorical models for schoolchildren, the curricular role for which the Latin fabulist probably wrote his fables. Henryson has raised the curricular stakes by writing forms of academic discourse *into* the fables rather than simply allowing those forms to be the subject of that discourse, anticipating the fact that the beasts in this collection will, like Chauntecleer, serve as scholastic debaters and commentators upon the texts that they are living. But if this idea begins as a wittily satirical displacement of scholarly *disputatio*, it is balanced by a serious indictment of sinfulness in lines 47–49 and the following stanza:

> Ne merveill is, ane man be lyke ane beist,
> Quhilk lufis ay carnall and foull delyte,
> That schame can not him renye nor arreist,
> Bot takis all the lust and appetyte,
> Quhilk throw custum and the daylie ryte
> Syne in the mynd sa fast is radicate
> That he in brutal beist is transformate. (50–56)

In his edition's notes to these lines, Fox cites the standard scriptural passages in which sinful men are compared to irrational beasts, 2 Peter 2:9ff. and Jude 10, but while these verses are certainly part of the broader background of Henryson's stanza, the idea of the incongruity of humans acting in beastly fashion could also have been borrowed from the second half of the *Auctores octo* introduction, reproduced in Appendix 3. This passage also shares with the final stanza of Henryson's prologue the emphasis on the

figurative nature of the poet's project ("Esope . . . be figure wrait his buke";
57, 59).

By the end of his prologue, then, Henryson has begun to sketch the role
of his narrator in the collection: that of a learned but modest man playing
the student before his superiors, while addressing spiritual concerns superior to his listeners. While they may be his "maisteris," mediators between
himself and higher authority, none of them is his lord. Henryson has acknowledged his familiarity with the classroom use of fables, but he will take
them beyond those traditional confines. And at this point we can see another dimension of modesty informing this project: its author does not
name himself within the collection, as Lydgate did. This collection initially
presents itself as a monument to Aesop, who duly appears in the fable
central to the collection, but thereafter the narrator's attitude toward both
his project and his *auctor* change dramatically.

The Scholastic Tradition and Henryson's Aesopic Fables: Artful Arbitrariness

I have chosen to divide my discussion of Henryson's neatly structured collection into a consideration first of his Aesopic fables and then those tales
borrowed from Reynardian literature. This division will allow us to examine how this poet understood and exploited the fable commentary tradition
in relation to the fable texts with which it was used originally before we
confront his innovative use of it to comment upon beast-epic tales.

Like the elegiac Romulus's first fable, Henryson's "The Cock and the
Jasp" tells of an ignorant creature who cannot see beyond extrinsic beauty
to intrinsic value. Having found a jasper while scraping for food in the
dunghill, the cock uses rather high rhetorical style to tell the stone that it is
useless to him. He concludes:

> "Quhar suld thow mak thy habitatioun?
> Quhar suld thow duell, bot in ane royall tour?
> Quhar suld thow sit, bot on ane kingis croun
> Exalt in worschip and in grit honour?
> Rise, gentill Iasp, of all stanis the flour,
> Out of this fen, and pas quhar thow suld be;
> Thow ganis not for me, nor I for the." (106–12)

Then the narrator interjects a self-conscious first-person sentence to point
out that he intends to explain the tale's moral:

> Bot of the inward sentence and intent

Of this fabill, as myne author dois write,
I sall reheirs in rude and hamelie dite. (117–19)

Here the narrator's change of tone and person is reminiscent of the Latin fable's original *moralitas,* in which the narrator uncharacteristically addresses the cock and the jacinth, telling them what they represent (Appendix 1, p. 196). In each case, the narrator apparently wants to guide his readers through the first interpretation. Henryson's transition from fable to *moralitas* offers an implicit warning, however, in that the narrator intends to write in the low style—"rude and hamelie dite"—unlike the cock, whose high-flown rhetoric masks his foolishness.

The *moralitas* begins with a stanza about the seven properties of jasper, information obviously borrowed from a lapidary. This stanza raises questions for Henryson's modern editor, Denton Fox, who writes, "It seems very possible that [this] is a fragment which Henryson intended to cancel or rewrite. This stanza treats the jasp as a magical stone and deals exclusively with earthly things, while in the following stanzas Henryson makes the jasp into a figure of wisdom and contrasts it to 'ony eirthly thing'" (n, line 120). In spite of his uncertainty about the textual integrity of the passage, Fox goes on to cite several English lapidaries. Of course we have seen that writers had recourse to lapidaries in describing the jewel both in the scholastic tradition (BL MS Add. 11897) and in at least one vernacular adaptation— John Lydgate's.[10] Since Lydgate's fables survive in only two manuscripts, both of which are miscellanies of his poetry, we cannot assume that the tales reached a large audience; therefore, Henryson's knowledge of them seems only slightly more plausible than his knowledge of the German manuscript. Regardless of whether Henryson was acquainted with either of these texts, their very existence suggests that for medieval readers the use of natural allegory in relation to this particular fable may not have seemed as odd as it does to modern readers.

Like Evax, Henryson mentions the jewel's color in the second verse of the stanza, and he may have been elaborating upon the line "Et tutamentum portanti creditur esse" in writing the following verses:

It makis ane man stark and victorious
Preseruis als fra cacis perrillous;
Quha hes this stane sall haue gud hap to speid,
Of fyre not fallis him neidis not to dreid. (123–26)

Henryson's next stanza contrasts the properties that God has given the jasper with those that the fabulist gives it in his poetry:

This gentill iasp, richt different of hew,
Betakinnis perfite prudence and cunning,
Ornate with mony deidis of vertew,
Mair excellent than ony eirthly thing,
Quhilk makis men in honour ay to ring,
Happie, and stark to haif the victorie
Of all vicis and spirituall enemie. (127–33)

Although Fox believes that line 130, the comparison with "ony eirthly thing," describes the jasper, it is more likely that this phrase describes virtue, since the subject of the comparison leads to victory over vices. We should note, too, that a jasper ornamented with virtue would help people to triumph over vices and their "spirituall enemie"; Henryson's jewel leads to a spiritual fortitude absent from the jasper in his source text, a stone symbolic only of moral wisdom.

Here is Henryson's first variation on the relationship between fable and moral. The relationship is mediated by natural allegory, which Henryson wants his reader to consider but turn away from, just as the cock has considered but rejected the stone itself. The reader must acknowledge that the jasper is an actual stone that occurs in nature, which can be read as a book of instruction. But that book has already been written by the divine hand, so the narrator leads his "maisteris" from the literal to the figurative, the natural to the fabular.

At this point the jasper is subsumed in the allegorical interpretation until the author has described the cock:

This cok, desyrand mair the sempill corne
Than ony iasp, may till ane fule be peir,
Quhilk at science makis bot ane moik and scorne,
And na gude can; als lytill will he leir—
His hart wammillis wyse argumentis to heir,
As dois ane sow to quhome men for the nanis
In hir draf troich wald saw the precious stanis. (141–47)

The closing lines of this stanza, which Fox identifies as a reference to Matthew 7:6, "Neither cast ye your pearls before swine," also echo the *Auctores octo* commentary as adapted from the Romulus LBG. In the plot summary of the fable, that commentator initially refers to the stone not as "*iaspis*," but only as "*margarita*." In his moralization he writes, "Per margaritam (intellige) sapientem." Just as Henryson alludes to the pearl of great price but returns to the jasper at the end of his *moralitas* (155ff.), the *Auc-*

tores octo commentator changes his pearl back to a jacinth at the end of his moralization, where he gives the etymology for the word *iaspis*.[11]

In general, Latin fable commentaries called several forms of interpretation into play early in the elegiac Romulus collection, thus familiarizing readers with several avenues of interpretive pursuit, any of which might be followed in subsequent fables. In the *moralitas* of "The Cock and the Jasp," Henryson appears to follow the example of scholastic commentators by giving several kinds of interpretation to the first fable in his collection: he uses more than one type of allegory and *auctoritas*, in this case the natural (the lapidary), the social (the earthly fool), and the biblical (the allusion to the pearl before swine). What to modern readers appears a confusing variety of allegorical forms created by Henryson may have suggested to medieval readers the multiplicity of interpretive approaches brought from Latin commentary for application to the vernacular translation of fable. But Henryson shows his narrator choosing among those types of interpretation in search of the one that best suits his purposes here and in the rest of the collection, in which natural allegory does not reappear.

Henryson's fable of the city mouse and the country mouse, a lengthy adaptation of the elegiac Romulus's twelfth fable, is not as clearly indebted to scholastic commentaries as most of Henryson's other fables, perhaps because the commentaries themselves generally offer only social interpretations similar to that provided in the verse fable itself. The *Auctores octo* commentary reads the country mouse as "bonos homines spirituales, de securitate semper letos" [good spiritual men always joyful about their security], and the city mouse as "pravos homines et seculares semper gaudentes tam de illecebris quam de utilitate" [crooked secular men always rejoicing as much from enticements as from useful things]. The BL MS Add. 11897 commentator repeats this interpretation. Henryson includes only a vague echo of this reading when writing the country mouse's farewell, after the cat has interrupted dinner: this speech contains the only mention of God by either of the characters: "Almichtie God keip me fra sic ane feist" (350). In the *moralitas*, Henryson's passing mention of "sickernes (with small possessioun)" (380) reflects the commentary's use of "*securitate*" quoted above, but this is the only word implying a debt to the commentary, and its repetition may well be coincidental.

Henryson concludes his *moralitas* by citing a biblical authority:

And Solomon sayis, gif that thow will reid,
"Vnder the hevin I can not better se
Than ay be blyith and leif in honestie."
Quhairfoir I may conclude be this ressoun:

Of eirthly ioy it beiris maist degre,
Blyithnes in hart, with small possessioun. (391–96)

Although this scriptural citation itself has not been identified with any certainty, Henryson's use of Solomon as *auctor* in his moral is clearly traceable to the commentary tradition, where he is quoted repeatedly in relation to *moralitates* as the author of proverbial wisdom literature.[12] In this moral we see the beginning of the narrator's shifting perception of his audience: he tells this fable to "friendis" (line 365), not the "maisteris" whom he initially addressed. There is also a strongly personal tone as the narrator chooses for himself a "merry hart with small possessioun" (388). The effects of his "education" already begin to make themselves apparent.

After the first triad of beast-epic fables, Henryson returns to the Latin fable collection as the source for "The Sheep and the Dog," which tells of a canine who falsely accuses a sheep of being in debt to him and who bribes false witnesses to support his claim in court. Perhaps to mark the change from one kind of source to another, this fable begins with an approximate translation of the standard introduction to comments in the *Esopus moralizatus*, "Hic autor ponit aliam fabulam." Henryson writes "Esope ane taill puttis in memorie" (1146), a phrase that evokes the scholastic practice of memorization. However, Henryson's version of the narrative is less a generalized scholastic fable than a pointed satire on legal corruption, devoting as much attention to the victimized sheep as to the corrupt court proceedings. In rewriting the fable as a satirical view of legal injustice, Henryson rejects the spiritual allegory available to him in some scholastic commentaries, where the trial is allegorically recast as judgment of a human soul.[13] Instead, Henryson opts for detailed social allegory: the sheep represents "the figure / Of pure commounis" (1258–59), the wolf is likened to "ane schiref stout" (1265), and the raven represents "ane fals crownair" (1272). Here Henryson is obviously not writing a fable general enough for all times and places: these are medieval characters in late-fifteenth-century Scotland.

Among the three roles, figurative specificity shifts widely. The role of a poor common person is used quite often in fable commentaries as "*paupes*" or "*impotens*," but a definite role for a powerful person almost never appears; these remain at the general level of "*potentes*" or "*tyranni*."[14] Evidently willing to sacrifice broader applicability at the altar of satire, Henryson goes against the precedent set by scholastic commentary when he assigns the wolf and the crow specific roles within the legal system. Perhaps because of this alteration, Henryson introduces the figurative roles differently. The sheep "may present the figure / Of pure commounis" (1258–59); the use of "may" is standard for the author as he introduces allegorical roles. However, turning to the other two animals, he writes, "This volf I likkin to ane schiref stout" (1265), and "This rauin I likkin to ane fals crownair" (1272). The narrator's personal intervention here might betray Henryson's discomfort with his substantial modifications of not only his source but also standard figurative treatments of the genre as a whole; these are very much his own readings, not those of Aesop as the imagined father of fable nor those from curricular discourse.

Once the figurative identities have been established, the sheep speaks up again in the middle of the *moralitas,* an interruption that strikes the modern reader as bizarre. In spite of our expectations, this kind of direct address in the *moralitas* had been established in scholastic commentaries before Henryson's day. For example, in the "Allegoria" section of the *Auctores octo* comment on Fable 35, "De Lupo et Capite," this sentence concludes the comment: "Lupus, id est deus, ait, 'O vos decores depicti huius mundi hominis, sed heu, sine voce, id est gratia mea et regno patris mei.'" [The wolf—that is, God—says, "Oh, elegant depictions of this world of men, but alas, without voice, that is, without my grace and the power of my father."] This kind of direct address must be based on the fact that the statement is general enough to fit the wolf as well as God (or in this case, Christ); in fact, only the first half of the wolf/deity's statement strikes the appropriate level of generality.[15] In Henryson's fable of the sheep and the dog, the animal's plaint is as appropriate to poor people as to himself, to the degree that he becomes confused about his own identity: the group on whose behalf he complains is "we pure pepill" (1317).

But Henryson's changes to the scholastic model are significant, for the sheep's plaint is not a mere repetition of what he has said in the fable. There, he has presented his case formally, using legal terminology. In the *moralitas* he bemoans his unjust sentence as symptomatic of the evil in the more powerful classes of society:

"Se how this cursit syn of couetice
Exylit hes baith lufe, lawtie, and law.
Now few or nane will execute iustice,
In falt of quhome, the pure man is ouerthraw.
The veritie, suppois the iugis knaw,
Thay ar so blindit with affectioun,
But dreid, for meid, thay thoill the richt go doun.

"Seis thow not, lord, this warld ouerturnit is,
As quha wald change gude gold in leid or tyn?
The pure is peillit, the lord may do na mis,
And simonie is haldin for na syn.

> Now is he blyith with okker maist may wyn;
> Gentrice is slane, and pietie is ago.
> Allace, gude lord, quhy tholis thow it so?" (1300–13)

In effect, this declamation, which continues to the end of the *moralitas*, is as truthful and relevant to the sheep's case as his speech before the court (1187–1201), and it could certainly have found a place in the fable narrative itself. Alternatively, the lines in the *moralitas* could have been left in the voice of the narrator, and their moral import would have been much the same. However, Henryson has marginalized the plaint, making the sheep the commentator on the fable in which he appears. This structure suggests that the universe defined by the fable is too corrupt to encompass certain truths: they must be marginalized in a world that is "ouerturnit," upside down. Ironically, however, the structure gives the sheep's voice greater authority, since it inhabits the *moralitas,* where the greatest wisdom of a fable lies.

Another of Henryson's innovations here is the narrator's claim that he sees and overhears the sheep complaining:

> Bot of this Scheip, and of his cairfull cry
> I sall reheirs; for as I passit by
> Quhair that he lay, on cais I lukit doun,
> And hard him mak sair lamentatioun. (1282–85)

The narrator thus marginalizes himself with the animal and lives the moral moment with him. Although Henryson's method of bringing the fable into "real" time is very different from the one employed by Chaucer's Nun's Priest when he assigns a day and date to Russel's attack upon Chauntecleer, the result here is at least partly the same: the unfortunate sheep is historicized, with the important difference that he occupies the same time and place as the narrator himself. Once again the "generic" requirement that a fable present a narrative that could not have happened is turned on its head as the narrator claims the suffering sheep as a contemporary. But in terms of fable as a discursive mode drawn from the scholastic tradition, the meaning of Henryson's innovation is clear: the fable "speaks" directly to the narrator in a way that circumvents any mediating entity whatsoever, including Aesop. This historical coincidence shows the degree to which the narrator has become a good reader of fable: his education is now well under way.

The exclusion of truth from its proper realm remains an important theme in the framing narrative of Fable 7, "The Lion and the Mouse," in which the narrator dreams that Aesop visits him and grudgingly tells a fable. Henryson

has constructed this fable to focus on the confrontation of classical authority and vernacular appropriation that informed the transmission and translation of this mode of discourse: Henryson rewrites both Aesopic fable and
Aesop himself. The fable therefore deserves examination not only in relation to the scholastic commentary tradition that informs it but also in light
of the strategies of authoritative appropriation employed by the vernacular
poet.

The dream-vision frame in "The Lion and the Mouse" is another aspect
of Henryson's fables that has bothered modern critics, notably Dieter Mehl,
whose article "Robert Henryson's *Moral Fables* as Experiments in Didactic
Narrative" includes perceptive readings of the lessons Henryson teaches.
However, because Mehl is unfamiliar with the variety of didactic experiments in scholastic fables and commentaries, he believes that the frame
undermines the possibility of unity among Henryson's fables as a collection.
Mehl writes, "The originality of the frame makes it very unlikely that the
poet wrote the fable as part of a collection; to justify its place in the
Bassandyne-order by pointing out that it stands exactly in the centre of the
thirteen tales is tempting, but does not explain the individual character of
the tale."[16] *Pace* Mehl, the elegiac Romulus fables, undeniably a collection,
include two framing narratives, in Fable 7, "De Femina et Fure," and Fable
50, "De Patre et Filio." In both of these, a wise man faced with a social
problem (a neighborhood potentially overrun by thieves, and a wayward
son, respectively) attempts to change his listeners' behavior by telling a
relevant fable. It would be unwise to deny the possibility, then, that
Henryson could have conceived of his framed fable as one in a collection.

Furthermore, extant scholastic commentaries include at least one example of a commentator sketching a framing narrative in which Aesop
himself tells a fable, as he does in Henryson's work. The Latin collection's
twenty-first fable, "De Terra Atheniensium Petente Regem," was apparently written to incorporate two fables, though some manuscripts divide
them. The first narrative accords with the title above, and the second tells
an analogous story of frogs begging Jupiter for a ruler, only to be given first
an inert log and then a hungry hydra. The fable as a whole begins with a sort
of promythion, two lines describing why fables were first created ("Fabula
nata sequi mores et pingere vitam, / Tangit quod fugias, quodque sequaris
iter"),[17] and the lines that serve as a transition between the two sections
mention Aesop himself ("Vrbem triste iugum querula cervige gerentem /
Esopus tetigit, consona verba movens").[18] In MS II.216 of the Biblioteca
Comunale Ariostea in Ferrara, the commentator believed the two stories
were one fable, the first describing the historical situation in which Aesop

himself came forward to tell the exemplum of the unfortunate frogs (f. 84v). That an Aesop figure should tell both the Italian commentator's version of the tale and Henryson's fable of the lion and the mouse is coincidental in subject matter as well, for both narratives are concerned with the need for just government. As is the case with MS Add. 11897, the Ferrara text pre-dates Henryson's *Fabillis* by about a century, but no clear link can be drawn between it and his fables; even so, the inspiration for having Aesop tell a fable may have been available to him in another commentary.

The Middle Scots fabulist carries the idea of a framing narrative much further than any extant commentary on fable, creating a complex series of negotiations between *auctor* and vernacular poet before the fable itself is told. These negotiations highlight the issues of authority inherent in the appropriation and translation of classical texts into the vernacular, issues discussed in the broader Aesopic tradition in Chapter 2. In relation to this fable in particular, Tim William Machan has perceptively developed ideas initially sketched by A. C. Spearing,[19] who, unlike Mehl, sees the fable as central to the collection not only numerically but also thematically. Machan describes the tensions between the dreaming narrator and the dreamed Aesop: for example, although the narrator realizes immediately that the man who "come[s] throw the schaw" (1347) is worthy of respect, the nar-rator does not rise to greet him; indeed, Aesop sits down beside the narrator. He also asks the visitor to list his "birth . . . facultye, and name" (1368) in a manner that does not befit a social inferior addressing a superior elder. Furthermore, he does not acquiesce to Aesop's initial refusal to tell a fable, and the narrator's insistence carries the day.[20]

One of Henryson's most radical appropriations of Aesopic authority results from complicating the identity of Aesop by making him a Christian born in Rome and therefore deserving an authority different from that belonging to pagans. His first words to the dreamer are "God speid, my sone" (1363), a greeting that puts the narrator at his ease, and Aesop says that he dwells in heaven (1374). But Aesop's Christianity is tinged with despair, as he betrays when replying to the dreamer's request for a fable:

Schaikand his heid, he said, "My sone, lat be,
For quhat is it worth to tell ane fenʒeit taill,
Quhen haly preiching may na thing auaill?

"Now in this warld me think richt few or nane
To Goddis word that hes deuotioun;
The eir is deif, the hart is hard as stane;
Now oppin sin without correctioun,

The e inclynand to the eirth ay doun.
Sa roustit is the warld with canker blak
That now my taillis may lytill succour mak." (1388–97)

Why would Henryson have decided to make Aesop Christian? He may have extrapolated the idea from a scholastic commentary. The *accessus* of neither the *Esopus moralizatus* nor the *Auctores octo* states that Aesop was a pagan, and in the latter work, the fables appear alongside several clearly Christian works including the *Facetus, De Contemptu Mundi, Tobias,* and the *Floretus.* Although the translation of Aesop from pagan to Christian is an innovation on Henryson's part, it is only one step beyond John Lydgate's translation of fable's father from a Greek to a Roman. If in one sense Aesop's putative Christianity grants him greater authority than he would have had as a pagan writer, in another it shows Henryson mastering Aesop in a way that we have seen before: his biography as well as his textual offspring can be appropriated and revised to suit the needs of the medieval fabulist.

Aesop's Christianity lends weight to his assertion that "haly preiching" is no longer efficacious. While the narrator does not go so far as to disagree with Aesop's appraisal, he persists in requesting a fable, asking, "Quha wait nor I may leir and beir away / Sum thing thairby heirefter may auaill?" (1402–3). This vague rebuttal, highlighting the persistence of fable in memory in a manner similar to curricular texts, persuades Aesop to begin recounting the fable.

The tale of "The Lion and the Mouse" is a narrative extension of the social concerns that Aesop initially raises as a reason for telling no more fables, but the fable works at another level as well. The mutable power relations in the fable, augmented by a number of details from the verse Romulus that Henryson altered, reinscribe in its broadest outlines the dynamics of authority and appropriation that the narrator and Aesop have already delineated: the lion is a figure of the authoritative, lordly Aesop, and the mouse a figure of Henryson's narrator. The commodity that the fable characters exchange is life itself, while the commodity exchanged by Aesop and Henryson's narrator is fable, the mode of discourse that is the textual life of both the father of fable and his literary children.

It is significant that according to the captured mouse, the troop of mice took the liberty of dancing on the sleeping lion because they thought the lion was dead, not to be revived ("3e lay so still and law vpon the eird / That be my sawll we weind 3e had bene deid" [1445]). The lion responds that he deserves consummate respect, whether dead or alive, and then, in a passage dissimilar to any available source material for this fable, the lion proposes an odd hypothesis:

"I put the cace, I had bene dede or slane,
And syne my skyn bene stoppit full off stra;
Thocht thow had found my figure lyand swa,
Because it bare the prent off my persoun,
Thow suld for feir on kneis haue fallin doun." (1449–53)

The lion makes of himself a monument, a preserved image of his authoritative "persoun" whom he claims would deserve adoration even if he were dead. Thus Henryson has cleverly described the two medieval attitudes toward Aesop outlined in Chapter 2: one is the dead Aesop on a monument, worthy of respect simply for his authority, but the other is very much alive, revived by a "vile vnworthie thing" (1427).

Henryson's fable diverges sharply from the version in the elegiac Romulus, in which the innately noble lion persuades himself that he will gain no glory by killing a lowly mouse (Appendix 1, p. 202). First, Henryson's mouse begs for mercy, but the lion promises "ane schamefull end / And deith" to the mouse. Henryson then rewrites the Latin fable so that the lion's self-persuasion is transferred to the voice of the rodent, who takes six stanzas to plead her case. The persuasion is so effective that "the lyoun his language / Paissit" (1503–4) and he grants the mouse mercy. In effect, the mouse buys her life with her rhetoric, changing the authoritative nature of the lion. This series of events reflects the dialogue between Aesop and the narrator earlier: the dreamer is rebuffed at his first request for a fable from Aesop, but he persuades the *auctor* to give him what he wants.

Another major difference between the Latin and Middle Scots fables lies in the lion's rescue. In the elegiac Romulus the mouse whose life was spared returns alone to free the lion from his bonds, but Henryson has the mouse gather the entire troop of mice to help (1549–58). Through this modification Henryson signals his awareness that no one inheritor of the Aesopic tradition can keep the authority figure alive; he can only be liberated from the bonds of literary "death" through the help of a larger group of usurpers of authority, dancers upon his literary corpus.

In the final stanza of the fable we are told that the lion is free "because he had pietie" (1569), pity similar to that which Aesop has taken upon the narrator in telling him the fable that he wanted to hear. Because the *auctor* has responded to the request by telling a fable, the narrator has returned the favor by keeping the fable alive, reporting it to his readers. It is noteworthy, however, that the narrator retains control in the final stanza of the narrative, perhaps even interrupting the fabulist to ask, with notable redundancy, whether the fable has a moral (1570–71). The narrator thus shows himself a worthy inheritor of this literature.

Aesop does not allow himself any first-person interventions in his fable: as the plot unfolds he never speaks of himself or his opinions about the narrative. This absence markedly contrasts the narrator's tendency to express opinions about and comment upon the fable plots as they progress, and sometimes to place himself in them. In light of Henryson's strategies of translation and appropriation, Aesop's "depersonalized" fable is surely significant: he has no fabulist predecessor against whom he needs to define himself, so his presence in the fable is not necessary. This is a fable on which appropriating readers or retellers can bring their own interests to bear.

The *moralitas* that Aesop gives the fable is purely social, tacitly acknowledging that the fable is no sermon. The lion represents royalty, and the mouse the common people. In his closest brush with more complex allegory, Aesop makes the forest stand for "the warld and his prosperitie, / As fals plesance, myngit with cair repleit" (1582–83). In one sense this role represents only an allegorical synecdoche based on place: the part represents the whole. However, the religious connotations of "the warld and his prosperitie" give the moralization a different twist, one that is anticipated in MS Ambrosiana I. 85 supra, copied by Johannes Brixianus (that is, of Brescia) in 1415. Like Henryson's Aesop, the manuscript asserts that the lion and the mouse represent earthly figures ("homo pius" and "homo paupertas"), but the forest represents "this world" ("per silvam habemus istam mundum"); the commentator has chosen the demonstrative adjective with slightly pejorative overtones, instead of the more neutral *hic*. He and Henryson's narrator share the medieval Christian contempt for that which is purely worldly, a sentiment that teachers may have wanted to inculcate in their pupils at an early stage.

The final stanza of the fable returns us to the dream-vision, in which Aesop bids farewell to the dreamer:

> Quhen this wes said, quod Esope, "My fair child,
> Perswaid the kirkmen ythandly to pray
> That tressoun of this cuntrie be exyld,
> And iustice regne, and lordis keip thair fay
> Vnto thair souerane lord baith nycht and day."
> And with that word he vanist and I woke;
> Syne throw the schaw my iourney hamewart tuke. (1615–21)

The double entendre when Aesop, the father of fable, calls Henryson's narrator his "fair child" is largely self-explanatory: in one sense the narrator is the object of Aesop's gracious condescension, but in another, the narrator as the reteller of Aesop's fables is indeed the ur-fabulist's offspring. Perhaps

Aesop is urging his textual "child" to preach to churchmen, inasmuch as a sermon should partly be a persuasion to prayer, but again Henryson colors Aesop's message with despair; instead of exhorting the narrator to preach to the lords who are apparently close to losing faith in their leader, Aesop tells him to preach to the clergy, as if preaching to the nobility were doomed to failure. (This injunction provides further evidence that the unnamed lord in the collection's prologue is not actually an earthly one, for here we learn that such nobles are beyond the help of fable.)

The full displacement of Aesop by the dreaming narrator of this fable occurs in the final lines above: when Aesop vanishes abruptly and the narrator wakes, he takes the path by which he has seen Aesop arrive, "throw the schaw."[21] Aesop will live not only through but as this narrator. Although the Middle Scots fabulist does not challenge Aesop by naming himself in his collection (as Marie de France and Lydgate did), Henryson exercises an even greater control over the material he inherits by implying that Aesop sees his mode of discourse as exhausted, in need of revivification. Henryson's narrator must liberate fable from him, cajoling him to give up his riches. And wonder of wonders, the fabular wealth that Aesop bestows looks remarkably like what Henryson has already written: a richly amplified fable in rhyme royal. Thus, even though Aesop first gave life to Henryson as a fabulist, Henryson now determines the form and content of the existence that Aesop will have as an *auctor* in Middle Scots literature. Aesop can only be subsumed in Henryson's work, not separately glorified by it.

If the fable of the lion and the mouse questions the efficacy of preaching, that question receives a bleak answer in the following fable, "The Preaching of the Swallow." In fact, even before the plot begins, the fable seems to focus on preaching, for it opens with a sermonic meditation on God's omnipotence as evidenced by nature and the seasons. This encomium serves as a transition to the fable narrative, but at fifteen stanzas, it is much longer than necessary if Henryson, a poet capable of impressive verbal economy, were not emphasizing its homiletic aims. Thus, by the time we reach the preaching swallow himself, we see similarities between the bird and the narrator. This resemblance is strengthened by the embellishment of both the narrator's and the swallow's sermons with quotations from classical curricular *auctores:* the narrator cites Aristotle's *Metaphysics* in line 1635, and the swallow has recourse to half of one of the distichs of Cato in line 1754. Both speakers fully understand the use of scholastic commenting techniques.

A further similarity unites the narrator and the bird: like the swallow, the narrator here is fully in the fable, living through the season during which he watches as the flax is planted, nurtured, harvested, and woven into nets.[22] While Henryson does not call dates and days of the week into play as we have seen in *The Nun's Priest's Tale,* his use of "real" time through which his narratorial persona lives achieves an effect that is related to Chaucer's historicizing gesture in his fable: the story occupies the same time continuum that human beings occupy, giving it more relevance to its readers. This continuity of time and space is particularly important for the narrator, as his animal *doppelgänger* in the fable is enacting the same type of morality that he hopes to realize among his audience. But the transference of fable into "real" time yet again flies in the face of the definition of fable as a story that could not have happened: for Henryson's narratorial persona, these events actually occurred, and allegorically they continue to occur on the human level.

This structure allows Henryson an added freedom: if his narrator actually lives through these events, they acquire the authority of personal experience and no longer require the authority of the name of Aesop; significantly, that name does not appear in the fable narrative. Instead, the book that Henryson's narrator reads here is the Book of Nature, in which God's authority is paramount, even in the presence of the evil bird-catcher. Thus the fable narrative represents a fulfillment of the appropriative gestures that the narrator has understood from the previous fable, as well as a reinforcement of the Christian concerns displayed there.

In commentaries written or printed in several countries during the century before Henryson wrote, the scholastic allegories for this fable are remarkably similar to each other and to Henryson's *moralitas:* the fabulist's debt to scholastic fable commentary is far clearer than has been acknowledged. The *Esopus moralizatus* commentary as published by Heinrich Quentell in Cologne in 1489 gives the following allegorization after the summary of the fable's plot:

> Allegorice per aves intelligere possumus peccatores, per hyrundinem vero spirituales, qui sepe ammonent peccatores ut desistant et abstineant a peccatis. Sed peccatores, spirituales ammonitiones spernentes, tandem per rethia capiuntur et eterno igni traduntur. (Appendix 2, p. 211)

> [Allegorically by the birds we are able to understand sinners, by the swallow spiritual men, who often admonish sinners to desist and abstain from sins. But the sinners, spurning the admonitions of the spiritual men, are finally captured by nets and given over to eternal fire.]

This is one of only nine spiritual allegories among the sixty fable interpretations in this commentary.

The *Auctores octo* commentary printed by Jehan de Vingle in Lyon in 1495 summarizes the plot and then turns to this allegory:

Allegoria: tu debes insudare bonis operibus, ne dyabolus te seducat ab eis. Per aves intelligimus peccatores, per irundinem spirituales qui semper monent eos ut se abstineant; illi vero respuentes monitionem, venit dyabolus et rapit per rhetia, id est per opera mala et deducit eos ad infernum." (Appendix 3, p. 217)

[Allegory: you ought to sweat over your good works, lest the devil seduce you from them. By the birds we understand sinners, by the swallow spiritual men who always warn them to abstain; when those people reject the admonition, the devil comes and captures them with a net, that is with their bad works, and he leads them to hell.]

Because BL MS Add. 11897 lacks the plot paraphrases used in the printed commentaries, its allegorical interpretation includes more details of setting and plot than do the other comments. The allegorizer offers spiritual meanings for nearly every aspect of the story.

Allegoria: per yrundinem intellige spiritualem praedicatorem qui a(d)-monet certas aves, id est homines, ut evellant linum, id est peccatum maximum cordis seu cogitationis que habent se, et seminaria aliorum peccatorum de agro cordis sui, ne agricola, id est dyabolus, ex eisdem diversa rethia, id est diversas temptationes quibus solet decipere homines, faciat. Sed ipsi homines consilium predicatorum spernentes sinunt crescat linum, id est peccata ex quibus dyabolus texit rethe. Quando illa capiant illos ducendo eos in consuetudinem peccandi et tandem reddens obstinatos in peccatis et finaliter impenitentes, ducit ipsos ad penas inferni eternales. (f. 8v)

[Allegory: by the swallow, understand a spiritual preacher who admonishes certain birds, that is to say men, to tear out the flax, which is the very great sin of the heart or of thought that they have within themselves, and the nursery of other sins in the field of the heart, lest the farmer, that is to say the devil, make from them diverse nets—that is, diverse temptations by which he is accustomed to deceive men. But the men themselves, spurning the counsel of the preachers, allow the linen to grow, that is, the sins from which the devil weaves nets. When the nets capture them by leading them into the habit of sinning and then imitating obstinate people in their sins and finally being impenitent, he leads them into the eternal pains of hell.]

Although this keenly detailed allegorization may exist in only one manuscript, it actually has more in common with Henryson's *moralitas* than does either of the comments from incunables, which Henryson was far more likely to have known. This allegory appears in other commentaries as well.[23]

Following the first stanza of the *moralitas* of "The Preaching of the Swallow," in which the poet eulogizes Aesop for the "morall edificatioun" inherent in his fables, the narrator states that the tale has "ane sentence according to ressoun" (1893–4). This gratuitous statement, unique among his fables, could be the poet's acknowledgment that the scholastic allegories associated with the fable are unusually uniform. The reason for this uniformity may not be far to seek: the figure of the bird-catcher was conventionally read as symbolic of the devil,[24] the interpretation that Henryson reproduces:

> This carll and bond, of gentrice spoliate,
> Sawand this calf, this small birdis to sla,
> It is the feind, quhilk fra the angelike state,
> Exylit is, as fals apostata,
> Quhilk day and nycht weryis not for to ga,
> Sawand poysoun and mony wickit thocht
> In mannis saul, quhilk Christ full deir hes bocht. (1895–1901)

The seed sown "in mannis saul" is substantially similar to that sown in the heart of sinners, mentioned in BL MS Add. 11897. That manuscript also emphasizes "consuetudinem peccandi," vocabulary duplicated in Henryson's next stanza:

> Ressoun is blindit with affectioun,
> And carnall lust grouis full grene and gay,
> Throw consuetude hantit from day to day. (1905–7)

The narrator goes on to tell us that wicked thoughts sown by the devil grow in the minds of sinners until "the feynd plettis his nettis scharp and rude" (1911), an action that also appears in the manuscript's allegorization quoted above ("linum . . . ex quibus dyabolus texit rethe").

Henryson then gives ornamented descriptions of the birds' allegorical roles as mentioned in the commentaries:

> Thir hungrie birdis, wretchis we may call,
> Ay scraipand in this warldis vane plesance,

Greddie to gadder gudis temporall,
Quhilk as the calf ar tume without substance. (1916–19)

As in the scholastic comments, the swallow as preacher is mentioned only in passing; Henryson devotes most of his attention to the pains that sinners will suffer at the hands of the devil.

This swallow, quhilk eschaipit is the snair,
The halie preichour weill may signifie,
Exhortand folk to walk, and ay be wair
Fra nettis of our wickit enemie
Quha sleipis not, bot ever is reddie,
Quhen wretchis in this warldis calf dois scraip,
To draw his net, that thay may not eschaip. (1923–29)

The narrator writes three more stanzas of exhortation to avoid sin, the last of which begins in the first-person plural but shifts to third-person singular at the end:

Pray we theirfoir quhill we ar in this lyfe
For four thingis: the first, fra sin remufe;
The secund is to seis all weir and stryfe;
The thrid is perfite cheritie and lufe;
The feird thing is, and maist for our behufe,
That is in blis with angellis to be fallow.
And thus endis the preiching of the swallow. (1944–50)

The abrupt change of person and focus from the allegorical mode to a homiletic tone shares formal similarities with the *Auctores octo* commentary, in which no transition helps the reader from the second-person command to the third-person allegorization.

The stanza shows the narrator following the instructions of Aesop in the final stanza of the previous fable: he is persuading people to pray. In doing so, he is transformed. His voice merges with that of the swallow, a transformation emphasized by the last line, in which the bird's preaching is said to end simultaneously with the narrator's. The reader has been partially prepared for the reappearance of an animal voice in the *moralitas* by the strange renaissance of the sheep in the final verses of the fable of the sheep and the dog, where the animal supplies the moral. In addition, the conjunction of human and animal voices recalls the human-into-beast translation described in Henryson's prologue. It is therefore appropriate that he use first-person plural in addressing his audience, for he, like us, has debased his human nature through beastly sinfulness. Here, then, is another type of *moralitas* that Henryson adds to his repertoire: unlike the moral of "The Sheep and the Dog," in which the narrator overhears the complaining animal, here the moral is provided by a narrator whose voice has merged with his subject, enacting the moral lesson that it, too, has learned.

The penultimate fable in the *Morall Fabillis,* "The Wolf and the Lamb," evidently owes little to the scholastic commentary tradition. Rather, it seems to have been placed here in order to summarize the moral interests of the three previous fables from the beast-epic tradition, all of which include wolves in their casts of characters. The figurative roles of the lamb as "pure pepill" (2707) and the wolf as "false extortioneris / And oppressouris of pure men" (2711–12) reflect the Latin fable's *moralitas* as much as any scholastic commentary. Indeed, the lengthy, formally structured description of the kinds of wolves that rule in the world (2714ff.) clearly grew from the final clause of the Latin moral "Hii regnant qualibet urbe lupi" (317). In this world of contemporary political concerns, however, there is no room for classical authority: Aesop is absent from this fable.

Henryson's version of the elegiac Romulus's third tale, "De Mure et Rana," rewritten as the final Middle Scots fable "The Paddock and the Mouse," evidently has an allegorical tradition nearly as unified as that for the fable of the swallow and the flax. In both printed commentaries the commentators include not only social but also spiritual allegories. The *Esopus moralizatus,* after an elaborately embellished plot summary, gives this allegorical reading:

> Allegorice per ranam potest intelligi caro humana; per murem autem intelligitur anima que adversus carnem semper militat. Caro concupiscit adversus spiritum et spiritus adversus carnem. Caro enim nititur trahere animam ad terrena, et carnales delectationes. Anima vero resilit ad bona opera. Et istis sic ligantibus venit milvus, id est diabolus, quasi bolus in morsus duorum, scilicet corporis et anime. Virtus aliter sicut tangitur in fine littere: per ranam intelligant[ur] deceptores bonum dicentes deceptationemque intendentes; conantur enim alios decipere. Et sic quandoque cadunt in insidias quos aliis paraverunt. Sic dicitur in psalmo, "Incidit in foveam," etc. (Appendix 2, p. 207)[25]

[Allegorically, by the frog can be understood human flesh; by the mouse, however, the spirit is understood, which always fights against the flesh. The flesh always strives against the spirit and the spirit against the flesh. The flesh also exerts itself to betray the spirit to earthly things and carnal delights. The spirit leaps back toward good works. And these having been thus bound, the kite comes, that is, the devil, like a morsel in two bites, namely of the body and the spirit. Otherwise, virtue is touched upon thus at the end of the writing: by the frog are understood deceivers, saying something good and intending deception; they certainly attempt to deceive others. And thus at some time or other they fall into the snares that they have prepared for others. As is said in the Psalms, "He falls into a trap," etc.]

Here the commentator has interpreted not only the fable but also his own interpretation, by writing a situational etymology for the "diabolus," which the kite is said to represent. This is an interesting example of the displacement of the authoritative source: the commentator finds his own text rather than the authoritative fable worthy of interpretation on the verbal level.

The *Auctores octo* commentator remains more faithful to the fable plot in his summary, and he gives much the same allegory as above:

> Allegoria: per ranam intellige corpus cuiuslibet hominis, per murem animam qui nititur ad bona opera vel ad regnum dei; sed corpus retrahit eam, et sic milvus, id est diabolus, venit utrunque rumpens, scilicet corpus et animam. Fructus talis est quod non promittamus prodesse cum possimus nosmetipsos iuvare et volumus obesse. (Appendix 3, p. 214)

> [Allegory: by the frog understand the body of any man, by the mouse a soul that strives toward good works or toward the kingdom of God; but the body drags it back, and thus the kite comes, that is to say the devil, tearing both apart, namely the body and the soul. The fruit is as follows: we shouldn't promise to be useful when we are able to help ourselves and we want to injure.]

As for other fables, BL MS. Add. 11897 gives a reading similar to that in the *Auctores octo* text, but the commentator allegorizes more of the elements of the plot, thus more closely approaching Henryson's *moralitas.*

> Allegoria: per mure intelligere possumus anima que ad bonum et ad celestia regna nititur et tendit, per rana corpus hominis quod vivit in deliciis presentis seculi, per lacum vero presens seculum aut mundum, deliciis et occupacionibus variis fluctuans. Unde sic rana promiserat mure velle transducere ipsum per lacum, licet [in]tendebat dolum quia nitebatur, per hoc murem submergere. Sic corpus humanum educatum in deliciis promittit animae servitutem in istis temporalibus, in quibus non est salus nec servitas. Anima non nititur in hereditatem celestibus. Iuxta illud ratio semper deprecatur ad optima. Et ita ipsis contra se reluctantibus, secundum quod dicit apostolus, "Caro concupiscit

adversus spiritum et spiritus adversus carnem." Tandem supervenit milvus rapax, id est diabolus, qui rapit utrunque et pena cruciat eternaliter. Fructus apologi est: Ne dum promittimus prodesse intendemus ut conemur obesse, ut dum nitimur decipere alios redundat pena in nosmetipsos. (f. 3r)

[Allegory: by the mouse we are able to understand the soul that strives toward and reaches the good and the celestial kingdom, by the frog the body of a man who lives in the delights of the present age, by the lake the present age or the world, changing in varied delights and employments. Whence thus the frog assured the rat that he wanted to help lead him across the lake, namely he intended pain, because he strove by means of this to submerge the mouse. Thus the human body brought up in delights promises service to the soul in those temporal things in which there is neither health nor service. The soul does not strive toward the inheritance in the skies. In a like manner reason always prays for the best. These having striven against each other, according to what the apostle says, "The flesh strives against the spirit and the spirit against the flesh." Then a rapacious kite comes up—that is, the devil—and carries off and punishes both with pain eternally. The fruit of the apologue is: When we promise to be helpful, we should not intend to undertake to do injury, lest when we strive to deceive others, the punishment flow back on ourselves.]

Again, we see the double *moralitas*, which includes both social figuration and spiritual allegory.[26] The same spiritual allegory, though not always accompanied by the social reading, can be found in numerous manuscripts.[27]

Henryson reproduces the two-fold structure of this interpretation, placing the social reading first. This *moralitas* is formally similar to that for the fable of the two mice: each of its first three stanzas, written in the eight-line ballade form, concludes with an identical message, in this case a warning about the evils of finding oneself with a wicked companion (Middle Scots "marrow"). The second of these stanzas reads as follows:

Ane fals intent vnder ane fair pretence
Hes causit mony innocent for to de;
Grit folie is to gif over sone credence
To all that speiks fairlie vnto the;
Ane silkin toung, ane hart of crueltie,
Smytis more sore than ony schot of arrow;
Brother, gif thow be wyse, I reid the fle
To matche the with ane thrawart fenyeit marrow. (2918–25)

It is possible that the image of the painful arrow of deceit has as its source an *auctoritas* from the commentary tradition; in BL MS Add. 11897, the same image, drawn from Geoffrey of Vinsauf's *Poetria Nova,* appears in marginalia adjacent to the *moralitas* of the fable. The gloss reads "Gaufredus in Poetria: Sepe sagittantem didicit referire sagitta," a reference to line 201 of Geoffrey's work.[28] If Henryson had this marginal gloss in mind, his warning against false friends tacitly includes its own warning to the liars themselves.

After the three ballade stanzas the poet marks a shift to a different type of reading by returning to rhyme royal, the first lines of which tell us a good deal about how fables were read in Henryson's day: "This hald in mynd; rycht more I sall the tell / Quhair by thir beistis may be figurate" (2934–35). Readers are meant to keep in mind both the social interpretation that the narrator has just concluded in the ballade stanzas and the spiritual allegory that immediately follows. Henryson expects us to balance these two forms of interpretation as we read, retaining both lessons as we should when studying the *Auctores octo* and MS Add. 11897 comments above. Henryson also could have borrowed from these commentators the idea that the narrator should make a self-conscious declaration that the type of figuration is about to change; as "Fructus talis est" prepares us for a different kind of allegorical exploration, so does Henryson's couplet.

Henryson translates the first of the comments' allegorized animal roles as follows:

The paddok, usand in the flude to duell,
Is mannis bodie, swymand air and late
In to this warld, with cairis implicate:
Now hie, now law, quhylis plungit vp, quhylis doun,
Ay in perrell, and reddie for to droun. (2936–40)

"Mannis bodie" is more directly indebted to the *Auctores octo* and MS Add. 11897 commentaries, which use the phrase "corpus (cuiuslibet) hominis" rather than "caro humana" in the *Esopus moralizatus.*

On the other hand, while the basic mouse/soul allegorization could have been taken from any of these sources, the concluding portion of this description seems to reflect the *Esopus moralizatus.*

This lytill mous, heir knit thus be the schyn,
The saull of man betakin may in deid—
Bundin, and fra the bodie may not twyn,
Quhill cruell deth cum brek of lyfe the threid—
The quhilk to droun suld ever stand in dreid

Of carnall lust be the suggestioun,
Quhilk drawis ay the saull and druggis doun. (2948–54)

The final verses of this stanza are quite close to the sentence in the *Esopus moralizatus* warning that the flesh strives to drag (*"trahere"*) the soul toward earthly things and carnal delights (*"carnales delectationes"*).

While Henryson's allegorization of the water as the world is a logical extension of the roles for the mouse and the frog, it also bears a striking resemblance to the description in BL MS Add. 11897.

The watter is the warld, ay welterand
With mony wall of tribulatioun,
In quhilk the saull and bodye wer steirrand,
Standand distinyt in thair opinioun:
The spreit vpwart, the body precis doun;
The saull rycht fane wald be brocht ouer, I wis,
Out of this warld into the heuinnis blis. (2955–61)

In both the poem and the manuscript comment the water is described with a present participle denoting motion (*"fluctuans"* and "welterand") associated with the troubles which the soul will find therein ("deliciis et occupacionibus variis" and "tribulations"), and both morals mention that the mouse/soul wants to cross the water in order to reach the heavenly kingdom ("hereditatem celestibus" and "heuennis blis"), an idea which in both texts exists independently of any directly stated allegorical correlation between the opposite bank and heaven.

Henryson's allegorization of the kite as death instead of the devil seems to be his own:

The gled is deith, that cummis suddandlie
As dois ane theif, and cuttis sone the battall:
Be vigilant thairfoir and ay reddie,
For mannis lyfe is brukill and ay mortall. (2962–65)

Because of the change of roles for the kite, Henryson's fable is more hopeful than is his source; the body and soul are taken by death rather than chewed to pieces by the devil, and the poet leaves the destiny of the soul to the imagination of the reader.[29]

Henryson works with the scholastic fable tradition in much the same way that modern scholars work with critical material: sometimes adopting it wholeheartedly with very few changes, at other times rejecting it entirely, but most often simply showing that the tradition has been understood and absorbed. Furthermore, the poet/schoolmaster must have felt comfortable enough with the structure and function of fable allegory (which he had probably taught many times) to detach it completely from fable and transfer it to beast-epic episodes, as the same variety of approach characterizes the *moralitates* of the six fables examined in the next section.

The Beast-Epic Fables: Extra-curricular Translation of Scholastic Commentary

That Robert Henryson should have used Latin scholastic fable commentaries in writing morals for vernacular translations of the same fables should not surprise us, for in his prologue he tells us plainly that he is doing "ane maner of translatioun," in the loose sense in which that term was generally understood in the Middle Ages. Six fables in the compilation, however, are drawn from sources other than the scholastic fables and therefore came to him without related commentary.[30] Henryson's *moralitates* for these tales appear original, as does the very idea of interpreting such works in terms of spiritual allegory. But if Henryson constructs his own *moralitates,* he uses recognizable building materials, many of which clearly come from the scholastic fable commentary tradition.

By including the beast-epic episodes in this collection, Henryson implies that this literature had acquired a certain authority of its own, augmented by the authority given it by Chaucer in *The Nun's Priest's Tale.* In relation to the commenting practices of late medieval readers, the presence of the beast-epic episodes adds yet another dimension to the collection: they show how a lengthy narrative was divided into units short enough to be treated thoroughly using principles of the scholastic commentary tradition. Indeed, the very act of dividing a long narrative into episodes of a brevity appropriate for individual interpretation, called *divisio,* was an important step in the scholastic practices that had to be mastered by young readers.[31]

Although Henryson's third fable, "The Cock and the Fox," is indebted to Chaucer in ways that have already received ample critical attention,[32] the Middle Scots author may have decided to include it in his collection because of its presence among the fables of Marie de France. Because of its mixed background as both Aesopic fable and offshoot of the beast-epic tradition, it is placed ideally here as a transition from one kind of fable to another. Henryson's reading of the fable is based upon simple allegory, with the cock representing "nyse, proud men, woid and vaneglorious / Of kin and blude, quhilk is presumpteous" (591–92), and the fox "flatteraris with plesand wordis quhyte" (601). The passing mention of the cock's pride offers Henryson the chance to address the vice in an apostrophe which comprises a quarter of the *moralitas:*

> Fy, puft vp pryde, thow is full poysonabill!
> Quha favoris the, on force man haif ane fall;
> Thy strenth is nocht, thy stule standis vnstabill.
> Tak witnes of the feyndis infernall,
> Quhilk houndit doun wes fra that heuinlie hall
> To hellis hole and to that hiddeous hous,
> Because in pryde thay wer presumpteous. (593–99)

In scholastic commentaries we have seen biblical events associated with fable plots, and perhaps Henryson had this exegetical type of allegory in mind here: the prideful Chauntecleer's fall in a sense figures the fall of Lucifer and his proud allies. However, the relationship of Henryson's citation of the story of the "feyndis infernall" to the story of the cock and the fox is left unclear, suggesting a metonymic relationship that the reader must determine.

Fable 4, "The Fox and the Wolf," resembles the fable of the two mice in that the *moralitas* is broadly general, making no use of allegory. The fable is, in the strictest sense, an exemplum, as the narrator tells us at the beginning of the brief, three-stanza *moralitas*, just after the wolf has shot the fox:

> This suddand deith and vnprouysit end
> Of this fals tod, without contritioun,
> Exempill is exhortand folk to mend,
> For dreid of sic ane lyke conclusioun. (775–78)

Here the impulse is toward simple figuration, but Henryson does not explicitly make the comparison between fox and human.

Henryson gives a more elaborate *moralitas* to the following fable, "The Trial of the Fox," which he links to the previous one by making the main character the natural son of the murdered hero of Fable 4 (796–800). He introduces the *moralitas* with yet another statement of the poetic theory informing the fables.

> Richt as the mynour in his minorall
> Fair gold with fyre may fra the leid weill wyn,
> Richt so vnder ane fabill figurall
> Sad sentence men may seik, and efter fyne,
> As daylie dois the doctouris of deuyne,
> That to our leuing full weill can apply
> And paynt thair mater furth be poetry. (1097–1103)

Although modern readers may first tend to interpret "doctouris of deuyne" as preachers, the title actually signifies university graduates. If we read this

passage in relation to the educational system of Henryson's day, we see that
he could be referring to the teachers who interpret fables, including those
responsible for commentaries.[33] This reading is supported by the fact that in
this *moralitas* Henryson first associates the beast-epic fable with the scholastic commentary tradition of allegorization. Devoting a stanza to the figurative or allegorical role which each character plays, he creates a measured,
formal exposition of the meaning of the narrative. The first character to be
allegorized is the judge in the trial, the lion:

> The lyoun is the warld be liklynace,
> To quhome loutis baith empriour and king,
> And thinkis of this warld to get mare grace,
> And gapis daylie to get mair leuing;
> Sum for to reull, and sum to raxe and ring,
> Sum gadderis geir, sum gold, sum vther gude;
> To wyn this warld, sum wirkis as thay wer wod. (1104–10)

The lion's allegorical role as the world alone recalls the phrase "delectatio
huius mundi," which is one of the most common allegorical roles in the
Auctores octo commentary and BL MS Add. 11897.[34] This corresponds to
the rather pejorative sense in which the concept is interpreted in this stanza.
By giving this role to the lion, Henryson immediately defines the fable society as rotten, for if this character is considered by those in the fable world
to be the greatest among them, their judgment is weak.

   In contrast to the lion is the virtuous mare:

> The meir is men of contemplatioun,
> Off pennance walkand in this wildernes,
> As monkis and othir men of religioun
> That presis God to pleis in euerilk place,
> Abstractit from this warldis wretchitnes. (1111–15)

This description belongs to the category of allegory with religious roles,
which features prominently in nearly all scholastic commentaries.[35]

   The comparison of the wolf to sensuality in the following stanza could
have its roots in scholastic commentary as well. In the BL MS Add. 11897
allegorization of the widow of Ephesus, for example, the body of the husband is said to represent "sensualitatem eius" (f. 20r). However, Henryson
describes the conflict between the wolf and the mare in more traditional
terms, relying on the age-old battle between sensuality and "ressoun"
(1124). The hoof with which the mare knocks out the wolf is described as
follows:

Hir hufe I likkin to the thocht of deid:
Will thow remember, man, that thou man de,
Thow may brek sensualiteis heid;
And fleschlie lust away fra the sall fle.
Fra thow begin thy mynd to mortifie,
Salomonis saying thow may persaif heirin,
"Think on thy end; thow sall not glaidlie sin." (1125–31)

Aside from the reference to Solomon, a commonplace of scholastic interpretation, Henryson uses a pattern of allegorization that could have come from similar sources. In the fable commentaries the end of life and concurrent confrontation with death shock characters into action or cause them to seek to better themselves. Two examples from the *Auctores octo* commentary will suffice. In Fable 29, the hares, who represent men, are frightened out of the forest by a noise, representing the end of life. This allegorization is related to the need for doing penance. Similarly, in Fable 48, the vain stag, allegorized as a prideful person, is at the spring, allegorized as "extremitate vite sue," when he discovers the beauty of his own horns, representing demons. BL MS Add. 11897 also uses temptation as an allegorical role in the same way that Henryson applies it to the fox. In the fable of the stag and the spring, the dogs that chase the animal are allegorized as "diversas temptationes" (f. 24r); both the dogs and the fox ultimately bring about the death of other characters. Henryson elaborates upon the role to the point that he returns the reader to contemplation of virtue before the final stanza, a prayer to Mary that, at the end of the five stanzas giving allegorical roles, balances the stanza at the beginning of the *moralitas*.

Henryson has structured the first three beast-epic fables as if to accustom his original readers gradually to the moralized aspect that he adds to them. The first two *moralitates* employ the simplest type of allegory, as if Henryson feels obliged to prove that a beast-epic episode can function as a relatively unadorned Aesopic fable. Only in the third beast-epic fable does the author move beyond simple allegory into the greater complexities available to him through scholastic commentary.

Following the central triad of Aesopic fables, Henryson places "The Fox, the Wolf, and the Cadger," a tale in which a fox successfully tricks an itinerant fishmonger out of all of his herring, but a wolf who has befriended the fox nearly loses his life while trying to win the man's "nekhering," which the wolf believes to be an even greater fish. (Denton Fox states that this obscure term means "a blow on the neck"; n, line 2089.) In trying to steal this exotic fish, the wolf is nearly beaten to death by the cadger, and the fox gets all the booty.

Henryson dispenses allegorical roles hastily in the first stanza of the *moralitas:*

> This taill is myngit with moralitie,
> As I sall schaw sumquhat, or that I ceis.
> The foxe vnto the warld may likkinit be;
> The reuand wolf vnto ane man, but leis;
> The cadgear, deith, quhome vnder all man preis—
> That euer tuke lyfe throw cours of kynd man dee,
> As man, and beist, and fische in to the see. (2203–9)

Although these roles were all part of the discourse of scholastic allegory that Henryson used in fables discussed earlier in this chapter, here the poet has chosen to reveal the allegorical roles by means of a structure more scholastic than poetic. In the previous beast-epic fable, Henryson gives each role a rather formal presentation in a full rhyme royal stanza (1104–38), but here he follows the example of scholastic commentaries by listing the roles and then retelling the story according to them. The poet assigns the only remaining role in the middle of the allegorized narrative.

> The warld, ʒe wait, is stewart to the man,
> Quhilk makis man to haif na mynd of deid,
> Bot settis for winning all the craftis thay can.
> The hering I likkin vnto the gold sa reid,
> Quhilk gart the wolf in perrel put his heid—
> Richt swa the gold garris landis and cieteis
> With weir be waistit daylie, as men seis.
>
> And as the foxe with dissimulance and gyle
> Gart the wolf wene to haif worschip for euer,
> Richt swa this warld with vane glore for ane quhyle
> Flatteris with folk, as thay suld failʒe neuer;
> ʒit suddandlie men seis it oft disseuer
> With tham that trowis oft to fil the sek—
> Deith cummis behin and nippis thame be the nek. (2210–23)

This type of retelling, with a list of allegorical roles followed by quick shifts back and forth between narrative and allegory, is typical of the style used in allegorical comments, but Henryson renders it more poetic through the use of simile rather than the grammatically disjunctive "id est" construction favored by the commentators.

The allegorical version of the fable is finally reduced to a warning about avarice:

The micht of gold makis mony men sa blind,
That settis on auarice thair felicitie,
That thay for3et the cadgear cummis behind
To stryke thame, of quhaat stait sa euer thay be:
Quhat is mair dirk than blind prosperitie?
Quhairfoir I counsell mychtie men to haif mynd
Of the nekhering, interpreit in this kynd. (2224–30)

Appropriately ambiguous, the final couplet of this stanza both serves as a *memento mori* and raises the problem of interpretation of worldly signs by focusing on the word "nekhering." The cadger has misinterpreted the fox's play-acting as death, and the wolf has misinterpreted the strange word as a fish, though they both know of the fox's lying nature. Henryson keeps his readers from falling victim to the same type of misinterpretation; they should see the end of life interpreted according to Christian ideology instead of attending to worldly concerns and forgetting their mortality.

The wolf is duped yet again in the next fable, "The Fox, the Wolf, and the Husbandman," a tale that Denton Fox traces to the *Disciplina clericalis* of Petrus Alfonsi and the *Roman de Renart*. The fable tells of a husbandman who grows so impatient with his team of young, ill-disciplined oxen that he finally shouts at them, "The volff . . . mot haue you al at anis!" (2244). A wolf, skulking with a fox in the woods nearby, hears the farmer's oath and asks him to keep his word. The husbandman asks whether the wolf has any witnesses to support the claim that the oxen should be handed over, at which point Lowrence the fox comes forth. When the disputants have agreed to abide by his judgment, he holds a brief conference with each of them. He makes the farmer promise to hand over a hen if the wolf can be persuaded to forsake his claim; the farmer agrees to hand over "sex or sevin / Richt off the fattest hennis off all the floik" (2326–27). Satisfied with the offer, the fox tells the wolf that the farmer wants to settle the claim by giving the wolf an enormous cheese weighing more than a stone. The wolf demands to see the cheese before making a decision, so the animals set off together and walk until nightfall. They arrive at a well, into which the fox asks the wolf to look; there he sees the reflection of the moon, which the fox says is the cheese. Of course when the wolf has descended into the well to get it, the fox leaves him there. As in the previous fable, the wolf's mistake is misinterpretation, though in this case he misinterprets not artificial signs but natural ones. His greed, also a central problem in the previous fable, leads him to mistake the reflection for food. As we shall see, the wolf's weak interpretive abilities continue in the next fable.

Henryson gives no overall social reading for this fable but opens his moral with social allegory that develops into spiritual allegory. He writes:

This wolf I likkin to ane wickit man
Quhilk dois the pure oppres in everie place,
And pykis at thame all the querrellis that he can,
Be rigour, reif, and vther wickitnes. (2427–30)

Beyond labeling the wolf a wicked man, this passage seems to offer little to elucidate the fable, since the narrative includes no real mention of the husbandman's poverty—and in fact, if he has a team of oxen, a plow, and a flock of chickens from which he can happily spare six or seven, he is hardly destitute. The description of the wolf who picks quarrels with and oppresses the poor is more likely to have been borrowed from scholastic commentary on the second fable in the elegiac Romulus, "The Wolf and the Lamb." In the *Esopus moralizatus,* the promyth introducing the plot summary states, "mali tyranni potentes de facili inveniunt causam nocendi pauperibus et impotentibus" (Appendix 2, p. 206) [evil, powerful tyrants easily light upon a cause for harming the poor and the powerless]. This lesson is rather different from that in the Latin fable, which focuses upon the lamb's innocence instead of its poverty. Like the *Esopus moralizatus,* BL MS Add. 11897 also summarizes the fable with an emphasis on the oppression of the poor rather than the innocent.

The reason for the wolf's slightly misaligned role in this fable is quite obvious: the next two tales in the *Morall Fabillis* involve evil wolves, and the second of these is "The Wolf and the Lamb," the moral of which tells us yet again that the wolf represents "fals extortioneris / And oppressouris of pure men" (2711–12). By giving the wolf's role this unusual slant and by ordering his fables as he did, Henryson makes a figurative role serve three fables at once: the one to which it is directly (though loosely) applied and the two which it precedes. This repetition gives cohesion to the *Morall Fabillis* as a collection and adds yet another type of structural variation to the compilation.

The description of the fox as the devil is too general to indicate any one comment as its source.

The foxe, the Feind I call into this cais,
Arctand ilk man to ryn vnrychteous rinkis,
Thinkand thairthrow to lok him in his linkis. (2431–33)

Although numerous comments allegorize foxes as devils (and Henryson would have been aware of this association from the *Esopus moralizatus* and the *Auctores octo*), scholastic allegory is too rich to allow any animal to become completely typecast; if the fox plays the devil in commentaries more often than certain other animals, it is simply because his most common fable role is that of villain. More helpful than the number of fox/devils in commentaries is the number of devils generally: in allegorizing the elegiac Romulus's sixty fables, the *Esopus moralizatus* finds six devils, the *Auctores octo* sixteen, and BL MS. Add. 11897 twenty-seven—or one in almost every other fable! The devils' ranks grow steadily over the two centuries during which these commentaries were written, showing the increasing interest in spiritual allegory. That concern was dominant by Henryson's day.

The husbandman in the fable acquires no new role in the *moralitas;* he is simply figurative of "ane godlie man" tempted by the devil. The hens, on the other hand, are given allegorical significance, insignificant though they are in the narrative. Henryson writes, "The hennis ar warkis that fra ferme faith proceidis" (2437). This kind of allegorization, part and parcel of the scholastic commentary tradition, has earned Robert Henryson the condescension of several generations of critics; one of the most recent, Stephan Khinoy, writes of this fable, "This is a case in which we smile at both the tale and the moral: the tale for its comic realism and inventiveness, the moral for its homely ingenuity (hens as good works, indeed!)"[36] I. W. A. Jamieson was so mystified by this allegorical correspondence that he did Henryson the disservice of suggesting to Douglas Gray that the choice of this role might represent a Protestant revision of Henryson's work.[37] But not only was the choice of allegorical role for the chickens ultimately Henryson's own; also, the "homely ingenuity" of this particular allegorical role belonged to the commentators. In the *Auctores octo* commentary characters in five fables are allegorized as "bona opera," and in BL MS. Add. 11897 six fables (four of these the same ones as in the *Auctores octo*) feature this role. In the fable of the fox and the eagle, for example, the eagle wants to feed the fox's cubs to her brood, but the fox wins them back; the eagle represents the devil, the fox a person, and the cubs that person's good works (BL MS. Add. 11897 f. 6r). Similarly, in the fable of the wolf who offers to help a sow in labor to deliver her piglets so that he can eat them, the wolf is the devil, the sow is a person, and the piglets are good works. In five of the seven examples of this kind of interpretation, what is allegorized as good works is a group of objects or animals, similar to the group of hens in Henryson's fable.[38]

Henryson also includes this allegory: "The woddis waist, quhairin wes the wolf wyld, / Ar wickit riches, quhilk all men gaipis to get (2441–42). This allegorical role is almost as generalized as that of the fox, so any single source would be difficult to locate. The commentaries contain several allegories which include "*voluptatibus*," "*delectationes*," or "*temporalia*," all of which can imply riches; however, the commentators leave these concepts vague and unexploited, unlike Henryson, who devotes an entire stanza to details about how riches trick and ensnare people.

The final stanza of the *moralitas* allegorizes something that does not actually exist in the fable: the cheese. Henryson constructs an interpretation based on the falseness and emptiness of the vice:

> The cabok may be callit couetyce,
> Quhilk blomis braid in mony mannis ee:
> Wa worth the well of that wickit vyce,
> For it is all bot fraud and fantasie,
> Dryuand ilk man to leip in the buttrie
> That dounwart drawis vnto the pane of hell—
> Christ keip all Christianis from that wickit well! (2448–54)

The practice of allegorizing objects or characters as vices or virtues was quite common. We have already seen the jasper allegorized as wisdom, and other virtues deployed in the *Auctores octo* and BL MS Add. 11897 commentaries include "*prudentia*," "*humilitas*," and "*fides*." However, in these commentaries the vices are far more popular than the virtues, and the greatest of these is "*superbia*," which appears three times in the *Auctores octo* and twice in BL MS Add. 11897.[39] But if these interpretations offer a possible source for this kind of allegory, they are certainly not the only such source, since the allegorization of vices and virtues, which achieved notoriety in Prudentius's *Psychomachia*, provided the foundation for allegorical discourse in the Middle Ages.

Continuing with allegorizing that which is not, in lines 2451–53 Henryson creates a metaphorical link between the nonexistent buttery, in which the unreal cheese is stored, and hell. Greed and gluttony are the first steps toward the inferno, the poet tells us, but in the closing couplet he leaves the allegorical parallel between hell and the well at a metaphorical level, strengthened by rhyme. This metaphor also serves to break the pattern of direct allegorical correspondence, preparing us for the next fable.

In Fable 11, "The Wolf and the Wether," a thieving wolf is so frightened by a sheep dressed in a dog skin that he befouls himself. However, the disguise having been discovered, the wolf exacts predictably murderous revenge on the sheep. Here we return to a homiletic tone with only the role of the dog's borrowed skin receiving a metaphorical interpretation. We are warned against "riches of array" that make poor people appear "presumpteous" (2595, 2596). This metaphor has significance only when placed alongside the larger metaphor of the natural order as a reflection of the social order, the comparison to which Henryson turns at the end of the fable.

> Thairfoir I counsell men of euerilk stait
> To knawe thame self, and quhome thay suld forbeir,
> And fall not with thair better in debait,
> Suppois thay be als galland in thair geir:
> It settis na seruand for to vphald weir,
> Nor clym sa hie quhill he fall of the ledder:
> Bot think vpon the wolf and on the wedder. (2609–15)

If the wolf is on Fortune's wheel in Fables 9, 10, 11, and 12, then this *moralitas* marks the beginning of his ascent, even though he is guilty of the same shortcoming, misinterpretation. Following his misinterpretation of word and nature, now he misinterprets appearance. However, he suffers only wounded pride, while the sheep must suffer violent death. In Henryson's hierarchy of sins, social climbing is apparently more serious than gullibility.

Again we are confronted by a *moralitas* as suitable for the next fable as for this one. The lamb in Fable 12 takes on his natural/social superior the wolf in the riverside debate, and the result is predictable.

Because Henryson has chosen to place the non-Aesopic material of beast epic in a collection that is primarily Aesopic, we should consider how he positions himself in these narratives in relation to the father of fable. It is noteworthy that in the first three beast-epic fables, the narrator does not mention Aesop at all; rather, he subjects these non-Aesopic neo-fables to scholastic commenting practices, effectively demonstrating that the texts can acquire a respectable veneer of moral didacticism. The narrator's encounter with Aesop in the dream-vision at the center of the collection and his subsequent appropriative gestures in "The Preaching of the Swallow" seem to give him greater confidence in relation to the second trio of beast-epic fables, for he attributes all of them to a greater authority. In "The Fox, the Wolf, and the Cadger," the narrator credits his story to "myne Author" (1952), whom the reader naturally assumes to be Aesop even if Henryson meant to allude to a beast-epic writer. "The Fox, the Wolf, and the Husbandman" begins, "In elderis dayis, as Esope can declair / Their wes ane husband" (2231–32); should the audience read this introduction as implying that Aesop could have told this fable, even if he did not? Similar lines introduce "The Wolf and the Wether": "Qwhylum thair wes, as Esope can report, / Ane scheipheird" (2455–56), but if they appear somewhat ambiguous about the tale's authorship, the first lines of the fable's *moralitas* do not:

> Esope, that poet, first father of this fabill,
> Wrait this parabole, quhilk is couenient,
> Because the sentence wes fructuous and agreabill,
> In moralitie exemplatiue prudent . . . (2588–91)

Henryson's iteration of "this fabill" and "this parabole" leaves little doubt that he intends for "The Wolf and the Wether" to be considered Aesopic.

Progressing from silence about the provenance of the first beast-epic fables to increasing confidence in attributing the second group to Aesop, Henryson's narrator demonstrates the power that comes with the appropriation of a textual tradition. If the narrator can adopt the voice and the authority of Aesop after "The Lion and the Mouse," then he can certainly contribute to the corpus of Aesopic literature; this is simply the next logical step in literary appropriation.

In the collection as a whole, Henryson astutely counterbalances his narrator's increasing authority in relation to Aesop with a declining authority in relation to his audience. As mentioned above, Henryson constructs his narrator at the beginning of his collection as inexperienced and sophomoric, addressing his "maisteris," and his audience seems to remain sizeable through "The Preaching of the Swallow."[40] There Henryson lays for him the Cassandrian trap of having an audience but no real listeners. Thereafter, the narrator narrows his sights to an audience of one, a companion rather than a congregation, whom he mentions in the moral of Fable 11, "The Wolf and the Wether," as "thow" (2595).[41] The narrator and his diminished audience are apparently the homiletic "we" to whom the moral of the next fable is addressed, for the audience of one remains in "The Paddock and the Mouse," where the narrator directs the moral only to "my brother" (2910), whom he addresses consistently with second-person singular pronouns "thow" and "the." At the end of this epimyth, the narrator strips himself of any remaining authority by telling his listener-reader that he will not complete the translation that he has undertaken:

> Adew, my freind, and gif that ony speiris
> Of this fabill, sa schortlie I conclude,
> Say thow, I left the laif vnto the freiris,
> To mak a sample or similitude. (2969–72)

At the end of the collection Henryson's narrator no longer tells fables for his "maisteris"; he has been educated beyond their classroom concerns. As a part of that education, he has learned from no less a personage than Aesop himself that fables lack efficacy when holy preaching can attract no followers; the narrator ultimately internalizes this lesson, too, and leaves the remaining fables not to denizens of the classroom like the "maisteris" whom he initially addresses, but to the preaching friars. Whether the narrator is satirizing the exemplum-loving friars is unclear,[42] but I think that Henryson most likely wanted to leave the tone of the bequest neutral in order to imply that the friars should accomplish as much with fable as they can, if this mode of discourse will make preaching more palatable than it has been in recent times. Regardless of the tone here, Henryson's narrator, like Aesop, has reached a point of exhaustion and perhaps frustration with his project.

Henryson's narrator has literally made his way through fable literature, experiencing it as neither the Nun's Priest nor Lydgate's trepidatious narrator has. His education leaves him a sadder and a wiser man, like the Aesop whom Henryson constructs, and if we carry this education to its logical conclusion, it must lead him to a level at which he will finish studying fable and turn away from it to other more advanced texts. Indeed, in a line that has received little critical attention, Henryson wrote that Aesop wrote "The Preaching of the Swallow" (and by extension, all of his fable) "[q]uhen that he waikit from mair autentik werk" (1890)—when he had free time from more authoritative work. This line could represent Henryson's allusion to the legendary Aesop's diplomatic career, in which fable featured only as a means to an end. But just as the father of fabular discourse engaged in more valuable types of work than fable telling, the narrator must progress to other types of work in which wisdom can be not only textualized but enacted.

In sum, Henryson exploits a remarkable range of scholastic practices in the *Morall Fabillis*. Among the most significant of these is the variety of relationships that he creates between the narratives and their morals—from straightforwardly social to deeply spiritual, from entirely imagined to fully experienced. He also explores the gamut of types of interpretation discussed in Chapter 3, and he brings that variety of reading to bear with a variety of degrees of specificity, from rather general moralizing that only partially reflects the complexity of the fable text to highly specific allegories that leave no aspect of the fable plot uninterpreted. Within the allegorical *moralitates*, Henryson's choices for the roles assigned to the characters of both the beast-epic tales and the Aesopic fables were largely but not entirely determined by what he had learned from the scholastic commentaries on the elegiac Romulus fables. While his debt to this source extends to the very roles in the allegories in at least two fables, he owes even more to fable commentary for the rhetorical constructs and discursive conventions that he employs in some of his *moralitates,* constructs and conventions that he transfers successfully to beast epic. To this spectrum of signification Henryson added another dimension to the complexity of his collection by using not only details of plot but also general (if sometimes slightly skewed) *moralitates* to link fables together. Thus some fables provide intertextual commentary on others.

By examining the elements of the *Morall Fabillis* that educated fifteenth- and sixteenth-century readers would have viewed as traditional but that we as modern readers find unsettling, we can begin to dispense with modern scholars' prejudices that Henryson was to some degree delighting in being perverse. Simultaneously we can begin to appreciate him both for making full use of the variety inherent in the scholastic fable tradition and for embellishing it in ways that would have had resonance for many of his original readers.

Afterword

Toward the Renaissance, Beyond Latin Curricular Fable

Having considered the fables of Chaucer, Lydgate, and Henryson as off-spring of the scholastic fable tradition, I would like to close this book by briefly comparing them to one another as translations, in the loose medieval senses of that term. Lydgate and Henryson both acknowledge in their prologues that their collections are translations, and although Chaucer's Nun's Priest does not, any reader of *The Canterbury Tales* who was familiar with Aesop would have seen the tale as a fable related to the classical tradition that he fathered.

In *Rhetoric, Hermeneutics, and Translation in the Middle Ages,* Rita Copeland has discussed the integral role that scholastic commentary plays in the medieval translation process. Differentiating between types of literary translations, Copeland posits two helpful categories that link the act of translation to scholastic practices:

> [P]rimary translation and secondary translation . . . denot[e] the degree to which the translation identifies itself with the exegetical practice of the schools, which is the "primary" point of departure for translation as a form of academic discourse. Primary translations . . . exhibit a close alliance with the aims and methods of exegetical practice, and like exegesis define their purpose in terms of service to a source text. Secondary translations . . . derive their essential methods and motive from exegesis, but stand in a "secondary" relationship to the exegetical tradition of the schools: they do not define themselves through exegetical methods of service or supplementation, but rather through rhetorical models of invention, that is, discovery of one's own argument or subject out of available topics or commonplaces.[1]

As a whole, the fable translation projects that I have examined here problematize these categories, for nearly every educated medieval reader had, at some point in his education, undertaken a primary translation of the elegiac Romulus under the eye of an authoritative schoolmaster who kept reading and interpretation within institutionally recognized boundaries. Such translating activity is inscribed in the Romulus epistle that commonly introduces this collection, practically demanding that a translator exercise imperious control over the text. For vernacular fabulists, there must have been little motivation to produce primary translations in the vernacular, because such work was the activity of children, artless though it must have been.

However, the very fact that curricular fable was a text that many readers had mastered in primary translations became part of the rhetorical invention in secondary translation: previous use becomes subject matter, uniting a community of educated readers. Henryson's narrator addresses just such a community of "maisteris," and both he and Lydgate allude to the scholastic practice of memorization. While the influence of scholastic practice on the structure of Chaucer's *Nun's Priest's Tale* is less immediately apparent, it has long been acknowledged that reading and interpretation are central to the subject matter of the tale. All of the fables are littered with the rhetorical markers of scholastic discourse—the conventional catchwords and phrases that signal scholastic readings in progress.

Lydgate's *Isope's Fabules,* in which the poet's narratorial persona says of Aesop that he will "folow þys poete / And hys fables in Englyssh . . . translate" (29–30), would superficially seem the vernacular collection that is most respectful of the textual tradition from which it is drawn: the author constantly pays verbal obeisance to his author, and he borrows from related scholastic commenting traditions both liberally and unimaginatively. However, he makes clear almost immediately that he is not creating a monument to Aesop when he inverts the moral of the well-known fable "The Cock and the Jacinth," a displacement legitimated by scholastic practice. Furthermore, the revision of the fables in order to highlight issues of law, tyranny, and "suffisaunce" represents the narrator's own interests. Here the fabulist positions himself in a predictable way in relation to his source: he praises its authority and acknowledges its historical importance, but he undermines it nevertheless.

Henryson's collection may include both types of translation: the two fables most clearly allied with scholastic exegesis, "The Preaching of the Swallow" and "The Paddock and the Mouse," might be considered primary translations in Copeland's paradigm, for Henryson not only cites the authoritative source for the fables but he also employs the authoritative commentary with which they were conventionally associated. Interestingly, both of these fables appear in the second half of his collection, after he has established himself in rhetorical territory that is independent of his source text. Of course Henryson does not conceal the source for the Aesopic fables, and he employs some of the tools of exegesis in the fables' *moralitates,* but the fables basically serve his social vision rather than the source text. The other half of Henryson's project, in which he borrows "fables" from a non-curricular tradition and imbues them with scholastic discourse, moves beyond Copeland's categories. If in one sense Henryson honors Aesop by expanding the corpus of his work, in another he undermines his authority by dressing these beast-epic crows in academic peacock feathers. This is surely an even greater challenge to Aesopic authority than Lydgate's inversion of the elegiac Romulus's first fable.

Ostensibly, Chaucer's *Nun's Priest's Tale* does not fit Copeland's categories at all, for its roots are not in school texts. However, it "exhibit[s] a close alliance with the aims and methods of exegetical practice," even if that alliance takes the form of parody. Even so, Chaucer concealed his debt to any preceding textual authority—even to the spirit of Aesop—just as he "concealed" the identity and interests of the tale's narrator. The fable's humorous reversal of "primary translation" practices relates to Copeland's other category, for in this case those scholastic practices become the "argument or subject [from] available topics or commonplaces" that is integral to Chaucer's project of rhetorical invention.

What I hope to indicate here is that these three medieval authors seem to have innately understood the categories that Copeland posits, because each of them used the transgression of the boundary between the categories as an integral part of his poetic invention. Chaucer blurs the distinction for the effect of humor, overloading his text with interpretive markers that ultimately leave the reader wondering which signs to follow. For Lydgate, the transgression seems to have been undertaken largely for moral or ethical reasons: he wants to imbue his fables with a situational inevitability that will occlude their original concerns. Henryson enacts the transgression as a part of the educational process: we see his narrator literally grow through and then out of the fables as they become part of his history.

In sum, fable as a mode of discourse for these vernacular authors asked to be situated in a rhetorical context that it had already occupied for each of them earlier in life: the context defined by scholastic practice. For each of these authors, that context commanded a different degree of authority, just as Aesop did, and each author succeeded in showing that he had learned his lessons fully enough to extend those practices beyond the world of the grammar school.

Henryson's *Morall Fabillis* represents both the zenith and the culmination of fable collections in any language in medieval Britain. His half-Reynardian project presents a tacit challenge to the curricular Latin Aesopic corpus, but ultimately it did less to supplant its source than did Steinhöwel's *Aesop,* the encyclopedic compilation that had been printed by Johann Zainer in Ulm in 1476–77 and reprinted; discussed in Chapter 2, this compilation, prefaced by the *Life of Aesop,* included most of the elegiac Romulus, Greek fables translated by Rinuccio d'Arezzo, the fables of Avianus, the *Disciplina Clericalis* of Petrus Alphonsus, and tales from Poggio Bracciolini's *Facetiae.*[2] As discussed above, this translated compilation was one of the most popular incunables in every European language in which it appeared. Even if Henryson did not use the English translation of this collection, Caxton's *Aesop,* as one of his sources,[3] it is noteworthy that the collection's concatenation of both Aesopic and patently non-Aesopic Latin "fables" embodies an impulse identical to Henryson's: the expansion of the authoritative Aesopic corpus with new, patently non-Aesopic material. The compilation represented the final moment of widespread popularity for the elegiac Romulus fables, which subsequently—and perhaps even consequently—disappeared from the European curriculum.

But the authority of the elegiac Romulus as the curricular Aesop ultimately received its strongest challenge not from any late medieval translation but from a competitor out of its own history. Greek reached the curriculum in most European countries by the mid-fifteenth century, after having taken root in Italy, where the earliest of the so-called Renaissance educators, Peter Paul Vergerius, began learning Greek at the age of fifty in Florence in 1397.[4] Later, a student at Padua, Vittorino da Feltre (b. 1378), came under Vergerius's influence and became one of the most important early teachers of Greek; under his tutelage students translated from Greek to Latin such works as the *Lives* of Plutarch, as well as the *Vita Aesopi.*[5] In 1422 educational reformer Battista Guarino set as an assignment for the twelve-year-old Ermolao Barbaro the translation of Greek Aesopic fables to Latin; the result of his labors survives in a single manuscript in the British Library, a unique document that should lead us to wonder how many similar translations did not survive. Within forty years, Greek had reached the cultural backwater of England: in 1465 Thomas Chandler, the Warden of New College, Oxford, introduced Greek lectures by the Italian Cornelio Vitelli, and William Grocyn became the first English teacher of Greek at Oxford in 1491.[6]

With the spread of Greek came the spread of the Greek Aesopic fables and the consequent diminution of interest in the obviously inauthentic Latin ones. The Greek fables required new scholastic approaches, for those used in medieval education in Latin largely grew out of Roman rhetorical practice,[7] which entailed methodologies that would have been inappropriate if retroactively applied to earlier Greek texts. Even so, the different language, new interpretive strategies, and changing views of the figure of Aesop himself did nothing to lessen the popularity of fable as classroom text, a role which it consistently played for centuries beyond the Middle Ages.

Appendix 1

Selected Fables from the Elegiac Romulus

Below are the fables translated by John Lydgate in *Isopes Fabules* and Robert Henryson in *Morall Fabillis*, along with my English translations. I have taken the fable texts from Léopold Hervieux, ed., *Les Fabulistes Latins depuis le siècle d'Auguste jusqu'à la fin du moyen âge* (Paris: Firmin Didot, 1883–94; reprint, New York: Burt Franklin, 1960), vol. 2, 316–25.

Prologue

Vt iuvet, ut prosit, conatur pagina presens:
    Dulcius arrident seria picta iocis.
Ortulus iste parit fructum cum flore, fauorem
    Flos et fructus emunt; hic nitet, ille sapit.
Si fructus plus flore placet, fructum lege; si flos
    Plus fructu, florem; si duo, carpe duo.
Ne mihi torpentem, sopiret inertia sensum,
    In quo peruigilet, mens mea mouit opus.
Vt messis pretium de uili surgat agello,
    Verbula sicca, Deus, complue rore tuo.

Verborum leuitas morum fert pondus honestum,
    Vt nucleum celat arida testa bonum.

    In order to please, in order to profit, the present work is attempted; serious matters embellished with humor please more sweetly. This little garden produces fruit along with flower; flower and fruit win favor; the flower is bright, the fruit has flavor. If fruit pleases more than flower, pick the fruit; if flower more than fruit, pick the flower; if both, pluck both. My mind begins a work at which it toils late into the night, lest inertia put the torpid senses to sleep. So that a harvest's reward may arise from a lowly little field, moisten with your dew, Lord, my dry words.
    The levity of words bears the honorable weight of morals, as a dry shell conceals a good kernel.

I. *De Gallo et Jaspide*

Dum rigido fodit ore fimum, dum queritat escam,
  Dum stupet inuenta iaspide Gallus, ait:
Res uili pretiosa loco, natique decoris,
  Hac in sorde manens, nil michi messis habes.
Si tibi nunc esset, qui debuit esse, repertor.
  Quem limus sepelit, uiueret arte nitor.
Nec tibi conuenio, nec tu mihi; nec tibi prosum,
  Nec mihi tu prodes; plus amo cara minus.

Tu Gallo stolidum, tu iaspide pulcra sophye
  Dona notes; stolido nil sapit ista seges.

The Cock and the Jacinth

While he digs in the dung with his stiff beak, while he seeks food,
when he is astounded at having come upon a jacinth, the rooster says,
"O precious thing in a vile place, endowed with natural beauty but
lying in filth, you have no harvest for me. If you now had a discoverer
as you ought to have had, the brilliance that slime has buried would
live through art. I am not fit for you, nor you for me; neither are you
useful to me, nor am I useful to you. I love more those things which are
less dear."

You, Cock, represent a stupid person; you, Jacinth, represent the
beautiful gifts of wisdom; that crop tastes of nothing to the stupid person.

II. *De Lupo et Agno*

Est Lupus, est Agnus: sitit hic, sitit ille; fluentum,
  Limite non uno, querit uterque siti.
In summo bibit amne Lupus, bibit Agnus in imo.
  Hunc timor impugnat, uerba mouente Lupo:
Rupisti potumque michi riuoque decorem.
  Agnus utrunque negat, se ratione tuens:
Nec tibi, nec riuo nocui; nam prona supinum
  Nescit iter, nec adhuc unda nitore caret.
Sic iterum tonat ore Lupus: Mihi dampna minaris?
  Non minor, Agnus ait. Cui Lupus: Immo facis.
Fecit idem tuus ante pater, sex mensibus actis.
  Cum bene patrixes, crimine patris obi.
Agnus ad hec: Tanto non uixi tempore, predo.

Sic tonat: An loqueris, furcifer? huncque vorat.

Sic nocet innocuo nocuus, causamque nocendi
  Inuenit. Hii regnant qualibet urbe lupi.

The Wolf and the Lamb

There is a wolf, there is a lamb; this one is thirsty, that one is thirsty. Each of the thirsty ones seeks a stream by a different path. The wolf drinks upstream, the lamb drinks downstream. Fear assails the lamb as the wolf speaks: "You have disturbed my drinking and the beauty of the river." The lamb denies each accusation, defending himself with reason: "I have harmed neither you nor the river, for the downward-flowing water does not know the way backwards, nor does it lack sparkle thus far." The wolf roars again, "Are you threatening me with injuries?" "I am not threatening," says the lamb. To which the wolf replies, "Rather, you're *doing* harm. Your father did the same thing six months ago. Because you act so like your father, die for the crimes of your father." The lamb retorts, "I have not been alive for so much time, robber!" The wolf roars, "Still chattering, gallows-bird?" And he devours him.

Thus a harmful one harms a harmless one, and he finds a reason for harming. Such wolves as these rule in any city.

III. De Mure et Rana

Muris iter rumpente lacu, uenit obuia Muri
  Rana loquax, et opem pacta nocere cupit.
Omne genus pestis superat mens dissona uerbis,
  Cum sentes animi florida lingua polit.
Rana sibi filo Murem confederat, audet
  Nectere fune pedem, rumpere fraude fidem.
Pes coit ergo pedi; sed mens a mente recedit.
  Ecce natant; trahitur ille, sed illa trahit.
Mergitur, ut secum Murem demergat; amico
  Naufragium faciens, naufragat ipsa fides.
Rana studet mergi; sed Mus emergit et obstat
  Naufragio: uires suggerit ipse timor.
Miluus adest, miserumque truci rapit ungue duellum:
  Hic iacet, ambo iacent, uiscera rupta fluunt.

Sic pereant, qui se prodesse fatentur, [et] obsunt.
  Discat in auctorem pena redire suum.

The Mouse and the Frog

As a mouse finds his path interrupted by a lake, a loquacious frog comes before the mouse and desires to harm while agreeing to help. A mind that does not accurately represent itself in words outranks every kind of pest, when a florid tongue embellishes the briars of the mind. The frog joins himself to the mouse with a thread; he dares to fasten the cord to his leg and to break faith by fraud. Foot comes together with foot, but mind recedes from mind. Behold, they swim; this one is betrayed, but that one betrays. The frog goes under so that the mouse sinks with him; fashioning ruin for a friend, he ruins faith. The frog strives to go down, but the mouse rises up and resists ruin: fear furnishes him with courage. A kite is present and seizes with fierce claws the wretched pair. She casts them down, both lie dead, ruptured viscera flow.

Thus perish those who claim themselves helpful but do harm. Let him learn that punishment returns to its author.

IV. *De Cane et Ove*

In causam Canis urget Ouem, sedet arbiter, audit.
    Reddat Ouis panem uult Canis; illa negat.
Pro Cane stat Miluus, stat Vultur, stat Lupus: instant
    Panem, quem pepigit reddere, reddat Ouis.
Reddere non debet nec reddere iure tenetur;
    Et tamen ut reddat, arbiter instat Oui.
Ergo suum, licet obstet yems, peruendit amictum,
    Et patitur Boream, vellere nuda suo.

Sepe fidem falso mendicat inertia teste,
    Sepe solet pietas criminis arte capi.

The Dog and the Sheep

A dog takes a sheep to court; a judge sits and hears their case. The dog wants the sheep to give back some bread; the sheep denies him. A kite, a vulture, and a wolf support the dog; they insist that the sheep give back the bread that he had contracted to give back. He is not obliged to give it back, nor is he constrained by law to give it back, and yet the judge presses the sheep to give it back. Therefore, though winter draws near, he sells his garments and, denuded of his fleece, suffers the North Wind.

Often laziness begs for faith from a false witness; often justice is wont to be captured by the deceit of crime.

V. *De Carne et Cane*

Dum Canis ore gerit carnem, caro porrigit umbram;
   Vmbra choeret aquis: has Canis urget aquas.
Spem carnis plus carne cupit, plus fenore signum
   Fenoris: os aperit; sic caro spesque perit.

Non igitur debent pro uanis certa relinqui.
   Non sua si quis auet, mox caret ipse suis.

The Meat and the Dog

As a dog carries some meat in his mouth, the flesh casts a shadow; the shadow unites with the waters, and the dog jumps at those waters. He desires the hope of meat more than meat, the image of gain more than gain. His mouth opens; thus flesh vanishes along with hope.

Therefore certainties should not be relinquished for vanities. If anyone pants after things that are not his own, soon he himself will lack his possessions.

VII. *De Femina et Fure*

Femina dum nubit Furi, uicinia gaudet;
   Vir bonus et prudens talia uerba mouet:
Sol pepigit sponsam. Iouis aures terra querelis
   Perculit, et causam, cur foret egra, dedit:
Sole necor solo; quid erit, si creuerit alter?
   Quid patiar? Quid aget tanta caloris yemps?

Hic prohibet sermo letum prebere fauorem
   Qui (his) male fecerunt, uel parant facta mala.

The Woman and the Thief

When a woman marries a thief, the neighborhood celebrates. A good and prudent man speaks thus: "The sun takes a spouse. The earth strikes Jove's ears with complaints, and she gives the reason that she might be ill: 'I'm slaughtered by one sun alone; what would happen if another should spring forth? What will such a storm of warmth do?'"

This speech prohibits the offering of joyful favor to those who have acted badly or who intend wrong deeds.

VIII. *De Lupo et Grue*

Arta Lupum cruciat uia gucturis osse retento:
   Mendicat medicam, multa daturus, opem.

Grus promissa petit, de faucibus osse reuulso.
    Cui Lupus: An uiuis munere tuta meo?
Nonne tuum potui morsu precidere collum?
    Ergo tibi munus sit tua meum uita.

Nil prodest prodesse malis: mens praua malorum

        Inmemor accepti non timet esse boni.

The Wolf and the Crane

The narrow passage of his throat tortures the wolf when a bone is stuck in it: he begs for medical help, promising a great deal. A crane seeks the promised reward when the bone has been pulled out of the wolf's gullet. To him the wolf says: "Don't you live in safety because of my reward? Couldn't I have snapped off your neck in a bite? Therefore let my reward to you be your life."

It is useless to be useful to evil people; the depraved mind of the evil does not fear being unmindful of goods received.

XII. *De Duobus Muribus*

Rvsticus urbanum Mus Murem suscipit, edem
    Commodat [et] mentem: menteque mensa minor.
In tenui mensa satis est immensa uoluntas,
    Nobilitat uiles frons generosa dapes.
Facto fine cibis, urbanum rusticus audit:
    Vrbani sotius tendit in urbis opes.
Ecce penum subeunt; inseruit amicus amico,
    Inuigilat mense; fercula mensa gerit.
Emendat conditque cibos clementia uultus,
    Conuiuam satiat plus dape frontis honor.
Ecce sere clauis inmurmurat, ostia laxat.
    Ambo timent, fugiunt ambo, nec ambo latent.
Hic latet, hic latebras cursu mendicat inepto,
    Assuitur muro reptile Muris onus.
Blanda penu clauso parcit fortuna timori;
    Ille tamen febrit, teste tremore, timor.
Exit qui latuit, timidum sic lenit amicum:
    Gaude, carpe cibos, hec sapit esca fauum.
Fatur qui timuit: Latet his in melle uenenum,
    Fellitumque metu non puto dulce bonum.
Quam timor obnubit, non est sincera voluntas;
    Non est sollicito dulcis in ore fauus.

Rodere malo fabam, quam cura perpete rodi;
  Degenerare cibos cura diurna facit.
His opibus gaude, qui gaudes turbine mentis;
  Pauperiem ditat pax opulenta michi.
Hec bona solus habe, que sunt tibi dulcia soli;
  Det pretium dapibus uita quieta meis.
Finit uerba, redit; preponit tuta timendis,
  Et quia summa timet, tutius ima petit.

Pauperies si leta uenit, ditissima res est:
  Tristior immensas pauperat usus opes.

The Two Mice

The country mouse receives the city mouse and accommodates him with food and magnanimity, but the magnanimity is greater than the repast. Abundant good will is enough at a poor table; a generous appearance ennobles cheap fare. When the end of dinner has been reached, the country mouse listens to the city mouse; the companion of the urban one is inclined to the wealth of the city. Behold, they approach the pantry; one friend serves the other, watches over the table; the table holds trays of food. Mildness of demeanor refines and spices the food, and distinction in appearance satisfies the guest more than the banquet. But lo, the key murmurs at the lock, opens the door. Both are frightened, both flee, but both do not hide. One hides, the other seeks hiding places on a useless course; the body of the creeping mouse tailors itself to the wall. The pantry having being closed, alluring fortune has spared the fearful ones; nevertheless their fear is feverish, as attested by their trembling. The one who was hidden comes out, and thus he soothes his frightened friend, "Rejoice, seize some nourishment, this food tastes of honeycomb!" The one who was frightened confesses, "Here poison is concealed in the honey; I do not consider a good thing sweet when it is made bitter by fear. That which fear obscures is not real good will; honeycomb is not sweet in a troubled mouth. I choose to gnaw a bean rather than to be gnawed by perpetual care; daily fear makes good food go bad. Enjoy these riches, you who enjoy confusion; sumptuous peace enriches my poverty. Have for yourself alone those goods which are sweet to you alone; a quiet life gives value to my meals." He finishes speaking and goes back home. He puts safe things before fearful things, and because he fears the heights, he seeks out the depths more safely.

If joyful poverty occurs, it is the richest thing; sadder experience impoverishes immense wealth.

XVIII. *De Leone et Mure*

Frigida sopito blanditur silua Leoni;
    Cursitat hic murum ludere promta cohors.
Pressus Mure, Leo Murem rapit; ille precatur,
    Ille precem librat, supplicat ira preci.
Hec tamen ante mouet animo: Quid Mure perento
    Laudis emes? summum uincere parua pudet.
Si nece dignetur Murem Leo, nonne Leoni
    Dedecus, et Muri ceperit esse decus?
Si uincat minimum summus, sic uincere uinci est.
    Vincere posse decet, uincere crimen habet.
Si tamen hoc decus est et laus sic uincere, laus hec
    Et decus hoc minimo fiet ab hoste minus.
De pretio uicti pendet uictoria: uictor
    Tantus erit, uicti gloria quanta fuit.
Mus abit, et grates reddit: si reddere possit
    Spondet opem. Solus fit mora parua dies.
Nam Leo rete subit, nec prodest uiribus uti,
    Sed prodest querulo murmure dampna loqui.
Mus redit, hunc reperit, cernit loca, uincula rodit;
    Hac ope pensat opem; sic Leo tutus abit.
Rem potuit tantam minimi prudentia dentis,
    Cui Leo dans ueniam se dedit ipse sibi.

Tu qui summa potes, ne despice parua potentem;
    Nam prodesse potest, si quis obesse nequid.

The Lion and the Mouse

A cool wood soothes a lion into sleeping. A quick troop of mice runs around playing. Brushed by a mouse, the lion seizes the mouse. One begs, the other weighs the plea; anger falls to its knees before the entreaty. Yet beforehand he thinks about this in his spirit: "What praise will you buy by destroying a mouse? The very great is ashamed to conquer the small. If a lion considers a mouse worthy of violent death, wouldn't shame fall to the lion and honor to the mouse? If the greatest conquers the smallest, then to conquer is to be conquered. To be able to conquer is fitting, to conquer is criminal. Yet if there is honor and praise in conquering thus, this honor and praise are diminished by the little enemy. Victory depends on the value of the conquered; the victor will be as great as the glory of the conquered is." The mouse leaves and gives thanks. He pledges help if he can give it in return. There is a short delay of only one day, until the lion is trapped in a net, and he cannot profit from using his strength, but it is helpful to speak of his suffering in a plaintive roar. The mouse comes back, discovers the lion, discerns the situation, gnaws the bonds. By this favor he recompensed a favor; thus the lion leaves, safe. The sagacity of the tooth of the smallest creature could do such a great deed, the one to whom the Lion gave favor, thus giving himself to himself.

You who can do very great things, do not despise anyone capable of small things, for he can be useful if someone refrains from harming him.

XX. *De Yrundine et Lino*

Vt linum pariat de lini semine, semen
   Nutrit humus; sed Aues tangit Hyrundo metu:
Hic ager, hoc semen nobis mala uincla minatur,
   Vellite pro uestris semina sparsa malis.
Turba fugit sanos monitus, uanosque timores
   Arguit; exit humum semen, et herba uiret.
Rursus Yrundo monet instare pericula; rident
   Rursus Aues. Hominem placat Yrundo sibi,
Cumque uiris habitans cantu blanditur amico;
   Nam prouisa minus ledere tela solent.
Iam metitur linum, iam fiunt retia, iam uir
   Fallit Aues, iam se conscia culpat Auis.

Vtile consilium [qui] spernit, inutile sumit.
   Qui nimis est tutus, retia iure subit.

The Swallow and the Flax

So that it may bring forth flax from the linseed, the soil nourishes the seed; but the swallow moves the other birds with fear: "This field, this seed threatens us with evil bonds, pluck out the seeds sown for your own harm!" The flock flies from sound admonitions and calls those fears empty; the seed comes out of the soil, and the plant is healthy. Again the swallow warns that danger is nigh; again the birds laugh. The swallow ingratiates himself to man, and when living among men, he soothes them with friendly song, for foreseen weapons usually do less injury. Now the flax is reaped, now nets are made, now man beguiles the birds, now each bird, conscious of his guilt, lays blame upon himself.

Whoever spurns useful advice employs useless advice. Whoever is too safe rightfully comes under the nets.

Appendix 2

Esopus moralizatus cum bono commento
(Cologne: Heinrich Quentell, 1489)

Quentell's edition of the *Esopus moralizatus* gives no titles for the fables, but in order to facilitate identification I have included the titles from Hervieux's edition, borrowed from Brussels Bibliothèque Royale MS Lat. 14381.

Accessus. Grecia, disciplinarum mater et artium, inter ceteros quos mundo tulit sapientes, virum edidit memorie digne, Esopum nomine. Erat enim ingenio clarus et studio sedulus, et placidus facundia. Qui inter cetera quae scripserat, utilia fabularum exempla utilibus plena etiam litteris commisit, et in unum redegit opusculum in quo parvuli diligentes instruantur et iocundi reddantur adulti. Liber igitur iste primo grece conscriptus est ab Esopo; post hoc a Romulo, imperatore romano, ad instruendum Tibarium, filium suum, in latinum venit. Deinde rex anglie Afferus in anglicam linguam eum transferri precepit.[1] Esopus itaque, de fabulis agens, res inanimatas introducit loquentes, videlicet et bestias et volucres, et fabulose de eis scripsit, sed de singulis moraliter concludit.

Comment on verse prologue. Antequam procedatur ad textum, aliqua sunt praemittenda, et primo de causis huius libri. Unde notandum quod praesentis libri, sicut et aliorum librorum, quattuor sunt cause, scilicet materialis, formalis, efficiens, et finalis. Unde causa materialis, sive subjectum huius libri, est sermo fabulosus in respectu ad virtutes morales. Causa formalis est duplex, secundum quod duplex est forma, scilicet forma tractatus et forma tractandi. Forma tractandi est modus agendi, qui in proposito est metricus. Sed forma tractatus consistit in compositione et explicabitur per continuationes et divisiones. Causa efficiens dicitur fuisse Esopus qui erat graecus; unde, ut fertur, praesens liber conscriptus erat in greco; sed postea jussu Rhomuli, imperatoris Romanorum, fuit translatus in latinum et hoc propter filios eius quos voluit instrui per doctrinas hujus libri. Causa finalis est duplex, scilicet intrinseca et extrinseca. Finalis intrinseca est cognitio eorum quae traduntur in hoc libro, sed extrinseca est ut nos per documenta et fabulas huius libri gradiamur ad bonos mores. Hiis visis accedendum est ad formam tractatus, scilicet divisionem libri.

Dividit igitur iste liber in duas partes principales, scilicet in partem prohemialem et partem executivam, secundam ibi, "Dum rigido . . ." [Fable I, *De Gallo et Jaspide*, line 1]. Pars prohemialis posset dividi in quattuor partes. Nam prima autor innuit delectationem et utilitatem huius libri. Similiter secundo tangit causam suscepti operis ibi, "Ne mihi torpentem . . ." [Prologue, line 8]. Tercio invocat divinum auxilium ibi, "Ut messis precium . . ." [Prologue, line 10]. Quarto excusat se de facilitate stili ibi, "Verborum levitas . . ." [Prologue, *moralitas*].

Notandum igitur quod autor dicat in textum praesens liber nedum est iocundus. Sed etiam etiam [*sic*] est utilis ad instructionem morum et ergo posset aperte subordinari philosophie morali. Est enim duplex poetria: quaedam est ad delectationem tam et talis non subordinatus alicui parti philosophie. Alia enim quae consistit ad utilitatem cuiusmodi est ista, unde Oratius, "Aut prodesse volunt aut delectare poete."[2] Et hoc est quod dicitur: "Ut iuvet et prosit," etc. [Prologue, line 1]. Pro quo notandum quod autor, declarans similiter delectationem et utilitatem huius libelli, innuit hanc sententiam, quod praesens pagina, i.e. praesens libellus debet describere fabulas ad delectationem et etiam ad vertutes morales quas sunt ad utilitatem. Si aliquis quaereret quare autor non tangit solum vertutes absque fabulis, ad hoc respondet autor cum subdit: "Dulcius arrident . . ." [Prologue, line 2]. Nam seria sive utilia magis delectant sive alliciunt quando sunt depicta rebus iocosis, et propter hoc in isto libello erunt vertutes commendabile cum fabulis premittendo, scilicet fabulas et subiungendo vertutes. Tunc ibi, "Ortulus iste parit . . ." [Prologue, line 3], autor magis declarat utilitatem libelli, dicens quod in isto libello est flos cum fructu qui faciunt hominem favorabilem; et qui vult capere fructum, capiat fructum; et qui florem, florem capiat; et qui utrunque, capiat utrunque. Et nota quod autor comparat sermonem fabulosum flori et per fructum dat intelligere vertutes morales, quia sicut flos est modici valoris sine fructu, sic etiam sermo fabulosus est modici valoris sine virtutibus quae trahuntur ex fabulis.

I. [*De Gallo et Jaspide*] Finita parte prohemiali, hic consequenter autor ponit partem executivam. Et potest dividi in tot partes quot ponit fabulas. Primo autor ponit unam fabulam cuius documentum est talem: quod stulto ac vitioso non valet scientia, vel quod stulti pervipendunt scientiam. Et hoc ostendit per quondam fabulam de gallo. Nam gallus quodam vicem, quaerens escam fodiendo fimum, invenit lapidem preciosum latentem in loco immundo. Cui dixit gallus, "Tu iaces in loco vili et immundo. Tu non es utilis mihi. Sed si aurifaber vel alium gemmarum cupidus te invenisset, per eum ad splendorem tuum venires et honores perciperes. Ego vero escam quaero et te non honorabo, quia tu non prodes mihi, nec ego prosum tibi. Nec de te curo, quia amo minus cara et vilia, videlicet grana et similia quae mihi prosunt ad nutrimentum." Deinde subdit doctrinam huius fabule, dicens quod per gallum debemus intelligere stultum, per lapidem preciosum scientiam vel sapientiam. Unde gallus sic spernit lapidem preciosum tamquam sibi non valentem neque utilem. Sic etiam stultus spernit sapientiam, eo quod non reputat eam necessariam neque utilem.

II. [*De Lupo et Agno*] Hic autor ponit aliam fabulam cuius documentum est quod mali tyranni potentes de facili inveniunt causam nocendi pauperibus et impotentibus. Istud innuitur nobis per lupum et agnum. Nam quodam tempore lupus et agnus comederunt et utroque sitiente similiter de rivo biberunt. Sed lupus stetit in parte superiori et agnus in inferiori. Lupus igitur cum haustum faceret, erixit se et dixit ad agnum, "Tu qui lanam portas, in deceptionem super meis offensis insistis." Agnus vero ad hanc vocem tremulum timide respondet et humiliter, "Domine potens et tremende, quare tam aspere mihi loqueris innocenti? Quas enim offensas ego parvulus tibi possem inferre?" Et lupus ait, "Tu turbas aquas quod inde gustare non possem." Repondetque agnus, "Mira sunt quae tu dicis, quia cum tu stans superius et ego inferius, quomodo possum tibi aquas turbare? Sed occasionem adversum me quaeris, sicut qui vult ab amico recedere." Tunc ergo exasperatus lupus ait iterum, "Tu nimis es garrulus et iurgia mecum multiplicare presumis. Sicut pater tuus, qui nondum transactus tribus mensibus de eo deinde hoc loco mihi forefecit, quod in te merito redundabit." Et ait miser agnus, "Cur sic in me patris culpas refundis, qui nondum natus eram?" "Sic mihi respondes in omnibus et reclamare non cessas." Irruensque in eum gutturis eius crudeliter apprehendit, et finem fecit verborum. Moraliter, sic tyranni faciunt, cum innocentum res vel mortem cupiunt; sive iuste sive iniuste, eos spoliant et opprimunt.

III. [*De Mure et Rana*] Hic autor ponit aliam fabulam cuius documentum est quod nemo debet promittere auxilium quod cor non intendit, quia tales bonum dicentes et malum cogitantes sepe cadunt in laqueos quos paraverunt. Sicut innuitur nobis per murem et ranam. Mure in ostio molendini super limen residente, supervenit rana de gurgite progressa et, mure salutato, cuius illa domus esset eum interrogavit, quam suam esse respondit. Rogavit ergo rana ipsum murem ut ipsam nocte illa in hospicio colligeret et benigne susciperet, cui mus benigne respondit et eam intrare iussit et adduxit eam superius. Facta quoque hora cene, apposuit ei grossam farinam et invitavit et rogavit eam diligenter ut comederet ea que haberet, dicens quod, "Si meliora essent in domo mea libenter apponeret ea." Et placuit rane locus et cibus. Sed cum potus diu expectatus non venit, rana, potus assueta et sicca, tristis recedit et potum deesse minus eque tulit et dixit quod mallet esse sub molendino absque tali cibo quam supra sine potu. Cui mus ait molestum sibi esse quod oblata sibi non placerent et iuravit se nunquam uno nocte tam bene procurata fuisse, et de impensa illa se velle recompensationem habere dixit. Talibus itaque auditis, rana dixit et respondit quod si secum ad sua vellet transire, sibi reddere vellet cibum cum potu administrans in copia. Favensque mus et dixit ei et se promittit iturum. Mane itaque facto, agressi sunt iter et rana per pratum rexit se ad fluvium mure comitante. Erat autem rore plenus et via muri difficilis, volebatque desistere. Sed ipsum rana confortavit et in vicino domum suam esse dixit. Tandem itaque prato a mure vix separato venerunt ad fluvium et ait rana, "Hic transeundi est nobis aqua [sic] ut ulterior ripa nos recipiat in qua est domus mea ad quam tendimus." Fessus igitur mus, ex longa via attediatus, ad ranam sic inquit: "Amiciciam tuam invite perdo, sed hospicium tuum adire nequeo quia rore prati adhuc gravioribus, aquis istis me committere non audeo." Ait ergo rana, "Turpe est modo desistere et viam brevem non perficere, quia si fessus es et debilis, ego fortior iuvabo te ne in aquam deficias. Sic ergo faciamus: filum nobis allegabimus, tu in collo et ego in pede meo, et trahendo remeabo." Sic et rana dixit et mus rem verbis optavit. Ipsis itaque in medio fluminis iam positis, rana loquax exclamavit, "Ego confisa nimis meis viribus iam deficio, et ad profundum ducor peritura." Sponteque se mergens mure machinata est naufragium. Mus autem rana trahente iam secundo submersus, sursum tamen rediens, male geri intellexit et litus relicturus et respiciens, illic redire voluit. Ortumque est ibi litigium illis in partes trahentibus; rana namque ad fundum tendebat, et mus ad littus tendebat. Dum enim sic distrahunt illi, aquila, que forte speculatrix erat, miserum dirimit duellum, murem unguibus arripiens et annexam ranam similiter trahens, que cum se ad mortem trahi videret, sic fertur locuta fuisse: qui socio suo parat opprobrium, non immerito cadit in laqueum. Allegorice per ranam potest intelligi caro humana; per murem autem intelligitur anima que adversus carnem semper militat. Caro concupiscit adversus spiritum et spiritus adversus carnem. Caro enim nititur trahere animam ad terrena, et carnales delectationes. Anima vero resilit ad bona opera. Et istis sic litigantibus venit milvus, id est diabolus, quasi bolus in morsus duorum, scilicet corporis et anime. Virtus aliter sicut tangitur in fine littere: per ranam intelligant deceptores bonum dicentes deceptationemque intendentes; conantur enim alios decipere. Et sic quandoque cadunt in insidias quos aliis paraverunt. Sic dicitur in psalmo, "Incidit in foveam," etc.[3]

IV. [*De Cane et Ove*] Hic autor ponit aliam fabulam dicens quod quodam tempore canis traxit ovem in causam pro pane quem se dixit illi concessisse, sed ovis hoc factum negavit, dicens se nunquam panem a cane mutuasse. Iudex ergo si testes haberet huiusmodi rei vel fide iussores canem interrogavit, qui tres testes nominavit, scilicet lupum, milvum, et vulturem. Et iudex ab illis veritatem requirit, at illi testimonium veritatis cani dederunt, quia partem habere sperabant in ove si damnaretur. Iudex ergo precepit quatenus de debito suo cani satisfaceret, ex quo ydoneis testibus convicta esset. Sed illa misera nihil habuit praeter lanam quod dare posset, et hyems erat et canis fortiter instabat. Ovis ergo lana exuens eam cani presentavit et nuda remansit. Canis autem hac satisfactione non contentus in pellem ipsius ait, et irruens super eam cum falsis testibus suis, lupo et milvo, miseram illam miseriorem redidit. Moraliter, sic perversi et fallaces faciunt quando res aliorum appetunt cum suis complicibus tractant et agunt qualiter iudiciis suis eos subvertere.

VI. [*De Carne et Cane*] Hic autor ponit aliam fabulam cuius documentum est quod homo prudens non debet dimittere certa, quamvis sint modica, pro incertis quae reputantur magna, quia modica res certa plus valet quam magna res incerta. Iuxta illud, plus valet in manibus passer quam sub dubio grus. Istud nobis innuitur per canem qui natavit per aquas, massas carnis in ore gerens, et vidit in aquis umbram carnis maiorem quam erat frustum quod habebat in ore. Et sic cupiens illud frustum magnum, aperit os ad capiendum illud, et sic tandem cum os aperavit, amisit tam carnem veram quam umbram carnis. Allegorice per canem intelligitur homo parcus vel avarus qui inter totiens quaerit bona aliena, et quoniam contingit quod talis ex nimia cupiditate amittit bona propria. Vel aliter per canem possumus intelligere hominem qui dimisso vero bono, inheret bonis terrenis, quae sunt tanquam umbre, quia felicitatem huiusmodi non quaerit nisi in bonis terrenis, ideo finaliter remanet vacuus. Eo quod ipso moriente summum bonum non quaesivit, unde bona temporalia dimittit moriens in manus aliorum, et sic a se transeunt bona temporalia sic acquisita, et sic amittuntur bona sempiterna.

VII. [*De Femina et Fure*] Hic autor ponit aliam fabulam cuius documentum est quod quodam tempore fur duxit uxorem, ad cuius nuptias vicini convenerunt gaudentes et letantes. Quod videns quidam vir discretus protulit hanc fabulam: "Quodam tempore sol debebat uxore ducere ut filios conformes procrearet. Quod audiens universa creatura per terram considerans periculum quod inde esset venturum, dixit ardores unius solis vix se tolerare posse; quid ergo erit si plures soles novi nascerentur? Et clamans in celum querulis vocibus, iovem summum deum invocavit, quatenus incommodum ammoveret. Jupiter igitur commotus precepit soli sine uxore permanere." Quasi diceret iste vir discretus, "O vos boni vicini, res vestras perditis per istum unum furem; quid ergo erit si fur alios fures generaret? Quare multum insipienter agitis quod ad nuptias eius pervenitis gaudentes et letantes?" Ista fabula docet etiam moraliter quod melius est habere unum principem quam plures, nam si plures sint, quilibet sibi vendicat servicium et honorem quibus sufficere nequeunt subditi, et illis pro honore discordantibus nescit populus cui adhereat vel sub quo tutius vivat. Et inde rapine, homicidia, etque plura mala oriuntur.

VIII. [*De Lupo et Grue*] Hic autor ponit aliam fabulam cuius documentum est quod non expedit malis hominibus benefacere quia sunt ingrati et beneficiorum immemores. Et istud innuitur nobis per lupum et gruem. Quodam tempore dum lupus sumptus carnibus os roderet, particula ossis gutturi eius inhesit, et magnum dolorem sibi intulit. Lupus ergo, potens in curia leonis regis ut summus prepositus regis, fecit omnes bestias congregari, sperans ab aliqua sui doloris et periculi medelam percipere. Quaesivit si aliqua bestiarum habuerit artem medicine quae suo dolori poterit subvenire. Adducta est itaque grus ad lupi infirmi presentia, quae salutiferam promittit lupo medicinam si de mercede esset certificata. Lupus ergo his consolatus dixit se in tanta necessitatem non velle parcere divitiis. Promittit ergo munera magna dummodo consequi possit sanitatem. Grus ergo, collo suo in gutture lupi immisso, causam doloris induxit, et sic lupus sanatus est. Quo facto, grus exigit a lupo promissa, cui respondit lupus, "Nonne magna mee pietatis munera recipisti, dum de gutture meo caput tibi sanum emisi? Si ergo sapiens esses, hoc munere contenta fores, cum tu manifeste scias gruinas carnes me maxime desiderare in ista infirmitate." Moraliter, per gruem intelliguntur pauperes et impotentes qui sunt sub potentioribus. Videtur enim potentioribus quod pauperes sufficientem mercedem recipiunt pro suis laboribus in hoc quod eos vivere promittunt et bona residua que habent non usurpant.

XII. [*De Duobus Muribus*] Hic autor ponit aliam fabulam cuius documentum est quod melius est possidere pauca cum libertate et securitate quam multa cum servitute et timore. Istud designatur nobis per mures duos, quorum unus est silvester, alter urbanus. Quodam tempore mus silvester recepit in domum suam murem urbanum et sibi prandium de suis cibariis quae habebat fecit, quae licet modica erant et minus preciosa habebat tamen cum eis securitatem et libertatem. Quaedam autem die cum ista cibaria muri urbano non placerent, redire voluit ad civitatem et duxit secum murem silvestrem et intraverunt pariter quoddam cellarium, quod in cunctis bonis sibi competentibus habundabat, et pinguia et delicata faciebant convivia, quae placuerunt muri silvestri. Dixit se non velle redire ad nemus, sed potius manere in civitate ubi habundabat deliciis—quia adhuc periculorum et adversitatum sibi imminentium erat ignarus. Cum autem isti duo mures comederunt deliciose et gauderent, supervenit famulus domus, ad cuius introitum prae nimio terrore ambo mures de sua mense fugerant. Mus autem urbanus qui erat ibi bene notus ad locum satis tutum fugit, sed mus silvester, angulis ignarus quo fugeret vel latitaret, locum non invenit, tamen ad obscuram currebat adherens pedibus suis parieti donec famulus exiret, quo recedente, ad mensam sunt reversi. Sed mus silvester tremens et territus atque tritis in fine mense sedit, cui mus urbanus dixit, "Cur sic sedes ad mensam tristis? Comede et gaude! Ista cibaria melle sunt dulciora." Respondit mus silvester, "Vere sub hoc melle latet venenum, nec possent esse dulcia cibaria, quia tali timore sunt mellita, nec est sincera voluptas quam tantus timor obscurat, nec possum esse cibus dulcis in ore sollicito. Tuque bono mihi modo ministrasti, sed mala et pericula quae latent non revelasti. Ego putavi tecum vivere in securitate et deliciis, et nunc video multiplices causas tue miserie; oportetque enim te timere homines et cattos, qui die ac nocte tibi insidiantur, quia *ve* vobis si in manus catti insideritis. Sint ergo bona vestra vobis simul et mala; habete quae natura concessit. Michi autem et nec multa commoda dedit natura nec magna mala contulit." His itaque dictis et similibus, mus silvester redit ad locum suum pristinum. Per hanc fabulam significatur moraliter quod melior est paupertas libera et secura quam divitie periculose et inanis gloria quae magno cum timore et dolore possidentur.

XVIII. [*De Leone et Mure*] Hic autor ponit aliam fabulam cuius documentum est quod divites et potentes debent pauperibus misereri, et si in parvo pauperes deliquerent, debent divites indulgere, quia poterunt in posterum pauperes divitibus prodesse. Istud nobis declaratur per leonem et murem, quia quodam tempore quidam leo dormivit in nemore ubi mures circumcirca cursitabant ludentes. Accidit autem quod quidam mus casu leonem tetigit et sic somnum eius turbavit. Leo igitur excitatus apprehendit murem, cui mus ait, "O leo, tua nobilitas mihi parcat, quia non malo animo sed mihi casualiter hoc accidit." Petiit itaque mus veniam. Leo igitur minime motus dimisit murem illesum, cogitans intra se quod esset sibi parva gloria si murem damnaret. Contigit autem postea quod idem leo transiens per silvam cecidit in laqueum qui non potuit laqueum suis dentibus dissolvere et sic se ab illa captivitate liberare, et ergo emisit rugitus et strepitus querulosus. Quibus auditis venit supradictus mus cui leo prius pepercit; vidensque leonem laqueatum eum agnovit et recordatus est beneficii leonis. Corrosit et dissolvit chordas rethis sive laquei, quibus dissolutis leo liber abscessit. Et ut dicit autor, ille leo dans grates muri, dedit seipsum ad nutum muris, eo quod mus liberavit eum a morte. Moraliter autem sic potentes non debent spernere debiles et impotentes, quia licet pauperes et impotentes quandoque nocumentum inferre non possent, quandoque tamen possunt potentibus prodesse.

XX. [*De Yrundine et Lino*] Hic autor ponit aliam fabulam cuius documentum est quod nullus debet contemnere concilium alterius, quia accidit multoties quod respuentes concilium fiunt inutiles unde frequenter eis malum evenit. Istud declaratur nobis per semen lini seminatum in terram, et per hyrundinem et alias aves. Nam quodam tempore ortulanus seminavit semen lini in agro suo, ad quem hyrundo et alie aves consueverunt venire pro necessariis. Hyrundo vero presciens futurum malum premonuit alias aves resistere huic seminationi dicens, "Hoc semen multiplex periculum nobis parabit; ergo evellamus illud ne malum inde venturum nobis adveniat." Quo audito, alie aves minus provide hyrundinis concilium contempserunt. Quo viso, hyrundo suum genus convocavit et federe pacis cum hominibus inivit. Erat autem forma pacis quod neutra pars in damnum alterius cogitaret, et sic hyrundines ex signo pacis in domibus nidificaverunt. Tempore ergo messis ortulanus colligit sibi linum seminatum, et inde rethia et laqueos fabricavit, per quos ipse ortulanus omnes alias aves capiebat, quae capte recognoverunt quod stulte spreverunt concilium hyrundinis. Allegorice per aves intelligere possumus peccatores, per hyrundinem vero spirituales, qui sepe ammonent peccatores ut desistant et abstineant a peccatis. Sed peccatores, spirituales ammonitiones spernentes, tandem per rethia capiuntur et eterno igni traduntur.

Appendix 3

Auctores octo: Fabularum Esopi
(Lyon: Jehan de Vingle, 1495)

(*Prologus*) In principio huius libri quinque sunt inquirenda, scilicet: causa efficiens, forma materialis, et finalis utilitas, et cui parti philosophiae supponitur, et quis titulus. Causa efficiens est duplex, scilicet movens et non mota et movens et mota. Movens et non mota fuit Theodosius ipse imperator et miles qui petiit Esopum ut sibi aliquas res iocosas componeret ad removendum curas publicas: qui recusare non valens hoc opus composuit in graeco; quia ipse fuit graecus, et ille fuit latinus; ut Socrates de graeco in latinum transtulit logicam. Alii dicunt quod Galterus anglicus fecit hunc librum sub nomine Esopi et sic habemus quod duplex est Esopus. In principio huius sunt multae fabulae et apologi vel materia quae continet utilitates in simplicibus dictis fabularum. Causa formalis est duplex: scilicet forma tractandi et forma tractatus. Forma tractatus est congregatio vel multiplicatio vel documenta quae in hoc libro continetur. Forma tractandi est modus vel materia, dispositio vel descriptio. Causa finalis sive utilitas est ut perlecto libro sciamus ea quae dicta sunt in libro. Titulus talis est: *Incipit Esopus* vel *Esopus* vel *Liber magistri Esopi*. Cui parti philosophiae supponitur? Ethicae, quia de moribus tractat. Ethis enim graece, mos dicitur esse latine: inde ethica, id est moralis scientia. Magister Esopus de civitate Atheniensi, auctor huius libri, volens omnes homines communiter informare quid agere et quid vitare debeant, hoc opus composuit in quo fingit bruta irrationalia animalia et inanimata loqui nobis; per hoc inconveniens docet nos cavere cavenda, et sectari sectanda: nam fingit gallum loqui et lupum, ut patet in littera; hoc est totum figurative: ut id quod minus videtur inesse inest et id quod magis. Istud autem opus fuit in greco sermone compositum: diu a latinis iacuit intemptatum, donec Tiberius quidam imperator romanorum rogavit magistrum Romulum ut sibi aliquas fabulas jocosas, ad removendum publicas curas, compleret et legeret; iste autem magister Romulus non audens precibus tanti viri contradicere, librum suum utpote auctenticum de graeco sermone in latinum transtulit, dicens, "O Tyberine, scribam calumnias malorum, verba blanda improborum, ut risus multiplicetur et ingenium acuatur per exempla."

I. (*De Gallo et Jaspide*) Notandum est quod auctor iste ponit utilitatem vel fructum in duobus versibus vel quattuor in fine cuiuslibet fabule. Fabula vero vel apologus est, vel in hoc apologo docet nos auctor quod non simus stulti sed sapientes, quia stulto nihil prodest sapientia, unde Salo, "Quid prodest stulto divitias querere cum non potest sapientiam emere, quia quicunque stultum de eius stultitia corrigit et castigat magis est inimicus quam amicus." Unde Salo, "Corrige stultum et habebis inimicum; corrige sapientem et habebis amicum." Et hoc probat per gallum, dicens quod in sterquilinio quidam gallus quesivit escam, et dum invenit margaritam in indigno loco iacentem qua uti non valuit eam, sic allocutus est: "O bona et preciosa margarita, cum in hoc stercore iaces, si te cupidus invenisset quanto gaudio rapuisset, et sic ad splendorem pristini modi, id est decoris, redires. Sed sicut ego tibi non prosum, sic nec tu mihi, sed potius escam quero, scilicet grana tritici." Allegoria: per gallum aliquem stultum intelligemus; per margaritam sapientem, donas gratiam dei vel regnum celorum, quod stultus est insensatus non curans de regno dei, sed sapiens vadit et vendit omnia que habet et emit regnum celorum. Unde scriptum est, "Vade et vende omnia que habes," etc.[1] Nota quod iaspis dicitur quasi "iacens inter aspides vel in fronte aspidis," vel dicitur ab "yos" grece, quod est "viride" latine, quia est viridi coloris.

II. (*De Lupo et Agno*) In hoc apologo docet nos auctor quod non debemus esse calumniantes sive calumniatores, quod probat per litteram, dicens quod lupus et agnus, post esum sitientes, venerunt ad quendam fluvium via tamen diversa, quia in superiori parte lupus bibit et in inferiori agnus potavit. Videns lupus agnum potantem ait, "Tu turbasti aquam et innudasti mihi rivum." Agnus utrunque negavit, dicens rationabiliter, "Quo modo potest hoc fieri cum non a me sed a te unda fluat? Nunquam aqua retrosum currere potest: hoc est eminens." Tunc dixit lupus agno, "Tu minaris." Respondit agnus, "Non minor nec incedo contra te." Dixit lupus, "Immo facis et non est mirum quod perimas: pater tuus docuit te nequitiam. Sex mensibus prosumpsit contra me litigare." Respondit agnus, "Non vixi tanto tempore quod dicas. Non fui tunc natus cum pater meus mortuus est." Ait lupus, "Nunquid non taces, furcifer." Apprehenso eo contra iusticiam, devoravit. Nota lupus dicitur a "lichon" vel "licham" grece, quod est lupus latine, inde dicitus "lichaon" a "licham" quod est lupus et on [*sic*] totus, quasi totus inimicus in luxum, quia virit de rapina, ut lupus. Agnus dicitur ab "agnos" grece, quod est "cognoscere" latine, quia solo balatu congnoscit matrem suam, vel dicitur ab "agnos" grece quod est "pius" latine, quia est animal valde pium. Allegoria: per agnum debemus intelligere deum creatorem nostrum, per lupum sinagogam, id est impios iudeos qui turpiter obiicientes

domino dixerunt, "Destruis nostras leges et violenta manu occiderunt eum."[2]
Fructus talis est: quod non simus calumniatores et non inferamus malum
alicui iniuste ut fecit lupus agno. Et tales homines sunt mali qui iniuste
opprimunt iustos et maxime potentes qui inferunt violenta pauperibus simplicibus, ut agnus.

III. (*De Mure et Rana*) In hoc apologo docet auctor ne cogitemus diversa de
salute alterius et ne promittamus prodesse cum velimus obesse. Et hoc
probat per mus pergens iter ad locum ubi obviavit rane, dicenti talia verba:
"O mure, transnata fluvium illum et ego te iuvabo," promittendo bonum
cum gereret fraudem. Dum ergo ligaret pedem pedi, ausa est fidem frangere.
Ecce natanti rana mergitur solito more. Sic ligantibus illis milvus supervenit
rapiens miserum duellum. Sic viscera rupta fluunt. Allegoria: per rana intellige corpus cuiuslibet hominis, per murem animam qui nititur ad bona opera vel ad regnum dei; sed corpus retrahit eam, et sic milvus, id est diabolus,
venit utrunque rumpens, scilicet corpus et animam. Fructus talis est quod
non promittamus prodesse cum possimus nosmetipsos iuvare et volumus
obesse.

IV. (*De Cane et Ove*) Hic auctor dicit quod non faciamus alicui misero nec
procuremus damnum, et hoc probat per litteram, dicens quod quidam canis
calumniosus pascebat panem ab ove, dicens causa mutui recepisse. Ovis
negavit se accepisse et negavit se velle reddere. Cum vero eam ad iudicium
traheret, introduxit plures testes, scilicet milvum, vulturem, et lupum, qui
partem canis affirmabant esse veram. Introductum habebat lupum in iudicem, sed tertius testis, scilicet vultur, ait, "Coram me accepit." Introductus
milvus ait, "Quare negas cum accepisti?" Et similiter lupus ait, "Iusta est
causa." Ergo ovis, coacta falsis testibus, suam lanam vendidit, licet iam
hyems instaret et reddidit quod non accepit. Allegoria: per iudicem intellige
deum qui dicit, "Qualem te invenio, talem te iudico." Per ovem intellige
hominem; per lupum diabolum qui artat nos; per testes, scilicet per milvum
angelum, per vulturem turpia peccata, per lupum conscientiam de illis que
minus circa falsitatem sepe exprimitur veritas. Unde Salomon, "Appetitus
rerum alienarum detrimentum facit propriarum."

V. (*De Carne et Cane*) In ista fabula docet nos auctor ut non admittamus
rem certam pro re incerta; sic careamus propriis dum aliena petimus, quod
probat per canem, dicens quod quidam canis gerebat in ore carnem et trans-
natabat quendam fluvium, et transnatando vidit in flumine umbram quam
volebat accipere. Et putando umbram accipere, perdidit carnem quam in

ore gerebat, et sic caruit utroque. Allegoria: per carnem debemus intelligere regnum celeste. Per umbram transitoria huius mundi, per fluvium corpus cuiuslibet hominis. Non amittamus ergo perpetua gaudia de quibus certi sumus, id est regnum celorum quod nobis paratum est ab origine mundi. Fructus talis est: pro rebus transitoriis huius mundi non ammitamus eternam gloriam.

VII. (*De Femina et Fure*) In hoc fabula docet nos auctor quod de pravitate malorum non debemus gaudere, et ut malis non gaudeamus, quod probat dicens vicini cuiusdam mulieris, celebrantis nuptias foris, gaudebant quia latronem ducebat, inter quos erat quidam sapiens qui dixit illis talem fabulam: "Sol debebat ducere uxorem, sed omnis terra interdixit et clamore magno iovi conquesta est. Cum iupiter vero audivit vocem querimoniae et causam quesivit, respondit terra quod, 'Per solem solum patior et tamen uror et pene deficior, sed quid fierit si sol generaret filios, et qui diverteretur hyems?'" Allegoria: per solem et per filios solis intelligimus filios latronis, per furem cuiuslibet hominis oculum, per sponsam delectationes huius mundi, que si pervenerit ad actum, tunc generabit filios qui opprimunt terram, id est rationem. Per virum prudentiam que semper suadet oculo ne videat vanitates huius mundi que cito trahunt et homines sepius ducunt ad lapsum peccatorum, et hoc est quod vult presens fabula.

VIII. (*De Lupo et Grue*) In ista fabula declarat auctor quod nihil prodest benefacere malis hominibus, licet in agone mortis sint, quod probat dicens quod cum quidam lupus maie et avide carne devorasset, sibi hesit os in gutture quod propriis viribus non potuit extrahere. Opem medicis quesivit, promittentes magnam pecunie summam, ad quem grus veniens, proprio collo in os eius positus, de gutture hos extrabit. Cumque egrotum sanus sit dominum, grus sollicitam pecuniam petiit lupo, cui lupus crudeli voce ait, "Munus meum tibi sit hoc: quod collum tuum non precidi cum posueras in gutture meum," etc. Allegoria: per lupum aliquem divitem et potentem in agone positum intelligimus, per gruem vero patrem spiritualem qui debet pro pravis aliquid facere, et iniungit cuiipso convalverit semper benefacere, sed cum ad sanitatem redditur deo auxiliante promissa minime adimplet, sed perseverat in suis malis operibus.

XII. (*De Duobus Muribus*) Hic docet auctor quod citius debemus diligere parvum cum securitate quam multum cum tribulatione et impedimento, quod probat litteram, dicens mus quidam urbanus iter agebat et repertus in hospitium muris agrestis, qui mensam sibi posuit, gaudens de adventu suo, ordea grana et talia multa intulit. Mus urbanus reddidit sibi grates scilicet rustico muri, et econverso petivit ut secum comederet. Cum vero agressi sunt quoddam celarium ubi ederat communia sua, venit dominus celarii et reseravit hostium, et mures perterriti ceperunt huc et illuc currere. Urbanus vero mus, notis cavernis securis, se abscondit; aggestis vero, ignorans ubi fugeret, per parietes fugit et vix non captus evasit. Postea, quando dominus celarii egit illud quod volebat facere, recessit, et clauso hostio iterum, convenerunt mures pariter, de quibus ait urbanus muri rustico, "Comede de istis epulis; abiice timores mos." Alter mus dixit, "In isto cibo latet amaritudo, quia comeditur cum timore. Certe malo rodere fabam in cavernula mea secure et vivere in paupertate quam si haberem omnes cibos de mundo." Et bis dictis, reversus est in domum suam. Allegoria: per murem rusticum intelligimus bonos homines spirituales de securitate semper letos, per urbanum pravos homines et seculares semper gaudentes tam de illecebris quam de utilitate.

XVIII. (*De Leone et Mure*) Hic docet nos auctor quod non offendamus miserum, sed simus misericordes simplicibus, quod probat dicens mures, leone dormiente in silva, contigit quod unus eorum curreret super caput leonis quem ille pede suo apprehendit, et ille ita comprehensus, rogavit veniam dicens, "Da mihi veniam eo quod te dormiente graviter offendi." Leo distulit cogitans utrunque, sicut: "Si ulcisci an ignoscem deberet, crimen est mihi magnum." Muri fere interfecto pepercit et eum dimisit. Post paucos vero dies leo incidit rethia, et suis viribus uti non potuit, et maxima voce rugiens, mus autem ut audivit ad eum impetuose veniens, inquit, "Ne timeas parceri; tibi gratiam reddam." Et incepit secare dentibus et rodere nervos sive cordas. Laxavit artus illius ingenio. Sic mus captum leonem liberavit, restituendo silvis, sic ne quis miseros ledat nam prodesse potest, si quis obesse nequit. Tunc ira preci supplicat, tunc preces ammituntur, etc. Allegoria: per leonem patientes, benignos, et nobiles intelligimus; per murem pauperes qui sepissime nobiles offendere prosumunt, quos homo nobilis posset defendere, sed non vult, cogitans, "Qualem laudem habeo in paupere si ledam eum, tandem ille nobilis opprimitur?" Et non potest penitentia uti, sed precibus pauperis liberabitur.

XX. (*De Yrundine et Lino*) Hic nos docet auctor ut non spernamus consilium bonum, quia qui bonum consilum spernit malum invenit; vel non spernamus consilia salutifera, recta, et utilia. Hoc est ne cadamus in opprobria, quod probat dicens cum aves essent pariter congregate et volentes ire ad spacium, invenerunt quendam rusticum seminantem linum in campo, et hoc pro nihilo tenuerunt. Videns hoc, irundo dixit aliis avibus, "Hoc est malum pro nobis, quia ex isto lino fient rethia cum quibus capiemur. Venite; evellamus eum." Aves vero irundinem deriserunt. Deinde ut fructificavit semen iterum irundo dixit eis, "Malum est hoc. Venite; evellamus illud. Nam cum creverit, ex inde fient rethia ut humanis possimus capi artibus." Omnes verba irundinis deriserunt, respuentes eius consilium. Videns hec irundo ad homines se transtulit sive transfert ut tuta esset, subiiciens se eis. Aves vero, que respuerunt modice valentes odientes consilium irundinis, rethibus retente sunt. Ille vero securus vivit qui non habet quid timeat. Allegoria: tu debes insudare bonis operibus, ne dyabolus te seducat ab eis. Per aves intelligimus peccatores, per irundinem spirituales qui semper monent eos ut se abstineant; illi vero respuentes monitionem, venit dyabolus et rapit per rhetia, id est per opera mala et deducit eos ad infernum.

Appendix 4

British Library MS Add. 33780

This is an Italian manuscript on parchment dating from the fourteenth century. Each comment follows its respective fable.

[2r] [*Accessus*]

Salon, quidem sapiens homo fuit qui ivit athenas, ibique invenit librum esopi greci poete prosaice scriptum et metrice de diversis fabulis, et iacebat quasi ex ille opus, cumque ibi cepisset legere et vidisset ad figuram posse converti, ad figuram versus carminis adduxit; fecit inde quemdam librum latinis versibus in quo quaedam libello sive liber .v. quaeruntur, videlicet que materia, que intentio, que utilitas, cui parti phylosophie supponatur, et quod sit libri titulus.

Materia huius libri est lxiiii fabulle. Intentio circa materiam versatur. Incepit enim illa superdicans fabulas describere ad fructum et utilitatem tocius humani generi. Utilitas magna est, quia viso et cognito libro isto, poterimus per ipsum vel per ipsas fabulas informare animum nostrum ad bonum vivendum.

Cui parti phylosophie supponatur: supponitur enim ethyce sive moralitati. Ethis enim grece latine mos interpretatur, quia totus iste liber de moribus tractat, licet fabullose.

Libri titulus talis est: "Incipit libri esopi greci poete," vel "Incipit liber salonis papiensis poete."

Dividitur iste liber totus in duas partes, scilicet in prologum et tractatum. Prologus enim hic incipit: "Ut iuvet et prosit . . ." Tractatus enim illic incipit: "Dum rigido fodit . . ." Iste prologus dividitur in tres partes: in prima, quarum dicit quod prosit iste liber, quia prodesse praestando delectationem ideo quia dicit, "Ut iuvet." Prodest in praestando fructum sive utilitatem, unde dicit Oratius, "Aut prodesse volunt aut delectare poete." In secunda vocat librum istum ortulum vitando arrogantiam. In tercia dicit librum hec non fuisse factam a se, sed a domino, scilicet quod ponitur, unde dicit "Ut messis precium," etc. [Auctor] dicit sicut dicans psalmista, "Qui convertit petram in stagnam aquarum, et rupem in fontes aquarum." Unde prima pars hic incipit: "Ut iuvet . . ."; secunda illic: "Ortulus iste parit . . ."; tertia illic: "Ne mihi torpentem . . ."

[2v] [I.] *De gallo et jaspide*

Legitur fabulose quod gallus querebat escam in fimo et invenit Jaspidem, lapidem preciosum, et nescivit nec voluit eum recipere. Utilitas est hec. Per gallum intellige stultum hominem vel stultum scolarem qui vadit ad scolas et invenit jaspidem sive sapientiam, et nescit recipere nec vult recipere. Quod satis bene declaratur per versus notabiles.

[3r] [II.] *De lupo et agno*

Legitur fabulose quod lupus et agnus sicientes petiverunt fluentum sive aquam in primum tramitem, i.[e.], primam viam, causa bibendi. Ceperunt enim bibere in ripa fluminis, lupus vero in superiore parte fluminis bibebat, agnus in inferiori parte bibebat. Lupus autem aspiciens inferius per flumen vidit agnum et ait ei, "Tu turbasti aquam et nitorem ipsius aque, i.[e.] pulchritudinem, ita quod bibere non valeo." Respondit agnus, "Non feci nec tibi nec acque nocui, quia aqua nescit redire ad fontem." Et sic defendebat se rationabiliter. Dixit autem lupus, "Tu minaris mihi," cui agnus dixit, "Non minor." Et lupus dixit, "Imo facis, et pater tuus fecit mihi illud idem. Cum bene patriças, crimine patris obi." Et ita devoravit eum absque mora. ¶ Per lupum intellige tyrannum, per agnum intellige innocentem hominem que tyrannus destruit et devorat absque mora sine culpa, quod satis bene declaratur per versus notabiles in fine positos.

[III.] *De mure et rana*

Legitur fabulose quod mus volebat ire Romam, et pervenit ad quendam magnum fluvium et non valens transire, cepit tristari. Quem videns [3v] rana locuta est ei, "Noli timere, quia te ultra flumen bene portabo. Et ero tibi navis, nauta, et navigium," tegens in corde magnam fraudem cupiens eum mortificare fraudullenter, dicensque ei, "Porige mihi pedem tuum, et ligabo eum cum meo pede, et sic transibimus cito et secure." Cumque transirent et essent in medio flumine, rana mergebat se et trahebat se murem ad fundum aque. Mus vero, videns quod rana decipiebat eum, defendebat se quantum poterat ne submergeretur, et ita magnum proelium erat inter ipsos. Mivus autem volans inde per aera vidit eos, et utrunque mortificavit. ¶ Per murem intellige fidelem et humilem virum et mulierem, que sine nocumento aliorum vivunt. Per ranam intellige virum fraudolosum et mulierem fraudosam, que cum suis fraudibus finaliter pereunt, quod satis bene declaratur per versus notabiles in fine positos.

[IV.] *De cane urgente ovem et arbitre existente in causam*

Legitur fabulose quod canis curabat, i.[e.], vexabat ovem de pane quem ovis debebat sibi abstulisse et induxit falsos testes ad probandum hoc coram arbitre sive iudice. Cepit loqui canis et inquid sic: "Domine, ovis debet mihi reddere panem quem pepigit, quia furata est mihi. Praecipite quod mihi reddat." Ovis cepit hoc totum negare, et isti falsi testes prohibuerunt falsum testimonium contra eam, et dixerunt quod totum erat verum quod canis dicebat. Et erant isti testes: milvus, vultur, et lupus. Et ita arbiter arbitratus est quod ovis reddat panem cani, et sic oportuit eam vendere lanam suam et emere panem et dare cani. Et ita fecit et nuda vellere [4r] suo sive lana passa est frigus et boream longo tempore. ¶ Per canem intelligitur homo nequam et mulier qui vel quae per nephas alios decipit omnibus modis. Per ovem intelligitur homo vel mulier simplex, qui vel quae nescit se defendere, quod satis bene, etc.

[VI.] *De cane gerente carnem in ore*

Hic tangitur fabula qualiter canis furatus est frustrum carnium, et fugi[4v]ens per quendam pontem, gerens ipsas carnes in ore. Aspiciens in aqua, vidit umbram carnium; credens illas carnes esse in aqua, amisit veras carnes pro vanis. Et recte ita facit fenerator qui feneratur praestans denarios quos habet pro spe futuri lucri, et sepe illos amittit. Per canem intellige hominem cupidum et insatiabilem, qui amittit res quas habet pro rebus quas non habet, quod satis bene declarat per versus, etc.

[VII.] *De femina nupto furi et de viro prudenti*

Hic tangitur fabula qualiter unus fur sive latro accipiebat uxorem et tota vicinia eius cepit gaudere, credens quod de certo non plus debent furari. Quidam autem sapiens vir, arguens praedictam viciniam, tetigit talem fabulam: "Sol volebat accipere uxorem, et terra percullit aures iovis, rogans ipsum quod non promitteret accipere uxorem, dicens quod si alius sol esset, conbureretur a nimio magno calore. Et ita Jupiter prohibuit quod sol non acciperet uxorem, precibus ipsius terrae." Et ita monens ille sapiens vicinos non debere gaudere quod fur acciperet uxorem, quia facere[n]t filios, et ita essent plus fures. ¶ Alegoria talis est: quod boni homines et bonae mulieres nunquam deberent dare favorem et auxilium malis et pravis. Vt faciant et fiant potentes et crescant numero, quod satis declaratur per versus notabiles in fine positos.

[VIII.] *De Lupo et Grua* [*sic*]

Hic tangitur fabulla qualiter lupus cruciabatur ab osse sibi retento in gutture [5r] sive nigula, querens autem medicum qui eum iuvaret de ista egritudine. Spondebat ei dare magnum praemium sive precium de labore suo. Audiens autem hoc, grus ait, "Si vis mi dare hoc quod promittis aliis, volo te liberare de ista egritudine." Respondit autem lupus, "Promitto, et iuro tibi dare quod spondere." Ciconia autem posuit rostrum suum in gula lupi et exemit os de gutture ipsius et liberatus est lupus. Grui vero petenti praemium de labore, ait lupus, "Nil volo tibi dare. Nonne ego potui praecidere collum tuum cum habui in ore? Cum ego non praeciderim, imputa hoc promitto tui laboris." ¶ Alegoria talis est: quod bonus homo non nitatur nec velit facere nec dare auxilium malis quia totum perditum est quod eis fit. Imo mali nituntur reddere malum pro bono, et non timent oblivisci bonorum quae sibi fiunt. Quod satis bene declaratur per versus notabiles.

[6v] [XII.] *De muribus rustico et urbanus*

Legitur fabulose quod mus urbanus ivit rus causa solaciandi, et rusticanus mus cepit eum gratanter, rogans ipsum quod sit secum in prandio, et ivit ad prandium secum. Rusticanus quoque mus gaudenti anima leta quae facie paravit omnia cibaria que potuit tamen crossa. Sicut rusticanus de villa non valebat enim urbanus mus comedere illa cibaria quia crossa erant, et quia non erat consuetus comedere talia cibaria crossa, tamen bona voluntas et clara rusticani muris nobilitabat illa vilia cibaria, et cum comedissent simul, dixit urbanus mus, "Rogo te, amice, ut mecum venias ad urbem, quia cupio tecum in urbe convivari." Acquievit quoque suis precibus, et secum ivit ad urbem, ducens eum ad campam cuidam magnatis, praestansque sibi divitem mensam munitam cibis diversorum generum. Et cum deberent comedere supervenit penullio, inponensque fere clavem, aperuit hostia latrantia, et mures perteriti ceperunt fugere. Urbanus mus latuit in cavo in quo solitus erat latere. Rurensis vero mus, non inveniens cavum in quo posset latere, [A]dhesit muro et febricitabat, semivivus iacens; totus merdatus est pro nimio timore. Et cum exisset penullio, exivit urbanus mus qui latuit. Vocans rurensem murem, cepit blandiri, rogans eum ut deberent gaudere et deberent bibere illa dulcia et amena cibaria, que ei in mensa propriaverat. Respondensque ei mus rurensis, "Tu solus habias [*sic*] talia cibaria timorosa periculosa, quia tibi soli placent. Ego autem volo ire ad villam, et illic rodere fabam pocius quam hic habere in civitate delicata et mori timore." ¶ Utilitas huius fabule est: Melius esse pauperitate quam dives in timore, secundum quod dicit proverbium, "Melius est plumbum in tranquillitate quam aurum in adversitate," quod satis bene declaratur per versus notabiles in fine positos.

[XVIII.] *De leone sopito in silva*

[9r] Legitur quod leo sopiebat in silva, et circa eum curebat [*sic*] turba murium cum pedibus faciendo magnum strepitum, excitatusque leo unum ex illis cepit et poterat eum interficere si volebat, sed pepercit sibi, considerando quod pocius resultabat sibi ad opprobrium quam ad honorem interficiendo eum, et ita dimisit eum vivere. Mus autem recessit, cogitando reddere si talionem de tanto bono pollicitus est, si opem et servicium in omni loco. Transacto autem parvo tempore, leo captus est, [9v] et retentus a rete. Videns eum, mus ad eum cucurit in occursum, notansque vinculum a quo leo detinebatur, corrodit funem, et liberatus est leo. ¶ Alegoria talis est: per leone intelligi vir fortis et potens et discretus qui sit tenere et servare parvos et pauperes apud se, a quibus recipit servicium et honorem et quidem vitam. Per murem intelligi homo parvus, humilis, et bonus, qui recognoscit bona quae sibi fuit, quod satis declaratur per versus notabiles in fine positos.

[XX.] *De yrundine, avibus, et de semine lini*

[10r] Legitur quod agricola more solito suum agrum seminavit de semine lini ut multum linum meteret in futuro. Hic autem videns, yrundo perterita fuit multum propter semen seminatum, considerans quod agricola faceret retia, cum quibus possum eam et alios aves capere et mortificare. Cucurit enim ad alias aves premonens eas ut semen seminatum evellerent. Alicquam exista causa mori possent. Aves autem spreverunt verba et sanum consilium illius. Semen cepit crescere. Rursus yrundo monet aves ut lini evellant. Rursus aves fugiunt sanum consilium. Irundo provida et sapiens vadit ad agricolam, rogans eum ut recipiat eam pro amica, que omni die fundet sibi melos, ut eam de certo non offendat. Agricola vero suis precibus acquievit. Linum vero metitur, retia fiunt ex eo, agricola capit aves. Aves seipsas inculpant et penitent eas non credidisse sano consilio irundinis. ¶ Alegoria est hic: per yrundinem intelligi homo qui videt suos defectus et pericula sibi iminencia, et sit invenire remedium. Per aves intelliguntur stulti qui nolunt credere sapientibus quando eis bene consolunt. Quod satis bene declaratur per versus notabiles in fine positos.

Appendix 5

Accessus to the Elegiac Romulus

Freiburg Universitätsbibliothek MS 21

Esopus progenie nobis magister atheniensis regione grecus studio facunda
moribus quam dictissimus. Autor huius libri volens homines informare quid
facere et quid vitare et sequi debent hoc opus composuit. In quo bruta
irrationabilia et inanimata fingit loqui nobis innuens cavere cavenda et
sequi sequenda. Namque fingit gallum et lupum etc. loqui. Hoc totum figur-
atum est ideo ut sic illud quod minus [vere] in esse insit et illud quod magis
vere inesse inerit. Istud autem opus con[tra]cedium fuit conponitum et diu
occultatum et interpretatum a latinis latuit quidem donec [T]iberius quidam
imperator romulum rogavit ut si aliquas fabulas iocosas ad removendum
publicas curas compileret et legeret. Ipse vero Romulus non audebat precibus tanti viri contradicere librum istum utpote autenticum ab esopo prius
compositum de greco sermone transtulit in latinum. [f. 1v]

Munich Bayerische Staatsbibliothek MS Clm. 16213

This accessus is preceded by the following heading: "Titulus huius libri est
'Incipit Apologus Esopi.' Et apologus est sermon rusticalis de brutis ani-
malibus agens ad instructionem homini. Et scientia presentis libri est ad
allegorias vel etsi ad sermonem moralem. Subordinatur philosophie morali."

Titulus huius libri est Incipit Ezopus nomine magistri sui nuncupatus. Dicitur ezopus ab ysopo tali herba propter similitudinem quia sicut ysopus dat
bonos et varios odores, sic Ezopus dat diversas vtilitates vtique per uersum.
Ysopus est herba, ezopus dat bona verba. Vtilitas talis est: vt perlecto hoc
libro informacionem diversarum virtutum et morum retineamus. Intentio
auctoris est hortari nos ad suum librum legendum et reservare virtutes et
sapientiam que in hoc libro continentur. Parti autem philosophye supponitur ethice quia presens liber tractat de informatione morum et virtutum,
etc. Subiectum istius libri est elegans moralitas per exempla fabularum in-
troducta pro quo Scienda sicut dicit Aristotiles 3° methaphisice et Commen-

tator 2° celi: non omnes homines accipiunt virtutem per eundem modum et
viam eandem. Vnde quidam accipiunt virtutem per modum de munera-
tionis, quidam per modum autoritatum, et quidam per modum fabularum.
hoc idem autor considerans presens Ezopus poeta eximius qui claruit tempore Tyberij regis persarum et erat vir grecus de civitate attica ingeniosus et
prudens qui cum vixit finxit quasdam fabulas in presenti libello contentas
elegancia fictionis insignis componuit de quo quidam metrice. Hic ayt:
Instruit appologus documenta benignus esopus. In quibus vtilitas fulget
quasi solet piropus. Liber ergo iste primo grece conscriptus est a magistro
predicto. post hoc a famulo imperatore Romano ad instruendam Tiberinum
filium suum in latinum venit. Deinde rex anglie afferens in anglicam
lingwam transferri precipit [f. 292r].

Wolfenbüttel Herzog August Bibliothek MS Helmstedter 185

Incipiunt fabule esopi ad detestationem viciorum et virtutum instructionem
finaliter ordinate qui modus instruendi conuertissumus est, quia intellectus
inter cognicionem rerum quam alie intelligentie habent a principio sui esse
actualiter habet similem disponitionem et aptitudinem qui aptitudo non
proprio studio ad laborem ducatur ad actum secundum idem boecii libro 3°
de consolatione metro undecimo heret profecto semen introrsum veri quod
excitatur ventilante doctrina. Et nichilominus mens humana corpori tanquam carceri mancipata ut non nec sensibus corporis quasi angustis qui-
busdam senestris res deforis conspiciat. Est insuper molle corporis sic
gravata ut non nec per sensibilia in cognicionem intelligibilium attingere
valeat. Tercio de anima Unde ostendit generaliter intellectum nostrum ad
hoc quod in cognita percipiat manu duci ex prius scilicet notis ut dicitur ex
primo posteriorum Rethores ergo ut sua eloquentia fiant persuasiva pro
diversis statibus personis et materiis diversis utuntur modis atque mediis.
Nunc exemplo enthimematico primo rethoricorum nunc methaphoris et
similitudinibus ibidem 3° Inter quos alias [quod?] rhetorice perswasionis
materias methaphoricus modis precipuus est et magis generalis secundum
quem rethor potest quarumcumque rerum tam naturalium quam artifi-
cialium uti similitudinibus pro cuiuslibet materia introductione. Dummodo
conversa sit methaphora id est ad propositum bene proportionata scilicet ut
materie et auditoribus contrariat prout late deducit Philosophus 3° rethoris
Est itaque modus ipse magis generalis quia ratione delectationis reddit audi-
torem attentum. Sed ratione evidentie reddit ipsum docilem et benivolen-
tem. Quare conversus videtur et valde proficium virtutum transplanta-
tionem per methaforam germinare et secundare si unicuique statui pro
morali ipsius instructionem de rebus scilicet magis notis similitudines et

exempla proponantur ut scilicet milites per similtudines suorum actuum militarium ad virtutum exercitia inducantur communitatum que rhetores, reges, et principes ex suis regiminibus politicis se ipsos regere discant secundum dictamen rationis et cuius statibus hoc enim intendit philosophus 3° rethoricorum dicens quod omnes methaphore sumende sunt a quantibus et manifestis. Ea propter, in presenti libello virtutum semina per quasdam methaphoras et fabulas ingeniose designatur ut ex processu apparebit [f. 110v–11r].

Notes

Introduction

1. Patavino, *Chronicle,* vii–xiv.

2. Ibid., 88.

3. Ibid., 89–90. The Latin fable text within Patavino's Italian chronicle reads as follows:

> Accipitrem, milui pulsurum bella, columbe
>> Accipiunt regem; rex magis hoste nocet.
> Incipiunt de rege queri, quod sanius esset
>> Milui bella pati, quam sine marte mori. (Muratori, 8, pt. 1:89;
> Hervieux, 2:327)

Patavino and presumably the "man of education" did not reproduce the epimyth of the fable, which warns that one should always anticipate the result of one's actions.

Joseph R. Berrigan's translation is based on L. A. Muratori, ed., *Rerum Italicarum Scriptores: Raccolta degli Storici Italiani* (1723–51; reprint, Città del Castello: Lapi, 1906), vol. 8, pt. 1: *Rolandini Patavini Chronica Marchie Trivixane;* episodes summarized here appear on pp. 89–90. While I have reproduced Berrigan's translation of this fable verbatim, I have taken the liberty of rendering it in prose instead of the six lines of verse which he uses, a form unrelated to the original.

4. Ibid., 90.

5. Ibid., 93–94.

6. For some descriptions of fable teaching, see Glauche, *Schullektüre im Mittelalter;* Thomson and Perraud, *Ten Latin Schooltexts of the Later Middle Ages,* 22; and Ziolkowski, *Talking Animals,* 2.

The uses of fables in sermons receives attention in Douglass, *Justification in Late Medieval Preaching,* 34; Kellogg, "Bishop Brunton and the Fable of the Rats"; Mosher, *Exemplum,* passim.

For discussions of beast fables in illuminated manuscripts, see Randall, *Images in the Margins of Gothic Manuscripts,* 97–98 and passim; for a description of the eleventh-century wall paintings of Aesop's fables at the monastery of Fleury at Saint-Benoît-sur-Loire, see Goldschmidt, *An Early Manuscript of the Aesop Fables and Related Manuscripts,* 44–47.

7. My list of manuscripts collates two sources: Hervieux, *Les Fabulistes Latins,* 1:472–684, which is a descriptive catalogue; it is supplemented by a list from Dicke and Grubmüller, *Die Fabeln des Mittelalters,* lxvi–lxviii.

8. Two extra fables were sometimes added to the end of the collection; *De Capone et Accipitre* and *De Pastore et Lupo* are reproduced by Hervieux (2:350–51). However, they appear in fewer than half of the extant exemplars of this collection, and their presence neither contributes to nor detracts from the understanding of fable provided by the sixty fables which apparently comprise the original collection. Because I am concentrating upon the fables translated by British writers, all of which come from Book 1 of the collection, I have given the two added fables no attention in this study.

9. Hervieux, 2:602–31, supplemented by entries under "Ésope de Phrygie: Anonymus Neveleti" in *Catalog Général des Livres Imprimés de la Bibliothèque Nationale,* vol. 48 (Paris: Imprimerie Nationale, 1912); and entries under "Aesop [Latin—Anonymus Neveleti Collection]" and *"auctores (octo)"* in *British Library General Catalogue of Printed Books to 1975* (London: Clive Bingley, 1979).

10. Julia Bastin, ed., *Recueil Général des Isopets* (Société des Anciens Textes de Français. Paris: Firmin Didot, 1930), and Karl Warnke, "Die Quellen des Esope der Marie de France," in *Forschungen zur Romanische Philologie: Festgabe für Hermann Suchier,* 161–284 (Halle: Max Niemeyer, 1900. Repr. Tübingen, 1978).

11. Hervieux, *Les Fabulistes Latins,* 1:475–95.

12. See Ashby, *The Fox and the Grapes,* 17–19.

13. Davis, "Education in Dante's Florence," 417–18; Hunt, *Teaching and Learning Latin,* 2:11; Gehl, *A Moral Art,* 120–34; Grendler, *Schooling in Renaissance Italy,* 17; Grubmüller, *Meister Esopus,* 77–85.

1. Figuring the Fable and Its Father

1. Nøjgaard, *La Fable Antique,* 41.

2. Perry, ed., *Babrius and Phaedrus,* 419–610.

3. *Studium Generale* 1 (1959): 17–37.

4. Ibid., 18.

5. *Bestia: Yearbook of the Beast Fable Society* 2 (1990): 4–18.

6. Ibid., 8–10; Ziolkowski offers further elaboration of these points.

7. At the end of the plot summary and reiterated epimyth, the commentator writes, "Notandum etiam quod secundum quondam praesens textus non praetendit fabulam. Immo potius veracitatem meram praetendit et hic nihil ponitur quod videtur includere impossibilitatem credendi." [It should be noted that according to some people the present text does not represent a fable. Rather, it represents pure truth, and here nothing is set forth that seems to necessitate the impossibility of being believed.] The commentator concludes by adding that some have linked the tale to Roman chronicles (Quentell, Fable 42, n.p.).

8. Ziolkowski, "The Form and Spirit of the Beast Fable," 17. The author admits that he has a personal interest in the creation of the category "beast literature": at the time that he wrote this essay, he was teaching a course of that title (16), and later

he published a book whose title includes a variation on the term, *Talking Animals: Medieval Latin Beast Poetry, 750–1150,* a study that focuses upon non-fabular literature and requires no justification for its self-definition beyond that given in its title.

9. "Literary Genres and Textual Genericity," 170.

10. *The Fable as Literature,* xi.

11. Ibid., xvii.

12. Tübingen: Max Niemeyer, 1959.

13. *Meister Esopus,* 1–40.

14. This article posits a very different basis for the consideration of genre than "Literary Genres and Textual Genericity"; indeed, the article on Aesop uncovers a unique "generic" essence for fable which seems somewhat inconsistent with Schaeffer's more general discussion.

15. Schaeffer identifies the Augustana as "a group of five classes of manuscripts, of which the oldest in subject matter and the most complete is formed by MS Augustanus 564 and MS Parisinus 690."

16. "*Aesopus auctor inventus,*" 347–49.

17. *Language, Counter-memory, Practice: Selected Essays and Interviews,* 123.

18. Schaeffer, "*Aesopus auctor inventus,*" 355.

19. Leibfried, ed., *Fabel,* 31–35.

20. Schaeffer, "*Aesopus auctor inventus,*" 356.

21. In *Talking Animals,* Ziolkowski discusses the uses of beast literature in satirical classroom drama in his chapter entitled "Dramatic and Dialogic Beast Poems," 131–52.

22. Schaeffer, "*Aesopus auctor inventus,*" 361.

23. Foucault, "What Is an Author?" 131.

24. I have reached the figure of fifty printings by adding to Hervieux's list of editions (2:602–34) evidence of a few more printings in the listings of the catalogues of the British Library and the Bibliothèque Nationale.

The British market for printed books in Latin was supplied largely by continental presses. Lotte Hellinga has studied this phenomenon in her essay "Importation of Books Printed on the Continent into England and Scotland before c. 1520"; she writes of the very limited book production in England in the fifteenth century, adding, "Almost all books in Latin were imported from abroad" (206). See *Printing the Written Word,* Sandra Hindman, ed., 205–24.

25. Hervieux, 2:602–19; *British Museum Catalogue,* cols. 11–15; *Catalog Général des Livres Imprimés de la Bibliothèque Nationale,* vol. 48, p. 158.

26. Österley, *Steinhöwels Äsop,* 1–3; Caxton, *Caxton's Aesop,* 5.

27. Hervieux, 2:602–19; *British Museum Catalogue,* cols. 11–15.

28. *Caxton's Aesop,* 4.

29. Holbek, *Æsops levned og fabler,* 2:117.

30. Beardsley, *Hispano-Classical Translations Printed between 1482 and 1699,* 20–21; Keller and Kincade, *Iconography in Medieval Spanish Literature,* 93.

31. Holbek, *Æsops levned og fabler,* 1:117.

32. Keller and Kincade, *Iconography in Medieval Spanish Literature*, 93.

33. Holbek, *Æsops levned og fabler*, 1:116.

34. This edition has been printed in a facsimile as part of the *Xilografies Gironines: Les Faules d'Isop*, Joan Amades, ed. (Girona: Gironella, 1947).

35. Holbek, 1:119. In the English summary of *Æsop's levned og fabler*, Holbek suggests the desperation surrounding the Danish publication of this Aesopic collection and its near-disappearance:

> The Danish humanist Christiern Pedersen, who died in 1554, left an unprinted translation of the German edition. . . . His German son-in-law Bastian Hülsebrock saw the book through the press in Malmö in 1556. The poor editorial circumstances (Chr. Pedersen was doting and perhaps never had the work quite finished, the printer was old, the editor was a German probably with little knowledge of the Danish language, and apparently the manuscript was difficult to read) are without doubt the cause of the poor quality of the text, which has a large number of misunderstandings and misprints.
>
> One copy only is known, presented to the Royal Library in Copenhagen by the Swedish book collector Count L. Manderström in about 1880. Twenty leaves are lacking. (2:295–96)

36. *Studies in the Text History of the Life and Fables of Aesop*, 26.

37. Ibid., 226, n. 16.

38. Calogerà, *Nuova Raccolta d'Opuscoli Scientifici e Filologici*, 4:151.

39. Perry, "The Text Tradition of the Greek Life of Aesop," 244.

40. In the examination of fable's pedigree, two important aspects of Aesop as a father figure should be mentioned. First, Aesop's own birth and childhood receive no attention in the *Life:* he is a man without an origin, as shown in this dialogue when Xanthus is deciding whether to buy Aesop as a slave:

> And he [Xanthus] asked what art thow / And Esope ansuerd / I am of flesshe and bone / And Exantus sayd / I demaunde the not that / but where were thou engendrid And Esope ansuerd / in thw wombe of my moder / And Exantus sayd / yet I aske the not that neyther / Butr I aske of the In what place thow were borne / And Esope sayd / My moder neuer told / ne assured me / whether she was delyuerd of me in her chambre or in the halle. (Caxton, 34)

Whether this Aesop knows his own genealogy seems less significant than the fact that we cannot.

Equally significant is his apparent inability to father literally, a problem which leads him into political trouble:

> by cause Esop had no children / he adopted a noble and yonge child to his sone / which child was named Enus / This Enus within a lytel whyle after / medled with the chamberere of Esope whiche he held for his wyf / and knewe her bodyly / And by cause he was in grete doubte that Esope wold auenge hym he accused Esope toward the kynge of cryme of lezemageste or treason / and

composed fals lettres shewynge by them to the kynge / how by the fables whiche he sente here and thyder he hadde bytrayd hym / and that he had conspyred his dethe. (Caxton, 60)

The king orders Aesop executed, but he is hidden by a servant who admires him and later is resurrected when needed for diplomacy.

41. Patterson, *Fables of Power,* 34–36.

42. Ibid., 38.

43. *The Fables of Aesop,* xiv.

44. *Studies in the Text History of the Life and Fables of Aesop,* 1.

45. Ibid., 2. Within the last fifty years, scholars have been less quick to pass judgment upon the *Life* and more likely to view it as not so naive as previously thought. Bengt Holbek characterized Steinhöwel's Aesop in its entirety as "popularized scholarship" (294). Most recently, historian Keith Hopkins has read the text for evidence of attitudes toward slavery in Roman society; he disagrees with Perry's view of the work's audience, stating, "The *Life* makes jokes about academic pedantry and the respect due from children to their professors, which may indicate its origins or circulation among students"; see "Novel Evidence for Roman Slavery," 11.

46. Von Kreisler, "An Aesopic Allusion in the *Merchant's Tale.*" This article will be discussed in Chapter 4.

47. Phaedrus, trans. B. E. Perry, *Babrius and Phaedrus,* 290–91.

48. Ibid., 246–49.

49. *Caxton's Aesop,* 67.

50. See Perry's comments in *Babrius and Phaedrus,* xcvii–xcviii.

51. This fable concludes the Phaedrian collection in Wolfenbüttel MS Gud. Lat. 148, a manuscript written in Lombardy in the tenth century but later belonging to the monastic school of Sts. Peter and Paul in Wittenberg (Hervieux, 2:267–76); the so-called Romulus of Vienna in Imperial Library MS 303, a fourteenth-century schoolbook that includes Cato, Avianus, and the *Physiologus* (Hervieux, 2:688–90); five manuscripts of the *Romulus ordinaire* (Hervieux, 2:331–490); and two of the three *Romulus Nilantii* manuscripts, both from the thirteenth century, Bodleian Digby MS 172 and Bibliothèque Nationale MS 18270 (Herviecux, 2:715–17).

52. Wolfenbüttel MS Gud. Lat. 148; Vienna Imperial Library MS 303; and four of the five *Romulus ordinaire* manuscripts (Hervieux, 1:331–490).

53. Thiele, *Der Lateinische Äsop,* xv.

54. Hervieux, 2:234.

55. *Caxton's Aesop,* 68–71.

56. In order to introduce and summarize the lengthy *Speculum historiale* along with its companion volumes, the *Speculum naturale* and the *Speculum doctrinale,* Vincent wrote his *Libellus totius operis apologeticus,* in which he cites the *Historia ecclesiastica Eusebii Cesariensis et Rufini Aquilensis* as one of his sources. See Lusignan, "Preface au *Speculum Maius* de Vincent de Beauvais," 137.

57. Hervieux, 2:245.

58. Minnis, *Medieval Theories of Authorship,* 2nd ed., 157.

59. Marie de France, *Les Fables,* ed. Charles Brucker, 49–50.

60. For example, a *"seigneur"* has power over a *"sergant"* (servant) in Marie's eighty-fifth fable, "Del vilein e des bus" (The Peasant and the Oxen).

61. Minnis, *Medieval Theory of Authorship*, 75–84.

62. Marie de France, *Fables*, ed. and trans. Harriet Spiegel, 4.

63. Marie de France, *Les Fables*, ed. Charles Brucker, 49, n. 3.

64. *Marie de France: Äsop*, 55, n. 1.

65. Brucker, 6–11; Spiegel, trans., 6–7.

66. *Studies in the Text History of the Life and Fables of Aesop*, 40–41, n. 44.

67. Brucker, 20–21.

68. Ibid., 10–11; Grubmüller, 74–77; text in Hervieux, 2:564–649.

69. *Rhetoric, Hermeneutics, and Translation in the Middle Ages*, 25.

70. Hervieux, 1:475–95.

71. The edition's place in literary history was guaranteed when it was chosen as a base text by La Fontaine, whose very French fabulistic achievement is thus made to spring from ostensibly German roots.

72. *L'Aesopus moralisatus stampato in Parma da Andrea Portilia nel 1481*, 19–21.

2. Theories of Fable: Telling Truth, Fearing Falsehood

1. Quoted in Demats, *Fabula: Trois Etudes de Mythographie Antique et Médiévale*, 2.

2. *Fabula: Explorations into the Uses of Myth in Medieval Platonism*, 5.

3. Ibid., 4.

4. *Old Concepts and New Poetics*, 4–6.

5. *Institutio Oratoria*, ed. M. Winterbottom: 1, ix. 2–3; trans. Ziolkowski, *Talking Animals*, 21.

6. "... [fabellae] ducere animos solent praecipue rusticorum et imperitorum, qui et simplicius quae fictae sunt audiunt, et capti uoluptate facile iis quibus delectantur consentiunt." [(Fables) usually beguile the minds of the rustic and the unlearned, who both lend an ear more naively to fiction, and also, for desire of pleasure, show favor readily to those things which bring gratification.] *Institutio Oratoria* 5.ii.19; vol. 1: 283.

7. Charles E. Little, *The "Institutio Oratoria" of Marcus Fabius Quintilianus*, vol. 2 (Nashville: Peabody Press, n.d.), 20–21.

Vincent of Beauvais was himself a fabulist; see Hervieux, 2:234–45.

8. Prisciani Caesariensis, *Opuscula*, vol. 1, ed. Marina Passalacqua, 33–34; *Readings in Medieval Rhetoric*, ed. Miller, Prosser, and Benson, 52–53.

9. Ziolkowski, *Talking Animals*, 21–22.

10. Hervieux, 3:463–64.

11. Macrobius, *Commentarii in Somnium Scipionis*, ed. Jacob Willis, I.ii.9; *Commentary on "The Dream of Scipio,"* trans. William Harris Stahl, 84–85.

12. *Contra Mendacium*, 469–528, in *Corpus Scriptorum Ecclesiasticorum Latinorum*, vol. 41, 508–509; trans. Rev. H. Browne, *Nicene and Post-Nicene Fathers of the Christian Church*, vol. 3: *St. Augustine: On the Holy Trinity, Doctrinal Treatises, Moral Treatises*, 494.

13. *Quaestiones evangeliorum*, ed. A. Mutzenbecher, *CCSL* 44 B (1980), 2.51 (pp. 116–17); qtd. in and trans. by Mehtonen, *Old Concepts and New Poetics*, 124.

14. *Isidori Hispalensis Episcopi: Etymologiarum Sive Originum*, ed. W. M. Linsay, I.xl.1; Irvine, trans., *The Making of Textual Culture: "Grammatica" and Literary Theory, 350–1100*, 237.

15. *Isidori Hispalensis Episcopi*, I.xl.3; Irvine, *The Making of Textual Culture*, 238.

16. Irvine, *The Making of Textual Culture*, 239.

17. *Accessus ad Auctores, Bernard d'Utrecht, Conrad d'Hirsau: Dialogus super Auctores*, ed. Huygens, 22.

18. This is a form of "type C" prologue; it is described fully by Minnis, *Medieval Theories of Authorship*, and in my discussion of the *accessus* to the verse Romulus in Chapter 3.

19. Dronke, ed. and trans., *Fabula: Explorations into the Uses of Myth in Medieval Platonism*, 17.

20. Ibid., 18.

21. See, for example, I Corinthians 3:2; I Peter 2:2; Hebrews 5:12; qtd. in Curtius, *European Literature and the Latin Middle Ages*, 134.

22. *Accessus ad Auctores, Bernard d'Utrecht, Conrad d'Hirsau: Dialogus super Auctores*, ed. Huygens, 86; Minnis and Scott, *Medieval Literary Theory and Criticism, c. 1100–c. 1375: The Commentary Tradition*, 48.

23. *Accessus ad Auctores*, 86; Minnis and Scott, *Medieval Literary Theory and Criticism*, 49.

24. Presumably the Aesopic collection to which Conrad refers is one of the "Romulus" group; it is obviously not Walter's verse collection.

25. Ibid., 87–88.

26. Ibid., 88.

27. Ibid., 89; Minnis and Scott, trans., *Medieval Literary Theory and Criticism*, 51.

28. Related to Conrad of Hirsau's *Dialogus* is the versified *Registrum Multorum Auctorum* of Hugo von Trimberg (c. 1230–c. 1313). Hugo's list of curricular authors and texts puts the *Disticha Catonis* before Aesop (in this instance the verse Romulus, as shown by the incipit below). However, because Hugo adheres to Conrad's preference for Avianus over Aesop, he describes the verse Romulus in only four verses.

Cathonem in ordine	sequitur Esopus,
Clara cuius carmina	lucent ut pyropus.
Fertur is in Frigia	quondam floruisse
Et fabularum carmina	dulcia finxisse.

Incipit Esopus:
Ut iuvat et prosit conatur pagina presens
Dulcius arrident seria picta iocis, etc. (ed. Langosch, lines 589–92, p. 185)

Avianus earns a description four times as long as this one.

For our purposes, this passage is of interest less for its theories of fable than for its reiteration of both Conrad's order of study (Cato, Aesop, and then Avianus) and his belief that Aesop came from Phrygia. Hugo may also have created the metaphorical rhyme comparing Aesop to bronze (*pyropus*) that appears, equally undeveloped, in some curricular manuscripts; see p. 94.

29. See Jeauneau, "L'Usage de la notion d'*integumentum* à travers les gloses de Guillaume de Conches."

30. The *"Parisiana Poetria" of John of Garland*, ed. and trans. Traugott Lawler, 104–105. I have followed Mehtonen's changes to Lawler's translation, leaving *appologus* as its English cognate "apologue"; see *old Concepts and New Poetics*, 141.

31. Minnis and Scott, *Medieval Literary Theory and Criticism*, 3.

32. *Aristoteles Latinus*, vol. 33, ed. Laurentius Minio-Paluello (Brussels and New Haven: Yale University Press, 1974; Paris: Desclée de Brouwer, 1968), 51–52; Minnis and Scott, trans., *Medieval Literary Theory and Criticism*, 299–300.

33. Trans. Charles G. Osgood, *Boccaccio on Poetry*, 48.

34. Ibid., 49.

35. Ibid., 51.

36. Ibid., 64–65.

3. Toward a Grammar of Medieval Fable Reading in Its Pedagogical Context

1. Bourdieu, *Language and Symbolic Power*, 58.

2. Ibid., 61.

3. Ibid., 60–61.

4. *Schools and Scholars in Fourteenth-Century England*, 157–67.

5. Ibid., 159.

6. "Schoolmasters, 1307–1509," in Cecil H. Clough, ed., *Profession, Vocation and Culture in Later Medieval England*, 223-25.

7. For a discussion of the dangers of such an attempt, see Woods, "Editing Medieval Commentaries."

8. *Ovid and Medieval Schooling*, 115.

9. Ibid., 78.

10. Qtd. in Woods, "Editing Medieval Commentaries," 135–36.

11. Under this rubric Dagenais places the "New Philology" issue of *Speculum* 65 (1) (January 1990).

12. *The Ethics of Reading in Manuscript Culture*, 14.

13. Ibid., 57.

14. *The Making of Textual Culture*, 2.

15. See, for example, Carruthers, *The Book of Memory*, 21–22, 204–205; see also Reynolds, *Medieval Reading*, 29.

16. In his study of surviving school manuscripts from trecento Florence, Paul F. Gehl indicates that the *Disticha Catonis*, the first text studied by grammar-school

pupils, could be copied easily onto a gathering of six to eight leaves; four of the seven manuscripts in his census were originally pamphlets of this format. See *A Moral Art: Grammar, Society, and Culture in Trecento Florence,* 113.

John Lydgate writes of translating a fable (though not his *Isopes Fabules*) from a pamphlet. In the fifth stanza of "The Churl and the Bird" (468–85), as he approaches the end of his prolix prohemium, Lydgate's narrator states:

> And heere I cast vnto my purpoos
> Out of Frenssh a tale to translate
> Which in a paunflet I radde and sauh but late. (lines 33–35)

17. Hunt, *Teaching and Learning Latin,* 2:11. Also apparently a student manuscript, British Library MS Add. 27625, a combination of paper and vellum, was written in the fourteenth century in inexpert, uneven script; jagged initials, adorned with smiling faces, have been added in red. Spilled ink has soaked through the first three folios. Although even in its original condition the copy would not have been a source of pride for an adult, its student-scribe has scrawled the colophon, "Finis. Ego F. feci hoc opus." The copy is now bound with Boethius's *Consolation of Philosophy.*

18. In *Virgil in Medieval England,* Christopher Baswell says that the Virgil manuscripts with glosses in English date from "well into the fourteenth century" (63); he discusses one that postdates the Peasants' Revolt of 1381 (146–47), roughly contemporaneous with MS Add. 10089.

Vernacular plot summaries also appeared in early printed schoolbooks; see Smith, "An Early Italian Edition of Aesop's Fables," 65–67. Smith describes several late-fourteenth- and early-fifteenth-century editions of the elegiac Romulus.

19. For an examination of *derivatio* in relation to Horace's *Satires,* see Reynolds, *Medieval Reading: Grammar, Rhetoric, and the Classical Text,* 77–81; for more general discussion, see Gehl, *A Moral Art,* 125.

20. Hervieux, 2:317.

21. In relation to Fable 50, "De Patre et Filio," in which young people are urged to respect their elders, this manuscript suggests that a pupil (*"discipulus"*) behave similarly toward his teacher (*"magister"*). The rarity of such direct discussion of the student-teacher relationship in fable manuscripts suggests that this injunction might be wishful thinking on the part of a teacher.

22. *Medieval Reading,* 116; cf. 117–20.

23. See, for example, J. W. Jones and E. F. Jones, eds., *The Commentary on the First Six Books of the "Aeneid" of Virgil, Commonly Attributed to Bernardus Silvestris* (Lincoln: University of Nebraska Press, 1977); this edition is translated in Earl G. Schreiber and Thomas E. Maresca, trans., *Commentary on the First Six Books of Virgil's "Aeneid" by Bernardus Silvestris.*

24. Source studies include Wright, "The 'Nuremberg' *Aesop* and Its Sources"; diachronic studies include Adalbert Elschenbroich, "Von unrechtem gewalte: Weltlicher und geistlicher Sinn der Fabel vom 'Wolf und Lamm' von der Spätantike

bis zum Beginn der Neuzeit," in *Sub tua platano: Festgabe für Alexander Beinlich* (Emsdetten: Verlag Lechte, 1981), 420–51; and Dietmar Peil, *Der Streit der Glieder mit dem Magen* (Frankfurt: Peter Lang, 1985).

25. Text from Österley, *Steinhöwels Äsop,* 3. For some textual variants in the Romulus epistle, see Thiele, *Der Lateinische Äsop,* 2–4.

26. Ibid., 2, n. 2.

27. Jongkees, "Translatio Studii: Les avatars d'un thème médiéval," 41–44; Copeland, *Rhetoric, Hermeneutics, and Translation in the Middle Ages,* 103–107.

28. Goez, *Translatio Imperii,* 378–81.

29. *A Moral Art,* 111.

30. Seeman, *Hugo von Trimberg und die Fabeln seines Renners,* 23–40. Seeman bases his assertions on the fact that plot summaries in elegiac Romulus commentaries sometimes retain elements of the plots from other Romulus collections. While the information that Seeman provides helps to elucidate the background of fable commentary, he seems intent upon denying the elegiac Romulus its own commentary tradition in favor of a tradition borrowed from earlier sources.

31. *Medieval Theory of Authorship,* 19.

32. In his exploration of authorship of the fables, Hervieux discusses the Italian tradition attributing the translation of Aesop's work to Salon (1:479–82); the attribution is lauded though not further substantiated by Ciavarella in *L'Aesopus moralizatus stampato in Parma,* 19–21.

33. In Hexter's first appendix of *accessus* texts, see *Epistulae ex Ponto,* Munich Bayerische Staatsbibliothek MS Clm. 14752 (220); the second half of the *accessus* introducing the *Tristia, Epistulae heroidum,* and *Amores* in Munich MS Clm. 631 (223); and the related *accessus* to *Epistulae ex Ponto* in Copenhagen MS Hafn. 2015 and Wolfenbüttel MS Guelf. 4459 (226). While none of these includes all of the *accessus* categories listed by Minnis, each clearly represents a fully developed "type C" *accessus.*

34. *Ovid and Medieval Schooling,* 11.

35. Ibid., 212.

36. Hervieux lists the contents of this manuscript (1:595).

37. Hervieux does not include this marker, but it is significant inasmuch as it appears alongside every moral in this manuscript of the fables; by extension, the scribe is thus implying that this is the maxim relating to fable reading which should be remembered from the *accessus.*

I read two words in this manuscript differently from Hervieux, and I include those differences in the text reproduced here. In the definition of anagogic interpretation, where I read "*sursum*" Hervieux read "*supra.*" More important is the second word in the penultimate sentence, written "*mōis*"; Hervieux expanded this abbreviation to "*moralibus,*" but in this context, "*modis,*" referring to the four modes of reading just defined, seems preferable.

38. Hervieux, 2:595–96.

39. Hervieux, 2:564.

40. *Medieval Theory of Authorship*, 28.

41. Wright reproduces a version of this *accessus* in his unpublished dissertation, "The 'Nuremberg' *Aesop* and Its Sources."

42. See, for example, Stuttgart Württembergische Landesbibliothek MS HB. XII.4.

43. *Medieval Theory of Authorship*, 30.

44. A similar "extrinsic" *accessus* appears in Munich Bayerische Staatbibliothek MS Clm. 14529.

45. Trier MS 132, f. 159r–v, Stuttgart MS HB.I.127, f. 135r–v.

46. Other commentaries in which the commentator simply paraphrases without elaborating upon the morals of the fables include: Paris Bibliothèque Nationale MSS Lat. 8023, 8259 (in which each summary precedes its fable) and 8509A; Besançon Bibliothèque Publique MS 534; Milan Biblioteca Nazionale Braidense MS AD.10.43.n2; Ferrara Bibloteca Comunale Ariostea MS II.216; and Berlin Staatsbibliothek Preussischer Kulturbesitz MS Germ. Qu.1145 and MS Lat. Oct. 87. Of these, BN MSS 8023 and 8259, Berlin SPK MS Lat. Oct. 87, and the Besançon manuscript are full or partial *libri catonianus*.

47. *Rhetoric, Hermeneutics, and Translation in the Middle Ages*, 83. The practice of paraphrasing is closely related to the imposition of the *ordo naturalis* on poetic syntax; see Reynolds, *Medieval Reading*, 118–19.

48. Another form of commenting, if not true commentary, shares conceptual similarities with the summaries described above. It is best exemplified by Wolfenbüttel MS 162 Gud., a fifteenth-century parchment manuscript. The scribe in this professionally produced manuscript has written titles so lengthy that they serve as highly abbreviated plot summaries. For example, the fable of the frog and the mouse is entitled "De milvo rapiente murem et ranam dolo societatem faciente" [Of the kite seizing the mouse and the frog creating a friendship by fraud] (f. 1v). This title, which reads the fable backwards, molds the reader's understanding of the plot before he reads it. The title and the two-line moral nicely encapsulate the fable.

Although this manuscript is quite luxurious, it was nonetheless used as a school-book at some point in its history; written upside down in the bottom margin of ff. 7v and 8r in a hand different from that of the scribe is the following sentence: "Ego novo proles canonicus sum."

49. The comments in BL MS Add. 33780 (Appendix 4) fit this description.

50. See also Appendix 4, Fable 1, in which the foolish cock can be read as a stupid man or a stupid pupil ("stultum hominem vel stultum scolarem").

51. The fables written by Odo of Cheriton in the early thirteenth century frequently employ this type of allegory, largely because Odo was writing for a clerical audience. Hervieux reproduces Odo's fables in *Les Fabulistes Latins*, 4:173–250; they have been translated by John C. Jacobs, who provides historical information about Odo and his collection; see *The Fables of Odo of Cheriton*.

52. *Reductorium morale, liber xv: Ovidius moralizatus, cap. 1: De formis figurisque deorum*, ed. J. Engels, 105.

53. Reproduced in Seeman, *Hugo von Trimberg und die Fabeln seines Renners*, 29.

54. In the appendix of this text, see Fables 3 and 6 for further examples of this allegorical form.

55. Bersuire, *Reductorium morale*, 96. This binarism also appears in treatments of classical texts that were viewed as more historical than fictional. See Baswell, "The Medieval Allegorization of the *Aeneid*." This important article, which includes commentary texts from the Peterhouse manuscript, cites allegorizations of the golden bough as either "virtues, by which men are liberated from the hell of this life and are borne to heaven" or "the riches which cast men down to hell" (187).

56. Hervieux, 2:341.

57. For Petronius's version, see *Petronius and Seneca: Apocolocyntosis*, trans. Michael Heseltine and W. H. D. Rouse (Loeb Classical Library; Cambridge: Harvard University Press, 1969), 269–77. A general thematic discussion of this and similar stories appears in E. Griesbach, *Die Wanderung der treulosen Witwe durch die Weltliteratur* (Berlin: N.p., 1976).

58. British Library MS Add. 11897 includes and even allegorizes the most common variant in the fable, four lines which Hervieux reproduces in his note to the fable (2:341, n. 1); in this variant the guard remembers that the body on the cross had been missing teeth, to which the widow responds that he should not be afraid. She picks up a stone and breaks the teeth of her husband's corpse. The MS Add. 11897 commentator, after providing an allegory very similar to that in the *Esopus moralizatus*, adds:

> Et evellat eius dentes, id est per remorsu conscientiae, amaritudine penitentie, confessione oris, et satisfactione in opere, deleat multitudinem peccaminum animam a diversis morsibus vulneracium. (20r)

> [And she removes his teeth, that is through remorse of conscience, bitterness of penitence, confession of mouth, and satisfaction in works, she destroys a multitude of little sins of woundings to the soul from different bites.]

The commentator uses the textual variant about the corpse's teeth as an opportunity for etymological wordplay on the Latin *remorsum*, derived from the verb *mordeo*, "to bite"; such wordplay is one of the foundations of allegory. For a discussion of the relationship between wordplay and allegory, see Quilligan, *The Language of Allegory*, 33–51.

59. "*Metamorphosis Ovidiana Moraliter Explanata*" (Paris, 1509) of Pierre Bersuire, and "*Libellus*" (Basel, 1509) of "*Albricus*," intro. Stephen Orgel (New York: Garland, 1979), lxxvi.

60. The widow-as-soul/soldier-as-body allegory appears in the printed *Auctores octo* commentary and, along with the manuscript cited in the previous note, the following manuscripts: Milan Biblioteca Ambrosiana I. 85 supra; Mainz Stadtbibliothek 540; Trier Stadtbibliothek MSS 132, 756, and 1109; Stuttgart Württembergische Landesbibliothek HB.I.127; Munich Bayerische Staatsbibliothek MSS Clm. 7680, 14703, 16213, 19667; Wrocław Biblioteka Uniwersytecka MSS

II.Qu.33, IV.Qu.81; IV.Qu.88; Berlin SPK MS Lat. Qu.382; Wolfenbüttel Herzog August Bibliothek MS 185 Helmst.; and Vatican MS Lat. 557.

The same allegory also appears in Munich Bayerische Staatsbibliothek MS 14529, but its appearance here deserves mention separately from other copies, as the scribe has moved the fable from its usual position as the forty-eighth or forty-ninth of the sixty fables in the collection. He has placed it last in the elegiac Romulus, perhaps suggesting that students are ready to confront both the narrative's literal meaning and the allegory's more complex structure only when they are about to complete their study of the collection.

Although this allegory dominates the scholastic commentary tradition, Freiburg Universitätsbibliothek MS 21 interprets the fable in the opposite way: there, in a very brief allegory, the corpse is the spirit of an evil man, and the soldier is a devil accepting the gift of the man from his widow and damning him to eternal death (f. 19r–v). Since the woman is not allegorized, the fable's anti-feminism is left to be read literally.

61. This allegory appears in a handful of fifteenth-century Italian manuscript commentaries and nearly all contemporaneous German ones. The Italian manuscripts include: Milan Biblioteca Ambrosiana MS I. 85 supra (dated 1415) and MS Trotti 161; Treviso Biblioteca Comunale MS 156 in both of its commentaries (61r and 72r); and Vatican MS Lat. 557. The German manuscripts include Berlin SPK MS Lat. Qu.18; Leipzig Universitätsbibliotek MS 1084; Mainz Stadtbibliothek MS 540; Munich Bayerische Staatsbibliothek MSS Clm. 609, 7680, 14529, 14703, 16213, 19667; Ottobeuren Stiftsbibliothek MS o.82; Prague Statni Knihovna MS XI.C.4; Stuttgart Württembergische Landesbibliothek MS HB.I.127 and HB.XII.4; Trier Stadtbibliothek MS 132/1197; Wolfenbüttel Herzog August Bibliothek MS Helmst. 185; and Wrocław Biblioteka Uniwersytecka MSS II.Qu.33, IV.Qu.4, IV.Qu.81, and IV.Qu.88. Also in Wolfenbüttel H.A.B. MS 81.16.Aug.fol., in which German plot summaries and comments are given for the Latin verse fables, the anti-Semitic reading is translated into the vernacular.

62. Hervieux, 2:338.

63. *Reductorium morale,* 101.

64. Cited in Baswell, *Virgil in Medieval England,* 66.

65. In the comment on the previous fable of the wolf and the lamb, this manuscript also lists some of the characteristics which Isidore attributes to wolves (65r).

Although this naturalistic interpretation of fable characters seems far removed from modern scholarly practice, within the last fifty years a similar approach has been taken to Chauntecleer in "The Nun's Priest's Tale." See Laila Phipps Boone's "Chauntecleer and Partlet Identified" (*MLN* 64 [1949]: 78–81), in which the author's goal is to classify the fictional rooster as a Golden Spangled Hamburg.

66. One more Latin "commentary" of unusual form deserves consideration here, though its audience sets it apart from the scholastic commentaries discussed above. After the elegiac Romulus in *Les Fabulistes Latins,* Hervieux reproduces verse *additiones* to the fables from Brussels Bibliothèque Royale MS 11193 (2:352–65),

a work nearly identical to Bibliothèque Nationale MS 1594 and the former MS Grenville XIII, now British Library MS Add. 33781. According to Hervieux (2:516–28), this trio of manuscripts was produced by the same scribe and illuminator in the second quarter of the fourteenth century; comprising both the elegiac Romulus and eighteen fables of Avianus, along with French translations and skilled illuminations, these volumes were not produced for schools. Rather, the manuscript now housed in the Bibliothèque Nationale was created for Jeanne de Bourgogne, wife of Philip VI of France. A lengthy epilogue entitled "Comment L'Acteur a Compilé ces Livres avecques Adicions Aucunes en l'Onneur de Madame La Royne" explains the history of the manuscript's creation and its author's goals (Hervieux, 2:524–26).

The additions to each fable, generally four lines appended to the *moralitas* and amplifying its concerns, are clearly related to the scholastic commentary tradition. For example, the addition to Fable 3, "De Mure et Rana," begins with the distich, "Incidit in foveam quam fecerit insidiator; / In laqueum fraudator cadit ipse suum" (Hervieux, 2:353). These lines paraphrase Psalm 7:16, which also appears in the comment to this fable in the *Esopus moralizatus* (Appendix 2, p. 208). The addition to Fable 45 of the war between the birds and quadrupeds includes the line, "Nemo potest dominis pariter servire duobus," a paraphrase of Matthew 6:24, the verse also used in the comment on the same fable in BL MS Add. 11897.

In vernacular translations of scholastic texts (including those undertaken by Lydgate and Henryson), the division between authoritative text and appended commentary is often blurred by the vernacular poet, but the commentator whose work appears in these three manuscripts makes a gesture apparently unique in the literature associated with the elegiac Romulus: he attempts to erase completely the division between the authoritative Latin verse fables and his moralizing comments added to them.

That this text was meant for a female audience raises interesting issues: Jeanne's Latin skills must have been quite advanced if the writer of the additions, or even only the scribe of the manuscript, believed that she would benefit from the lengthening of the fables.

67. This citation represents either a generalized paraphrase from *De Beneficiis* or the commentator's unsuccessful attempt to reproduce a memorized passage, as it does not duplicate any identifiable sentence in that work.

68. The quotation from "Salo" is in the comment on Fable 40, "De Mustella et Rustice," where the commentator writes, "Quicquid agant homines intentio iudicat omnes." Although the commentator elsewhere cites Solomon, for which "Salo" is a plausible abbreviation, this passage resembles nothing in any of the biblical books attributed to Solomon in the Middle Ages.

69. Among the commentaries that I have seen, Trier Stadtbibliothek MS 1109, a manuscript written in a largely illegible hand, uses *auctoritates* most heavily, to the degree that they threaten to overwhelm the commentator's engagement with the fable plots. For example, in relation to Fable 3, "De Mure et Rana," the commentator quotes from Aristotle four times, Seneca three times, Matthew of Vendôme's

Tobias once, Cato once, and Boethius once. The next fable comment includes ten *auctoritates,* and the next cites eleven.

70. "Sic etiam ex proposito autor noster, volens nos hortari ad bonos mores, primo promittit fabulas, tamquam quendam praeludia, et deinde subiungit doctrinas tanquam exercitia neccessaria et utilia scientia, quia omnia denominanda sunt a fine" (f. 99r).

71. These include Berne Bibliothèque Cantonale MS 688, from the thirteenth century; Laon Bibliothèque Municipale MS 462, a fourteenth-century manuscript that once belonged to the abbey of Cuissy; and Munich Bayerische Staatsbibliothek MS 5311, dated 1449 (Hervieux, 1:601, 539, 563).

The scribe of Bibliothèque Nationale MS Lat. 15135 gave the morals double emphasis, first by marking the lines of each distich with the red carets and then by reproducing at the end of the collection a list of the title and moral of each fable.

72. The isolated quotations in the list of *auctoritates* appear on ff. 243v, 255v–56r, and 256v; the list of distichs from the elegiac Romulus covers ff. 261r–63v.

73. These are numbered XXII, XXV, XXIII, and XVIII in Hervieux's edition.

74. For discussions of the importance of "play" in relation to medieval literature, see Olson, *Literature as Recreation in the Middle Ages,* especially pp. 90–109. Ludic aspects of medieval drama are discussed in Kolve, *The Play Called Corpus Christi,* Chapter 2: "The Drama as Play and Game" (8–32).

75. Gehl, *A Moral Art,* 127–28.

76. Berlin SPK MS Lat. Qu.18 and MS Lat. Oct. 87, and Augsburg MS II.1.4°.11.

77. Bibliothèque Nationale Lat. 8259, British Library MS Add. 11897, and Wrocław Biblioteka Uniwersytecka MSS IV.Qu.4 and IV.Qu.64.

78. Both Lambeth Palace MS 431 and Biblioteca Marciana MS XIV, cod. 289, add *"sed"* to the quotation, but both spell the name of the herb and the human identically, that is, the former manuscript states, "Ysopus est herba, sed ysopus dat bona verba."

79. *The Book of Memory,* 165.

80. See Erwin Leibfried, ed., *Fabel* (Bamberg: C. C. Buchner, 1984), 31–35.

81. Rumination upon hyssop/Aesop involved the displacement of Avianus from the standard curriculum, and according to Hugo von Trimberg, the movement of the displaced fabulist farther down the ruminative chain. Hugo etymologizes Avianus's name with a grossly unflattering reference to his writing style: "scribens enim ut ipsius avi tonat anus" [writing truly like the anus of a grandfather alone thunders] (qtd. in Grubmüller, *Meister Esopus,* 92).

82. Quoted in Carruthers, *Book of Memory,* 219; the text is slightly modified from the translation by Aldo Bernardo, *Letters on Familiar Matters,* 3 vols. (Baltimore: Johns Hopkins University Press, 1975–85).

83. Much the same unacknowledged ruminative incorporation of fable occurs in a curricular text popular contemporaneously with the elegiac Romulus, Alain of Lille's *Parabolae,* 5.2. Warning against provoking ridicule for putting on airs, Alain paraphrases the fables of the ass in the lion's skin from Avianus (Fable 5) and of the

frog and the ox from a Romulus collection. See *Doctrinale altum seu parabolum liber* in *Patrologiae cursus completus,* ed. J. P. Migne, vol. CCX, cols. 581 ff.; translated by Thomson and Perraud, *Ten Latin Schooltexts,* 312.

84. The eleventh-century grammarian Aimeric had used evaluative categories based on metals in his *Ars lectoria* of 1086, but his classifications are based upon the Christian authority of the listed writers rather than their era; after gold and silver, his third category is tin, and to it he consigns Cato, Avianus, and Aesop. See Curtius, *European Literature and the Latin Middle Ages,* 464.

85. *Virgil in the Middle Ages,* 159–60.

86. *The Ethics of Reading in Manuscript Culture,* 27.

87. Baswell, *Virgil in the Middle Ages,* 166.

4. Commentary Displacing Text: *The Nun's Priest's Tale* and the Process of Reading Curricular Fable

1. The information on Stephen Patrington is a collation of the entries on him in both *The Dictionary of National Biography* (Oxford: Oxford University Press, 1917), 15:492–93, and A. B. Emden, ed., *A Biographical Register of the University of Oxford* (Oxford: Clarendon Press, 1959), 3:1435–36.

2. The proverb, "Ne confidatis secreta nec hiis detegatis, / Cum quibus egestis pugnae discrimina tristis," is used twice in the *Directorium Humanae Vitae;* see Hervieux, 5:473, 727.

3. "Qui plus posse putat, sua quam natura ministrat, / Posse suum superans, se minus ipse potest" (Hervieux, 2:332).

4. See J. Burke Severs's account of the *Melibee*'s relation to its source in W. F. Bryan and Germaine Dempster, *Sources and Analogues of Chaucer's "Canterbury Tales"* (1941; reprint, New York: Humanities Press, 1958), 561–66.

5. Cited in *The Riverside Chaucer,* note on lines 1568–69, p. 887.

6. "An Aesopic Allusion in the *Merchant's Tale,*" 34.

7. This manuscript is discussed in Chapter 1.

8. Chaucer alludes to a Romulan fable later in *The Merchant's Tale,* when Damian, squire in Januarie's household and May's lover, is compared to "the naddre in the bosom sly untrewe" (1786). However, since this reduction of the fable had become proverbial by Chaucer's day, he need not have had the fable in mind when he penned the line. See the note in *The Riverside Chaucer,* p. 887.

9. In his editions of Chaucer's work, Thomas Speght clearly categorized the *Nun's Priest Tale* as a beast fable by choosing the following rubric for the work: "Of a Cocke and an Henne: the morall whereof is to embrace true friendes, and to beware of flatterers" (*A Variorum Edition of the Works of Geoffrey Chaucer,* vol. 2, part 9: *The Nun's Priest's Tale,* ed. Derek Pearsall, 139). Not only does Speght's rubric provide an all-too-clear fabulistic moral, but it also translates the conventional Latin construction for fable titles, "*De . . . . et . . . . ,*" into which the names of the animal characters are inserted. Eight manuscripts, including Ellesmere and Hengwrt, give the tale titles including the phrase "of the cock and hen": MSS Bo1, Cn, Ds1, El, Ha4, Hg, Ln, Ma. See Sir William McCormick and Janet E. Heseltine,

The Manuscripts of Chaucer's Canterbury Tales (Oxford: Clarendon Press, 1933).

10. "Three Old French Sources of the Nonnes Preestes Tale," parts 1 and 2.

11. Ibid., 427.

12. Ibid., 646.

13. For the tale's relation to patristic writings, see Lenaghan, "The Nun's Priest's Fable"; and Manning, "Fabular Jangling and Poetic Vision in *The Nun's Priest's Tale.*"

14. P. 82. Travis's other articles on this tale include "Chaucer's Trivial Fox Chase and the Peasants' Revolt of 1381," and "Learning to Behold the Fox: Poetics and Epistemology in Chaucer's *Nun's Priest's Tale.*"

15. "*The Nun's Priest's Tale* as Grammar-School Primer," 85.

16. Ibid., 87.

17. Gehl, *A Moral Art*, 122–27.

18. The most interesting of these that I have studied, Venice Biblioteca Marciana MS 4658, is described in Chapter 3. In their catalogue, Dicke and Grubmüller list four other manuscripts containing fable commentaries but not the fables (lxviii).

19. Wrocław Biblioteka Uniwersytecka MS II.Qu.33, the so-called Breslauer-Äsop, a fifteenth-century manuscript which also includes German verse translations of the fables; and Berlin SPK MS Lat. Oct. 87, which formerly belonged to the Benedictine monastery of St. Peter at Erfurt. In *Die Handschriften des Benediktinerklosters S. Petri zu Erfurt* (Leipzig: Otto Harrassowitz, 1920), Joseph Theele asserted that the Berlin manuscript dated from the twelfth century, but on the basis of the scribal hand and the work's condition, I think that it is more likely a product of the thirteenth or even fourteenth century.

20. "Talking Back to the Text," 128.

21. In "Talking Back to the Text," Baswell quotes similarly structured character-voiced comments from a Norwich commentary on the *Aeneid* and adds that Ralph Hexter mentions "a similar Ovidian case" on pages 57–60 of *Ovid and Medieval Schooling* (128).

22. *The Riverside Chaucer*, 253, line 4014. Later references to the *Nun's Priest's Tale* are made by line number within the body of the chapter. I have used the Chaucer Society lineation, marked by asterisks in the Benson edition, as it is used exclusively in Pearsall's *Variorum Edition* of the tale.

23. Kate Oelzner Petersen, *On the Sources of the "Nonne Prestes Tale,"* 48.

24. Treviso, Biblioteca Comunale, MS 156, fols. 71v, 72r.

25. Peter Travis, comparing Chauntecleer to Nicholas in *The Miller's Tale*, points out that both characters are expert in mathematics, music, and astronomy, but then he states, "It is only geometry, the most theoretical and regal of the four mathematical arts, that appears beyond the ken or interest of our two scholar-lovers" ("*The Nun's Priest's Tale* as Grammar-School Primer," 81). However, the description of the cock's architectonic comb lies too close in both form and proximity to the other three representative elements to be ignored. Syntactically, Chauntecleer's voice is initially described using exactly the comparative adjectival structure that is employed in describing his comb ("His voys was murier than the murie orgon" [4041];

"His coomb was redder than the fyn coral" [4049]); these descriptions enclose the other two.

Chaucer's understanding of the relationship between geometry and architecture is demonstrated in the description of Theseus's call for craftsmen to build the lists for Palamon and Arcite's duel. The Knight states, "in the lond ther was no crafty man / That geometrie or ars metrike kan" who was not employed in the project (lines 1897–98). For a discussion of the study of geometry in relation to architecture, see "Constructive Geometry" (209–12) in Leon Shelby's chapter on the discipline in David L. Wagner, ed., *The Seven Liberal Arts in the Middle Ages.*

26. The Hengwrt manuscript uses the grammatical variant "say" instead of "saugh" in this line (Variorum Edition of *The Nun's Priest's Tale*), though Benson fails to mention this difference. The word may represent a pun, since Chauntecleer is "saying" his vision of the beast, thus highlighting the textuality of the picture that he paints.

27. *Rhetoric, Hermeneutics, and Translation in the Middle Ages,* 83.

28. Walter Clyde Curry, *Chaucer and the Medieval Sciences,* 2nd ed. (New York: Barnes and Noble, 1960), 199–218; Kenneth Sisam, ed., *Chaucer: The Nun's Priest's Tale* (Oxford: Clarendon, 1927), 35.

29. *Commentary on the Dream of Scipio,* 88.

30. Ibid., 84–85.

31. The conjunction of dream and fable is made explicit in the *Roman de Renart,* where Chauntecleer, skeptical of the prophetic force of the dream, says that it has turned into a fable ("A fable est li songes tornez"; quoted in Pratt, "Old French Sources," 428).

32. For a discussion of the use of the *Disticha Catonis* in the medieval curriculum, see Thomson and Perraud, *Ten Latin Schooltexts,* 52–54, and Gehl, *A Moral Art,* 107–20.

33. "Some Latin Sources of the Nonnes Preest on Dreams," 538–58.

34. Marie de France began her fable collection with the fable of the cock and the jewel in the dung-heap, as most revisers of the Romulan fables did. Furthermore, her *Del cok e del gupil,* clearly one of Chaucer's sources, begins with the image of the cock sitting atop a dung-heap ("*femer*"); see *Marie de France: Fables,* ed. and trans. Harriet Spiegel, 168. Chaucer's displacement of the dung-heap from the animal realm in his source fable to the human realm in the exemplum doubtless serves to reaffirm Chauntecleer's regal nature.

35. In the *Variorum Edition of The Nun's Priest's Tale,* Derek Pearsall points out that in the Hengwrt manuscript this line concludes the last verse paragraph in the pilgrimage exemplum, but most modern editors have placed it at the beginning of the next verse paragraph (186). I agree with Pearsall that the Hengwrt paragraphing suits the sense of the passage best.

36. In *The Nun's Priest's Tale* this inexorable destiny has a metaphorical dimension as well in the repetitive history of successive generations of roosters: Russell

hopes that Chauntecleer will adequately "countrefete" his father, who also fell to the fox's predations (4485–4511).

37. *The Minor Poems of John Lydgate,* part 2: *Secular Poems,* ed. Henry Noble McCracken, 566–99.

38. Citing Plato's *Phaedrus,* Mary Carruthers discusses classical and medieval attitudes toward the superiority of memory as the primary site of knowledge, where it can be used as "living discourse" between two or more people (a use that is clearly appropriate to fable as a mode of discourse). The act of reading a written text, on the other hand, must be solitary, and overreliance upon writing may keep the reader from fully learning the text. See *The Book of Memory,* 30–32.

39. *The Poems of Robert Henryson,* ed. Denton Fox.

40. *The Ethical Poetics of the Later Middle Ages.*

41. *The Ethics of Reading in Manuscript Culture,* 21.

42. Equally laden with *auctoritates,* the commentary in Biblioteca Marciana MS 4658 includes aphorisms from Peter of Blois, Boethius, Egidius, Augustine, Cato, Seneca, Prudentius, and the Bible; it also cites Aristotle ("Philosophus") and Cassiodorus twice each, and Cicero ten times.

Although his fable commentary has apparently not survived, Stephen Patrington's *Ecloga* commentary cites Boethius, Isidore, Seneca, and Bernardus Silvestris, among other *auctores;* see Thomson and Perraud, *Ten Latin Schooltexts,* 121–22. Patrington may have ornamented his commentary on the elegiac Romulus fables with similar citations.

43. See Chapter 3, pp. 85–86.

44. See Maria Chiara Celletti, "Santi Rolando, Olivero e compagni," and Alberto Del Monte, "Apologia di Orlando."

45. Leipzig Universitätsbibliothek MS 1084, f. 115v. The same amplified plot summary appears in Augsburg Universitätsbibliothek MS II.1.4°.27; Munich Bayerische Staatsbibliothek Clm. 4409 and 22404; Ottobeuren Stiftsbibliothek 0.82; Freiburg Universitätsbibliothek MS 21; and Prague Statni Knihovna MS XI.C.4. All of these manuscripts date from the fifteenth century.

46. Baswell, *Virgil in Medieval England,* 144–46.

47. Cf. lines 3141–48, describing Andromache's premonitory dream of Hector's death; 3228–29, the comparison of Russell to Sinon, discussed above; 3355–59, the shrieking of the Trojan women at the death of Priam.

48. See, for example, Lynn Staley [Johnson], "'To Make in Som Comedye': Chauntecleer, Son of Troy"; see also Baswell, *Virgil in Medieval England,* 221.

49. This type of comment is part of what Baswell calls "pedagogical exegesis"; see *Virgil in Medieval England,* Chapter 2: "Pedagogical Exegesis of Virgil in Medieval England: Oxford, All Souls College 82."

50. Chaucer's humorous blurring of the distinction between *fabula* and *historia* exemplifies a tendency studied by Päivi Mehtonen, who asserts that such generic distinctions all became "poeticized" within the medieval rhetorical tradition, "[leading] to more straightforward articulations of *poetica narratio* and its detachment

from rhetorical commitments and oratorical circumstances." He cites eleventh- and twelfth-century commentaries on the *Rhetorica ad Herennium* and Cicero's *De inventione* as seminal in these developments, but by Chaucer's day "we can see that commentary practices relating to other texts have contributed as well" (*Old Concepts and New Poetics,* 31).

51. Chaucer's use of the word "reccheless" in the Nun's Priest's moral has no precedent in his sources, and he may have chosen it as a play on the verb "recche" in line 4086, Chauntecleer's first words in the tale and indeed its central concern: "'Now God,' quod he, 'my swevene recche aright.'" In the extant corpus of Chaucer's work this is the only use of "recche" to mean "interpret" (Larry D. Benson, *A Glossarial Concordance to the Riverside Chaucer* [New York: Garland, 1993], "recchen," v. [1]). Chauntecleer's desire for proper interpretation is flouted by the Nun's Priest in relation to the tale as a whole; the fable, like Chauntecleer's dream, concludes without interpretation that engages the text fully.

52. Baswell sees a similar conflation of roles in the figure of Geffrey in *The House of Fame;* Geffrey is envisioning and later narrating a dream, within which there are moments when he "is rather more a reader . . . than a narrator. His interjections, his constant recursion to his own emotional response, get him lost in glossating rather than moving along with his story" (*Virgil in Medieval England,* 235).

5. John Lydgate's *Isopes Fabules:* Appropriation through Amplification

1. See, for example, Ebin, *John Lydgate,* 9–16; John H. Fisher, "A Language Policy for Lancastrian England," *PMLA* 107, 5 (October 1992): 1168–80; Lee Patterson, "Making Identities in Fifteenth-Century England: Henry V and John Lydgate," in Jeffrey N. Cox and Larry J. Reynolds, eds., *New Historical Literary Study: Essays on Reproducing Texts, Representing History* (Princeton: Princeton University Press, 1993), 69–107; Pearsall, "Lydgate as Innovator." A helpful earlier study is J. W. McKenna, "Henry VI of England and the Dual Monarchy: Aspects of Royal Political Propaganda," *Journal of the Warburg and Courtauld Institute* 28 (1965): 145–62.

2. Shirley states that the fable of the dog and the cheese was "made at Oxforde," an assertion reproduced by John Stow in MS Trinity R.3.19. For further information on Lydgate's life, see the biographical chapter that opens Ebin's *John Lydgate,* 1–19.

3. See Pearsall, "Lydgate as Innovator," especially 13–22.

4. On Lydgate's extensive use of amplification, see Pearsall, *John Lydgate,* 129–37 and 143–50.

5. Lydgate's use of Marie's fables was identified at least as early as the 1880s, by Sauerstein in his dissertation, *Über Lydgates Æsopübersetzung,* 24–40.

6. All references to *Isopes Fabules* are by line numbers as they appear on pages 566–99 of *The Minor Poems of John Lydgate,* Henry Noble McCracken, ed.

7. Lydgate might have intended for *Isopes Fabules* to include his popular *The Churl and the Bird,* which survives in sixteen manuscripts and several printings. It

accords with the fables in its rhyme royal stanzaic form, though at fifty-five stanzas it is a good deal longer than the longest of *Isopes Fabules,* that of the dog and the sheep, which is only thirty-three stanzas. For a description of this work and its sources, see Lenora D. Wolfgang, "'Out of the Frenssh': Lydgate's Source of *The Churl and the Bird,*" *ELN* (March 1995): 10–22).

8. The titles given to Lydgate's fables differ markedly in the two copies. MS Trin. Coll. R.3.19 gives each fable a lengthy heading which incorporates moralizing information similar to that found in a commentary promythion; for example, the first fable is headed "The Tale of the Cok, that founde a precyous stone, groundyd by Isopus, the phylosopher of Rome, that yche man shuld take in gree suche as God sent." Instead of headings like this one, the Harley manuscript provides a very brief prose summary in the margin adjacent to the end of the fable. At the end of the first fable is written, "Here endith the tale of Isope how that the cok founde a joconet stone in þe dunghill." It goes no farther toward identifying the next fable than simply stating, "The secunde tale of Isopos." This difference is almost certainly scribal, perhaps reflecting the scribes' dissatisfaction with the generic titles which might have been supplied by the author. In this chapter, for the sake of brevity, I will use the modern English titles created by McCracken.

9. Pearsall, *John Lydgate,* 193. Pearsall asserts that in both manuscripts the first four fables follow "the traditional order of the Aesop-collections," though only the Trinity College manuscript actually does, and he also implies that the Trinity manuscript contains all three of the shorter fables, though it lacks "The Marriage of the Sun."

10. Sauerstein's study of the fables is typical of its period in concentrating on their pedigree as Aesopic fable rather than upon how Lydgate made the fables his own. In *John Lydgate: A Study in the Culture of the XVth Century,* Walter F. Schirmer mentions *Isopes Fabules* several times in passing, but only to identify them as possibly Lydgate's earliest work, not to discuss the text. In *The Poetry of John Lydgate,* Alain Renoir briefly examines the prologue to the fables alongside "The Churl and the Bird," but mainly in terms of their similar modesty topoi. Pearsall's *John Lydgate* devotes six pages to the fables, but Pearsall gives most of his attention to comparing the work unfavorably to Robert Henryson's *Morall Fabillis;* Ebin offers a very similar but briefer comparison in *John Lydgate,* which is largely a compilation of the three earlier books on the author.

11. See, for example, the allegories for the fable of the Widow of Ephesus discussed in Chapter 3.

12. This punctuation is my own. I take issue with McCracken's editorial decision to put closing quotation marks at the end of line 581, thereby giving the next two verses to the narrator. Line 584, "The iuge, abraidyng, axed of the hounde . . . ," indicates that the judge remains central in these two stanzas. Although Lydgate is given to excessive moralizing, even he would probably not break the judge's speech in half in order to insert a mere two lines of narratorial opinion. Furthermore, the narrator (never given to denying his own authority) but not the judge is privy to the knowledge that two lines are disproven by the action of the fable, for the law shows itself to be unjust.

13. Although Fable 5 begins the second group of *Isopes Fabules* in the Trinity College manuscript, its first stanza implies the cohesion of the collection:

> In Isopus forther to proced,
>> Towchynge the vyce of wnkyndenesse,
> In this tretes a lytyll fabill I rede
>> Of engratytude, ioynyd to falsenesse,
>> How that a wolff, of cursyd frowardnesse
> Was to the crane, of malyce, as I fynde,
> For a good torne falce founden and wnkynd. (750–56)

"Forther" in the first verse tells the reader that Lydgate did not mean for this fable to stand on its own. Equally telling is the "frowardnesse" attributed to the wolf, a quality associated with this animal twice in Fable 2 ("a froward beste of kynde" [251], "froward of condicion" [253]) and once by implication in Fable 4, in which he is one of the false witnesses called "froward folkis" in the opening line (526). After the first stanza of Fable 5, the quality is linked to the wolf twice directly (775, 818) and once indirectly (779).

14. See lines 204ff., 222ff., 341ff., 356, and 512ff.

15. Tierney, *Medieval Poor Law*, 28.

16. Qtd. in Tierney, 29.

17. *De Gemmis Scriptum Evacis Regis Arabum* (Lubeck: H. Rantzovii, 1575), n.p.

18. Hervieux, 2:565.

19. Sauerstein, *Über Lydgates Æsopübersetzung*, 33.

20. *Ropertus Holkot super libros sapientie.* Hagenau: Gerard Leeu, 1494.

21. See "Martialis" in F. Edward Cranz and Paul Oskar Kristeller, eds., *Catalogus Translationum et Commentariorum: Mediaeval and Renaissance Latin Translations and Commentaries* (Washington, D.C.: Catholic University of America Press, 1980), vol. 4, pp. 250–51; "Martial" by M. D. Reeve, in L. D. Reynolds, ed., *Texts and Transmissions: A Survey of the Latin Classics* (Oxford: Clarendon Press, 1983), 239–44.

6. Robert Henryson's *Morall Fabillis:* Reading, Enacting, and Appropriating

1. A detailed discussion of the structure of Henryson's fables and its significance appears in the introduction to the facing-page translation by George Gopen, *The Moral Fables of Aesop by Robert Henryson,* 17–24. See also Fox's introduction, pp. lxxv–lxxxi, in *The Poems of Robert Henryson.*

2. *Robert Henryson,* 125–28.

3. See, for example, Kinsley, *Scottish Poetry;* Murtaugh, "Henryson's Animals," 408–9; and Wood, *Two Scots Chaucerians,* 17.

4. "Henryson's *Fables,*" *ELH* 29 (1962): 337–56.

5. All quotations of Henryson's work, cited by line number, are taken from *The Poems of Robert Henryson,* ed. Denton Fox.

6. Augustine, *Contra Mendacium,* 508–9; Macrobius, *Commentary on the Dream of Scipio,* I.ii.9. These passages are discussed in Chapter 2.

7. For a description of the categories used in this type of prologue, see Chapter 3. See also Minnis, *Medieval Theory of Authorship,* 28–29.

8. Fox discusses the term's scholastic usage in his edition of Henryson's poems (xv).

9. *The Latin Element in the Vocabulary of the Earlier Makars Henryson and Dunbar,* 57.

10. See Chapter 5, 136–38. Fox also cites Lydgate's description of the stone in his note for line 131.

11. "Nota quod jaspis dicitur quasi 'iacens inter aspides vel in fronte aspidis,' vel dicitur ab 'yos' grece, quod est viride latine, quia est viridi coloris" (Appendix 3, p. 213).

12. In his article "Chaucer's Influence on Henryson's Fables: The Use of Proverbs and Sententiae," Donald MacDonald cites Chaucer as the source for Henryson's repeated use of proverbial *auctoritates* such as this reference to Solomon, but it seems equally possible that Henryson, at least in this work, picked up the technique from scholastic commentary. In the *Auctores octo* commentary, for example, Solomon is quoted four times, one instance of which appears in the comment on the fable following that of the two mice.

13. See, for example, the *Auctores octo* comment (Appendix 3, p. 214).

14. In the *Esopus moralizatus,* these roles appear in Fables 2, 5, 8, 13, and 14.

15. For other examples of direct address used by characters in *moralitates,* see Fables 18, 22, 32, 34, 38, 41, and 61 in the *Auctores octo.* In these examples, it is not the fable character but rather the figurative or allegorical representative who speaks, generally paraphrasing something which the fable character has said. While these examples do not represent exactly the technique employed by Henryson, they show the manner in which commentators made the division between fable character and its figurative or allegorical analogue less distinct.

This technique is also reminiscent of the commenting technique used in some commentary on Ovid's *Heroides,* in which Dido provided her own commentary on her letter to Aeneas. See Baswell, "Talking Back to the Text," 128.

16. Mehl, 87.

17. Hervieux, 2:325.

18. Ibid., 326.

19. *Medieval to Renaissance in English Poetry,* 195–99.

20. "Robert Henryson and Father Aesop: Authority in the *Moral Fables,*" 209–10.

21. This repeated vocabulary contrasts with the narrator's description in the fable's prologue of the site of his stroll and nap as "ane wod" (1327).

22. See, for example, lines 1720–33, 1776–89, and 1823–24; also, in lines 1874–75, the narrator implies that he suffers while watching the birds trapped and killed ("Allace, it wes grit hart sair for to se / That bludie bowcheour beit thay birdis doun"), after which he watches the swallow fly away for the last time (line 1887).

23. Some commentaries including the allegory of the swallow as a religious person or preacher, the other birds as sinners, and the man as the devil appear in the following manuscripts: Augsburg Universitätsbibliothek MS II.1.4°.27; Basel Universitätsbibliothek MS F.IV.50; Berlin Staatsbibliothek Preussischer Kulturbesitz MSS Lat. Qu.18 and Lat. Qu.382; Freiburg Universitätsbibliothek MS 21; Halle Universitäts-und Landesbibliothek Sachsen-Anhalt MS Stolb.Wern. Za 64; Leipzig Universitätsbibliothek MS 1084; Mainz Stadtbibliothek MS 540; Milan Biblioteca Ambrosiana MS I. 85 supra, and MS Trotti 161; Munich Bayerische Staatsbibliothek Clm. 609, 7680, 14529, 14703, 16213, 19667, and 22404; Stuttgart Württembergische Landesbibliothek MSS HB XII.4 and HB.I.127; Treviso Biblioteca Comunale MS 156; Trier Stadtbibliothek MSS 132, 756, and 1109; Wolfenbüttel Herzog August Bibliothek MS 185 Helmst.; Wrocław Biblioteka Uniwersytecka MSS II.Qu.33, IV.Qu.81, and IV.Qu.88.

24. See B. G. Koonce, "Satan the Fowler."

25. This phrase appears in Psalm 7:16, part of a passage referring to God's punishment of a wicked man:

> 15. Behold, he hath been in labour with injustice; he hath conceived sorrow, and brought forth iniquity.

> 16. He hath opened a pit and dug it: and he is fallen into the hole [incidit in foveam] he made.

> 17. His sorrow shall be turned on his own head: and his iniquity shall come down upon his crown. (Douay-Rheims)

26. In his brief exploration of the similarities between scholastic commentaries and Henryson's fables, Douglas Gray also makes this point (127).

27. The same allegory, though not always the same two-fold interpretation, is reproduced in all but three of the manuscripts listed in note 23; those lacking the allegory are Augsburg Universitätsbibliothek MS II.1.4°.27; Munich Bayerische Staatsbibliothek Clm. 22404; and Stuttgart Württembergische Landesbibliothek MS HB XII.4. Like the allegory for the preaching of the swallow, this one probably appears in other manuscripts as well.

28. Of course the similarity of this imagery may be entirely coincidental, since each of these stanzas features a rhyme word at the conclusion of the sixth line which anticipates "marrow"; Henryson also uses "barrow" and "tarrow." Even though he could certainly have arrived at the use of this word without external influence, the numerous similarities of the *Morall Fabillis* to BL MS Add. 11897 make this coincidence worth a passing mention.

29. Ian W. A. Jamieson, in his dissertation "The Poetry of Robert Henryson: A Study of the Use of Source Material," notes the similarity between Henryson's *moralitas* and that given for the same fable in MS 141, No. 328 of the Municipal Library of Bern (qtd. by Fox in *Henryson*, 325, n. 1). The fabulist responsible for this collection, which Hervieux called the "Bern Romulus," wrote after his very brief version of the fable, "Sic maiores et minores inter se disceptantes. Sic etiam dyabolus animam et corpus dissipat" (Hervieux, 2:738). Jamieson could not ex-

plain the relationship between this fifteenth-century manuscript, of which only one copy is extant, and Henryson's *Morall Fabillis*, but a similar branch of fable commentary doubtless explains the resemblance.

30. See Fox's discussion of the *Roman de Renart* as source text for these fables (*The Poems of Robert Henryson*, xlvii–xlviii).

31. See Baswell, *Virgil in Medieval England,* 165–66; in *The Book of Memory* Carruthers also discusses the efficacy of *divisio* in medieval reading, but she is primarily concerned with its relation to memory (79, 86, passim).

32. See, for example, Donald MacDonald, "Chaucer's Influence on Henryson's *Fables*" and "Henryson and Chaucer: Cock and Fox."

33. Mehl argues that Henryson's "reference to 'doctouris of deuyne' in support of his method [of interpretation] rather encourages our scepticism because it reminds us of the vain out-witted Wolf whom the Fox mockingly addresses as 'newmaid doctour off diuinitie'" (1052). However, since the honorific itself must be morally neutral, we should look at the voice behind it rather than at the term itself. The fox indeed uses it as a joke, but he is making fun of the wolf, not educated people; because the wolf is so far from deserving the title, the animals in the court understand the humor in the misnomer, and they laugh (1054). No such irony is implied in the *moralitas,* where the narrator goes on to make use of the kind of teaching popularized by these doctors. In light of Henryson's debt to the scholastic tradition and his apparently serious attempt to moralize beast-epic fables, I find it difficult to read this passage as ironic.

34. In the *Auctores octo* commentary, the phrase appears once in each of the comments on Fables 7, 25, and 33, and twice in those on Fables 27 and 28.

35. See, for example, Fables 51 and 61 in the *Esopus moralizatus,* and Fables 17, 30, 37, and 51 in the *Auctores octo* commentary.

36. "Tale-Moral Relationships in Henryson's *Moral Fables,*" 110.

37. *Robert Henryson,* 129, n. 6.

38. The other allegories of this type which both commentaries have in common are for Fable 25, "De Lupo et Sue Pariente"; Fable 49, "De Viro et Uxore"; and Fable 52, "De Lupo et Ovibus." The *Auctores octo* commentator finds goods works in his interpretation of Fable 36, "De Mula et Musca," and the BL MS Add. 11897 commentator sees this meaning in Fable 5, "De Carne et Cane."

This allegorical structure also has an *in malo* form whereby groups of animals or things are allegorized as "*peccata*" or "*opera illicita,*" as the eagle chicks are called in the fable described above.

39. In the *Auctores octo* pride is represented by the heifer in Fable 6, "De Ove et Capra"; the boar in Fable 16, "De Leone et Apro"; and the inflated frog in Fable 41, "De Rana et Bove." In BL MS Add. 11897, the horns of the stags in Fables 47 and 58, "De Cervo et Canibus" and "De Cervo et Bove," are allegorized as pride; such uniformity of interpretation, along with the exclusion of any other representative of the vice, suggests that an external metaphorical meaning has been brought to bear here.

40. See, for example, the narrator's addresses to his "Freindis" (365), "worthie folk" (586), "gude folke" (789), and "us synnaris" (1141).

41. Between the end of "The Preaching of the Swallow" and the conclusion of the compilation, only one construction appears that could be construed as implying an audience of more than one: "ye wait" in line 2210. However, this is most likely a metrical filler, for when the narrator counsels "mychtie men" at the end of the moral, he seems to use apostrophe to address absent people.

42. Denton Fox, who disagrees with John MacQueen's assertion that the line is "a dig at the over-ingenuity of the friars," remarks in his note on these lines that the moral of "The Paddock and the Mouse" is itself neither short nor simple.

Afterword

1. Pp. 6–7.

2. Österley, *Steinhöwels Äsop*, 1–3; Caxton, *Caxton's Aesop*, 5.

3. MacQueen in *Robert Henryson: A Study of the Major Narrative Poems*, McDiarmid in *Robert Henryson*, and other scholars have assumed that the poet used Caxton's *Aesop* as a source, but Denton Fox has argued convincingly against this view; see Fox, "Henryson and Caxton."

4. Leach, *The Schools of Medieval England*, 247.

5. William Harrison Woodward, *Studies in Education during the Age of the Renaissance* (New York: Russell and Russell, 1968), 11–18.

6. Leach, *The Schools of Medieval England*, 247.

7. Copeland, *Rhetoric, Hermeneutics, and Translation in the Middle Ages*, Chapters 1–2.

Appendix 2

1. In the epilogue to her fables, Marie de France writes that King Alfred ("li reis Alfrez") translated Romulus's fables into English (lines 16–17); the name of the king here may be a variant of "Alfred."

2. Horace, *Ars Poetica*, line 333.

3. Psalm 7:15–17, referring to the wicked man:

15. Ecce parturiit iniustitiam et concepit dolorem et peperit iniquitatem;

16. Lacum aperuit et effodit eum et incidet [*sic*] in foveam quam fecit.

17. Convertetur dolor eius in caput eius et in veticem ipsius iniquitas eius descendet.

Appendix 3

1. Matthew 19:21: "Ait illi Iesus si vis perfectus esse vade vende quae habes et da pauperibus et habebis thesaurum in caelo et veni sequere me."

2. This sentence may be based upon Romans 3:31, the only verse in the Bible to use the verb "destruo" and the object "lex." Here Paul responds to the Jews' accusation that Christians threaten laws regarding circumcision: "Legem ergo destruimus per fidem abiit sed legem statuimus."

Bibliography

Aesop. See Hervieux, *Les Fabulistes Latins.*

L'Aesopus moralisatus stampato in Parma da Andrea Portilia nel 1481. Parma: Istituto Statale d'Arte "P. Toschi," 1961.

Alan of Lille. *Anticlaudianus.* Ed. R. Bossuat. Paris: J. Vrin, 1955.

———. *Anticlaudianus, or the Good and Perfect Man.* Trans. James J. Sheridan. Toronto: Pontifical Institute of Mediaeval Studies, 1973.

———. *The Complaint of Nature.* Trans. Douglas M. Moffat. *YSE* 36 (1908). Reprint, Hamden, Conn.: Archon Books, 1972.

Alford, John A. "The Grammatical Metaphor: A Survey of Its Use in the Middle Ages." *Speculum* 57 (1982): 728–60.

Allen, Judson Boyce. *The Ethical Poetics of the Later Middle Ages* Toronto: University of Toronto Press, 1982.

———. *The Friar as Critic.* Nashville: Vanderbilt University Press, 1971.

———. "The Ironic Fruyt: Chauntecleer as Figura." *Studies in Philology* 66 (1969): 25–35.

Alton, E. H., and D. E. W. Wormell. "Ovid in the Medieval Schoolroom." Parts 1 and 2. *Hermathena* 94 (1960): 21–38; 95 (1961): 67–82.

Amsler, Mark. *Etymology and Grammatical Discourse in Late Antiquity and the Early Middle Ages.* Amsterdam and Philadelphia: John Benjamins, 1989.

Ashby, Anna Lou. *The Fox and the Grapes: Aesop through the Ages: A Checklist of Aesopic Fables in the Pierpont Morgan Library.* New York: Pierpont Morgan Library, 1995.

Ashby-Beach, Genette. "Les *Fables* de Marie de France: Essai de grammaire narrative." In *Epopée animale, fable, fabliau,* ed. Gabriel Bianciotti and Michel Salvat, 13–29. Paris: PU de France, 1984.

Auctores octo. Fabularum Esopi. Lyon: Jehan de Vingle, 1495.

Auerbach, Erich. "Figura." In *Scenes from the Drama of European Literature,* trans. Ralph Manheim. New York: Meridian Books, 1959.

Augustine. *Contra Mendacium.* In *Corpus Scriptorum Ecclesiasticorum Latinorum,* vol. 41, 469–528. Leipzig: Freytag, 1900.

———. *On Christian Doctrine.* Trans. and intro. D. W. Robertson, Jr. Indianapolis: Bobbs-Merrill, 1958.

Avianus. *Fabulae Aviani.* See Duff, *Minor Latin Poets.*

Babrius. *Babrius and Phaedrus.* Ed. and trans. Ben Edwin Perry. Loeb Classical Library. Cambridge: Harvard University Press, 1935.

Baird-Lange, Lorrayne Y. "Christus Gallinaceus: A Chaucerian Enigma; or the Cock as Symbol of Christ in the Middle Ages." *Studies in Iconography* 9 (1983): 19–30.

Banks, Mary Macleod. *An Alphabet of Tales: An English Translation of the "Alphabetum Narrationum" of Etienne de Besançon.* EETS, o.s., 126–27, 1904–5. Millwood, N.Y.: Kraus Reprint, 1972.

Barney, Stephen A. "The Plowshare of the Tongue: The Progress of a Symbol from the Bible to *Piers Plowman.*" *Mediaeval Studies* 35 (1973): 261–93.

Bastin, Julia, ed. *Recueil General des Isopets.* Vols. 1 and 2. Société des Anciens Textes de Français. Paris: Champion, 1929–1930.

Baswell, Christopher. "The Medieval Allegorization of the *Aeneid:* MS Cambridge, Peterhouse 158." *Traditio* 41 (1985): 181–237.

———. "Talking Back to the Text: Marginal Voices in Medieval Secular Literature." In *The Uses of Manuscripts in Literary Studies: Essays in Memory of Judson Boyce Allen,* ed. Charlotte Cook Morse et al., 121–60.

———. *Virgil in Medieval England: Figuring the Aeneid from the Twelfth Century to Chaucer.* Cambridge: Cambridge University Press, 1995.

Baugh, Albert C., and Thomas Cable. *A History of the English Language.* 3rd ed. London: Routledge and Kegan Paul, 1978.

Bauman, Richard. "The Folktale and Oral Tradition in the Fables of Robert Henryson." *Fabula* 6 (1963): 108–24.

Baxter, J. H., and Charles Johnson. *Medieval Latin Word-List.* London: Oxford University Press, 1934.

Beardsley, Theodore S., Jr. *Hispano-Classical Translations Printed between 1482 and 1699.* Pittsburgh: Duquesne University Press, 1970.

Beer, Jeanette M. A. *Narrative Conventions of Truth in the Middle Ages.* Geneva: Droz, 1981.

Bennett, J. A. W. *Poetry of the Passion: Studies in Twelve Centuries of English Verse.* Oxford: Clarendon Press, 1982.

Berrigan, Joseph, trans. *Fabulae Aesopicae Hermolai Barbari et Gregorii Corrarii.* Lawrence, Kans.: Coronado, 1977.

Bersuire, Pierre. *Reductorium morale, liber xv: Ovidius moralizatus, cap. 1: De formis figurisque deorum.* Ed. J. Engels. Utrecht: Rijksuniversiteit Instituut voor Laat Latijn, 1966.

Bethurum, Dorothy, ed. *Critical Approaches to Medieval Literature.* New York: Columbia University Press, 1960.

Biblia Sacra: Iuxta Vulgata Versionem. Stuttgart: 1969.

Black, Robert. "The Curriculum of Italian Elementary and Grammar Schools, 1350–1500." In *The Shapes of Knowledge from the Renaissance to the Enlightenment,* ed. Donald Kelley, 137–63. Dordrecht, Boston: Kluwer Academic Publishers, 1991.

Blackham, H. J. *The Fable as Literature*. London: Athlone, 1985.

Bland, Cynthia Renee. *The Teaching of Grammar in Late Medieval England: An Edition, with Commentary, of Oxford, Lincoln College MS. Lat. 130*. East Lansing, Mich.: Colleagues Press, 1991.

Bloomfield, Morton W. "Allegory as Interpretation." *New Literary History* 3 (1972): 301–17.

Boccaccio, Giovanni. See Osgood, *Boccaccio on Poetry*.

Bonaventure, Brother, F.S.C. "The Teaching of Latin in Later Medieval England." *Mediaeval Studies* 23 (1961): 1–20.

Bonner, Stanley F. *Education in Ancient Rome*. London: Methuen, 1977.

Bourdieu, Pierre. *Language and Symbolic Power*. Ed. John B. Thompson, trans. Gino Raymond and Matthew Adamson. Cambridge: Harvard University Press, 1991.

Calogerà, Angelo. *Nuova Raccolta d'Opuscoli Scientifici e Filologici*. Vol. 4. Venice: Simone Occhi, 1758.

Cameron, Alan. "Macrobius, Avienus, and Avianus." *Classical Quarterly*, n.s. 17 (1967): 385–99.

Caoursin, Guillaume. *The Siege of Rhodes (1482) and Aesopus' The Book of Subtyl Histories and Fables of Europe (1484)*. Facsimile Reproductions. Delmar, N.Y.: Scholars' Facsimiles and Reprints, 1975.

Carnes, Pack. *Fable Scholarship: An Annotated Bibliography*. New York: Garland, 1985.

Carruthers, Mary. *The Book of Memory: A Study of Memory in Medieval Culture*. Cambridge: Cambridge University Press, 1990.

Catalogue Général des Livres Imprimés de la Bibliothèque Nationale. Paris: Imprimerie Nationale, 1912.

Caxton, William. *Caxton's Aesop*. Ed. R. T. Lenaghan. Cambridge: Harvard University Press, 1967.

Celletti, Maria Chiara. "Santi Rolando, Olivero e compagni." *Bibliotheca sanctorum* 9 (1968): 303–6.

Chaucer, Geoffrey. *The Riverside Chaucer*. 3rd ed. Ed. Larry Benson. Boston: Houghton Mifflin, 1987.

———. *A Variorum Edition of the Works of Geoffrey Chaucer*. Vol. 2: *The Canterbury Tales*. Part 9: *The Nun's Priest's Tale*. Ed. Derek Pearsall. Norman: University of Oklahoma Press, 1984.

Clark, George. "Henryson and Aesop: The Fable Transformed." *English Literary History* 43 (1976): 1–18.

Clifford, Gay. *The Transformations of Allegory*. London: Routledge and Kegan Paul, 1974.

Clogan, Paul M. "Literary Genres in a Medieval Textbook." *Medievalia et Humanistica*, n.s. 11 (1982): 199–209.

Copeland, Rita. *Rhetoric, Hermeneutics, and Translation in the Middle Ages: Academic Traditions and Vernacular Texts*. Cambridge: Cambridge University Press, 1991.

Courtenay, William J. *Schools and Scholars in Fourteenth-Century England.* Princeton: Princeton University Press, 1987.

Curtius, Ernst Robert. *European Literature and the Latin Middle Ages.* Trans. Willard R. Trask. Princeton, N.J: Princeton University Press, 1953.

Dagenais, John. *The Ethics of Reading in Manuscript Culture: Glossing the "Libro de Buen Amor."* Princeton: Princeton University Press, 1994.

Dahlberg, Charles. "Chaucer's Cock and Fox." *Journal of English and Germanic Philology* 53 (1954): 277–90.

Dane, Joseph A. "Integumentum as Interpretation: Note on William de Conches' Commentary on Macrobius (I, 2, 10–11)." *Classical Folia* 32 (1978): 201–15.

Davis, Charles T. "Education in Dante's Florence." *Speculum* 40 (1965): 415–35.

Delaney, Sheila. "'*Mulier est hominis confusio*': Chaucer's Anti- Popular '*Nun's Priest's Tale.*'" *Mosaic* 17 (1984): 1–8.

Del Monte, Alberto. "Apologia di Orlando." *Filologia Romanza* 4 (1957): 225–34.

Demats, Paule. *Fabula: Trois Etudes de Mythographie Antique et Médiévale.* Geneva: Droz, 1973.

Dicke, Gerd, and Klaus Grubmüller. *Die Fabeln des Mittelalters und der Frühen Neuzeit: Ein Katalog der deutschen Versionen und ihrer lateinischen Entsprechungen.* Munich: Wilhelm Fink, 1987.

Dithmar, Reinhard. *Die Fabel: Geschichte, Struktur, Didaktik.* Paderborn, Germany: Ferdinand Schoningh, 1974.

Douglass, E. Jane Dempsey. *Justification in Late Medieval Preaching: A Study of John Geiler of Keiserberg.* Leiden: E. J. Brill, 1966.

Dronke, Peter. *Fabula: Explorations into the Uses of Myth in Medieval Platonism.* Leiden: E. J. Brill, 1974.

———. "New Approaches to the School of Chartres." *Annuario de estudios medievales* 6 (1971): 117–40.

Duff, J. Wight, and Arnold M. Duff, eds. and trans. *Minor Latin Poets.* Loeb Classical Library. Cambridge: Harvard University Press, 1934.

Du Méril, Edelestand. *Poésies Inédites du Moyen Age.* Paris: Franck, 1854. Reprint, Geneva: Slatkine, 1977.

Ebin, Lois A. "Henryson's 'Fenyeit Fabils': A Defense of Poetry." *Actes du 2e Colloque de Langue et de Littérature Ecossaises (Moyen Age et Renaissance).* Strasbourg: University of Strasbourg, 1978: 222–38.

———. *John Lydgate.* Boston: Twayne, 1985.

Ellenberger, Bengt. *The Latin Element in the Vocabulary of the Earlier Makars Henryson and Dunbar.* Lund Studies in English 51. Lund: C. W. K. Gleerup, 1977.

Escallier, E. A. *Remarques sur le patois suivies du vocabulaire Latin-Français de Guillaume Briton.* Douai: D'Aubers, 1851.

Esopus moralizatus cum bono commento. Cologne: Heinrich Quentell, 1489.

Evax. *De Gemmis Scriptum Evacis Regis Arabum.* Lubeck: H. Rantzovii, 1575.

Faral, Edmond. *Les Arts poétiques du XIIe et du XIIIe siècle.* Paris: Honore Champion, 1958.

Fischer, Nancy. "Handlist of Animal References in Middle English Religious Prose." *Leeds Studies in English* 4 (1970): 49–110.

Fitz Stephen, William. *Norman London*. Intro. F. Donald Logan. New York: Italica Press, 1990.

Fletcher, A. *Allegory: The Theory of a Symbolic Mode*. Ithaca: Cornell University Press, 1964.

Foerster, Wendelin. *Lyoner Yzopet*. Reprint, Wiesbaden: Martin Sandig, 1968.

Foucault, Michel. "What Is an Author?" In *Language, Counter- Memory, Practice: Selected Essays and Interviews,* ed. Donald F. Bouchard, 113–38. Trans. Donald F. Bouchard and Sherry Simon. Ithaca: Cornell University Press, 1977.

Fox, Denton. "Henryson and Caxton." *Journal of English and Germanic Philology* 67 (1968): 586–93.

Fradenburg, Louise O. "Henryson Scholarship: The Recent Decades." In *Fifteenth-Century Studies: Recent Essays,* ed. Robert F. Yeager, 65–92. Hamden, Conn.: Archon Books, 1984.

Frese, Dolores Warwick. *"The Nun's Priest's Tale:* Chaucer's Identified Master Piece?" *Chaucer Review* 16 (1982): 330–43.

Gehl, Paul F. *A Moral Art: Grammar, Society, and Culture in Trecento Florence*. Ithaca: Cornell University Press, 1993.

Ghisalberti, Fausto. "Arnolfo d'Orleans, un cultore di Ovidio nel s. XII." *Memorie del Reale Istituto Lombardo di Scienze e Lettere* 24 (1932): 157–234.

Glauche, Günter. *Schullektüre im Mittelalter: Entstehung und Wandlungen des Lektürekanons bis 1200 nach den Quellen dargestellt*. Münchener Beiträge zur Mediävistik und Renaissance-Forschung. Munich: Arbeo-Gesellschaft, 1970.

Goez, Werner. *Translatio Imperii*. Tübingen: Mohr, 1958.

Goldschmidt, Adolph. *An Early Manuscript of the Aesop Fables and Related Manuscripts*. Studies in Manuscript Illuminations 1. Princeton: Princeton University Press, 1947.

Goossens, Jan, and Timothy Sodmann, eds. *Proceedings of the Third International Beast Epic, Fable, and Fabliau Colloquium Munster, 1979*. Cologne: Bohlau, 1981.

Gopen, George D. "The Essential Seriousness of Robert Henryson's *Moral Fables:* A Study in Structure." *Studies in Philology* 82 (1985): 42–59.

The Gospel of Nicodemus. Ed. H. C. Kim. Toronto: Pontifical Institute of Mediaeval Studies, 1973.

Graesse, Benedict, Plechl. *Orbis Latinus*. Braunschweig: Klinkhardt and Biermann, 1972.

Gray, Douglas. *Robert Henryson*. Leiden: E. J. Brill, 1979.

Green, Richard Hamilton. "Classical Fable and English Poetry in the Fourteenth Century." In *Critical Approaches to Medieval Literature,* ed. Dorothy Bethurum, 110–33. New York: Columbia University Press, 1960.

Greentree, Rosemary. *Reader, Teller, and Teacher: The Narrator of Robert Henryson's "Moral Fables."* Frankfurt am Main: Peter Lang, 1993.

Grendler, Paul F. *Schooling in Renaissance Italy: Literacy and Learning, 1300–1600*. Baltimore: Johns Hopkins University Press, 1989.

Grubmüller, Klaus. *Meister Esopus: Untersuchungen zu Geschichte und Funktion der Fabel im Mittelalter.* Munich: Artemis, 1977.

Halm, Karl Felix von, ed. *Rhetores Latini Minores.* Leipzig: Teubner, 1863.

Hellinga, Lotte. "Importation of Books Printed on the Continent into England and Scotland before c.1520." In *Printing the Written Word: The Social History of Books, circa 1450–1520,* ed. Sandra Hindman, 205–24. Ithaca: Cornell University Press, 1991.

Henderson, Arnold Clayton. "Animal Fables as Vehicles of Social Protest and Satire: Twelfth Century to Henryson." In *Proceedings of the Third International Beast Epic, Fable and Fabliau Colloquium, Munster, 1979,* ed. Jan Goossens and Timothy Sodmann, 160–73. Cologne: Bohlau, 1981.

———. "Medieval Beast Fables and Modern Cages: The Making and Meaning in Fables and Bestiaries." *PMLA* 97 (1982): 40–49.

———. "'Of Heigh or Lough Estat': Medieval Fabulists as Social Critics." *Viator* 9 (1978): 265–90.

Henryson, Robert. *Aesop: The Morall Fabillis of Esope the Phrygian (Edinburgh 1570).* New York: Da Capo, 1970.

———. *Moral Fables of Aesop.* Ed. and trans. George Gopen. Notre Dame, Ind.: University of Notre Dame Press, 1987.

———. *The Poems of Robert Henryson.* Ed. Denton Fox. Oxford: Oxford University Press, 1981.

Hervieux, Léopold, ed. *Les Fabulistes Latins depuis le siècle d'Auguste jusqu'à la fin du moyen âge.* Vols. 1–5. New York: Burt Franklin, 1960.

Hexter, Ralph J. *Ovid and Medieval Schooling: Studies in Medieval School Commentaries on Ovid's "Ars Amatoria," "Epistulae ex Ponto" and "Epistulae Heroidum."* Münchener Beiträge zur Medievalistik und Renaissance-Forschung 38. Munich: Arbeo-Gesellschaft, 1978.

Holbek, Bengt. *Æsops levned og fabler: Christiern Pedersens oversættelse af Stainhöwels Æsop.* 2 vols. Copenhagen: J. H. Schultz, 1962.

Holkot, Robert. *Ropertus Holkot super libros sapientie.* Hagenau: Gerard Leeu, 1494.

Hopkins, Keith. "Novel Evidence for Roman Slavery." *Past and Present* 138 (1993): 3–27.

Horace. *Satires, Epistles, and Ars Poetica.* Trans. H. Rushton Fairclough. Loeb Classical Library. Cambridge: Harvard University Press, 1926.

Hugo von Trimberg. "*Das 'Registrum Multorum Auctorum' des Hugo von Trimberg.*" Ed. Karl Langosch. *Germanische Studien* 235. Nedeln/Liechtenstein: Kraus Reprint, 1969.

Hunt, R. W. "The Introductions to the *Artes* in the Twelfth Century." In *Studia Medievalia in Honorem R. J. Martin,* 85–112. Bruges: N.p., 1948.

Hunt, Tony. "*Prodesse et delectare:* Metaphors of Pleasure and Instruction in Old French." *Neuphilologische Mitteilungen* 80 (1979): 17–35.

———. *Teaching and Learning Latin in Thirteenth-Century England.* 3 vols. Cambridge: D. S. Brewer, 1991.

Huygens, R. B. *Accessus ad Auctores, Bernard d'Utrecht, Conrad d'Hirsau: Dialogus super Auctores*. Leiden: E. J. Brill, 1970.

Irvine, Martin. "'Bothe Text and Gloss': Manuscript Form, the Textuality of Commentary, and Chaucer's Dream Poems." In *The Uses of Manuscripts in Literary Studies: Essays in Memory of Judson Boyce Allen*, ed. Charlotte Cook Morse et al., 81–120.

———. *The Making of Textual Culture: "Grammatica" and Literary Theory, 350–1100*. Cambridge: Cambridge University Press, 1994.

Isidore of Seville. *Isidori Hispalensis Episcopi: Etymologiarum Sive Originum*. Ed. W. M. Linsay. Oxford: Clarendon Press, 1911.

Jacobs, Joseph. *William Caxton: The Fables of Aesop*. Vol. 1: *History*. London: D. Nutt, 1889.

Jambeck, Karen K. "The *Fables* of Marie de France: Base Text and Critical Text." *TEXT: Transactions of the Society for Textual Scholarship* 2 (1985): 83–91.

James, Montague Rhodes, trans. *The Apocryphal New Testament*. Oxford: Clarendon Press, 1924.

———. *A Descriptive Catalogue of the Manuscripts in the Library of Lambeth Palace*. Cambridge: Cambridge University Press, 1930.

Jamieson, Ian W. A. "The Beast Tale in Middle Scots: Some Thoughts on the History of a Genre." *Parergon* 2 (1972): 26–36.

———. "The Poetry of Robert Henryson: A Study of the Use of Source Material." Ph.D. diss., University of Edinburgh, 1964.

Jauss, Hans Robert. *Untersuchungen zur Mittelalterlichen Tierdichtung*. Tübingen: Max Niemeyer, 1959.

Jeauneau, Edouard. "L'Usage de la notion d'*integumentum* à travers les gloses de Guillaume de Conches." *Archives d'Histoire Doctrinale et Littéraire du Moyen Age* 32 (1957): 35–100.

John of Garland. *Integumenta Ovidii: Poemetto inedito del secolo XIII*. Ed. Fausto Ghisalberti. Testi e documenti inediti o rari, 2. Messina: G. Principato 1977.

———. *The "Parisiana Poetria" of John of Garland*. Ed. and trans. Traugott Lawler. New Haven: Yale University Press, 1974.

———. "Poetria magistri Johannis Anglici arte prosayca metric et rithmica." Ed. Giovanni Mari. *Romanische Forschungen* 13 (1902): 883–964.

Johnson, Lynn Staley. "'To Make in Som Comedye': Chauntecleer, Son of Troy." *Chaucer Review* 3 (1985): 225–44.

Jongkees, A. G. "Translatio Studii: Les avatars d'un thème médiéval." In *Miscellanea Mediaevalia in memoriam Jan Frederik Niermeyer*, 41–51. Groningen: J. B. Wolters, 1967.

Juvencus, Caius Vettii Aquilini. *Libri Evangeliorum IIII*. Ed. Karl Marold. Leipzig: Teubner, 1886.

Keller, John E., and L. Clark Keating, eds. and trans. *Aesop's Fables: With a Life of Aesop*. Lexington: University Press of Kentucky, 1993.

Keller, John E., and Richard P. Kincade. *Iconography in Medieval Spanish Literature*. Lexington: University Press of Kentucky, 1984.

Kellogg, Eleanor H. "Bishop Brunton and the Fable of the Rats." *PMLA* 50 (1935): 57–68.

Kennedy, Leonard A. "Late Fourteenth-Century Philosophical Scepticism at Oxford." *Vivarium* 23 (1985): 124–51.

Khinoy, Stephan. "Tale-Moral Relationships in Henryson's *Moral Fables*." *Studies in Scottish Literature* 17 (1982): 99–115.

Kindrick, Robert L. *Henryson and the Medieval Arts of Rhetoric*. New York: Garland, 1993.

———. *Robert Henryson*. Boston: Twayne, 1979.

Kinsley, James, ed. *Scottish Poetry: A Critical Survey*. London: Cassell, 1955.

Klingender, Francis. *Animals in Art and Thought to the End of the Middle Ages*. Cambridge: M.I.T. Press, 1971.

Kolve, V. A. *The Play Called Corpus Christi*. London: Edward Arnold, 1966.

Koonce, B. G. "Satan the Fowler." *Mediaeval Studies* 21 (1959): 176–84.

Kratzmann, Gregory. "Henryson's Fables: 'The Subtle Dyte of Poetry.'" *Studies in Scottish Literature* 20 (1985): 49–70.

Kretschmar, William A., Jr. "The Literary-Historical Context of Henryson's 'Fabillis.'" Ph.D. diss., University of Chicago, 1980.

Lander, J. R. *Conflict and Stability in Fifteenth-Century England*. London: Hutchinson, 1969.

Landwehr, John. *Fable-Books Printed in the Low Countries: A Concise Bibliography until 1800*. Nieuwkoop: B. de Graaf, 1963.

Lange, Karl. "Geistliche Speise: Untersuchungen zur Metaphorik der Bibelhermeneutik." *Zeitschrift für Deutsches Altertum und Deutsches Literatur* 45 (May 1966): 81–122.

Leach, A. F. *The Schools of Medieval England*. London: Methuen, 1915.

Leibfried, Erwin, and Josef M. Werle, eds. *Texte zur Theorie der Fabel*. Stuttgart: J. B. Metzler, 1978.

Lenaghan, R. T. "The Nun's Priest's Fable." *PMLA* 78 (1963): 300–307.

Levrault, Leon. *La Fable: Evolution du Genre*. Paris: Delaplane, n.d.

Leyser, Polycarp. *Historia Poetarum et Poematum Medii Aevi*. Halle a.d. Saale: N.p., 1721. Reprint, Bologna: Forni, 1969.

Lubac, Henri de, S.J. *Exégèse médiévale: Les quatressens de l'écriture*. 4 vols. Paris: Aubier, 1959–64.

Lusignan, Serge. "Preface au *Speculum maius* de Vincent de Beauvais: Réfraction et diffraction." *Cahiers d'études médiévales* 5. Montreal: Bellarmin, 1979.

Lyall, R. J. "Henryson and Boccaccio: A Problem in the Study of Sources." *Anglia* 99 (1981): 38–59.

Lydgate, John. *The Minor Poems of John Lydgate*. Ed. Henry Noble McCracken. EETS, o.s., 192. London: 1934.

MacDonald, Donald. "Chaucer's Influence on Henryson's *Fables*: The Use of Proverbs and Sententiae." *Medium Aevum* 39 (1970): 20–27.

———. "Henryson and Chaucer: Cock and Fox." *Texas Studies in Literature and Language* 8 (1966): 451–61.

Machan, Tim William. "Robert Henryson and Father Aesop: Authority in the *Moral Fables.*" *Studies in the Age of Chaucer* 12 (1990): 193–214.

MacQueen, John. *Allegory.* Critical Idiom Series 14. London: Methuen, 1970.

———. *Robert Henryson: A Study of the Major Narrative Poems.* Oxford: Oxford University Press, 1967.

Macrobius, Ambrosius Theodosius. *Commentarii in Somnium Scipionis.* Ed. Jacob Willis. Leipzig: Teubner, 1970.

———. *Commentary on "The Dream of Scipio."* Trans. William Harris Stahl. Records of Civilization, Sources, and Studies 48. New York: Columbia University Press, 1952.

Mann, Jill. "The *Speculum Stultorum* and *The Nun's Priest's Tale.*" *Chaucer Review* 9 (1974–75): 262–82.

Manning, Stephen. "Fabular Jangling and Poetic Vision in *The Nun's Priest's Tale.*" *South Atlantic Review* 52 (1987): 3–16.

———. "The Nun's Priest's Morality and the Medieval Attitude toward Fables." *Journal of English and Germanic Philology* 59 (1960): 403–16.

Marie de France. *Die Fabeln der Marie de France.* Ed. Karl Warnke. Halle: Max Niemeyer, 1898.

———. *Les Fables: Edition critique accompagneé d'une introduction, d'une traduction, de notes, et d'un glossaire.* Ed. Charles Brucker. Louvain: Peeters, 1991.

———. *Fables.* Ed. and trans. Harriet Spiegel. Toronto: University of Toronto Press, 1987.

McDiarmid, Matthew P. *Robert Henryson.* Edinburgh: Scottish Academic Press, 1981.

McDonald, Craig. "The Perversion of Law in Robert Henryson's Fable of the Fox, the Wolf, and the Husbandman." *Medium Aevum* 49 (1980): 244–53.

McGregor, James H. "Ovid at School: From the Ninth to the Fifteenth Century." *Classical Folia* 32 (1978): 29–51.

McKenzie, Kenneth, and William A. Oldfather, eds. "Ysopet-Avionnet: The Latin and French Texts." *University of Illinois Studies in Language and Literature* 5 (1919): 5–274.

McMahon, Clara P. *Education in Fifteenth-Century England.* Baltimore: Johns Hopkins University Press, 1947.

Mehl, Dieter. "Robert Henryson's 'Moral Fables' as Experiments in Didactic Narrative." In *Functions of Literature: Essays Presented to Erwin Wolff on His Sixtieth Birthday,* ed. Ulrich Broich et al., 81–99. Tübingen: Niemeyer, 1984.

Mehtonen, Päivi. *Old Concepts and New Poetics: Historia, Argumentum, and Fabula in the Twelfth-and Early-Thirteenth- Century Latin Poetics of Fiction.* Commentationes Humanarum Litterarum 108. Helsinki: Societas Scientarum Fennica, 1996.

Middleton, Anne. "The Clerk and His Tale: Some Literary Contexts." *Studies in the Age of Chaucer* 2 (1980): 121–50.

Miller, Joseph M., Michael H. Prosser, and Thomas W. Benson, eds. *Readings in Medieval Rhetoric.* Bloomington: Indiana University Press, 1973.

Miner, John N. *The Grammar Schools of Medieval England: A. F. Leach in Histo-riographical Perspective.* Montreal and Kingston: McGill-Queens University Press, 1990.

Minnis, A. J. *Medieval Theory of Authorship: Scholastic Literary Attitudes in the Later Middle Ages.* London: Scolar Press, 1984.

———. "A Note on Chaucer and the *Ovide moralisé.*" *Medium Aevum* 48 (1979): 254–57.

Minnis, A. J., and A. B. Scott, with David Wallace. *Medieval Literary Theory and Criticism, c. 1100–1375: The Commentary-Tradition.* Oxford: Clarendon Press, 1988.

Moran, Joann H. *Education and Learning in the City of York, 1350–1560.* Borthwick Papers, No. 55: 1979.

Morse, Charlotte Cook, Penelope Reed Doob, and Marjorie Curry Woods, eds. *The Uses of Manuscripts in Literary Studies: Essays in Memory of Judson Boyce Allen.* Studies in Medieval Culture 31. Kalamazoo, Mich.: Medieval Institute Publications, 1992.

Mosher, J. A. *The Exemplum in the Early Religious and Didactic Literature of England.* New York: Columbia University Press, 1911.

Murphy, James J., ed. and trans. *Quintilian on the Teaching of Speaking and Writ-ing.* Carbondale: Southern Illinois University Press, 1987.

———. "The Teaching of Latin as a Second Language in the Twelfth Century." *Historiographica Liguistica* 7 (1980): 159–75.

Murrin, Michael. *The Veil of Allegory: Some Notes toward a Theory of Allegorical Rhetoric in the English Renaissance.* Chicago: University of Chicago Press, 1969.

Murtaugh, Daniel M. "Henryson's Animals." *Texas Studies in Language and Lit-erature* 14 (1972): 405–21.

Muscatine, Charles. *Chaucer and the French Tradition.* Berkeley: University of California Press, 1957.

Newlyn, Evelyn S. "Affective Style in Middle Scots: The Education of the Reader in Three Fables by Robert Henryson." *Nottingham Medieval Studies* 26 (1982): 47–56.

Niermeyer, F. *Mediae Latinitatis Lexicon Minus.* Leiden: E. J. Brill, 1976.

Noel, Thomas. *Theories of the Fable in the Eighteenth Century.* New York: Colum-bia University Press, 1975.

Nøjgaard, Morten. *La Fable Antique: La Fable Grecque avant Phèdre.* Copenhagen: NYT Nordisk Forlag, 1964.

Odo of Cheriton. *The Fables of Odo of Cheriton.* Trans. and intro. John C. Jacobs. Syracuse: Syracuse University Press, 1985.

Olson, Glending. *Literature as Recreation in the Middle Ages.* Ithaca: Cornell Uni-versity Press, 1982.

Orme, Nicholas. *Education and Society in Medieval and Renaissance England.* London and Ronceverte, W.Va.: Hambledon Press, 1989.

———. *English Schools in the Middle Ages.* London: Methuen, 1973.

———. "Schoolmasters, 1307–1509." In *Profession, Vocation and Culture in Later*

Medieval England: Essays Dedicated to the Memory of A. R. Myers, ed. Cecil H. Clough, 218–41. Liverpool: Liverpool University Press, 1982.

Osgood, Charles G. *Boccaccio on Poetry.* 2nd ed. New York: Bobbs- Merrill, 1956.

Österley, Hermann. *Steinhöwels Äsop.* Tübingen: Litterarischer Verein, 1873.

Owst, G. W. *Literature and Pulpit in Medieval England.* 2nd ed. Oxford: Blackwell, 1961.

———. *Preaching in Medieval England.* New York: Russell and Russell, 1965.

Paetow, L. J. "The Arts Course at Medieval Universities with Special Reference to Grammar and Rhetoric." *University of Illinois University Studies* 3 (1910), vol. 7.

Parry. A. W. *Education in England in the Middle Ages.* London: University Tutorial Press, 1920.

Patavino, Rolandino. *The Chronicles of the Trevisan March.* Trans. and intro. Joseph R. Berrigan. Lawrence, Kans.: Coronado Press, 1980.

Patterson, Annabel. *Fables of Power: Aesopian Writing and Political History.* Durham, N.C.: Duke University Press, 1991.

Pearsall, Derek. *John Lydgate.* Charlottesville: University Press of Virginia, 1970.

———. "Lydgate as Innovator." *MLQ* 53 (1992): 5–22.

Peck, Russell A. "St. Paul and the *Canterbury Tales.*" *Mediaevalia* 7 (1981): 91–131.

Perry, Ben Edwin. *Aesopica: A Series of Texts relating to Aesop or Ascribed to Him or Closely Connected with the Literary Tradition That Bears His Name.* Urbana: University of Illinois Press, 1952.

———. "Some Traces of Lost Medieval Story-Books." In *Humaniora: Essays in Literature, Folklore, and Bibliography Honoring Archer Taylor on His Seventieth Birthday,* ed. Wayland O. Hand and Gustave O. Arlt, 150–60. Locust Valley, N.Y.: J. J. Augustin, 1960.

———. *Studies in the Text History of the Life and Fables of Aesop.* Lancaster, Pa.: Lancaster Press, 1936. Reprint, Chico, Calif.: Scholars Press, 1981.

———. "The Text Tradition of the Greek Life of Aesop." *Transactions and Proceedings of the American Philological Association* 64 (1933): 198–244.

Peters, F. J. J. "Chaucer's Time in the *Nun's Priest's Tale.*" *Studia Neophilologica* 60 (1988): 167–70.

Petersen, Kate Oelzner. *On the Sources of "The Nonne Prestes Tale."* Radcliffe College Monographs 10. Boston: Ginn, 1898. Reprint, New York: Haskell House, 1966.

Phaedrus. *Babrius and Phaedrus.* Ed. and trans. B. E. Perry. Cambridge: Harvard University Press, 1965.

———. *The Fables of Phaedrus.* Trans. P. F. Widdows. Austin: University of Texas Press, 1992.

Physiologus. Trans. Michael J. Curley. Austin: University of Texas Press, 1979.

Plessow, Max. *Geschichte der Fabeldichtung in England bis zu John Gay (1726).* Berlin: Mayer & Müller, 1906.

Powell, Marianne. *Fabula Docet: Studies in the Background and Interpretation of Henryson's "Morall Fabillis."* Odense University Studies in English 4. Odense: Odense University Press, 1983.

Pratt, Robert A. "Some Latin Sources of the Nonnes Preest on Dreams." *Speculum* 52 (1977): 538–70.

———. "Three Old French Sources of the 'Nun's Priest's Tale.'" *Speculum* 47 (1972): 422–44, 646–68.

Prisciani Caesariensis. *Opuscula*. Vol. 1. Ed. Marina Passalacqua. Rome: Edizioni di Storia e Letteratura, 1987.

Quain, Edwin A., S.J. "The Medieval *Accessus ad Auctores*." *Traditio* 3 (1945): 215–64.

Quilligan, Maureen. *The Language of Allegory: Defining the Genre*. Ithaca: Cornell University Press, 1979.

Quintiliani, M. Fabi. *Institutionis Oratoriae* I. Ed. M. Winterbottom. Oxford: Clarendon, 1970.

Randall, Lillian. *Images in the Margins of Gothic Manuscripts*. Berkeley: University of California Press, 1964.

Renoir, Alain. *The Poetry of John Lydgate*. Cambridge: Harvard University Press, 1967.

Reynolds, Suzanne. *Medieval Reading: Grammar, Rhetoric, and the Classical Text*. Cambridge: Cambridge University Press, 1996.

Robert, A. C. M. *Fables inédites des XIIe, XIIIe et XIVe siècles, et Fables de La Fontaine*. Vol. 1. Paris: Etienne Cabin, 1825.

Rowland, Beryl. *Blind Beasts: Chaucer's Animal World*. Kent, Ohio: Kent State University Press, 1971.

Runte, Hans R. "'Alfred's Book,' Marie de France, and the Matron of Ephesus." *Romance Philology* 36 (1983): 556–64.

Sauerstein, Paul. *Über Lydgates Æsopübersetzung*. Halle a.d. Salle: Karras, 1885.

Scanlon, Larry. *Narrative, Authority, and Power: The Medieval Exemplum and the Chaucerian Tradition*. Cambridge: Cambridge University Press, 1994.

Schaeffer, Jean-Marie. "*Aesopus auctor inventus:* Naissance d'un genre: La fable ésopique." *Poétique* 63 (1985): 345–64.

———. "Literary Genres and Textual Genericity." Trans. Alice Otis. In *The Future of Literary Theory*, ed. Ralph Cohen, 167–87. New York: Routledge, 1989.

Schaff, Philip, ed. *Nicene and Post-Nicene Fathers of the Christian Church*. Vol. 3: *St. Augustine: On the Holy Trinity, Doctrinal Treatises, Moral Treatises*. New York: Scribners, 1917. Reprint, Grand Rapids, Mich.: Wm. B. Eerdmans, 1980.

Scheler, M. Aug. *Lexicographie Latine du XIIe et du XIIIe Siècle*. Leipzig: F. A. Brockhaus, 1867.

Scheps, Walter. "Chaucer's Anti-Fable: *Reductio ad Absurdum* in The Nun's Priest's Tale." *Leeds Studies in English,* n.s., 4 (1970): 1–10.

Schirmer, Walter F. *John Lydgate: A Study in the Culture of the XVth Century*. Berkeley: University of California Press, 1961.

Schirokauer, Arno. "Die Stellung Äsops in der Literatur des Mittelalters." In *Festschrift für Wolfgang Stammler*, 179–91. Berlin: Erich Schmidt, 1953.

Schrader, Richard J. "Some Backgrounds of Henryson." *Studies in Scottish Literature* 15 (1980): 124–38.

Seeman, Erich. *Hugo von Trimberg und die Fabeln seines Renners.* Munich: Callwey, 1921.

Seneca, Lucius Annaeus. *Moral Essays.* Trans. John W. Basore. Loeb Classical Library. London: Heinemann, 1928.

Shallers, A. Paul. "The 'Nun's Priest's Tale': An Ironic Exemplum." *ELH* 42 (1975): 319–37.

Silverstein, Theodore. "Allegory and Literary Form." *PMLA* 82 (1967): 28–32.

Silvestris, Bernardus. *Commentary on the First Six Books of Virgil's "Aeneid."* Trans. Earl G. Schreiber and Thomas E Maresca. Lincoln: University of Nebraska Press, 1979.

Simrock, Karl. *Die Deutschen Sprichworter.* 4th ed. Basel: Benno Schwabe, 1881.

Smalley, Beryl. *English Friars and Antiquity in the Early Fourteenth Century.* Oxford: Blackwell, 1960.

Smith, H. E. "An Early Italian Edition of Aesop's Fables." *Modern Language Notes* 25 (1910): 65–67.

Smith, M. Ellwood. "Aesop, a Decayed Celebrity." *PMLA* 46 (1931): 225–36.

Soudée, Madeleine. "Le dédicataire des *Ysopets* de Marie de France." *Lettres Romanes* 35 (1981): 183–98.

The Southern Passion. Ed. Beatrice Daw Brown. EETS, o.s., 169. London: Oxford University Press, 1927.

Spearing, A. C. *Medieval to Renaissance in English Poetry.* Cambridge: Cambridge University Press, 1985.

Speckenbach, Klaus. "Die Fable von der Fabel: Zur Uberlieferungsgeschichte der Fabel von Hahn und Perle." *Frümittelalterliche Studien* 12 (1978): 178–229.

Spitz, Hans-Jorg. *Die Metaphorik des Geistigen Schriftsinns.* Munich: Wilhelm Fink, 1972.

Stephen, Leslie, and Sidney Lee. *The Dictionary of National Biography.* Oxford: Oxford University Press, 1917.

Strubel, Armand. "Exemple, fable, parabole: Le récit bref figuré au moyen âge." *Le Moyen Age* 94 (1988): 341–61.

Thiele, Georg. *Der Lateinische Äsop des Romulus und die Prosa- Fassungen des Phaedrus.* Heidelberg: Carl Winter, 1910.

Thomas, Paul R. "Cato on Chauntecleer: Chaucer's Sophisticated Audience." *Neophilologus* 72 (1988): 278–83.

Thomson, David. *A Descriptive Catalogue of Middle English Grammatical Texts.* New York: Garland, 1979.

Thomson, Ian, and Louis Perraud. *Ten Latin Schooltexts of the Later Middle Ages: Translated Selections.* Lewiston, N.Y.: Edwin Mellen Press, 1990.

Tierney, Brian. *Medieval Poor Law: A Sketch of Canonical Theory and Its Application in England.* Berkeley: University of California Press, 1959.

Toliver, Harold. "Robert Henryson: From Moralitas to Irony." *English Studies* 46 (1965): 300–309.

Travis, Peter W. "Chaucer's Trivial Fox Chase and the Peasants' Revolt of 1381." *Journal of Medieval and Renaissance Studies* 18 (1988): 195–220.

———. "Learning to Behold the Fox: Poetics and Epistemology in Chaucer's *Nun's Priest's Tale.*" In *Poetry and Epistemology: Turning Points in the History of Poetic Knowledge,* ed. Roland Hagenbuchle and Laura Skandera, 30–45. Regensburg: Pustet, 1986.

———. "*The Nun's Priest's Tale* as Grammar-School Primer." *Studies in the Age of Chaucer: Proceedings* 1 (1984): 81–91.

Trimpi, Wesley. "The Quality of Fiction: The Rhetorical Transmission of Literary Theory." *Traditio* 30 (1974): 1–118.

Tuve, Rosemond. *Allegorical Imagery: Some Mediaeval Books and Their Posterity.* Princeton: Princeton University Press, 1966.

Van Dijk, S. J. P. "An Advertisement Sheet of an Early Fourteenth-Century Writing Master at Oxford." *Scriptorium* 10 (1956): 47–64.

Van Dyke, Carolynn. *The Fiction of Truth: Structures of Meaning in Narrative and Dramatic Allegory.* Ithaca: Cornell University Press, 1985.

Von Kreisler, Nicolai. "An Aesopic Allusion in *The Merchant's Tale.*" *Chaucer Review* 6 (1971): 30–37.

Wagner, David. L. *The Seven Liberal Arts in the Middle Ages.* Bloomington: Indiana University Press, 1983.

Walther, Hans. *Proverbia Sententiaeque Latinitatis Medii Aevi.* Gottingen: Vandenhoek & Ruprecht, 1963.

Warnke, Karl. "Die Quellen des Esope der Marie de France." In *Forschungen zur Romanische Philologie: Festgabe für Hermann Suchier,* 161–284. Halle: Max Niemeyer, 1900. Reprint, Tübingen, 1978.

Welter, J. T. *L'Exemplum dans la Littérature Réligieuse et Didactique du Moyen Age.* Geneva: Slatkine Reprints, 1973.

Wentersdorf, Karl P. "Symbol and Meaning in Chaucer's *Nun's Priest's Tale.*" *Nottingham Medieval Studies* 26 (1982): 29–46.

Wetherbee, Winthrop. *Platonism and Poetry in the Twelfth Century: The Literary Influence of the School of Chartres.* Princeton: Princeton University Press, 1972.

White. T. H. *The Book of Beasts.* Gloucester, Eng.: Alan Sutton, 1954.

Whitesell, Frederick R. "Fables in Mediaeval Exempla." *Journal of English and Germanic Philology* 46 (1947): 348–66.

Whitman, Jon. *Allegory: The Dynamics of an Ancient and Medieval Technique.* Cambridge: Harvard University Press, 1987.

Wilson, R. M. *The Lost Literature of Medieval England.* London: Methuen, 1952.

Wood, H. Harvey. *Two Scots Chaucerians.* London: Longmans, 1967.

Woods, Marjorie Curry. *An Early Commentary on the "Poetria Nova" of Geoffrey of Vinsauf.* New York: Garland, 1985.

———. "Editing Medieval Commentaries: Problems and a Proposed Solution." *TEXT: Transactions of the Society for Textual Scholarship* 1 (1981): 133–45.

Woolf, Rosemary. "The Theme of Christ the Lover-Knight in Medieval English Literature." *Review of English Studies,* n.s., 13 (1962): 1–16.

Wright, Aaron E., Jr. "The 'Nuremberg' *Aesop* and Its Sources." Ph.D. diss., Princeton University, 1991.

Wright, Thomas. *A Volume of Vocabularies*. Library of National Antiquities, vol. 1. Liverpool: Privately printed, 1857.

Yates, Donald N. "Chanticleer's Latin Ancestors." *Chaucer Review* 18 (1983): 116–26.

Zarncke, Friedrich. "Weitere Beiträge zum Mittellateinische Spruchpoesie." In *Berichte über der Verhandlungen d. Kgl. Sachs.* Leipzig: N.p., 1863.

Ziolkowski, Jan. "The Form and Spirit of the Beast Fable." *Bestia: Yearbook of the Beast Fable Society* 2 (1990): 4–18.

———. *Talking Animals: Medieval Latin Beast Poetry, 750–1150*. Philadelphia: University of Pennsylvania Press, 1993.

Index

Baswell, Christopher, 95–96, 104, 117–
18, 235n. 18, 238n. 55, 243n. 21,
246n. 52; on "pedagogical exegesis,"
245n. 49
Bernard of Clairvaux, 113
Berrigan, Joseph R., 227n. 3
Bersuire, Pierre, 80, 84, 86
Bestiaries, 78, 86–87, 136
Bible, 88, 113
Blackham, H. J., 11–12
Boccaccio, Giovanni, 49–50, 69, 94
Boethius, 89, 90, 113, 235n. 17, 240n.
69; commentary of, on Porphyry's
Isagogue, 66
Boner, Ulrich, 63
Book of Good Love, 56
Bourdieu, Pierre, 52–54
Bouyer, Jean, 103
Bracciolini, Poggio, 19, 193
Bradwardine, Bishop Thomas, 113
Brucker, Charles, 27–28
Brutus, 114
Bury St. Edmunds, 124

Carruthers, Mary, 93, 254n. 38
Cato, 108, 240n. 69, 242n. 84
Caxton, William, 19, 29, 193, 252n. 3
Chandler, Thomas, 193
Chaucer, Geoffrey: and the Host, 120–21;
House of Fame, 246n. 52; Manciple's
Tale, 98, 119; Merchant's Tale, 99–100,
120, 242n. 8; Monk's Tale, 107; Nun's
Priest's Tale, 18, 28, 97–123, 124, 125,
136, 147, 161, 168, 177, 192
(differences from source texts, 101;
dream in, 106–7; structure of, 103–4);
Summoner's Tale, 57; Tale of Melibee,
99; Troilus and Criseyde, 107; Wife of
Bath, 145
Ciavarella, Dr., 30, 236n. 32
Cicero, Marcus Tullius, 90, 108, 109,
245n. 50
Circutio, 62
"City Mouse and Country Mouse, The,"
90; elegiac Romulus text, 200–201; in
Henryson's Morall Fabillis, 158; Latin
commentary texts, 209–10, 215–16,
221

Cock and the Jewel, 76, 115, 185; elegiac
Romulus text, 196; in Lydgate's Isopes
Fabules, 129–30, 191; in Henryson's
Morall Fabillis, 155–58; Latin
commentary texts, 205–6, 213, 219
Commentarii in Somnium Scipionis, 38,
43–44, 48–49, 107
Commentary, scholastic; on fable, 62–96,
236n. 30; paraphrase in, 76–77;
transmission of, 56; vernacular plot
summaries in, 235n. 18; passim. See
also Appendixes 2–5, pp. 204–25
Conrad of Hirsau, 44–46, 233n. 28
Consolation of Philosophy, 89, 90, 235n. 17
Constructiones, 60
Contra Mendacium, 39–41
Copeland, Rita, 29, 77, 107, 190–92
Courtenay, William J., 55
"Crow and the Peacock, The," 93–94, 99

Dagenais, John, 56, 84, 95, 112, 234n. 11
Daun Burnel the Asse, 119
De anima (Aristotle), 90
De beneficiis (Seneca), 88–89
De Capone et Accipitre, 228n. 8
De contemptu mundi, 164
De divinatione (Cicero), 109
De gemmis (Evax), 87
De genealogia deorum gentilium, 49–50
Demats, Paule, 32
Denominatio, 62
Derivatio, 60, 235n. 19
Dialogus super Auctores, 44–46
Dido, 104, 249n. 15
Disciplina clericalis, 19, 182, 193
Distichs of Cato (Disticha Catonis), 88,
90, 107–8, 167, 233n. 28, 234n. 16
Divisio, 177, 251n. 31
"Dog and the Cheese, The": in Lydgate's
Isopes Fabules, 133, 147. See also
"Meat and the Dog, The"
"Dog and the Sheep, The," 79; elegiac
Romulus text, 198; in Henryson's
Morall Fabillis, 159–61, 172; Latin
commentary texts, 208, 214, 220; in
Lydgate's Isopes Fabules, 132–33,
140–44
"Doves and the Hawk, The," 2–3

Index of Manuscripts

Edward Wheatley is associate professor of English at Hamilton College in Clinton, New York.